Next-Generation Systems and Secure Computing

Scrivener Publishing
100 Cummings Center, Suite 541J
Beverly, MA 01915-6106

Advances in Cyber Security

Series Editors: Rashmi Agrawal and D. Ganesh Gopal

Scope: The purpose of this book series is to present books that are specifically designed to address the critical security challenges in today's computing world including cloud and mobile environments and to discuss mechanisms for defending against those attacks by using classical and modern approaches of cryptography, blockchain and other defense mechanisms. The book series presents some of the state-of-the-art research work in the field of blockchain, cryptography and security in computing and communications. It is a valuable source of knowledge for researchers, engineers, practitioners, graduates, and doctoral students who are working in the field of blockchain, cryptography, network security, and security and privacy issues in the Internet of Things (IoT). It will also be useful for faculty members of graduate schools and universities. The book series provides a comprehensive look at the various facets of cloud security: infrastructure, network, services, compliance and users. It will provide real-world case studies to articulate the real and perceived risks and challenges in deploying and managing services in a cloud infrastructure from a security perspective. The book series will serve as a platform for books dealing with security concerns of decentralized applications (DApps) and smart contracts that operate on an open blockchain. The book series will be a comprehensive and up-to-date reference on information security and assurance. Bringing together the knowledge, skills, techniques, and tools required of IT security professionals, it facilitates the up-to-date understanding required to stay one step ahead of evolving threats, standards, and regulations.

Publishers at Scrivener
Martin Scrivener (martin@scrivenerpublishing.com)
Phillip Carmical (pcarmical@scrivenerpublishing.com)

Next-Generation Systems and Secure Computing

Edited by

Subhabrata Barman

Santanu Koley

and

Subhankar Joardar

Scrivener Publishing

WILEY

This edition first published 2025 by John Wiley & Sons, Inc., 111 River Street, Hoboken, NJ 07030, USA and Scrivener Publishing LLC, 100 Cummings Center, Suite 541J, Beverly, MA 01915, USA

For more information about Scrivener publications please visit www.scrivenerpublishing.com.

Wiley Global Headquarters
111 River Street, Hoboken, NJ 07030, USA

For details of our global editorial offices, customer services, and more information about Wiley products visit us at www.wiley.com.

Library of Congress Cataloging-in-Publication Data

ISBN 978-1-394-22826-3

Front cover images supplied by Adobe Firefly
Cover design by Russell Richardson

Set in size of 11pt and Minion Pro by Manila Typesetting Company, Makati, Philippines

Printed in the USA

10 9 8 7 6 5 4 3 2 1

Contents

Preface

The rapid evolution of technology has brought us to an era where the convergence of systems, computing, and security is no longer an isolated domain, but an integral aspect of every facet of our digital lives. From advanced data analytics and machine learning to decentralized systems and cloud computing, we are witnessing a profound transformation in how we interact with technology, communicate, and conduct business.

Next-Generation Systems and Secure Computing represent the frontier of this digital revolution, shaping not only how we develop and deploy technology, but also how we protect it. The growing complexity of modern systems demands innovative approaches to both functionality and security, ensuring resilience against increasingly sophisticated threats. As we integrate more sophisticated algorithms, artificial intelligence, and distributed architectures into our systems, the stakes in safeguarding data and infrastructure have never been higher.

This book provides an in-depth exploration of these critical topics, with contributions from leading experts in the fields of systems design, cyber security, and computational theory. It offers a comprehensive look at the cutting-edge technologies that are defining the next generation of secure computing systems, from block chain and quantum computing to advanced cryptography and AI-driven security protocols.

By addressing both the theoretical underpinnings and practical applications of secure computing in modern systems, this book aims to equip researchers, practitioners, and students with the knowledge and tools to tackle the challenges of tomorrow's digital ecosystem. The chapters presented here cover a broad spectrum of topics, from the evolution of security paradigms to novel approaches in securing data, communications, and infrastructures.

The following research topics are well covered in this book:

Video Steganography
Watermarking
Malware Analysis
Cryptography

Cybersecurity and Block Chain
Cybersecurity and law
Secured Communication Systems
Security in Wireless Networks
Security in IoT Systems
Security in Mobile Crowd Sensing
Multimedia Security
Sentiment Analysis in Social Media

We believe that the integration of security at the very foundation of system design, coupled with the innovative solutions presented in this work, will lay the groundwork for the development of resilient, trustworthy, and future-proof systems. As we look ahead to a world increasingly reliant on interconnected technologies, the need for secure, efficient, and scalable computing systems has never been more urgent.

We hope this book serves as both a valuable reference and an inspiring resource for the next generation of technologists, researchers, and innovators working at the intersection of systems engineering and secure computing. Together, we can build a safer, more robust digital future.

1

Yet Another Move Towards Securing Video Using Sudoku-Fernet

Sunanda Jana[1], Swarnajit Bhattacharya[1], Mrinmoy Sen[1*], Abhinandan Khan[2], Arnab Kumar Maji[3] and Rajat Kumar Pal[2]

[1]*Haldia Institute of Technology, WB, India*
[2]*University of Calcutta, Kolkata, India*
[3]*North-Eastern Hill University, Meghalaya, India*

Abstract
In this era of digital communication and multimedia content sharing, ensuring the security and privacy of sensitive video data is of utmost importance. Symmetric key encryption is a widely used technique for securing video content; however, the generation of secure and unpredictable encryption keys remains a challenge. This study proposes a novel approach that employs Sudoku puzzles as a mechanism for generating symmetric keys. Then, by passing the key through fernet module, the Sudoku-Fernet cipher key was extracted for video encryption. The Sudoku puzzle's inherent properties of uniqueness, complexity, and nonlinearity make it an ideal candidate for key generation. The proposed method combines the strength of the Giant Sudoku instance of size 25 × 25 with a cryptographic fernet module to enhance the security of video encryption systems, offering an innovative solution to protect sensitive video content without affecting cost and time.

***Keywords*:** Symmetric key, fernet, sudoku-fernet cipher key, video encryption, security

1.1 Introduction

Sudoku puzzle [1] is a popular logic-based number-placement game that has gained worldwide popularity. Its structure consists of an $n \times n$ square

**Corresponding author*: mrinmoy.sen@gmail.com

Subhabrata Barman, Santanu Koley and Subhankar Joardar (eds.) Next-Generation Systems and Secure Computing, (1–16) © 2025 Scrivener Publishing LLC

grid, containing some clues as preassigned, forming a Sudoku puzzle, where n is an integer and $\sqrt{n}$ is an integer. Thus, minigrids are formed with size $\sqrt{n} \times \sqrt{n}$. In each minigrid, each integer between 1 and n appears only once. Standard Sudoku consists of a 9 × 9 grid divided into nine 3 × 3 subgrids. The goal is to fill in the empty cells with digits from 1 to 9, ensuring that each row, column, and subgrid contains every digit exactly once. Sudoku puzzles can be of various sizes and configurations beyond the classic 9 × 9 grid. Some common Sudoku types are based on different grid sizes [10]:

1. **Classic 9 × 9 Sudoku:** This is the standard version of Sudoku, where the puzzle is presented on a 9 × 9 grid divided into nine 3 × 3 subgrids. The objective is to fill in the grid such that each row, column, and 3 × 3 subgrid contains numbers 1 through 9 with no repetition.
2. **Mini Sudoku (4 × 4):** In Mini Sudoku, the puzzle is played on a 4 × 4 grid, divided into four 2 × 2 subgrids. Each row, column, and 2 × 2 subgrid contain numbers 1 through 4.
3. **6 × 6 Sudoku:** In 6 × 6 Sudoku, the grid is 6 × 6 in size and is divided into six 2 × 3 subgrids. Each row, column, and 2 × 3 subgrid must contain numbers 1–6.
4. **Samurai Sudoku:** Samurai Sudoku is a variant that consists of five overlapping 9 × 9 grids. The objective is to fill in the entire arrangement so that each row, column, and 3 × 3 subgrid in each of the five grids contains numbers 1–9.
5. **Hyper Sudoku (4 × 4 regions):** Hyper Sudoku uses a 9 × 9 grid, but the subgrids are irregular and can have different shapes. In addition, there were four 2 × 2 subregions within the grid. The objective was the same as that of the classic Sudoku.
6. **Giant Sudoku:** Giant Sudoku puzzles have larger grids, often ranging from 12 × 12 to 25 × 25, or even larger. Larger grid sizes provide more challenging puzzle-solving experience.
7. **Diagonal Sudoku:** In Diagonal Sudoku, along with the usual rows, columns, and 3 × 3 subgrids, the diagonals must also contain numbers 1 through 9 (or the corresponding numbers for different grid sizes).
8. **Irregular Sudoku:** Irregular Sudoku, also known as Jigsaw Sudoku, has irregularly shaped subgrids instead of standard 3 × 3 boxes. The objective remains the same: each row, column,

and irregular subgrid must contain numbers 1 through 9 (or the corresponding numbers for different grid sizes).

9. **Killer Sudoku:** Killer Sudoku combines elements of Sudoku and Kakuro. Kakuro is a crossword number puzzle in which each number word must add up to the number provided as a clue above or to the left of it. In this variant, you are given additional information in the form of "cages" that represent the sum of the numbers within that cage. The objective was to fill the grid with numbers that satisfied the sum constraints for each cage.

3D Sudoku [11] is a variation of the classic Sudoku puzzle that adds an extra dimension to the game. Instead of the usual 9 × 9 grid, 3D Sudoku is played on a 9 × 9 × 9 grid, which means that it has nine 3 × 3 × 3 cubes. The objective is the same as that of traditional Sudoku: fill in the grid so that every row, column, and 3 × 3 × 3 cube contains the numbers 1 through 9 with no repetition.

Figure 1.1 shows a 25 × 25 Sudoku instance where clues are highlighted in red, whereas Figure 1.2 provides a solution to that Sudoku instance. Although Sudoku puzzles are primarily enjoyed as recreational games,

1		4	20	25	24		15	17	10		8	18	14	22	6	12	9	3	16	2	7		23	5
5	2		23	24	8	22	12	9	3	16	6	7	20	17	18	21	25	14	13	10	11	4	1	15
17	14		6	3	25	21	5	7	20	11			1	13	4	8					12	16	22	19
16	7	21	8	18	4	2	13	11	23	5	19	15	24		10	20	17	22	1	9	6	25		3
10	13			22	14	1		6	16	23	9	25	4	3	7	5	19	11	2	8	24	20		17
12	1	11	10	6	5	13	23	24	15			8	17	21	25	19	3	4			14	2	20	18
8	19	13	21	9	16	4	25	12	2	15	3	5	11	20	14			18	22	1	10	7	24	6
4	17		18	7	9	3	22	21	19	25	1	24	2	23	5	13	20	10	6	16	15	8	11	12
22	3	24	15		18	20			7	10	13	4	6	14	16	2	12	21	8	5	19			9
20	16	2	25	5	10	8	6	14	17	9	22	12			1	11	15	7	24	3	23	21	13	4
13	25	3	5	10	2	23	14	4	18	22	15	17	19	24	20	7	1	9	21	12	16	6	8	11
14	23	1	24	12	19	16	8			2	7	20		10	3	4	13	17	11	21	9	5	18	22
7	8			17	20	24	21	22	9	3	4	1		16	2	6				25	13	15	10	
2	22	16	9	21	17	11	7	10	25	8	5	14	13	6	12	24	18	15	23	19	4	1	3	
6	15	20	19	4	13	12	3	5	1	18			21	9	8	22	16	25	10	7	17	24	2	14
21	18	12	2	16	7	10	19	3	13	1	24	22	9	4	11	15	6	20	14	17	8	23	5	25
9			13	1	6	25	4	20	12	17	14			18	23	16		5	19	11	21		15	2
23	10	22	7	15	21			18	14	6	20	16	8	11	17	1		13	25	4	3		12	24
25	5	6	14	11	1	17	2	8	24	13			23	15	9	3		12	4	20	18	22	16	7
3	20	17	4	19	22	15	16	23	11	12	25	10	5	2	21	18	8	24	7	6	1	14	9	13
19	6	23		8	15	18	1	25	4	14	2	9	3	7	13	10	11		20	24			17	21
15	4	5	17	14	3	7		19	8	20	23	11	10	25	22	9		1	12	13	2	18	6	16
11	12	7	16		23	6		2	21	24	18	13	15	1	19	25	5	8	3	14	22	9	4	10
18	9	25	1	2	11	14		13	22	4	12		16	5		23	7	6	17	15			19	8
24	21	10	3	13	12	9	20	16	5	19	17	6	22	8	15	14	4	2	18	23	25	11	7	1

Figure 1.1 An instance of a 2D Sudoku puzzle of size 25 × 25 with clues highlighted in red.

1	11	4	20	25	24	19	15	17	10	21	8	18	14	22	6	12	9	3	16	2	7	13	23	5
5	2	19	23	24	8	22	12	9	3	16	6	7	20	17	18	21	25	14	13	10	11	4	1	15
17	14	9	6	3	25	21	5	7	20	11	10	2	1	13	4	8	24	23	15	18	12	16	22	19
16	7	21	8	18	4	2	13	11	23	5	19	15	24	12	10	20	17	22	1	9	6	25	14	3
10	13	15	12	22	14	1	18	6	16	23	9	25	4	3	7	5	19	11	2	8	24	20	21	17
12	1	11	10	6	5	13	23	24	15	7	16	8	17	21	25	19	3	4	9	22	14	2	20	18
8	19	13	21	9	16	4	25	12	2	15	3	5	11	20	14	17	23	18	22	1	10	7	24	6
4	17	14	18	7	9	3	22	21	19	25	1	24	2	23	5	13	20	10	6	16	15	8	11	12
22	3	24	15	23	18	20	11	1	7	10	13	4	6	14	16	2	12	21	8	5	19	17	25	9
20	16	2	25	5	10	8	6	14	17	9	22	12	18	19	1	11	15	7	24	3	23	21	13	4
13	25	3	5	10	2	23	14	4	18	22	15	17	19	24	20	7	1	9	21	12	16	6	8	11
14	23	1	24	12	19	16	8	15	6	2	7	20	25	10	3	4	13	17	11	21	9	5	18	22
7	8	18	11	17	20	24	21	22	9	3	4	1	12	16	2	6	14	19	5	25	13	15	10	23
2	22	16	9	21	17	11	7	10	25	8	5	14	13	6	12	24	18	15	23	19	4	1	3	20
6	15	20	19	4	13	12	3	5	1	18	11	23	21	9	8	22	16	25	10	7	17	24	2	14
21	18	12	2	16	7	10	19	3	13	1	24	22	9	4	11	15	6	20	14	17	8	23	5	25
9	24	8	13	1	6	25	4	20	12	17	14	3	7	18	23	16	22	5	19	11	21	10	15	2
23	10	22	7	15	21	5	9	18	14	6	20	16	8	11	17	1	2	13	25	4	3	19	12	24
25	5	6	14	11	1	17	2	8	24	13	21	19	23	15	9	3	10	12	4	20	18	22	16	7
3	20	17	4	19	22	15	16	23	11	12	25	10	5	2	21	18	8	24	7	6	1	14	9	13
19	6	23	22	8	15	18	1	25	4	14	2	9	3	7	13	10	11	16	20	24	5	12	17	21
15	4	5	17	14	3	7	24	19	8	20	23	11	10	25	22	9	21	1	12	13	2	18	6	16
11	12	7	16	20	23	6	17	2	21	24	18	13	15	1	19	25	5	8	3	14	22	9	4	10
18	9	25	1	2	11	14	10	13	22	4	12	21	16	5	24	23	7	6	17	15	20	3	19	8
24	21	10	3	13	12	9	20	16	5	19	17	6	22	8	15	14	4	2	18	23	25	11	7	1

Figure 1.2 A solution instance of 2D Sudoku puzzle of size 25 × 25 given in Figure 1.1.

they have also found interesting applications in various fields. One such application is video encryption, in which Sudoku-based algorithms can be utilized to secure video content.

A Sudoku instance can be solved in multiple ways because we can start from any given clue present in the minigrids. However, in contemporary literature, no technique has been described to determine the number of starting cells. The starting cell becomes fascinating to a mathematician only if it follows a minimal route, and the removal or inclusion of a single clue may generate another Sudoku instance for which other new solutions may exist. Moreover, no current technique can determine the minimum number of clues to be provided to the cells. This accounts for the maximum number of variations in Sudoku puzzle instances. The authors in [8] stated that a minimum of 17 clues are needed to ensure that a Sudoku instance, if solvable, has only one unique solution. Therefore, any Sudoku puzzle instance with fewer than 17 givens, if valid, must have more than one solution. However, a valid Sudoku instance may have multiple correct solutions even if the instance includes more than 17 clues. Several techniques exist for the solving a Sudoku puzzle, which differ depending on the difficulty level of the puzzle. According to contemporary literature, the level of difficulty of a Sudoku puzzle is governed by its number of clues [9]. The relationship between the difficulty level of a Sudoku puzzle and the number of clues presented is shown in Table 1.1.

In addition to the number of clues, the position of the empty cells also influences the difficulty level. For any two Sudoku puzzle instances with the same number of clues, the puzzle where the clues are present in clusters/groups is assigned a higher difficulty level than the puzzle with an even distribution of clues. According to the row and column constraints presented in [9], the minimum possible number of clues, in each row and column for different difficulty levels is set as given in Table 1.2.

Sudoku can also be used for video encryption. Sudoku puzzles have a unique property that can be used to scramble and encrypt data. Sudoku puzzles can be used to create a 9 × 9 matrix that can be used to map the pixels of a video frame to new positions. This scrambling process makes it difficult for unauthorized users to decrypt a video without the correct key.

Table 1.1 Definition of the Sudoku instance difficulty level according to the number of given clues.

Difficulty level	Number of clues
1 (Extremely Easy)	>46
2 (Easy)	36–46
3 (Medium)	32–35
4 (Hard)	28–31
5 (Evil)	17–27

Table 1.2 Minimum possible number of clues, in each row and column of a Sudoku instance for different levels of difficulty.

Difficulty level	Minimum possible number of clues in each row and column
1 (Extremely Easy)	05
2 (Easy)	04
3 (Medium)	03
4 (Hard)	02
5 (Evil)	00

There are several different ways to use Sudoku puzzles for video encryption. A common method is to use the Sudoku matrix to create a permutation function. This function can then be applied to the pixels of a video frame to scramble them. Another common method is to use a Sudoku matrix to create a substitution function. This function can then be used to replace pixel values with new values. Sudoku-based video encryption is a relatively new and an emerging field. However, they have enormous potential advantages over other encryption methods. For example, Sudoku-based encryption is relatively simple to implement and does not require specialized hardware or software. In addition, Sudoku-based encryption is highly resistant to attacks.

Here are some of the potential applications of Sudoku-based video encryption:

- Securing confidential video communications
- Protecting copyrighted video content
- Enhancing the security of video surveillance systems

Video encryption involves the process of transforming a video file into ciphertext, which can only be deciphered with a corresponding decryption key. This ensures that unauthorized individuals cannot access or understand video content. Traditional encryption methods often employ complex mathematical algorithms; however, Sudoku-based encryption offers an alternative approach that combines simplicity and security. Sudoku-based encryption provides several advantages. First, it offers a visually pleasing and challenging encryption method that can engage users in solving the Sudoku puzzle to decrypt a video. Second, the simplicity of Sudoku rules and transformations makes them easier to implement and understand than the complex mathematical algorithms used in traditional encryption methods. Finally, Sudoku-based encryption can provide a level of security suitable for certain applications, particularly when combined with other encryption techniques and key management practices. This study used Giant Sudoku to generate the key. As for 25×25 Sudoku 7.5×10^{22}, possible Sudoku solution grids are there, which is huge. Therefore, extracting a key is impossible for an attacker.

1.2 Literature Survey

Sudoku has enormous applications in the fields of cryptography [12], steganography [2], and encryption of messages, texts, images, audio, and videos. In today's digital world, securing data from all possible attacks is very crucial. The proposed method works on a video file to transmit the file securely. Data security is of paramount concern in the digital age. As the volume of information exchanged online continues to increase, so do the risks associated with unauthorized access and tampering. Traditional encryption methods rely on complex algorithms and mathematical operations. Many researchers are exploring this area to make today's digital world more secure.

In 2018, Rupali *et al.* [6] encrypted a digital video by applying a Simplified Data Encryption Standard and the chaotic map concept. In their work, the RSA algorithm was used to exchange keys. In 2019, Jana *et al.* [2] developed a video steganographic scheme that uses color videos and hides values in 9 × 9 Sudoku. To hide the video into 9 × 9 Sudoku, every time this 9 × 9 Sudoku needs to be replicated to continue the procedure. The time required for our proposed method is less than that required in their work without compromising video quality.

To protect data in the cloud, especially images, Tyagi *et al.* [3] developed a hybrid algorithm by combining AES and Fernet incorporating double-level encryption with CNN Auto-Encoders. This model provides a more secure cloud computing model than the other existing models. The original images are processed as input, encrypted/decrypted, converted into bitmap images as outputs that are decrypted by users with 'key' when needed. The developed model primarily focuses on pre-processing the original images and passing them to double-level encryption, where the Fernet and Advanced Encryption Standard (AES) algorithms are utilized as hybrid models. Using this two-level encryption method, the image is passed through the CNN and is initially trained. Once the encryptions (Fernet and AES) are successful, the images are stored and accessed through decryption. AES and Fernet algorithms were applied, and the vector image was processed and regenerated as the original image (bitmap) to obtain the output in a secure manner.

In 2021, Haridas *et al.* [5] developed a Quasigroup Video Encryption Scheme (QuVench). Using this method, near-real-time secure processing of video data was achieved. In this encryption method, compressed video is considered. The authors proposed a novel approach using Sudoku, which offers a unique and intriguing alternative for video encryption. Here, the complexity of key extraction was very high. Therefore, it is very difficult for an attacker to extract an encryption key.

In another study, Matin *et al.* [7] described the encryption and compression properties of a CCRM camera. In this case, it appears to be a formidable imaging system for applications demanding highly encrypted and compressed data acquisition at high frame rates. The experiments demonstrated that the original data could only be recovered using the encryption key observed by the detector. In their study, the authors introduced an amplitude-encoding technique for the encryption and compression. Introducing the same, the key-space has been significantly extended, and the risk of brute-force attacks on data recovery is substantially reduced.

Recently, research has been conducted on 3D Sudoku because its application can potentially revolutionize different application domains. Various 3D puzzles are being applied in ongoing research, including structural control in metal additive manufacturing [13], historical artifacts [14], image steganography [15], and various security issues.

1.3 Proposed Methodology

In this study, we perform video encryption, which transforms a video file into ciphertext with the help of Sudoku-Fernet. Fernet is a symmetric encryption algorithm [4] that is a part of the cryptography library in Python. It is designed to provide secure and fast encryption and decryption of the data. Fernet uses symmetric key cryptography, in which the same key is used for both encryption and decryption. When using Fernet, a key can be generated using the Fernet.generate_key() method, which produces a random 256-bit key encoded in URL-safe base 64. This generated key is typically used to encrypt and decrypt data. However, Fernet also allows the use a user-generated key instead of a random key. To use a user-generated key with Fernet using Sudoku, we used the correct format where our generated key is a URL-safe, base 64 encoded 256-bit key. Using a user-generated key, we can have more control over the encryption process. However, this work uses the *i*th solution of a 25 × 25 Sudoku puzzle and 'diamond-plus' pattern to produce the elements to form the strongest key. The security of encrypted data depends on the strength and confidentiality of the key. Our proposed method generates a Sudoku-Fernet, which makes data secure because it is very difficult to break. Our key generation algorithm and video encryption process are described in *Section 1.3.1.*

1.3.1 Proposed Algorithm for Generating Sudoku-Fernet Cipher Key

To generate the 44-byte long key for video data encryption, we consider the *i*th solution of a 25 × 25 Sudoku puzzle. We derive the first 25 elements (1 byte each) from the *i*th solution and, to that end, we take center elements from each of the 25 mini-grids. The *i*th solution and the center elements of the mini-grids are shown in Figure 1.3. The center elements are shown in gray cells and

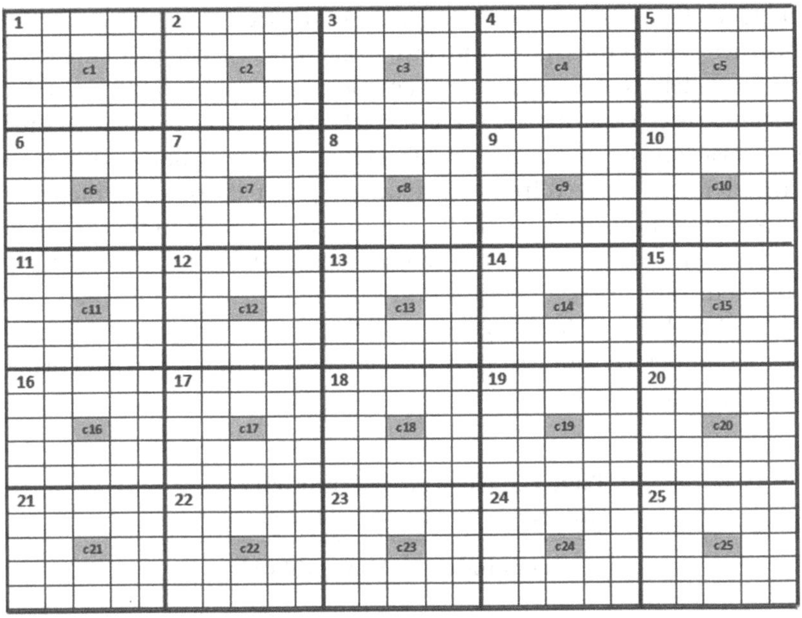

Figure 1.3 The *i*th solution of a 25 × 25 Sudoku puzzle and the 25 center elements of the mini-grids.

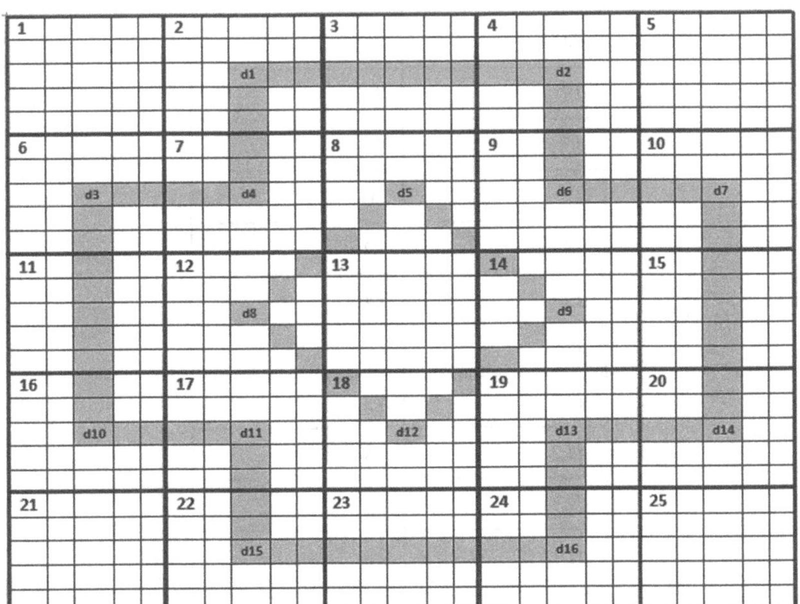

Figure 1.4 The *i*th solution of a 25 × 25 Sudoku puzzle and the 16 elements forming the diamond plus pattern.

numbered *c1* to *c25* in the Sudoku grid. The mini-grid index is shown at the top left corner of each mini-grid. The next 16 elements (1 byte each) are derived from the pattern that we address as diamond-plus, as shown in Figure 1.4. The remaining three elements are three special characters (1 byte each). Finally, this 44-byte long key is passed through a fernet for encryption purposes.

The elements derived from the diamond plus pattern are affiliated with the following mini-grids in the *i*th solution of the Sudoku puzzle, and are described in Table 1.3. All 16 elements were the central elements of the concerned mini-grids. Elements derived from diamond plus pattern are identified with the index range *d1* to *d16* in the gray region of Figure 1.4, and are numbered from 1 to 16, which is shown at the upper-left corner of each of the mini- grids.

Table 1.3 Elements and their mini-grid indices in diamond plus pattern.

Element index	Mini-grid index
d1	2
d2	4
d3	6
d4	7
d5	8
d6	9
d7	10
d8	12
d9	14
d10	16
d11	17
d12	18
d13	19
d14	20
d15	22
d16	24

Algorithm 1: Algorithm for generating Cipher Key CK for video encryption using Sudoku in Fernet.

Require: *ISL*, the *i*th solution of a 2D Sudoku matrix of dimension 25 × 25
Ensure: 44-byte long Cipher Key *CK*
Definition: In this algorithm, a minigrid is a 5 × 5 matrix; minigrid indices are considered row wise, left to right
Assign: Tag numbers at the top left corner cell of each mini grid

```
Initialize CK []
    m= 25
    for i in m do:
        CK.append(c_i)
    // c_i is of 1 byte and each element is the centre element of the mini
    grid of the ISL //
    n = 16
    for i in n do:
        CK.append(d_i)
    // d_i is of 1 byte and each element is the center element of the min-
    igrid lying on the 'diamond plus' pattern of ISL as shown in Figure
    1.4; mini grid indices are shown in Table 1.3 //
    P = 3
    for i in p do:
        CK.append(s_i)
    // s_i is a special character of 1 byte; i ranges from 1 to 3 //
    Finally, CK is derived as follows:
        CK = (c1:c25) + (d1: d16) + (s1: s3)
    // CK is a 44-byte long cipher key and is passed through the fernet
    to do the needful //
```

1.3.2 Encryption Process

After the generation of the key, the data are passed through the fernet skeleton. The encryption of the video data is performed using the Fernet object that we have already generated using our Giant Sudoku Fernet cipher key. Before encrypting video data, Fernet applies a sequence of operations to prepare the data for encryption:

a. *Fernet pads the data*: The video data are padded to meet the encryption block-size requirement. Fernet uses the PKCS7 padding scheme, which adds bytes to the input data to ensure that it is a multiple of the encryption block size (in this case, 128 bits or 16 bytes for the AES-128 encryption used by Fernet).

b. *Fernet generates an initialization vector (IV)*: An IV is a random value used as an additional input during the encryption process to ensure that each encryption produces a unique ciphertext, even for the same input. IV is generated securely and is unique for each encryption operation.

c. *Fernet constructs the encryption payload*: The encryption payload consists of the IV, padded video data, and other necessary information required for decryption.

Fernet performs symmetric encryption: Fernet uses AES in Cipher Block Chaining (CBC) mode with a 128-bit key size. The AES algorithm was applied to the encryption payload using a Fernet key. The CBC mode encrypts each block of data with the previous ciphertext block, ensuring that changes in one block affect the encryption of subsequent blocks, thereby enhancing security.

The encrypted ciphertext is returned: The resulting ciphertext obtained by applying AES encryption to the encryption payload, is the encrypted version of the video data.

1.4 Result Analysis

The use of giant Sudoku in the field of encryption is rare, particularly when using a Fernet key. Fernet uses a 44-byte long encryption key. In our study, we derive a 44-byte long encryption key that is passed through a Fernet for video encryption and decryption.

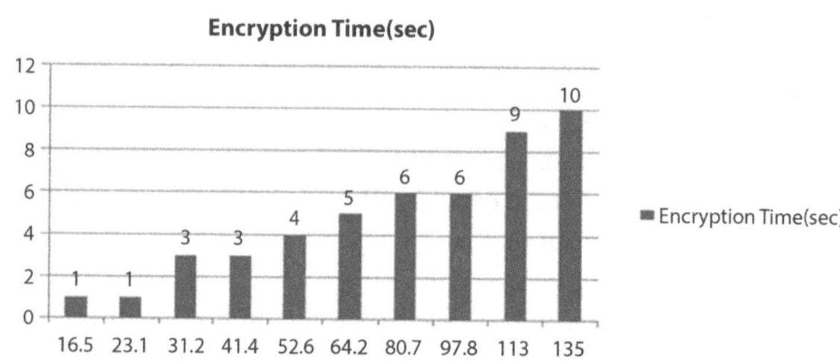

Figure 1.5 Video size vs. encryption time.

To that end, a graph is provided in Figure 1.5, based on the data available in Table 1.4, to judge the feasibility of the video size vs. encryption time. The specifications of the test bed and the video clips taken for the experiment are provided in Tables 1.5 and 1.6.

Table 1.4 Video sizes (mb) and corresponding encryption times (s).

Sl. no.	Video clip size (mb)	Encryption time (s)
1	16.5	1
2	23.1	1
3	31.2	3
4	41.4	3
5	52.6	4
6	64.2	5
7	80.7	6
8	97.8	6
9	113	9
10	135	10

Table 1.5 Hardware test-bed specification.

Hardware resource	Specification
Processor	Intel® Core™ i5-7200U
CPU speed	2.50 GHz
RAM	8 GB
OS	Windows (64-bit)
Python coding platform	Anaconda 3

Table 1.6 Video clip specification.

Video parameter	Specification
Video codec	AVC
Video encoding type	H264
Audio codec	mp3
Audio encoding type	stereo
Video quality	1,080 p
Audio channel	dual stereo
Video type	Full HD
Audio type	Dolby Atmos 5.1 surround channel
Video frame height	1,920
Video frame width	1,080

1.5 Computational Complexity

The complexity of video encryption using the Fernet cryptographic module depends on several factors, including the size of the video file (n), encryption algorithm used (e.g., AES-128 in Fernet), and underlying implementation details. The time complexity for reading a video file is typically $O(n)$, where n represents the size of the video file. This is because reading the entire file requires iteration over each byte or block of data. The time complexity of the encryption process is influenced by the encryption algorithm used (e.g., AES-128) and block size of the algorithm. For example, if we consider AES-128, which operates on 128-bit blocks (16 bytes), the time complexity for encryption can be expressed as $O(n / 16)$, where 16 is the block size. This indicates that the encryption time increases linearly with the size of the video file but with a smaller constant factor due to the block size. Overall, the time complexity of video encryption using Fernet is $O(n)$, assuming that the encryption process dominates the time complexity.

1.6 Conclusions

The generation of secure and unpredictable encryption keys remains challenging. In this study, a novel approach is proposed that employs Sudoku puzzles as a mechanism for generating symmetric keys. The cipher key is extracted by video encryption by passing the key through the Sudoku-Fernet fernet module, cipher key is extracted for video encryption. This study uses one of the solutions of Giant Sudoku of size 25 × 25, which is very difficult to identify and break owing to its uniqueness and difficult-to-solve property. The proposed method ensures the strength of Sudoku puzzles with cryptographic fernet modules to enhance the security of video encryption systems, thereby offering an innovative solution to protect sensitive video content.

A 25 × 25 Sudoku grid offers a high level of complexity and provides a large key space. This complexity can make it challenging for attackers to guess or brute-force a key. Sudoku involves nonlinear relationships between the numbers in each row, column, and subgrid. This nonlinearity of Giant Sudoku also enhances the security of the key generation process. The filled cells in the Sudoku grid can be considered pseudo-random sequences. This adds an element of unpredictability to the key-generation process. With a 25 × 25 grid, there are many possible ways to arrange numbers, creating a vast number of potential keys. We have used "diamond plus" pattern by applying a new key generation idea. This variability makes it more difficult for attackers to analyze or predict key structures. Thus, this algorithm secures the video in the strongest way by adding extra security to the Fernet cryptographic module during encryption.

References

1. Nishikawa, K. and Toda, T., Exact Method for Generating Strategy-Solvable Sudoku Clues. *Algorithms*, *13*, 7, 171, 2020.
2. Jana, S., Maji, A.K., Pal, R.K., A novel spn-based video steganographic scheme using Sudoku puzzle for secured data hiding. *Innov. Syst. Softw. Eng.*, 15, 1, 65–73, 2019.
3. Tyagi, S.S., Enhancing security of cloud data through encryption with AES and Fernet algorithm through convolutional-neural-networks (CNN). *Int. J. Comput. Netw. Appl.*, 8, 4, 288–299, 2021.
4. John, N. and Philip, A., FERNET System. *Proc. Natl. Conf. Emerging Comput. Appl. (NCECA)*, 3, 1, 215–217, 2021.

5. Haridas, D., Kiran, D.S., Patel, S., Raghavendra, K., Venkatraman, S., Venkatraman, R., Real-time compressed video encryption: Based on quasigroup on system on chip (SOC). *SN Comput. Sci.*, 2, 5, 408, 2021.
6. Hole, R.N. and Kolhekar, M., Robust encryption of uncompressed videos with a selective frame scheme, in: *2018 3rd International Conference for Convergence in Technology (I2CT)*, IEEE, pp. 1–7, 2018.
7. Matin, A. and Wang, X., Video encryption/compression using compressive coded rotating mirror camera. *Sci. Rep.*, 11, 1, 23191, 2021, doi: 10.1038/s41598-021-02520-8. PMID: 34848771; PMCID: PMC8633330.
8. McGuire, G., Tugemann, B., Civario, G., There is No 16-Clue Sudoku: Solving the Sudoku Minimum Number of Clues Problem, via Hitting Set Enumeration. *Experimental Mathematics*, 23, School of Mathematical Sciences, University College Dublin, 2012, 10.1080/10586458.2013.870056.
9. Lee, W.-M., *Programming Sudoku*, Apress, USA, 2006.
10. Maji, A.K., Jana, S., Pal, R.K., An algorithm for generating only desired permutations for solving sudoku puzzle. *Procedia Technol.*, 10, 392–399, 2013.
11. Jana, S., Mallik, M., Khan, A., Maji, A.K., Pal, R.K., Design and Analysis of a Modified 3D Sudoku Solver. *IEEE Access*, 11, 27352–27368, 2023.
12. Sharma, N., A review of information security using cryptography technique. *Int. J. Adv. Res. Comput. Sci.*, 8, 4, 323–326, 2017.
13. Ikeo, N., Fukuda, H., Matsugaki, A., Inoue, T., Serizawa, A., Matsuzaka, T., Ishimoto, T., Ozasa, R., Gokcekaya, O., Nakano, T., 3d puzzle in cube pattern for anisotropic/isotropic mechanical control of structure fabricated by metal additive manufacturing. *Crystals*, 11, 8, 959, 2021.
14. Capece, N., Erra, U., Gruosso, M., Anastasio, M., Archaeo puzzle: An educational game using natural user interface for historical artifacts, in: *Eurographics Workshop on Graphics and Cultural Heritage*, The Eurographics Association, 2020.
15. Xia, B., Wang, A., Chang, C.-C., Liu, L., An image steganography scheme using 3d-sudoku. *J. Inf. Hiding Multim. Signal Process.*, 7, 4, 836–845, 2016.

2

Watermarking: Characteristics, Methods, and Evaluation

Soumitra Roy[1]* and Bappaditya Chakraborty[2]

[1]Dept. of CSE, Dr. Sudhir Chandra Sur Institute of Technology & Sports Complex, Dum Dum, Kolkata, India
[2]Maulana Abul Kalam Azad University of Technology, Kolkata, India

Abstract

In the last decade, digitization of multimedia data (video, audio, images) is a common factor for the cost, space, and more significantly time effective business models with the swift progression of communication networks. In this counterfeit planet, counterfeiting, forging, alteration, and limitless replication of digital data are produced by illegitimate users with easily available user-friendly software and hardware materials. These criminal-minded people use the modern web network to distribute altered digital data in a smooth, errorless, and economical way. Thus, the main flaw for this transmitted digital data is not have inbuilt inherent security. Recently researchers suggested that this inbuilt inherent security can be provided to digital data if they satisfied confidentiality, integrity, and authenticity features. Stopping unlawful access by illegitimate consumers is confidentiality whereas locating the alteration of digital content by unlawful users is integrity. Authentication prevents countless illicit distributions of copyrighted digital materials. Both the cryptography and steganography mechanisms guaranteed confidentiality features. The foremost shortcoming of the cryptographic and steganographic methods is that the disclosed/decrypted data suffers from counterfeit alteration and plagiarized redistribution of digital data. Nowadays all the security domain researchers recommend that it would be not better but best if security is embedded before the transmission of digital signal not during transmission. This proves that the digital watermarking concept where the watermark is embedded logically or physically into the digital object can easily attain the confidentiality, integrity, and authenticity features. This watermarking research domain initiates with spatial domain watermarking methods where watermark embedding is done

**Corresponding author*: mousinapur.sou@gmail.com

Subhabrata Barman, Santanu Koley and Subhankar Joardar (eds.) Next-Generation Systems and Secure Computing, (17–38) © 2025 Scrivener Publishing LLC

by transforming the host image pixel data. Modern researchers logically explained the drawback of these types of schemes where geometric attacks on host images can remove that inserted watermarks. To make the watermark untraceable in the host object watermark is inserted asymmetrically inside transformed objects coefficients for the transformed domain schemes. In conclusion, modern researchers are interested in developing transform domain-based watermarking schemes. During the design of different watermarking schemes, it is found that the cover object is modified permanently which is known as the irreversible watermarking method. Where the cover object is also important like medial and military watermarking techniques reversible watermarking will be a better approach there. Another crucial dispute that arises during designing a watermarking is that an adequate amount of information should be inserted to be robust against small alterations without annihilating the existing watermark in the cover object. A high-capacity watermarking scheme may become visually imperceptible. This conflict fabricates another issue during the design of the watermarking scheme. To evaluate the proposed watermarking algorithms important characteristics are (i) Imperceptibility, (ii) Robustness, and (iii) Embedding capacity.

Keywords: Watermarking, reversible watermarking, irreversible watermarking

2.1 Introduction

In the modern social media and digital era, assuring the copyright protection/authenticity, integrity, and confidentiality of communicated social media content (e.g., Twitter, Facebook, ChatGPT, WeChat, and Ding Talk in the form of audio, video, and images) is of supreme significance. However, this speedily mounting electronic data of social media and relentlessly rationalized data interaction, authenticity, and sheltered communication of these data will, of course, face new problems, as predicted. The swift progress in social media has endorsed images as prominent social media information carriers. On the other hand, throughout the procedure of image communication, images are enormously disposed to a diversity of premeditated/intentional attacks [1], which causes issues in the integrity and authenticity of the communicated image data. Sometimes, it becomes harmful for people's personal protection, political affairs, and civilization of society, etc., if this premeditated alteration modifies the court proof, medical analysis report, or any other crucial image content. The discussion concludes that ensuring the safety of image communication and maintaining the authenticity of these communicated image resources is a vital crisis that should be addressed [2]. As truthful, multimedia information such as images play a very important role in applications, including health care, military communication, security observation, and education. Owing to the natital security deficiency of open Internet channels, several cryptographic techniques [3] are used to protect digital data while they are being transmitted. The confidentiality of digital data is protected by a number of data encryption or cryptographic algorithms, including the Data Encryption Standard (DES), Advanced Encryption Standard (AES), CAST (named after Carlisle Adams and Stafford Tavares), RSA (named after Ron Rivest, Adi Shamir, and Leonard Adleman), International Data Encryption Algorithm (IDEA), and others. To protect data confidentiality, users typically send sensitive information to approved recipients in encrypted form. Due to the simple accessibility of multimedia modification tools, there is no control in these types of apps to monitor the unauthorized re-sharing of decrypted digital information once it has been unlocked. Security risks in this case are related to integrity, copyright protection, or authentication [3].

Both robust and fragile watermarking techniques are applied to preserve the authenticity, reliability, and integrity of multimedia data [1]. Digital watermarking [5] involves inserting data within the cover image that may later be retrieved or recognized to safeguard the authenticity and/or integrity of the cover object. The legitimacy of the watermarked information is guaranteed by robust watermarking algorithms [4], which makes it impossible to completely erase the copyright data, even after any sort of change to the corresponding watermarked image. However, under a fragile watermarking system, the watermark containing copyright metadata is lost whenever the watermarked image is changed in any way. The watermarked image's integrity was guaranteed by this feature. Fragile watermarkings [6] are typically employed in important applications such as healthcare imaging and forensic picture preservation, wherein reliability is crucial, given that any tampering to the dataset results in incorrect conclusions or judgments in the medical sector or unlawful offense, respectively. Watermark evidence ought to remain undetectable after being inserted within the cover image, for example, and tampering should be localized even following the watermarked image's alteration or modification. These are the common requirements for fragile watermarking.

(i) Protecting the ownership rights of digital materials and (ii) maintaining digital content integrity are the two main goals of robust and fragile watermarking. However, the semi-fragile watermarking approach partially complements the traits of robust and fragile watermarking. These

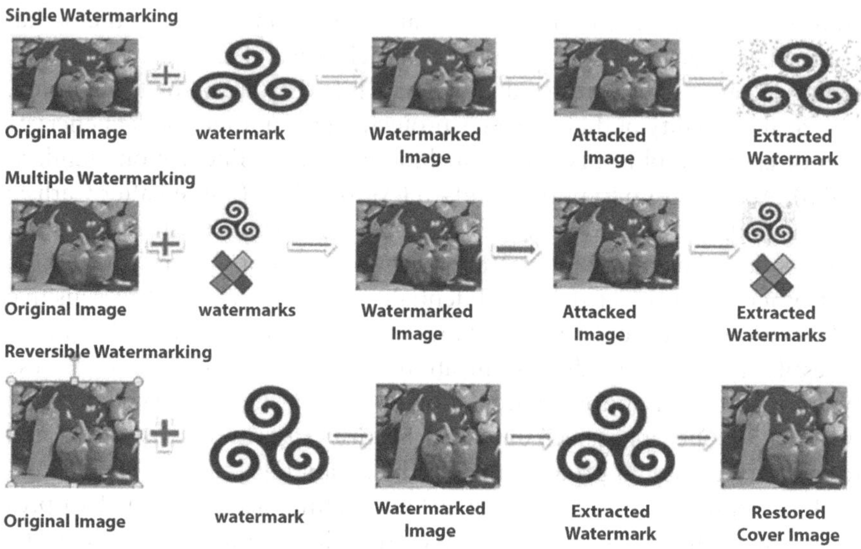

Figure 2.1 Basic watermarking steps.

types of watermarking may withstand a limited number of attempts at picture manipulation and are suitable for identifying modified image regions.

2.1.1 Chapter Organization

The remainder of this study is structured as follows. *Section 2.2* gives a watermark definition with its various applications. The distinctiveness of the digital watermarking technique is discussed in *Section 2.3*. *Section 2.4* represents a classification of digital watermarking. To evaluate various watermarking systems, *Section 2.5* discusses several types of watermarking attacks. This chapter is concluded in *Section 2.6*.

2.2 Watermark Definition

In general, a digital watermark is unique code that identifies the owner, creator, authorized user, or distributor of a digital file. Digital watermarking is a process in which this digital watermark is inserted imperceptibly into cover objects for applications such as content authentication, copyright protection, illegal copying, fingerprinting, content archiving, broadcast monitoring, distribution, and tampering of digital objects.

In the digital watermarking technique, the cover object is sometimes permanently marked because in irreversible watermarking techniques, the watermark is inserted with a slight modification of the cover object, and in the case of reversible watermarking schemes, the digital host object is restored after the recovery of the watermark on the receiver side. However, for joint endeavors or collaborative projects, a single watermark containing information connected to one creator cannot be embedded in the cover material. For such usage, the cover media should have several mutually exclusive watermarks to provide intrinsic security and protect the ownership interests of different owners.

2.2.1 Digital Watermarking Applications

Modern industries have used digital watermarking to secure multimedia data. Here, we briefly discuss a few ways in which watermarking [7] is used to safeguard multimedia data in many different applications.

2.2.1.1 Copyright Protection

Among the most effective uses of digital watermarking is for copyright safeguarding of digital data, in which the user embeds copyright protection sequences, such as a corporation or sender's emblem or signature, within the original cover medium to demonstrate who created the digital content. Copyright protection can limit some of the most significant illicit processes such as digital data manipulation, duplication, and content circulation. Unauthorized copies of the material can even be regulated and tracked by encoding the identity of the buyer and the legal ownership of the copyright holder.

2.2.1.2 Fingerprinting

A fingerprint timestamp/watermark functions similarly to an interim watermark. This aids in locating the source of the data that is repeated without permission. The container will have unique watermarks for different owners. The foundation from which the information is copied is determined using a fingerprinting technique. The proprietor or different intermediary layer clients/recipients implant their identification data/information into the cover material using the appropriate watermarking method throughout the fingerprinting integrating chain methodology. The holder can recreate the knowledge about the central-level embedding network and reconstruct the initial cover media on the receiver side. By disclosing details to another party, it permits the owner to recognize clients who have wrecked the terms of the license. If someone abuses digital data, it is simple or perhaps extremely simple to find the responsible client.

2.2.1.3 *Broadcast Monitoring*

Certain advertisers use this program to televise watermarked content at a precise time and location. The use of watermarking reveals that it tracks or observes data being broadcast, noting the time and place of broadcasting.

The broadcasted stations were being observed using specialized devices. In addition, it assists in identifying those responsible for transmitting copyright content. An autonomous observation system determines whether broadcast commercials follow the contract before adding a watermark to them. Every time a product is broadcast, owners of exclusive videos must pay royalties.

2.2.1.4 *Tamper Proofing*

When information is intentionally faked maliciously and purposefully, tamper-proofing is used to detect it by embedding a watermark that can be easily removed by a small implementation. As an illustration, a security tool such as CCTV has evolved from an analog-to-digital (A/D) system, yet all data are recorded in digital form. One significant disadvantage is that a regular user with a system can operate using digital information. Digital video recording devices, digital cameras, and other tools of various kinds are used in these methods.

2.3 Properties of Watermarking

Any proposed watermarking system must have a few fundamental characteristics in order to increase security and improve efficacy. However, the nature of an application determines the requirements for each characteristic. The following are some of the crucial features of the watermarking system:

(i) Imperceptibility: The Human Visual System (HVS) do not distinguish between authentic and watermarked information if it is imperceptible. The resulting modification of subjective picture quality (using the suggested watermarking approach) should be assessed to calculate the invisibility/imperceptibility assessment. To determine the perceptual resemblance between the host picture and watermarked picture, the peak signal-to-noise ratio (PSNR) was used. The criteria in support of the effective invisible watermarking approaches are

(a) *Embedded watermark data must be invisible/imperceptible* according to the normal *HVS and should be ensured by (b) standard typical benchmark PSNR data.*

PSNR data are presented in decibels (dBs). According to Petitcolas [8], the lowest permissible PSNR value for optimum imperceptibility was 38 dB. Given that PSNR is not a useful limitation when considering geometric distortions, this convention is questionable [9].
PSNR is defined as follows:

$$PSNR = 10 \times \log_{10} \frac{\max(x(i,j))^2}{MSE} \tag{2.1}$$

Where the following definition applies to the mean square error (MSE) involving the host image x and the watermarked image $\bar{x}$:

$$MSE = \frac{1}{M \times N} \sum_{i=1}^{M} \sum_{j=1}^{N} (x_{ij} - \bar{x}_{ij})^2 \tag{2.2}$$

Here, the numerals M and N represent the width and height of the image and x_{ij} is the image pixel intensity measurement of the original image's coordinates (i, j) and $\bar{x}_{ij}$ is equivalent to the consequent watermarked image's value. In simple terms, the PSNR was calculated to assess the perceived value of the cover image and the watermarked image after the watermark was embedded.
The PSNR for a color image is defined as follows:

$$\text{PSNR} = 10 \times \log_{10} \frac{255^2 \times 3}{\text{MSE(R)} + \text{MSE(G)} + \text{MSE(B)}} \tag{2.3}$$

When comparing the host image and watermarked public image, the mean square error (MSE) involving the red (R), green (G), and blue (B) constituents is described by the following formula:

$$\text{MSE} = \frac{1}{M \times N} \sum_{i=1}^{M} \sum_{j=1}^{N} (x_{ij} - \bar{x}_{ij})^2 \tag{2.4}$$

Here, the numerals M and N stand for an image's width and height, x_{ij} is the image pixel intensity measurement of the original image's coordinates (i, j) in blue/green/red section of original image and $\bar{x}_{ij}$ is equivalent to the consequent watermarked image's value.

(ii) Robustness: To determine the resilience benchmark feature of the suggested approach, bit-error-rate (BER) and normalized correlation (NC) data involving the original watermark and recovered deformed watermark (after implementing various types of planned attacks/without attacks) are examined. BER and NC can be defined as follows:

$$\text{BER} = \frac{\text{Number of error bits}}{\text{Total bits transmitted}} = \frac{\text{Number of error bits per second}}{\text{Data rate per second}} \tag{2.5}$$

$$\text{NC}(w, \bar{W}) = \frac{\sum_{i=1}^{M} \sum_{j=1}^{N} [w(i,j) - \mu_w] \times [\bar{w}(i,j) - \mu_{\bar{w}}]}{\sqrt{\sum_{i=1}^{M} \sum_{j=1}^{N} [w(i,j) - \mu_w]^2} \times \sqrt{\sum_{i=1}^{M} \sum_{j=1}^{N} [\bar{w}(i,j) - \mu_{\bar{w}}]^2}} \tag{2.6}$$

Here, the numerals N and M characterize an image's height and width, w(i,j) = The starting watermark's pixel intensity assessment at coordinates (i, j), $\overline{w}(i, j)$ = the watermark extraction pixel's intensity measurement at positions (i, j), μ_w = original watermark mean, $\mu_{\overline{w}}$ = extracted watermark mean correspondingly.

(iii) Embedding capacity: The carrying quantity of a watermark, also known as the watermark payload, redirects the quantity of data that must be implanted as a watermark for the receiver to successfully retrieve the watermark. Because raising the incorporated watermarking capacity of the data increased the watermarking scheme's robustness, which could impair the data's imperceptibility, there must be a trade-off/adjustment involving embedding capacity, robustness and imperceptibility. Therefore, a compromise among these three features is required to develop a successful watermarking system.

(iv) Readily embeddable and extractable: The suggested watermarking techniques must be simple to embed and extract watermark data.

(v) Computational complexity: The phrase "computational complexity" relates to the time and effort required to embed and extract watermarks from digital object content, and it is expressed in terms of actual CPU cycles. Computational complexity is another crucial criterion for assessing the effectiveness of watermarking algorithms.

2.4 Categorization of Watermarking

Watermarking approaches can be grouped into many different categories based on diverse qualities. Watermarking can be categorized into non-visible and visible watermarking based on how people perceive it. The cover image contains a visible watermark in the visible watermarking method; however, the major concerns in the non-visible watermarking method are the maintenance of the visual superiority of the watermark objects and the invisibility of the watermark emblem (by human sensibility). Depending on the details required for the detection method, watermarking systems may also be categorized into three categories: non-blind, semi-blind, and blind. In the blind method, neither the original information nor the watermark multimedia object's information is required for recognition. In the semi-blind method, the original multimedia object's information and, occasionally, watermark data are vital. In contrast, in the non-blind method, the original multimedia object's information and watermark object/data are required for detection. Several types of watermarking schemes, including text, audio, image, and video watermarking systems, depend on the type of material that needs to be sheltered. Watermarking techniques can be separated into two types based on their application: robust watermarking techniques and fragile watermarking techniques. Robust digital watermarking methods are used to protect copyrights. When using robust digital watermarking technology, the implanted watermark information nearly maintains the perceived quality of the watermarked image while fending off various attacks and modifications. Tamper detection and data authentication frequently employ fragile watermarking techniques. The goal of fragile watermarking techniques is to incorporate a watermark that is vulnerable to basic signal-processing assaults. A hybrid of a robust and fragile watermarking scheme, a semi-fragile watermarking procedure is created in accordance with the cover object's integrity property. Comparable to the robust watermarking method and a semi-fragile watermarking may introduce some degree of legitimate deformation into the watermarked item, whereas fragile watermarking can identify the part of the item that has been altered by illegal deformation and distinguish it from the original or unmodified area. Overall, watermarking techniques classified as irreversible watermarking eternally alter the cover data's content when the watermark is included in the cover item. However, permanent

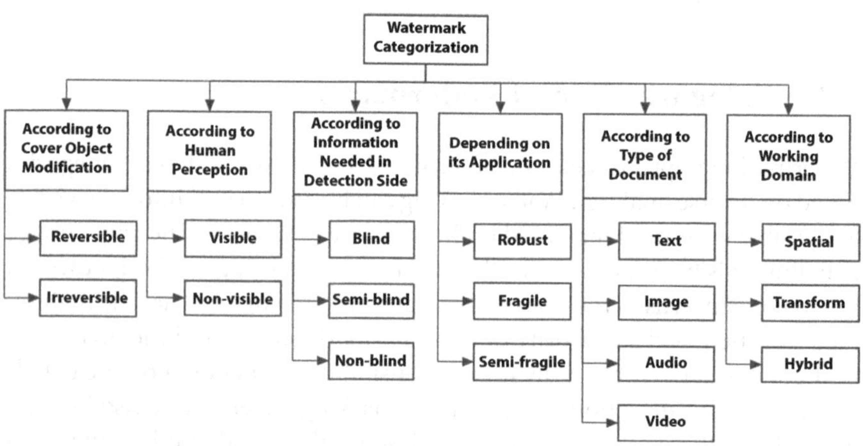

Figure 2.2 Classifications of watermarking.

deformation is prohibited in specialized applications. Therefore, reversible watermarking seems to be the answer to these situations, where it is possible to precisely reconstruct the initial cover material. Watermarking techniques can be divided into three types based on their working domains: transform, spatial, and hybrid domains. In a spatial domain watermarking approach, watermark information is added by simply modifying the cover object's pixel level. When using transformation domain watermarking methods, watermark data are incorporated into the coefficients of a changed cover object, whereas a hybrid domain watermarking method is created using compatible functioning domain approaches from two or three different domains. Following the above discussion, we discuss various proposed watermarking approaches.

2.4.1 Related Works on Watermarking

Because integrated watermark information in digital watermarking techniques virtually completely preserves the perceptual features of the image while defending against various forms of attacks on the watermarked image, scientists have recently presented a large number of efficient watermarking systems for grayscale images. It begins with spatial domain watermark insertion methods [10–13], in which watermark information is added by amending the data for the pixels of the host image's gray level. There are significant disadvantages for spatial domain watermarking systems because recent research has revealed that geometric attacks can be used to manipulate spatial domain watermarking methods. However, the current work discovered that watermark information is placed asymmetrically within the coefficients of a modified image, which may not be readily detectable and flexible in transformed domain watermarking methods. Consequently, the discrete cosine transform [14, 15], discrete Fourier transform [16], ridgelet transform [17], discrete wavelet transform [18], and redundant discrete wavelet transform [19] are some of the watermarking algorithms that are created in the transform domain. Singular value decomposition (SVD)-oriented transform domain watermarking schemes have recently gained popularity because they simplify the extraction of geometric characteristics from images [20]. However, the study discovered that the SVD-based method has three significant flaws: (i) Lower invisibility [21] because one single value update changes all values in a pixel matrix, there is less invisibility in the watermark representation; (ii) the false positive detection issue [22] is present in the greater part of SVD-oriented watermarking processes; and (iii) a diagonal line [23] may be created in the recovered watermark if the SVs developed from

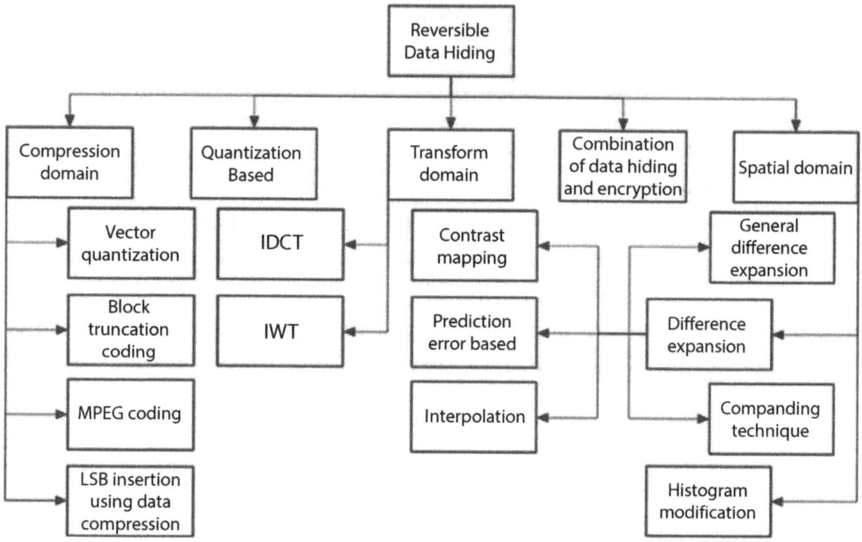

Figure 2.3 Different reversible watermarking methods.

the cover picture and the watermark image are changed. Researchers have recently established watermarking systems employing two or three transform domain methods to produce superior robustness and high imperceptibility [1, 24–26]. The results of these hybrid domain strategies were superior to those of their single equivalents. Because color images are prevalent in daily life, it is crucial to develop color image watermarking schemes. Some color image watermarking methods have been suggested in earlier studies [2, 27–35]. As previously discussed, for joint endeavors or collaborative projects, a single watermark that contains information connected to one creator cannot be embedded in the cover element. For these types of appliances, the cover of the media should have several mutually exclusive watermarks to provide intrinsic security and protect the property rights of different owners. These multiple watermarking-based algorithms were described in [4, 36–42]. Modern researchers have expanded these watermarking algorithms to provide medical images with built-in security. These specialized watermarking-based algorithms were found in [43–48]. The permanently altered, irreversible watermarking scheme-based images presented above cannot be used for investigative or decisive purposes, such as deep space research of military images. Reversible watermarking is a better option for medical and military applications. According to their characteristics, reversible watermarking can be divided into five categories: (i) compression domain

[49–54], (ii) transform domain [55–58], (iii) quantization-based [59–63]; (iv) combination of data hiding and encryption [64, 65]; and (v) spatial domain [66–74].

2.5 Attacks on Watermarking

Watermarked data could have been illegally altered while being transmitted through the internet. All of the irreversible watermarking strategies that have been developed have been tested against different attacks for the assessment of performance and accurate benchmarking.

According to [9], the Stirmark benchmark symbolizes a watermarking method benchmark that breaks down various image watermarking process attacks interested in groups resembling signal enhancement, rotation, scaling, shearing, linear transformations, cropping, other geometric transformations, compression, and combined attacks. The above designated attacks were further decomposed into a few sectors by Kutter *et al.* [8] based on their characteristics. Nearly all suggested solutions were tested for resistance to these attack metrics.

2.5.1 Enhancement Technique Attacks

(i) Low-pass filtering: To eliminate high-frequency noise from a signal, low-pass filtering was performed. Gaussian low-pass filtering attacks with various dimension constraints (2×2, 3×3, 4×4, etc.) were performed on the chosen standard test images to demonstrate the robustness of all the offered techniques versus low-pass filters.

(ii) Median filtering: In common applications for image improvement, a median filter is frequently employed for noise reduction instead of blurring. In essence, a median filter replaces the central pixel value of the window with the center value from the ordered value of the pixels. With various window dimensions (2×2, 3×3, etc.), all the proposed techniques were tested for resistance to median filtering assaults.

(iii) Wiener filtering: A Wiener filter is used to model the impact of two-dimensional linearly probabilistic image coding. The model became closer to the watermarked image chunk when the predictive filter order dimension was improved. One malicious attack that uses estimation is image denoising. Under various size settings, all these irreversible approaches are tested in opposition to Wiener filtering attacks.

(iv) Average filtering: Most designated attacks on denoising, as well as one of the best-known image-enhancing approaches, are average filtering. Each example of the watermarked image was subjected to an average filter, which substituted the average quantity commencing the range of W window dimensions (i.e., $W \times W$ adjacent pixels) for each sample. Each proposed solution was tested against a typical average-filtering attack.

(v) Image sharpening: To identify high-frequency noise created by unauthorized users, a sharpening attack is employed. These suggested techniques were examined in relation to sharpening procedures.

(vi) Histogram modification: Sometimes, the histogram of a picture is altered to compensate for the sharpness and brightness. Any image can be visually enhanced using the histogram alteration enhancement approach. Each proposed watermarking method was evaluated in compared with histogram modification.

(vii) Gamma correction: Gamma correction is a frequently used method for improving the quality of an image with poor projection. Additionally, power-law modification or gamma rectification techniques can occasionally be used to enhance images, whether intentionally or accidentally. Each of the suggested strategies was tested against gamma attacks by using various gamma values.

2.5.2 Noise Addition Attacks

(viii) Noise addition: In signal processing, the addition of uncorrelated multiplicative noise and additive noise is a non-geometrical attack that has received the most attention. Almost all of the proposed techniques have been evaluated against Gaussian noise, salt-and-pepper, and speckle noise. These methods provide protection from noise attacks because of their imperceptibility.

2.5.3 Geometric Transformation Attacks

(ix) Rotation: There are not many differences between an image's economic value and that of its small rotated form. However, a slight rotation can affect the watermark data. All of the suggested techniques are evaluated in opposition to rotation attacks by modifying various rotation angles in both anticlockwise and clockwise directions to confirm resilience against rotation geometric threats.

(x) Cropping: Cropping and focusing are performed on the necessary portion of an object to be photographed, leaving off the remainder of the object or image. Cropping is also used to alter an image's aspect ratio or enhance the frame of a picture. By altering the cropping window dimension, the robustness of the proposed approaches towards cropping operations was evaluated.

Such cropping windows may also be white or black.

(xi) Scaling: An image can be scaled uniformly or inconsistently, either consciously or unconsciously. Scaling an image, for instance, is a typical case when scanning a hard-copy document. To demonstrate the resilience and imperceptibility features against scaling, irreversible suggested methods were evaluated against scaling operations.

(xii) Deletion of lines or columns: Quite often, either purposefully or unintentionally, a portion of the image is destroyed or removed. One of the most extensively used geometric transformation attacks against several basic copyright protection systems is this one.

(xiii) Translation: Sometimes, a component of an object is deleted, and the remaining portion of the image is geometrically transformed such that it appears as though the image has been transferred to a new coordinate. Some of the suggested strategies were tested against translation attacks to determine which ones performed better by altering the translated coordinates.

(xiv) Shearing: Irreversible reported techniques have been evaluated against image shearing with various parameter settings to substantiate their robustness in opposition to the shear procedure. Shearing an image refers to its distortion in either the y-, x-, or both directions.

2.5.4 Compression Attack

(xv) JPEG compression: One of the most popular manipulation/compression attacks is the JPEG compression. A good watermark should have some degree of rigidity or compression. By altering the quality factor values, all the suggested reversible and irreversible watermarking systems were compared to JPEG compression.

2.5.5 Combinational Attacks

Some combinations of the aforementioned attacks are used against all common test images as part of a robustness test. Although there are many different combinations of attacks, the following four are presented here:

(xvi) Combining one attack using an enhancement approach and one attack using a geometric approach
(xvii) Combining one attack using a geometric approach and one attack using a geometric approach
(xviii) Combining one attack using a compression approach and one attack using a geometric approach
(xix) Combining one attack using any noise addition attack approach and one attack using a geometric approach.

2.6 Chapter Summary

This chapter explores various watermarking properties that may be beneficial for different applications as well as the concepts of watermarking and metrics for evaluating watermarks. Any watermarking technique must withstand both intentional and accidental attacks. Therefore, modern researchers have plenty of room to experiment with new attacks and develop more effective watermarking techniques in this field. To provide an adequate degree of security in numerous applications, watermarking can be further investigated in the near future using different datasets and in diverse contexts.

References

1. Roy, S. and Pal, A.K., A robust blind hybrid image watermarking scheme in RDWT-DCT domain using Arnold scrambling. *Multimed. Tools Appl.*, 76, 3, 3577–3616, 2017.

2. Roy, S. and Pal, A.K., An SVD based location specific robust color image watermarking scheme using RDWT and Arnold scrambling. *Wireless Pers. Commun.*, 98, 2223–2250, 2018.
3. Stallings, W., *Cryptography and Network Security: Principles and Practices*, 5th ed., Pearson Education, India, 2007.
4. Roy, S. and Pal, A.K., A blind DCT based color watermarking algorithm for embedding multiple watermarks. *AEU Int. J. Electron. Commun.*, 72, 149–161, 2017.
5. Lian, S., *Multimedia Content Encryption: Techniques and Applications*, CRC Press, New York, 2009.
6. Qin, C., Ji, P., Zhang, X., Dong, J., Wang, J., Fragile image watermarking with pixel-wise recovery based on overlapping embedding strategy. *Signal Process.*, **138**, 280–293, 2017.
7. Cox, I., Miller, M., Bloom, J., Honsinger, C., Digital watermarking. *J. Electron. Imaging*, 11, 3, 414–414, 2002.
8. Kutter, M. and Petitcolas, F.AP., Fair benchmark for image watermarking systems, in: *Electronic Imaging'99*, International Society for Optics and Photonics, pp. 226–239, 1999.
9. Voloshynovskiy, S., Pereira, S., Pun, T., Eggers, J.J., Su, J.K., Attacks on digital watermarks: classification, estimation based attacks, and benchmarks. *IEEE Commun. Mag.*, 39, 8, 118–126, 2001.
10. Swanson, M.D., Zhu, B., Tewfik, A.H., Transparent robust image watermarking, in: *Image Processing, 1996. Proceedings., International Conference on*, vol. 3, IEEE, pp. 211–214, 1996.
11. Hussein, J.A., Spatial domain watermarking scheme for colored images based on log-average luminance. arXiv preprint arXiv:1001.3496, 2010.
12. Langelaar, G.C., Van Der Lubbe, J.CA., Biemond, J., Copy protection for multimedia data based on labeling techniques, in: *Symposium on Information Theory in the Benelux*, Citeseer, pp. 33–40, 1996.
13. Nikolaidis, N. and Pitas, I., Copyright protection of images using robust digital signatures, in: *Acoustics, Speech, and Signal Processing, 1996. ICASSP- 96. Conference Proceedings., 1996 IEEE International Conference on*, vol. 4, IEEE, pp. 2168–2171, 1996.
14. Barni, M., Bartolini, F., Cappellini, V., Piva, A., A dctdomain system for robust image watermarking. *Signal Process.*, 66, 3, 357–372, 1998.
15. Pal, A.K. and Roy, S., A robust and blind image watermarking scheme in DCT domain. *Int. J. Inf. Comput. Secur.*, 10, 4, 321–340, 2018.
16. Premaratne. A novel watermark embedding and detection scheme for images in DFT domain, in: *Image Processing And Its Applications, 1999.* Seventh International Conference on (Conf. Publ. No. 465), vol. 2, pp. 780–783. IET, 1999.
17. Campisi, P., Kundur, D., Neri, A., Robust digital watermarking in the ridgelet domain. *IEEE Signal Process Lett.*, 11, 10, 826–830, 2004.

18. Ouhsain, M. and Hamza, A.B., Image watermarking scheme using nonnegative matrix factorization and wavelet transform. *Expert Syst. Appl.*, 36, 2, 2123–2129, 2009.
19. Lagzian, S., Soryani, M., Fathy, M., A new robust watermarking scheme based on rdwt-svd. *Int. J. Intell. Inf. Process.*, 2, 1, 22–29, 2011.
20. Ali, M., Ahn, C.W., Pant, M., A robust image watermarking technique using svd and differential evolution in dct domain. *Optik-Int. J. Light Electron. Opt.*, 125, 1, 428–434, 2014.
21. Qingtang, S., Niu, Y., Zou, H., Liu, X., A blind dual color images watermarking based on singular value decomposition. *Appl. Math. Comput.*, 219, 16, 8455–8466, 2013.
22. Zhang, X.-P. and Li, K., Comments on an svd-based watermarking scheme for protecting rightful ownership. *IEEE Trans. Multimed.*, 7, 3, 593–594, 2005.
23. Roman, R., Comments on An SVD-based watermarking scheme for protecting rightful ownership. *IEEE Trans. Multimed.*, 9, 2, 421–423, 2007.
24. Ling, H.C., Phan, R.C.W. and Heng, S.H., Comment on "Robust blind image watermarking scheme based on redundant discrete wavelet transform and singular value decomposition". *AEU-Int. J. Electron. Commun.*, 67, 10, 894–897, 2013.
25. Singh, A.K., Dave, M., Mohan, A., Hybrid technique for robust and imperceptible image watermarking in dwt–dct–svd domain. *Natl. Acad. Sci. Lett.*, 37, 4, 351–358, 2014.
26. Roy, S. and Pal, A.K., An indirect watermark hiding in discrete cosine transform–singular value decomposition domain for copyright protection. *R. Soc. Open Sci.*, 4, 6, 170326, 2017.
27. Chou, C.-H. and Wu, T.-L., Embedding color watermarks in color images. *EURASIP J. Appl. Signal Process.*, 2003, 32–40, 2003.
28. Su, Q., Niu, Y., Wang, Q., Sheng, G., A blind color image watermarking based on dc component in the spatial domain. *Optik-Int. J. Light Electron. Opt.*, 124, 23, 6255–6260, 2013.
29. Roy, S. and Pal, A.K., A. Hybrid Domain Color Image Watermarking Based on DWT–SVD. *Iran. J. Sci. Technol. Trans. Electr. Eng.*, **43**, 201–217, 2019, https://doi.org/10.1007/s40998-018-0109-x.
30. Yin, C.-q., Li, L., Lv, A.-q., Qu, L., Color image watermarking algorithm based on dwt-svd, in: *Automation and Logistics, 2007 IEEE International Conference on*, IEEE, pp. 2607–2611, 2007.
31. Sun, G. and Yu, Y., Dwt based watermarking algorithm of color images, in: *Industrial Electronics and Applications, 2007. ICIEA 2007. 2nd IEEE Conference on*, IEEE, pp. 1823–1826, 2007.
32. Yang, W.-M. and Jin, Z., A watermarking algorithm based on wavelet and cosine transform for color image, in: *Education Technology and Computer Science, 2009. ETCS'09. First International Workshop on*, vol. 2, IEEE, pp. 899–903, 2009.

33. Golea, N.E.-H., Seghir, R., Benzid, R., A blind rgb color image watermarking based on singular value decomposition, in: *Computer Systems and Applications (AICCSA), 2010 IEEE/ACS International Conference on*, IEEE, pp. 1–5, 2010.
34. Dharwadkar, N.V. and Amberker, B.B., An efficient and secured non blind watermarking scheme for color images using dwt and arnold transform. *Int. J. Comput.*, 9, 2, 183–191, 2010.
35. Santhi, V. and Thangavelu, A., Dc coefficients based watermarking techniquefor color images using singular valuedecomposition. *Int. J. Comput. Electr. Eng.*, 3, 1, 8, 2011.
36. Shieh, C.-S., Huang, H.-C., Wang, F.-H., Pan, J.-S., An embedding algorithm for multiple watermarks. *J. Inf. Sci. Eng.*, 19, 2, 381–395, 2003.
37. Mascher-Kampfer, A., Stögner, H., Uhl, A., Multiple rewatermarking scenarios, in: *Proceedings of the 13th International Conference on Systems, Signals, and Image Processing (IWSSIP 2006)*, pp. 53–56, Budapest, Hungary, 2006.
38. Mark, D., Uhl, A., Wernisch, H., Experimental study on watermark interference in multiple re-watermarking. *Security, Steganography, and Watermarking of Multimedia Contents IX*, vol. 15, p. 6505, 2007.
39. Woo, C.-S., Du, J., Pham, B.L., Multiple watermark method for privacy control and tamper detection in medical images, in: *Workshop Proceedings: WDIC 2005 APRS Workshop on Digital Image Computing*, pp. 43–48, University of Queensland, 2005.
40. Ganic, E., Dexter, S.D., Eskicioglu, A.M., Embedding multiple watermarks in the dft domain using low-and high-frequency bands, in: *Electronic Imaging 2005*, International Society for Optics and Photonics, pp. 175–184, 2005.
41. Lu, C.-S. and Liao, H.-Y.M., Multipurpose watermarking for image authentication and protection. *IEEE Trans. Image Process.*, 10, 10, 1579–1592, 2001.
42. Frikken, K. and Atallah, M., Cropping-resilient segmented multiple watermarking, in: *Workshop on Algorithms and Data Structures*, Springer, pp. 231–242, 2003.
43. Singh, A.K., Improved hybrid algorithm for robust and imperceptible multiple watermarking using digital images. *Multimedia Tools Appl.*, 76, 6, 8881–8900, 2017.
44. Singh, A.K., Kumar, B., Dave, M., Mohan, A., Multiple watermarking on medical images using selective discrete wavelet transform coefficients. *J. Med. Imaging Health Inf.*, 5, 3, 607–614, 2015.
45. Singh, A.K., Dave, M., Mohan, A., Robust and secure multiple watermarking in wavelet domain. *J. Med. Imaging Health Inf.*, 5, 2, 406–414, 2015.
46. Singh, A.K., Dave, M., Mohan, A., Hybrid technique for robust and imperceptible multiple watermarking using medical images. *Multimed. Tools Appl.*, 75, 14, 8381–8401, 2016.
47. Pandey, R., Singh, A.K., Kumar, B., Mohan, A., Iris based secure nroi multiple eye image watermarking for teleophthalmology. *Multimedia Tools Appl.*, 75, 22, 14381–14397, 2016.

48. Singh, A.K., Kumar, B., Dave, M., Mohan, A., Robust and imperceptible dual watermarking for telemedicine applications. *Wireless Pers. Commun.*, 80, 4, 1415–1433, 2015.
49. Yang, B., Lu, Z.-M., Sun, S.-H., Reversible watermarking in the vqcompressed domain, in: *Proceedings of the Fifth IASTED International Conference on Visualization, Imaging, and Image Processing, Benidorm, Spain*, pp. 298–303, 2005.
50. Lu, Z.-M., Wang, J.-X., Liu, B.-B., An improved lossless data hiding scheme based on image vq-index residual value coding. *J. Syst. Software*, 82, 6, 1016–1024, 2009.
51. Wang, J.-X. and Lu, Z.-M., A path optional lossless data hiding scheme based on vq joint neighboring coding. *Inf. Sci.*, 179, 19, 3332–3348, 2009.
52. Chang, C.-C., Lin, C.-Y., Fan, Y.-H., Lossless data hiding for color images based on block truncation coding. *Pattern Recognit.*, 41, 7, 2347–2357, 2008.
53. Mobasseri, B.G. and Cinalli, D., Lossless watermarking of compressed media using reversibly decodable packets. *Signal Process.*, 86, 5, 951–961, 2006.
54. Goljan, M., Fridrich, J.J., Du, R., Distortion-free data embedding for images, in: *International Workshop on Information Hiding*, Springer, pp. 27–41, 2001.
55. Plonka, G. and Tasche, M., Integer dct-ii by lifting steps. *International Series of Numerical mathematics*, pp. 235–252, 2003.
56. Yang, B., Schmucker, M., Funk, W., Busch, C., Sun, S., Integer dct-based reversible watermarking for images using companding technique, in: *Electronic Imaging 2004*, International Society for Optics and Photonics, pp. 405–415, 2004.
57. Yang, B., Schmucker, M., Niu, X., Busch, C., Sun, S., Integer-dct-based reversible image watermarking by adaptive coefficient modification, in: *Electronic Imaging 2005*, International Society for Optics and Photonics, pp. 218–229, 2005.
58. Xuan, G., Yao, Q., Yang, C., Gao, J., Chai, P., Shi, Y.Q., Ni, Z., Lossless data hiding using histogram shifting method based on integer wavelets, in: *International Workshop on Digital Watermarking*, Springer, pp. 323–332, 2006.
59. Cheung, Y.-. and Wu, H.-t., A sequential quantization strategy for data embedding and integrity verification. *IEEE Trans. Circuits Syst. Video Technol.*, 17, 18, 1007–1016, 2007.
60. Saberian, M.J., Akhaee, M.A., Marvasti, F., An invertible quantization based watermarking approach, in: *Acoustics, Speech and Signal Processing, 2008. ICASSP 2008. IEEE International Conference on*, IEEE, pp. 1677–1680, 2008.
61. Lee, J.-D., Chiou, Y.-H., Guo, J.-M., Reversible data hiding based on histogram modification of smvq indices. *IEEE Trans. Inf. Forensics Secur.*, 5, 4, 638–648, 2010.
62. Ko, L.-T., Chen, J.-E., Shieh, Y.-S., Scalia, M., Sung, T.-Y., A novel fractional-discrete-cosine-transform-based reversible watermarking for healthcare information management systems. *Math. Probl. Eng.*, 2012, 1, 757018, 2012, doi:10.1155/2012/757018.

63. Ko, L.-T., Chen, J.-E., Shieh, Y.-S., Hsin, H.-C., Sung, T.-Y., Nested quantization index modulation for reversible watermarking and its application to healthcare information management systems. *Comput. Math. Methods Med.*, 2012, 1, 839161, 2012, doi:10.1155/2012/839161.
64. Zhang, X., Reversible data hiding in encrypted image. *IEEE Signal Process Lett.*, 18, 4, 255–258, 2011.
65. Zhang, X., Separable reversible data hiding in encrypted image. *IEEE Trans. Inf. Forensics Secur.*, 7, 2, 826–832, 2012.
66. Tian, J., Reversible watermarking by difference expansion. *Proc. Workshop multimedia Secur.*, 19, 2002.
67. Tian, J., Reversible data embedding using a difference expansion. *IEEE Trans. Circuits Syst. Video Technol.*, 13, 8, 890–896, 2003.
68. Weng, S., Zhao, Y., Pan, J.-S., Ni, R., A novel reversible watermarking based on an integer transform, in: *Image Processing, 2007. ICIP 2007. IEEE International Conference on*, vol. 3, IEEE, pp. III–241, 2007.
69. Coltuc, D. and Chassery, J.-M., Very fast watermarking by reversible contrast mapping. *IEEE Signal Process Lett.*, 14, 4, 255–258, 2007.
70. Thodi, D.M. and Rodríguez, J.J., Reversible watermarking by predictionerror expansion, in: *Image Analysis and Interpretation, 2004. 6th IEEE Southwest Symposium on*, IEEE, pp. 21–25, 2004.
71. Abadi, M.A.M., Danyali, H., Helfroush, M.S., Reversible watermarking based on interpolation error histogram shifting, in: *Telecommunications (IST), 2010 5th International Symposium on*, IEEE, pp. 840–845, 2010.
72. Ni, Z., Shi, Y.Q., Ansari, N., Su, W., Sun, Q., Lin, X., Robust lossless image data hiding designed for semi-fragile image authentication. *IEEE Trans. Circuits Syst. Video Technol.*, 18, 4, 497–509, 2008.
73. Lee, S.-K., Suh, Y.-H., Ho, Y.-S., Reversiblee image authentication based on watermarking, in: *Multimedia and Expo, 2006 IEEE International Conference on*, IEEE, pp. 1321–1324, 2006.
74. Tseng, H.-W. and Chang, C.-C., An extended difference expansion algorithm for reversible watermarking. *Image Vision Comput.*, 26, 8, 1148–1153, 2008.

3

A Comprehensive Study on Deep Learning and Artificial Intelligence for Malware Analysis

Tukkappa Gundoor* **and Sridevi**

Department of Computer Science, Karnatak University, Dharwad, Karnataka, India

Abstract

This chapter offers a thorough review of the use of deep learning and artificial intelligence (AI) in malware analysis, emphasizing the essential methods, uses, difficulties, and prospects. It explains that essential ideas for feature extraction and malware classification, including convolutional neural networks (CNNs), recurrent neural networks (RNNs), and generative adversarial networks (GANs), are examples of neural networks. The categorization of malware using supervised learning techniques like CNNs and RNNs as well as the identification of anomalies using unsupervised learning methods like auto encoders and GANs are also covered in this chapter. It solves issues such as the lack of labeled malware samples and the constantly changing nature of malware. The necessity of interpretable deep learning models to comprehend identified malware is also emphasized in this chapter. Deep learning and AI present significant opportunities for improving malware detection, classification, and dynamic analysis, ultimately enhancing the security of computer systems and networks against the risks posed by harmful software.

Keywords: Attacks, artificial intelligence, deep learning, machine learning, malware, security

**Corresponding author*: gundoortukaram@gmail.com

Subhabrata Barman, Santanu Koley and Subhankar Joardar (eds.) Next-Generation Systems and Secure Computing, (39–60) © 2025 Scrivener Publishing LLC

3.1 Introduction

Over time, there has been a considerable increase in harmful cybersecurity activities, and threats have become more complex and ubiquitous. Malware is one of the most difficult enemies that both individuals and organizations must deal with. Ransomware, viruses, worms, Trojan horses, and other types of harmful software are all included in the term "malware." These harmful programs are designed to enter computer networks, corrupt data, and stop vital processes, all of which can have disastrous effects on finances, reputation, and operations. Traditional cybersecurity techniques such as signature-based detection and heuristic analysis have been used to address this ever-developing threat. However, these traditional techniques are becoming less successful owing to the rapid development of malware variants and the introduction of stealthy, polymorphic, and zero-day assaults [1–13].

Deep Learning and Artificial Intelligence (AI) have recently emerged as game-changing technologies with the ability to completely change malware analysis and detection. A branch of machine learning known as deep learning focuses on using neural networks to directly learn intricate patterns and representations from unprocessed data. On the other hand, AI covers a wider range of algorithms and methods that try to imitate human intellect, making it perfect for addressing complex and dynamic cybersecurity concerns. When used for malware analysis, deep learning and AI provide several benefits over the conventional methods. The first benefit of using these approaches is that they make it possible to build complex models that can distinguish between different types of malware based on learned patterns rather than on pre-established criteria. These models may continuously change and successfully fend off new dangers because of their versatility. Deep learning and AI also equip malware analysts with effective tools to manage enormous volumes of data, enabling a scalable and real-time approach to quickly detect and address threats [14–22].

3.2 The Evolving Landscape of Malware Threats

The panorama of malware threats is constantly changing in cybersecurity. Malware an abbreviation for malicious software refers to a wide range of harmful programs designed to undermine, exploit, or disrupt computer systems, networks, or other technologies. Malware assaults have become significantly more sophisticated, diverse, and frequent over time, posing serious problems to people, businesses, and governments.

3.2.1 Polymorphic and Metamorphic Malware

Polymorphic viruses change each copy of their code to avoid anti-malware protection, whereas metamorphic viruses rewrite their code at each iteration. A polymorphic virus changes its code using an encryption key, whereas a Metamorphic Virus rewrites its code. Writing a Metamorphic Virus is far more complex for a coder than constructing a polymorphic virus because many conversion mechanisms must be employed. The methods used to identify these two viruses differ. In the case of polymorphic viruses, such approaches as generic description technology and input point algorithms are required. The employment of emulators for tracking and geometric detection is required in the case of metamorphic viruses [23–25].

3.2.2 Advanced Persistent Threats (APTs)

Attacks by advanced persistent threats (APTs) are well-planned and extremely sophisticated cyber-attacks that target specific targets such as governmental institutions, critical infrastructure, or significant enterprises. APTs may entail persistent and covert infiltration into the target's network, allowing attackers to steal important data, disrupt operations, or obtain unauthorized access over a long period without being detected [26, 27].

3.2.3 Fileless and Memory-Based Attacks

A type of harmful software known as "fileless malware" functions entirely in the computer memory, leaving no traces on the file system. It uses scripting languages such as PowerShell to run malicious code directly in memory, evading detection by traditional security solutions that rely on file-based scanning methods. This stealthy technique presents a significant issue for cybersecurity because it allows hackers to carry out their operations without leaving observable evidence, necessitating the employment of memory-focused security solutions to combat this threat [28–32].

3.2.4 Ransomware and Cryptojacking

Ransomware has developed into a prevalent and profitable malware category. It encrypts the victim's data, making it unavailable, and demands a ransom for the decryption key. On the other hand, cryptojacking stealthily exploits the victim's computational resources for Bitcoin mining, causing system slowdowns and increased energy usage. Both threats pose substantial hazards to the digital ecosystem, affecting the data security and system performance.

3.2.5 Supply Chain Attacks

Malicious actors are increasingly focusing their efforts on software supply chains to infiltrate genuine software products with malware. Exploiting flaws in trustworthy software providers or their update procedures allows for broad, covert infection. Such assaults jeopardize the integrity of updates, possibly harming many companies and individuals who install tainted updates unknowingly. Protecting the software supply chain has emerged as a significant problem in cybersecurity, which requires robust security measures and constant monitoring to combat supply chain threats.

3.2.6 IoT and Mobile Malware

Mobile and Internet of Things (IoT) devices have become popular targets for hackers because of their prevalence. IoT devices frequently lack strong security safeguards, making them vulnerable to attack. Simultaneously, the growing use of mobile devices, which frequently store sensitive personal and financial information, has resulted in an increase in mobile malware, including spyware specifically designed to infiltrate smartphones and tablets, posing significant security challenges in the interconnected mobile era.

3.2.7 Zero-Day Exploits

Zero-day exploits allow attackers to take advantage of previously unknown software flaws, thereby giving them an advantage before security updates are released. These vulnerabilities are unknown to both program providers and the general public, making them incredibly desirable assets for cybercriminals. By exploiting these loopholes, attackers can launch catastrophic assaults, possibly inflicting considerable harm and causing data breaches. The race to uncover, report, and address zero-day vulnerabilities is a vital component of cybersecurity because it reduces the window of opportunity for bad actors to wreak havoc in the digital realm [33, 34].

3.3 The Role of Deep Learning and AI in Enhancing Cybersecurity

Deep learning and artificial intelligence (AI) are critical for increasing the agility and efficacy of cybersecurity. They enable firms to strengthen their security measures to combat the ever-changing cyber-threat scenario. AI and deep learning can enhance cybersecurity solutions by enhancing the detection, response, and prevention of threats. These technologies offer proactive and adaptive defenses and protect crucial data, networks, and systems from a wide range of attacks. In essence, AI and deep learning strengthen cybersecurity by improving its capacity to combat the dynamic characteristics of current cyber-attacks [35–37].

3.3.1 Advanced Threat Detection

Traditional cybersecurity systems typically utilize preset signatures and rule-based strategies to detect known threats. Deep learning and AI-based models can assess large amounts of data, including network traffic, system logs, and user behavior, to uncover patterns suggestive of cyber threats. By constantly reacting to new attack routes and learning from earlier data, these models can detect both known and unknown threats, including zero-day attacks and advanced persistent threats (APTs).

3.3.2 Real-Time Response and Mitigation

Deep learning and artificial intelligence (AI) are used in real-time cyber threat analysis to quickly identify and mitigate security issues. AI-powered systems may detect abnormal activities independently significantly reducing the time between danger discovery and mitigation. This timely response is crucial for averting significant harm from cyberattacks and mitigating the consequences of successful breaches. It helps enterprises proactively protect against changing threats, improving the overall cybersecurity posture.

3.3.3 Behavioral Analysis

AI-powered cybersecurity solutions excel at behavioral analysis, monitoring, and identifying abnormalities in user and system activities. By establishing baselines for expected behavior, these models can quickly identify deviations, allowing for the early detection of insider threats and compromised user accounts. This proactive strategy uses machine learning to improve cybersecurity by offering real-time information on prospective breaches and harmful intent.

3.3.4 Anomaly Detection

Deep learning models, particularly those intended for anomaly detection, are durable in large and complex datasets. They excel in detecting abnormalities in network traffic, system logs, and application activities in the context of cybersecurity. This skill is useful for identifying new attack patterns that may have avoided traditional security measures. Furthermore, these models dramatically reduce the occurrence of false positives and improve the accuracy and dependability of the threat detection systems. Organizations may reinforce their cybersecurity posture by proactively detecting tiny deviations from established standards using deep learning.

3.3.5 Predictive Security

AI-powered predictive security forecasts possible cyber risks by leveraging historical data and current behavioral trends. Machine learning algorithms sift through massive datasets to uncover new attack routes and vulnerabilities. With these predictive insights, enterprises may harden their defenses, fix vulnerabilities, deploy proactive security measures, and stop possible attacks before they occur. By leveraging AI's predictive capabilities, cybersecurity systems become nimbler and more capable of keeping ahead of hostile actors, improving the overall defense against emerging threats in the volatile battlefield of cyber warfare.

3.3.6 Reducing False Positives

Leveraging AI for threat detection provides a significant advantage in decreasing false positives, which frequently delay cybersecurity operations. AI can automatically distinguish and filter out innocuous events from serious dangers using powerful machine learning techniques. This functionality enables security analysts to focus their attention on key occurrences and optimize resource allocation and reaction times. AI improves the precision and efficiency of threat detection by reducing the noise from false alarms, resulting in more effective and proactive cybersecurity actions. This smart use of AI technology strengthens a company's security against cyber-attacks, while improving operational operations.

3.3.7 Continuous Learning and Improvement

Deep learning and artificial intelligence (AI) models support malware analysis by using methods for continual learning and development. They analyzed and integrated new data to help them adapt to changing dangerous environments. This flexibility is important in cybersecurity, because AI-powered solutions must remain successful in the face of new threats.

Models' capabilities are constantly improved by repeatedly upgrading their internal representations with the most up-to-date information. This enables them to develop more accurate forecasts, identify sophisticated malware variants, and maintain cybersecurity efficacy over time. The iterative learning process keeps models at the forefront of malware identification and analysis.

3.4 Deep Learning Models for Malware Analysis

Deep learning models and AI techniques have altered malware analysis, providing more powerful and precise tools for recognizing, categorizing, and interpreting malware. These technologies, which use neural networks and cutting-edge algorithms to evaluate vast volumes of complex data, assist cybersecurity specialists in staying ahead of ever-evolving malware threats. Here is a rundown of some of the most important deep learning models and AI technologies used in malware research.

3.4.1 Convolutional Neural Networks (CNNs)

Convolutional Neural Networks (CNNs) or ConvNet are complicated feed-forward neural networks used in machine learning. CNNs have been utilized for picture categorization and identification because of their great accuracy. It was proposed in the late 1990s by computer scientist Yann LeCun, who was motivated by the human visual experience of identifying objects. Convolutional Neural Networks (CNNs) are invaluable in malware analysis because they adopt a hierarchical model resembling a funnel. They culminate in a fully connected layer, where neurons interconnect with the process output. Although malware data are primarily binary, leveraging the CNN's image-processing prowess can yield impressive results. CNNs automatically learn and extract pertinent features from visual malware representations by encoding malware as images. This innovative approach harnesses CNNs' advanced image-analysis capabilities, making them potent tools for identifying and analyzing malware and effectively unraveling its hidden patterns and traits [38, 39].

Convolutional neural networks (CNNs) are used to handle malicious picture data shown in the Figure 3.1. Cybersecurity experts may employ CNNs to better detect and categorize malware by utilizing image-based representations.

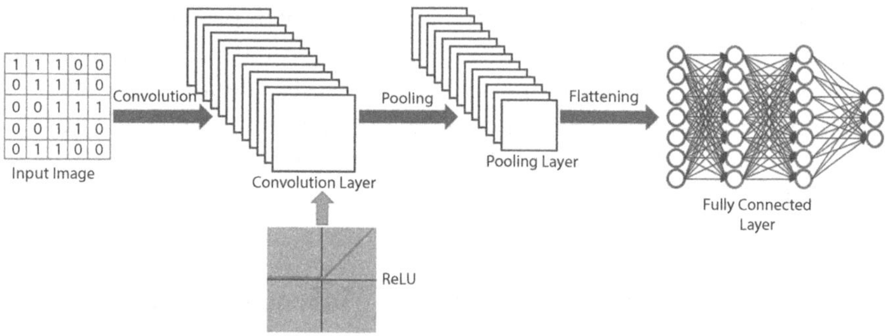

Figure 3.1 Convolutional neural networks architecture [40].

3.4.2 Recurrent Neural Networks (RNNs) for Malware Analysis

Recurrent Neural Networks (RNNs) are essential tools in malware research, particularly for sequential data analysis. The Figure 3.2, RNNs were built to deal with dynamic and time-sensitive features of malware activity. They work by remembering previous states, allowing them to consider the entire history of the incoming data. RNNs can successfully mimic the sequential nature of system calls, API invocations, or network traffic patterns associated with malicious software in the context of malware investigation. This temporal awareness allows RNNs to detect complicated malware activities and identify abnormalities by identifying departures from predicted sequences, considerably adding to the strong security against emerging cyber threats.

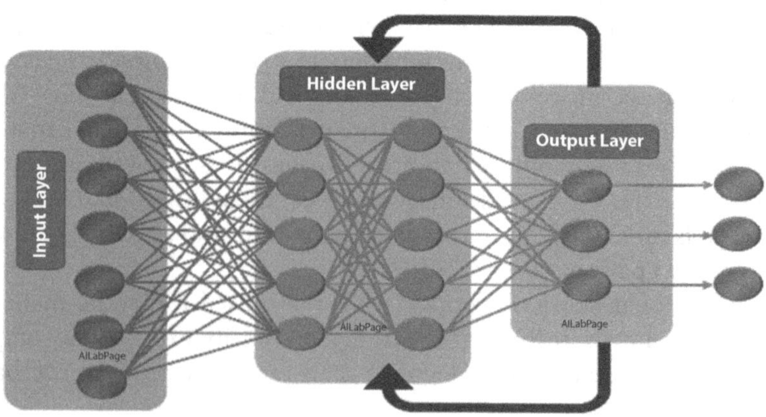

Figure 3.2 Recurrent neural networks [41].

Explorers discovered that RNNs are a particular category of neural networks designed to manage sequential inputs. RNNs maintain a hidden state that enables them to acquire data from previous time steps in a sequence, in contrast to traditional feedforward networks.

3.4.3 Long Short-Term Memory Networks (LSTMs)

Long Short-Term Memory Networks (LSTMs) are significant tools in malware research because of their capacity to learn and store vital information over long periods. The Figure 3.3, LSTMs, as opposed to standard Recurrent Neural Networks (RNNs), are designed to capture long-term relationships and recall prior data, making them particularly excellent for processing time-series data, a feature frequently encountered in malware. The input, forget, update, and output gates are all interconnected in a chain-like arrangement. These layers work together to handle sequential data efficiently. LSTMs can be used to examine the behavior of dangerous software over time in the context of malware investigation. They initially filter out extraneous information from prior states before selectively updating the cell state values to adapt to the present situation. This versatility enables them to detect small changes in malware activity, thereby assisting in the detection and categorization of dangerous actions. Although LSTMs are more commonly associated with tasks such as voice recognition, music composition, and pharmaceutical research, their application in malware analysis stems from their unique ability to process and learn from dynamic, time-dependent data, ultimately improving the accuracy and efficiency of malware detection and classification [42, 43].

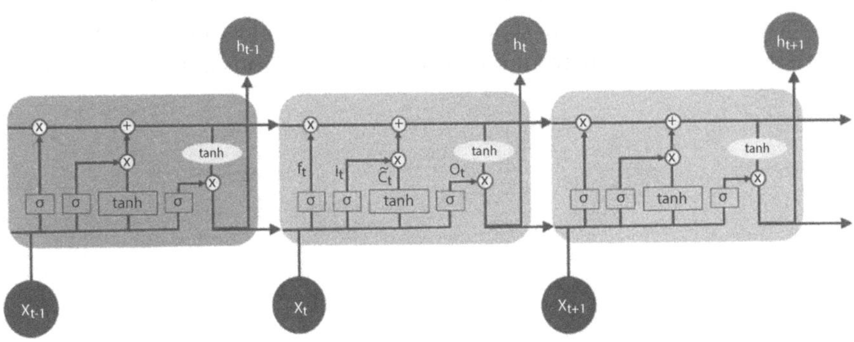

Figure 3.3 Long short-term memory networks (LSTMs) [44].

3.4.4 Generative Adversarial Networks (GANs)

Although Figure 3.4, Generative Adversarial Networks (GANs) are best recognized for producing synthetic data in the context of malware research, they may also be used to improve malware analysis and detection. GANs are composed of two main parts: a generator and discriminator. The generator generates synthetic malware instances in the program, and the discriminator's purpose is to discriminate between actual malware samples and those created by the generator. During the training process, the generator first creates bogus malware data; however, the discriminator quickly learns to distinguish it from genuine malware. As training advances, the discriminator's capacity to recognize these bogus instances increases, forcing the generator to tweak its output until it is indistinguishable from the actual malware.

GANs can be used to expand the dataset for malware analysis by iterating this process, creating synthetic malware samples that closely match existing threats. These synthetic samples can be used to train and fine-tune malware detection algorithms, allowing them to become more resilient and capable of detecting new and emerging malware types. Finally, GANs improve cybersecurity solution resilience by simulating and tackling new threats in the malware field.

3.4.5 Radial Basis Function Networks (RBFNs)

Convolutional Neural Networks (CNNs) use a hierarchical architecture similar to a funnel in malware analysis, ending in a fully connected layer where neurons interact for data processing. CNNs have emerged as powerful tools for malware analysis via image-based inspection. Although malware is largely binary data, it may be encoded and processed as pictures by utilizing CNN's sophisticated image processing skills. CNNs' usefulness for this purpose is ascribed to their inherent ability to gather and extract relevant characteristics independently from the visual representations of malware strains.

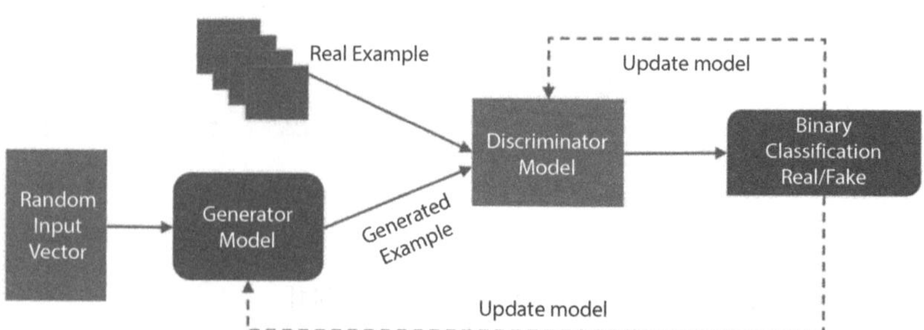

Figure 3.4 Generative adversarial networks (GANs) [44].

Figure 3.5, CNNs excel in detecting and analyzing malware because of their versatility, making them vital weapons in cybersecurity armory [45, 46].

3.4.6 Deep Belief Networks (DBNs)

Deep Belief Networks (DBNs) are generative models comprising numerous layers of stochastic latent variables, also known as hidden units, that have binary values. These networks are composed of layered Boltzmann Machines linked across layers to allow communication between them. DBNs are utilized in malware research in several fields, including image recognition, video recognition, and motion capture data processing. DBNs are learned using greedy learning algorithms that generate weights layer-by-layer. Gibbs sampling was used to draw samples from Restricted Boltzmann Machines (RBMs) on the top two hidden layers. DBNs assist in the inference of latent variable values in this manner by allowing for a single efficient bottom-up pass shown in the Figure 3.6.

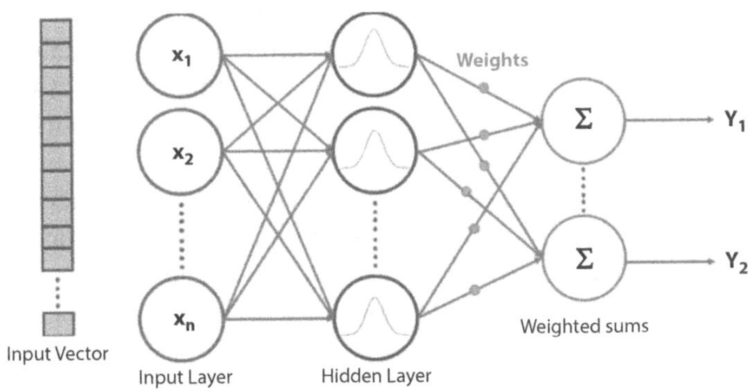

Figure 3.5 Radial basis function networks (RBFNs) [44].

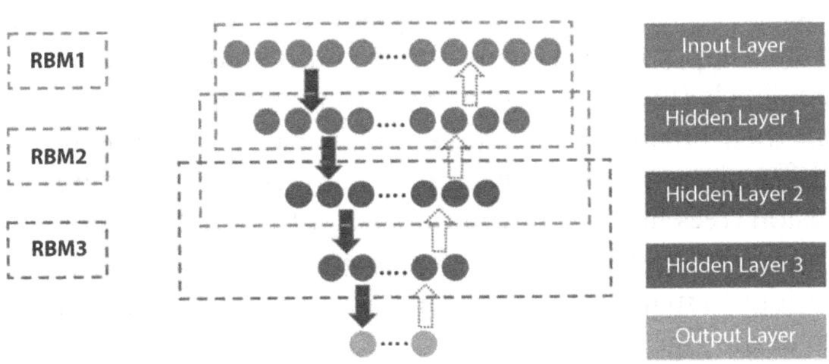

Figure 3.6 Deep belief networks (DBNs) [44].

3.5 AI Techniques in Malware Analysis

Machine learning, according to AI pioneer Arthur Samuel, is a combination of approaches that enables computers "the ability to learn without being explicitly programmed." In other words, a machine-learning algorithm identifies and formalizes the principles underlying the data it observes. The program can then explain the quality of previously unseen samples using this information. A previously unknown sample may represent a new file for malware detection. A concealed attribute may be be malicious or non-malicious. The model is a mathematically structured collection of underlying principles for data attributes. Instead of a single strategy, machine learning employs a wide range of approaches for problem-solving. These techniques have various capabilities and tasks that are best suited to them.

3.5.1 Unsupervised Learning

Unsupervised learning is a critical machine-learning method in the field of malware investigation. This entails working with unlabeled datasets to discover data structures and patterns, such as grouping similar malware samples. Clustering assists in categorizing malware without prior knowledge of its properties, thereby reducing the time-consuming manual labeling effort. Furthermore, representation learning, as demonstrated by autoencoder models, aids in the creation of informative features from low-level descriptions, thereby increasing the effectiveness of threat detection. Once informative embeddings are in place, they reduce the demand for labeled samples in subsequent supervised learning, in which both data and proper labels are accessible for training models to categorize new malware cases [47–49].

3.5.2 Supervised Learning

Supervised learning in malware analysis can be divided into two stages training and application. During the training phase, a model is trained to predict labels (malware or benign) for unseen objects (malicious files) based on their attributes (file content or behavior) such as file statistics and API function usage. Various model families, such as neural networks and decision trees have been studied, each with its own set of parameters. The training phase attempts to determine the best model and parameter combinations to make accurate predictions on the reference dataset which is shown in the Figure 3.7.

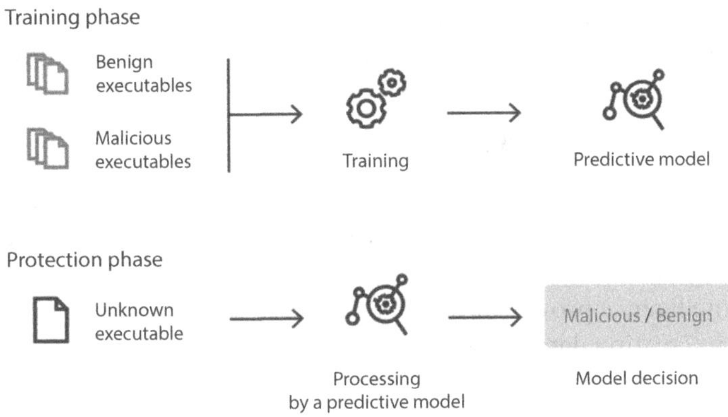

Figure 3.7 Malware detection algorithm life cycle.

Once a model has been trained and certified for quality, it is placed in the application phase, where it provides predictions that serve as the foundation for malware prevention. Users are provided with trained models and the product makes decisions autonomously based on these predictions.

3.5.3 Deep Learning

Deep learning, a subset of machine learning, is particularly effective in extracting abstract characteristics from low-level data. Although it has achieved remarkable success in fields such as computer vision, speech recognition, and natural language processing, its use in cybersecurity, particularly malware analysis, is gaining traction. Deep learning helps to distinguish high-level patterns from low-level data, making it a useful tool for malware detection. Deep learning facilitates the integration of many malware detection procedures into a single cohesive solution by training the end-to-end models. This method enables cybersecurity firms to build robust systems that learn complicated feature hierarchies and improve the accuracy and efficiency of malware analysis.

3.6 Challenges and Limitations in Malware Family Classification

Owing to the constantly changing nature of malware and the wide variety of threat actors' strategies, it is difficulty to classify malware families. Although machine learning and AI have greatly increased the precision and effectiveness of categorization, certain issues and restrictions still need to be resolved. Typical obstacles to overcome, along with solutions:

3.6.1 Lack of Labeled Data

Because some malware families are rare or there are not many ground truth labels available, obtaining a large, varied collection of labeled malware samples may be challenging. Active data collection, cooperation with threat intelligence providers, and the use of data augmentation techniques can aid in creating datasets that are more thorough and representative.

3.6.2 Imbalanced Data

Unbalanced data in malware analysis is frequently caused by a lopsided distribution of malware samples across distinct families. Some families are overabundant, whereas others are underabundant. To offset the effects of this imbalance and avoid model bias towards the majority classes, strategies such as data resampling, class weighting, and ensemble methods are used to guarantee that the machine learning model handles the entire spectrum of malware families.

3.6.3 Feature Engineering

Selecting and constructing informative aspects for malware categorization can be challenging, and certain traits may become obsolete as malware evolves. Emphasize The use of dynamic behavioral features is emphasized to record malware interactions and behaviors as they occur. Deep learning models can be utilized for autonomous feature extraction, which helps to address feature engineering challenges.

3.6.4 Adversarial Attacks

Adversarial assaults in malware analysis entail the production of samples tailored to circumvent categorization algorithms. Malware developers use various strategies to avoid detection. Countermeasures such as adversarial training and other defensive tactics can be used to improve the model resilience to escape. These tactics entail training machine-learning models to recognize and reject hostile samples, thereby increasing the resilience of malware detection systems.

3.6.5 Generalization to New Variants

Convolutional Neural Networks (CNNs) have demonstrated their effectiveness in malware analysis by responding to the dynamic environment of malware families. These dynamic networks use transfer and continuous learning methodologies and add novel malware samples to improve their capacity to detect previously unknown strains. Upgrading the model with new data improves its capacity to generalize and categorize previously undiscovered harmful codes, thereby increasing its usefulness in cybersecurity protection.

3.6.6 Real-Time Analysis

Real-time analysis is critical for malware analysis. A strong model should provide quick predictions for instant malware classification without sacrificing the precision. To achieve this, the model architecture must be optimized, hardware accelerators must be included, and lightweight models or model quantization approaches must be considered. These techniques improve inference speed and ensure speedy danger identification while retaining an acceptable degree of accuracy. By balancing the efficiency and accuracy, the model can successfully identify and classify malware in real time, enabling quick responses to cybersecurity threats, a vital feature of current malware analysis and mitigation.

3.6.7 Interpretability

Deep learning model interpretability is a major challenge because of the frequently considered "black box" character. These models produce complicated, non-linear judgments, making it difficult to understand the factors driving data categorization. Using explainable AI approaches, such as feature visualization or attention processes, we can learn about the inner workings of these models. This openness improves our knowledge of the principles that guide decisions and fosters trust and confidence in their data classifications. Interpretable deep learning models have become more approachable and valuable in various technical and practical applications by demystifying the decision-making process.

3.6.8 False Positives and False Negatives

Mitigating the impact of false positives and false negatives in malware analysis is critical for improving the system security. Balancing precision and recall necessitates continuous evaluation of the model's performance, fine-tuning of hyperparameters, and rigorous model validation, reducing the likelihood of incorrectly classifying benign files as malware (false positives) or failing to detect actual malware (false negatives). This recurrent method enables an appropriate trade-off between malware detection accuracy and comprehensiveness, thereby improving the overall cybersecurity.

3.6.9 Overfitting

Overfitting is a key challenge in malware investigations that utilize deep-learning models. When these models are overtrained on a single dataset, they become highly specialized and may fail to generalize to unknown malware samples. Practitioners must use techniques such as validation data, cross-validation, and regularization during model training to reduce overfitting. Validation data were used to monitor the model's performance on independent samples, whereas cross-validation data were used to evaluate resilience. By contrast, regularization limits the model's complexity, preventing it from fitting noise in the training data. These tactics are critical for improving deep learning models' generalization capabilities in malware analysis.

3.7 Future Directions

Ongoing learning will be more crucial than ever in the context of malware analysis to keep up with the dynamic and ever-evolving nature of cyberthreats. To increase the precision of detection, models are often updated and adapted to new malware strains and attack strategies. Federated learning enables collaborative model training across several enterprises without disclosing private information. This strategy can improve the collective intelligence and precision of malware detection systems while protecting data privacy. Using Generative Adversarial Networks (GANs) to create artificial adversarial examples during adversarial training improves protection against complex attacks may be achieved. As explainable AI research advances, cybersecurity professionals will be able to trust the results of AI-driven malware analyses and obtain deeper insights into model choices. AI-powered technologies will increasingly work with human analysts to streamline the analysis process and provide actionable insights to help with decision making. Privacy concerns in AI-driven malware analysis will lead to the development of privacy-preserving approaches to safeguard sensitive data during model training and inference.

Malware analysis has been transformed by AI and deep learning, which now offers effective methods for identifying, categorizing, and attributing malware threats. AI has shown considerable potential for recognizing malware behaviors and patterns using convolutional neural networks (CNNs) for image analysis, recurrent neural networks (RNNs) for sequence analysis, and transformer-based models for text analysis.

3.7.1 Conclusion

Threat detection, analysis, and mitigation have undergone fundamental changes owing to the integration of AI and deep learning in malware analysis and cybersecurity. Deep learning models, an AI-driven method, have shown impressive abilities in classifying malware families, attributing assaults, and enhancing overall cybersecurity defenses. Ongoing research is necessary for progress in AI-driven cybersecurity. AI models must adjust to new attack methods and continue to be resilient to adversarial attempts as malware and cyber threats change. Continuous research into creating AI models that are easier to understand, more transparent, and more ethical supports the responsible use of AI and increases confidence in its judgments. Additionally, for AI-driven cybersecurity systems to become more accurate and effective, research initiatives addressing issues such as data bias, privacy protection, and false positives/negatives are essential. Given the complexity and dynamics of cybersecurity, collaboration is equally important. A comprehensive approach to cybersecurity is fostered through cooperative efforts among AI developers, cybersecurity professionals, threat intelligence providers, legislators, and ethicists. Sharing threat intelligence, working together on research initiatives, and exchanging best practices can result in defensive plans that are more thorough and potent.

References

1. Gorment, N.Z., Selamat, A., Cheng, L.K., Krejcar, O., Machine Learning Algorithm for Malware Detection: Taxonomy, Current Challenges, and Future Directions. *IEEE Access*, 11, 141045–141089, March 2023, doi: 10.1109/ACCESS.2023.3256979.
2. Balan, S. and Howell, P., *A Machine Learning Approach for Network Traffic Analysis using Random Forest Regression. ACET Journal of Computer Education & Research*, vol. 13, no. 1, p.1, 2019.

3. Lee, L., Artificial intelligence and the future of cybersecurity. 3, January, 159–163, 2017.
4. Das, R., Sandhane, R., Artificial Intelligence in Cyber Security. *J. Phys. Conf. Ser.*, 1964, 4, 2021, doi: 10.1088/1742-6596/1964/4/042072.
5. Pupillo, L., Fantin, S., Ferreira, A., Polito, C., Centre for European Policy Studies, *Artificial Intelligence and Cybersecurity. Technology, Governance and Policy Challenges*, 2021. *Intereconomics*, vol. 59, no. 1, pp. 10–13, 2024, doi: 10.2478/ie-2024-0004.
6. Zabidi, M.N.A., Maarof, M.A., Zainal, A., Challenges in high accuracy of malware detection. *Proc. - 2012 IEEE Control Syst. Grad. Res. Colloquium, ICSGRC 2012*, pp. 123–125, 2012, no. Icsgrc, doi: 10.1109/ICSGRC.2012.6287147.
7. Jones, K.J. and Wang, Y., Malgazer: An Automated Malware Classifier with Running Window Entropy and Machine Learning. *2020 6th Int. Conf. Mob. Secur. Serv. MOBISECSERV 2020*, 2020, doi: 10.1109/MobiSecServ48690.2020.9042957.
8. Kuraku, S., Kalla, D, Emotet Malware - A Banking Credentials Stealer. *IOSR J. Comput. Eng.*, 22, 4, 31–40, 2020, doi: 10.9790/0661-2204023140.
9. Chen, Y.C., Chen, H.Y., Takahashi, T., Sun, B., Lin, T.N., Impact of Code Deobfuscation and Feature Interaction in Android Malware Detection. *IEEE Access*, 9, 123208–123219, 2021, doi: 10.1109/ACCESS.2021.3110408.
10. Udayakumar, N., Subbulakshmi, T., Dr & Mishra, A., Mishra, S., Jain, P., Malware category prediction using KNN and SVM classifiers. *Int. J. Mech. Eng. Technol.*, 10, 787–797, 2019.
11. Gundoor, T.K. and Sridevi, Optimized Feature Selection and classification for Non-Portable Executable Malware. *Int. J. Commun. Netw. Inf. Secur.*, 16, 4, 546–552, 2024.
12. Goosen, R., Rontojannis, A., Deutscher, S., Rogg, J., Bohmayr, W., Mkrtchian, D., Artificial Intelligence Is a Threat to Cybersecurity. It's Also a Solution. *BCG Bost. Consult. Gr.*, 6, 2018, [Online]. Available: http://image-src.bcg.com/Images/BCG-Artificial-Intelligence-Is-a-Threat-to-Cyber-Security-Its-Also-a-Solution-Nov-2018_tcm9-207468.pdf.
13. Wiafe, I., Koranteng, F.N., Obeng, E.N., Assyne, N., Wiafe, A., Gulliver, S.R., Artificial Intelligence for Cybersecurity: A Systematic Mapping of Literature. *IEEE Access*, 8,146598–146612, 2020, doi: 10.1109/ACCESS.2020.3013145. ACCESS.2020.3013145.
14. Fang, Y., Zhang, W., Li, B., Jing, F., Zhang, L., Semi-Supervised Malware Clustering Based on the Weight of Bytecode and API. *IEEE Access*, 8, 2313–2326, 2020, doi: 10.1109/ACCESS.2019.2962198.
15. Singh, J. and Singh, J., A survey on machine learning-based malware detection in executable files. *J. Syst. Archit.*, 112, July, 101861, 2021, doi: 10.1016/j.sysarc.2020.101861.
16. Higuera, J.B., Aramburu, C.A., Higuera, J.R.B., Urban, M.A.S., Montalvo, J.A.S., Systematic approach to Malware analysis (SAMA). *Appl. Sci.*, 10, 4, 1–31, 2020, doi: 10.3390/app10041360.

17. Karunanithi, D., Sg, A., Technology, I., Attacks on Artificial Intelligence Applications through Adversarial Image. 118, 20, 4491–4495, 2018.
18. Akhtar, M.S. and Feng, T., Malware Analysis and Detection Using Machine Learning Algorithms. *Symmetry (Basel).*, 14, 11, 1–11, 2022, doi: 10.3390/sym14112304.
19. De Andrade, C.A.B., De Mello, C.G., Duarte, J.C., Malware automatic analysis. *Proc. - 1st BRICS Ctries. Congr. Comput. Intell. BRICS-CCI 2013*, pp. 681–686, 2013, doi: 10.1109/BRICS-CCI-CBIC.2013.119.
20. Archana, P., Divyabharathi, P., Camry Joshya, Y., Sudha, Artificial Neural Network Model for Predicting Fraudulent Attacks. *J. Phys. Conf. Ser.*, 1979, 1, 1–9, 2021, doi: 10.1088/1742-6596/1979/1/012016.
21. Hemalatha, J., Roseline, S.A., Geetha, S., Kadry, S., Damaševičius, R., An efficient densenet-based deep learning model for Malware detection. *Entropy*, 23, 3, 1–23, 2021, doi: 10.3390/e23030344.
22. Osho, O., An Overview: Stochastic Gradient Descent Classifier, Linear Discriminant Analysis, Deep Learning and Naive Bayes Classifier Approaches to Network Intrusion Detection. 10, 04, 294–308, 2021.
23. Sridevi and Gundoor, T.K., Artificial Intelligence Knowledge Management and Industry Revolution 4.0. In: *Knowledge Management and Industry Revolution 4.0*, R. Kumar, V. Jain, V.C. Ibarra, C.A. Talib and V. Kukreja (eds.), 24264, 1,.ch6, 2024 https://doi.org/10.1002/9781394.
24. Liu, D., Wang, H., Stavrou, A., Detecting malicious javascript in PDF through document instrumentation. *Proc. Int. Conf. Dependable Syst. Networks*, pp. 100–111, 2014, doi: 10.1109/DSN.2014.92.
25. Talukder, S., Talukderm Z., A Survey on Malware Detection and Analysis Tools. *Int. J. Netw. Secur. Its Appl.*, 12, 2, 37–57, 2020, doi:10.5121/ijnsa.2020.12203.
26. Liu, Q., Li, P., Zhao, W., Cai, W., Yu, S., Leung, V.C.M., A survey on security threats and defensive techniques of machine learning: A data-driven view. *IEEE Access*, 6, 12103–12117, 2018, doi: 10.1109/ACCESS.2018.2805680.
27. Mukesh, S.D., An Analysis Technique to Detect Ransomware Threat. *2018 Int. Conf. Comput. Commun. Informatics, ICCCI 2018*, pp. 1–5, 2018, doi: 10.1109/ICCCI.2018.8441502.
28. Gibert, D., Mateu, C., Planes, J., The rise of machine learning for detection and classification of malware: Research developments, trends and challenges. *J. Netw. Comput. Appl.*, 153, 2019, 102526, 2020, doi: 10.1016/j.jnca.2019.102526.
29. Heinl, C.H., Artificial (intelligent) agents and active cyber defence: Policy implications. *Int. Conf. Cyber Conflict, CYCON*, 2014, 53–66, 2014, doi: 10.1109/CYCON.2014.6916395.
30. Hossain, G.M.S., Deb, K., Janicke, H., Sarker, I.H., PDF Malware Detection: Toward Machine Learning Modeling With Explainability Analysis. *IEEE Access*, 12, 13833–13859, 2024, doi: 10.1109/ACCESS.2024.3357620.

31. Sharma, P. and Arora, J., A Review on Malware Detection Schemes Using Machine Learning Techniques. *Int. J. Eng. Dev. Res.*, 4, 2, 2321–9939, 2016, [Online]. Available: https://www.ijedr.org/papers/IJEDR1602028.pdf.
32. Gundoor, T.K., IoT-Enabled 5G Networks for Secure Communication. *Information Security Practices for the Internet of Things, 5G, and Next-Generation Wireless Networks*. IGI Global, 1-29, 2022.
33. Panchariya, H. and Bharkad, S., Comparative Analysis of Feature Extraction Methods for Optic Disc Detection. *IOSR J. Comput. Eng.*, 16, 3, 49–54, 2014, doi: 10.9790/0661-16334954.
34. Gundoor, T.K. and Sridevi, Identification of Dominant Features in Non-Portable Executable Malicious File, *2022 Second International Conference on Computer Science, Engineering and Applications (ICCSEA)*, Gunupur, India, 1–6, 2022.
35. H. A. K. and T. M. A., Machine Learning Techniques for Malware Detection. *Int. J. Sci. Res. Sci. Eng. Technol.*, 4099, 70–76, 2021, doi: 10.32628/ijsrset21858.
36. Torres, M., Alvarez, R., Cazorla, M., A Malware Detection Approach Based on Feature Engineering and Behavior Analysis. *IEEE Access*, 11, 105355–105367, 2023, doi:10.1109/ACCESS.2023.3319093.
37. Tao, F., Akhtar, M., Jiayuan, Z., The future of Artificial Intelligence in Cybersecurity: A Comprehensive Survey. *EAI Endorsed Trans. Creat. Technol.*, 8, 28, 170285, 2021, doi: 10.4108/eai.7-7-2021.170285.
38. Eswara Narayanan, M. and Muthukumar, B., Malware Classification Using Xgboost With Vote Based Backward Feature Elimination Technique. *Turk. J. Comput. Math. Educ.*, 12, 10, 5915–5923, 2021, [Online]. Available: https://turcomat.org/index.php/turkbilmat/article/view/5412.
39. Sahay, S.K., Sharma, A., Rathore, H., Evolution of Malware and Its Detection Techniques. *Adv. Intell. Syst. Comput.*, 933, 139–150, 2020, doi: 10.1007/978-981-13-7166-0_14.
40. Sinchana, C., Sinchana, K., Afridi, S., Pooja, M.R., Artificial intelligence applications in defense. *Lect. Notes Netw. Syst.*, 89, 2, 727–734, 2020, doi:10.1007/978-981-15-0146-3_68.
41. Fadadu, F., Handa, A., Kumar, N., Shukla, S.K., Evading API Call Sequence Based Malware Classifiers. *Lect. Notes Comput. Sci. (including Subser. Lect. Notes Artif. Intell. Lect. Notes Bioinformatics)*, 11999 LNCS, 18–33, 2020, doi: 10.1007/978-3-030-41579-2_2.
42. Jahromi, A.N., Hashemi, S., Dehghantanha, A., Parizi, R.M., Choo, K.K.R., An Enhanced Stacked LSTM Method with No Random Initialization for Malware Threat Hunting in Safety and Time-Critical Systems. *IEEE Trans. Emerg. Top. Comput. Intell.*, 4, 5, 630–640, 2020, doi: 10.1109/TETCI.2019.2910243.
43. Soni, J., Prabakar, N., Upadhyay, H., Behavioral analysis of system call sequences using LSTM seq-seq, cosine similarity and jaccard similarity for real-time anomaly detection. *Proc. - 6th Annu. Conf. Comput. Sci. Comput. Intell. CSCI 2019*, pp. 214–219, 2019, doi: 10.1109/CSCI49370.2019.00043.

44. De La Rosa, L., Kilgallon, S., Vanderbruggen, T., Cavazos, J., Efficient Characterization and Classification of Malware Using Deep Learning. *Proc. Resil. Week 2018, RWS 2018*, pp. 77–83, 2018, doi: 10.1109/RWEEK.2018.8473556.
45. Kruczkowski, M. and Niewiadomska-Szynkiewicz, E., Comparative study of supervised learning methods for malware analysis. *J. Telecommun. Inf. Technol.*, 2014, 4, 24–33, 2014.
46. Akhtar, N. and Mian, A., Threat of Adversarial Attacks on Deep Learning in Computer Vision: A Survey. *IEEE Access*, 6, 14410–14430, 2018, doi: 10.1109/ACCESS.2018.2807385.
47. Gibert, D., Mateu, C., Planes, J., The rise of machine learning for detection and classification of malware: Research developments, trends and challenges. *J. Netw. Comput. Appl.*, 153, 102526, 2020, doi: 10.1016/j.jnca.2019.102526.
48. Rodrigo, C., Pierre, S., Beaubrun, R., El Khoury, F., Brainshield: A hybrid machine learning-based malware detection model for android devices. *Electron.*, 10, 23,1–19, 2021, doi: 10.3390/electronics10232948.
49. Bajcsy, Peter *et al.* Designing Trojan Detectors in Neural Networks Using Interactive Simulations. *Appl. Sci. (Basel, Switzerland)*, 11, 4, 2021. doi:10.3390/app11041865.

4

Transmit Texts Covertly Using Trigonometric Functions and Pythagorean Theorem

Nagadevi Bala Nagaram*, R. Narmada Devi and S. Karpagam

Department of Mathematics, Vel Tech Rangarajan Dr. Sagunthala R&D Institute of Science and Technology, Avadi, Chennai, Tamil Nadu, India

Abstract

Cryptography is the technique of encrypting messages in order to provide secrecy to information security. Information can be obtained through cryptography by being changed into a format that only those who understand the process of encoding can decipher. The initial information is referred to as plaintext, while the encoded version is referred to as ciphertext. The method by which plaintext is transformed into ciphertext is known as encryption. The calculation or code used to do so is referred to as an algorithm. Decryption is a reverse of encryption, which converts ciphertext back to plaintext. An article titled "A mathematical theory of cryptography" was written by Shannon who had considered the inventor of cryptography while he was a long-time employee at Bell Labs. The Egyptians employed hieroglyphic writing to send messages to one another around 4,000 years ago. Only the scribes, who used to send communications on the kings' behalf, were aware of this code's existence. Someone must understand the information or know how to convert it back to plain text in order to decode it. Decoding often includes both the algorithm and a key. Every day, people and organizations use cryptography to safeguard their privacy and maintain the secrecy of their communications and data. By encrypting communicated messages with an algorithm and Encryption is decryption with a key known only to the sender and the recipient which maintains confidentiality. In India, Indian Institute of Technology Kharagpur is best for cryptography. Kirchhoff's principle is used to describe that the message's secrecy should always depend on the confidentiality of the key, not the encryption algorithm.

**Corresponding author*: nagaramnagadevibala@gmail.com

Subhabrata Barman, Santanu Koley and Subhankar Joardar (eds.) Next-Generation Systems and Secure Computing, (61–78) © 2025 Scrivener Publishing LLC

Use ciphers that have been openly analyzed and recognized as standards, which is related to the aforementioned. In the same way that the Caesar cypher may be broken once the scheme is known, using "secret crypto" is dangerous. For instance, if your key is hacked, a hacker could view your messages, if the hacker can breach the cryptography system as a whole, they can get access to the plain text of every message that system has ever encrypted, not just those for a single user. In our day to life every nonliving things like mobile, computer, car, locker require security to protect from the hackers. Mathematics play a tremendous role in cryptography. A subfield of mathematics called trigonometry studies the correlations between angle and length ratios. The sine, cosine, tangent, co-secant, secant, and cotangent are the six trigonometric functions. Trigonometric functions are used to calculate unknown lengths from known or measured angles in geometric forms. The aim of this chapter is to encrypt the secret code by using trigonometric functions and by using Pythagorean theorem to decrypt the secret code.

Keywords: Cryptography, data encryption, decryption, trigonometric function, pythagorean

4.1 Introduction

In mathematics, trigonometry focuses on certain functions with angles, and how to use them in computations. Greek terms trigonon, the term refers to "triangle" and metron the term refers to "to measure," are the source of the word trigonometry. Trigonometry was primarily used to calculate the triangle's missing values in numerical form or any other form that may be divided into triangles by knowing the values of the other parts until around the 16th century. For instance, if the lengths of the first two sides of a triangle are known, the third side and two remaining angles can be found, and the enclosed angle is known. These computations set trigonometry apart from geometry, which focuses primarily on qualitative relations. Naturally, there is no absolute difference. Employing the Pythagorean theorem, for instance, is a quantitative statement concerning the lengths of the three sides of the right triangle. Naturally, this difference is not always clear. Consider the Pythagorean theorem, which is a quantitative statement concerning the lengths of the three sides of the right triangle. However, trigonometry was essentially a branch of geometry in its original form; the two were not separated into their own mathematical disciplines until the 16th century.

In trigonometry, the angle can have six common functions. The terms sine (sin), cosecant (csc), cosine (cos), secant (sec), tangent (tan), and cotangent (cot) are their names and abbreviations, respectively. The graph shows the trigonometric functions (TF) with respect to a right triangle. When a triangle has an angle A, for instance, the sine of A, or sin A, is the ratio of the side opposing A to the side opposite the right angle (hypotenuse). This definition also applies to the other TF's. These functions, which are characteristic of angle A regardless of triangle size, were computed and tabulated for several angles prior to computers rendering trigonometry tables superfluous. The TF in geometric figures can be used to derive unknown angles and distances from known or measured angles. The need to compute angles and distances for artillery range finding, mapping, surveying, and astronomy has led to the development of trigonometry.

Trigonometry is concerned with the relationship between a triangle's angles and its sides. The initial and terminal sides interact to produce an angle. When a side ray approaches the positive x-axis and its vertex is at the origin, the side is said to be in a fixed position. The angle was measured by the amount of rotation from the beginning to the terminal side. A rotation in the clockwise direction creates a negative angle, and a rotation in the counterclockwise direction creates a positive angle. Angles were measured in degrees and radians. The angles can be assigned numerical values by choosing a unit of measurement. Degree and radian are the most often used units. The entire revolution was 360°, with each degree being further split as 60′ (min) and every minute into 60″ (s). Radians are the most

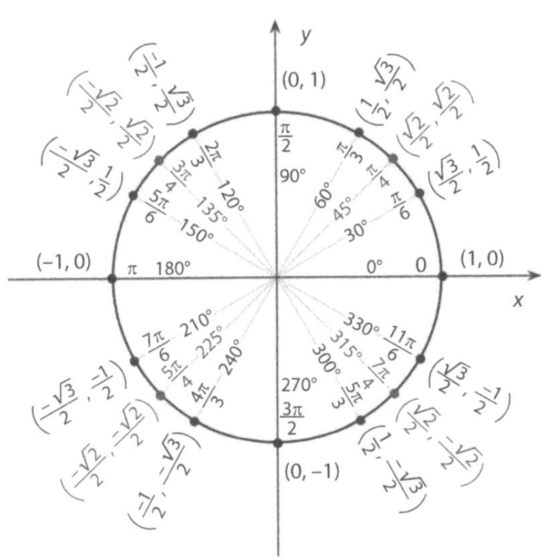

Figure 4.1 The angles in radius and degrees in the unit circle for TR. Source: https://en.wikipedia.org/wiki/Trigonometric_functions#/media/File:Unit_circle_angles_color.svg.

practical units while working in theory. The relationship between degrees and radians is $1° = \frac{\Pi}{180°}$ radians [10]. Figure 4.1 is expressed the unit circle with the center at the origin and is expressed to define the Trigonometric Ratios (TR).

The six TR in trigonometry connect the right triangle's angle measurements to the lengths of its sides, an initial side 'x' and a terminal side 'r.' The r refers to the right triangle's radius and hypotenuse, which is combined to create a right triangle. Because $x^2 + y^2 = r^2$, according to the Pythagorean theorem, $r = \sqrt{x^2 + y^2}$. An angle that is not straight is denoted by θ (theta). The side-length ratio was determined using any of the six TF. Sine (sin), cosecant (csc), cosine (cos), secant (sec), tangent (tan), and cotangent (cot) are the functions. Every coterminal angle in the TF has the same value. Therefore, sin (A ± 360n) = sin A when n is an integer and analogous relations hold for the other five functions. One way to describe these findings is to claim that the TF has a periodic period of 360° or 180° [11]. The ratios of these functions were created as follows.

The Cartesian coordinates of the unit circle were used to represent the six TF in Figure 4.2 for any given angle θ. A, B, and D have ordinates of sin

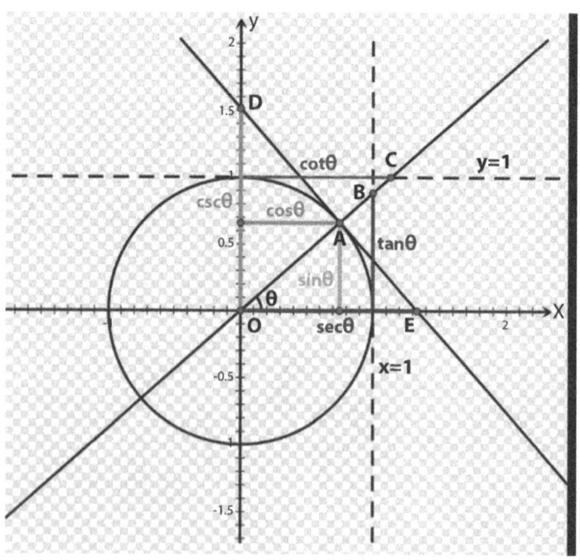

Figure 4.2 Unit circle values of trigonometric functions. Source: https://en.wikipedia.org/wiki/Trigonometric_functions#/media/File:Unit_Circle_Definitions_of_Six_Trigonometric_Functions.svg.

θ, tan θ, and csc θ, respectively, and the abscissas of cos θ, cot θ, and sec θ, for A, C, and E.

$$\sin\theta = \frac{opposite\,side}{hypotenuse}$$

$$\cos\theta = \frac{adjacent\,side}{hypotenuse}$$

$$\tan\theta = \frac{opposite\,side}{hypotenuse}$$

$$\cos ec\theta = \frac{hypotenuse}{opposite\,side}$$

$$\sec\theta = \frac{hypotenuse}{adjacent\,side}$$

$$\cot\theta = \frac{adjacent\,side}{opposite\,side}$$

Trigonometric function values should be easily accessible for every angle to be useful. Numerous trigonometric identities demonstrate that the values for angles ranging from 0° to 45° can be used to quickly ascertain the function values for every angle. For any angle between 0° and 45°, which are integral multiples of a handy unit (i.e., 1′), it is sufficient to record the sine, cosine, and tangent values in a table. Astronomers, surveyors, and engineers may benefit from such trigonometry tables until computers become obsolete in the late 20th century. Table 4.1 expresses the values of the six trigonometric functions between 0° and 90°.

The table for natural trigonometry functions is given below.

Table 4.1 Natural trigonometric functions.

function θ	**0°**	**30°**	**45°**	**60°**	**90°**
sine	0	$\frac{1}{2}$	$\frac{\sqrt{2}}{2}$	$\frac{\sqrt{3}}{2}$	1

(Continued)

Table 4.1 Natural trigonometric functions. (*Continued*)

function θ	**0°**	**30°**	**45°**	**60°**	**90°**
cosine	1	$\frac{\sqrt{3}}{2}$	$\frac{\sqrt{2}}{2}$	$\frac{1}{2}$	0
tangent	0	$\frac{\sqrt{3}}{3}$	1	$\sqrt{3}$	undefined
cosecant	undefined	2	$\sqrt{2}$	$\frac{2\sqrt{3}}{3}$	1
secant	1	$\frac{2\sqrt{3}}{3}$	$\sqrt{2}$	2	undefined
cotangent	undefined	$\sqrt{3}$	1	$\frac{\sqrt{3}}{3}$	0

The trigonometric functions that are most often used in contemporary mathematics are sine, cosine, and tangent functions. Their corresponding reciprocals are cotangent, secant, and cosecant, which are less frequently employed. There is an analog in the hyperbolic functions and a matching inverse function for each of the six trigonometric functions.

Only acute angles are included in the first formulations of the trigonometric functions, which are associated with right-angle triangles. Utilizing the conventional unit circle is frequently employed to describe the entire real line by sine and cosine functions geometrically, in this case, by removing a few isolated points in the real line, which gives as the domain of another TF. TFs are expressed as an infinite series. This allows the domains of the other TF, excluding a few isolated points, to be expanded to include the whole complex plane, including the domains of the sine and cosine functions. The progression of the cosine in notation is comparable to that of the sine [12].

The definitions of sine, cosine, and tangent may be easily remembered using the acronym SOHCAHTOA. This represents next-over-hypotenuse for cosine, opposite over adjacent for tangent, and opposite over hypotenuse for sine functions. Another significant related definition of the word "tangent" is a line or plane that contacts a certain curve or solid at a particular point. Then, we refer to these geometrical objects as tangent planes or lines [13].

The practice of securing data by converting them into a format that uninvited parties cannot decipher is known as cryptography. An initial human-readable communication, known as plaintext, is transformed into something that would appear to an untrained observer to be gibberish in cryptography using an algorithm or sequence of mathematical operations. This gibberish is known as ciphertext. For communication to be encrypted and used by the intended recipient, cryptographic systems require a technique to decrypt the ciphertext back into plaintext. This method is typically required, but not always. Julius Caesar employed it for his private communication, so it is known as the Caesar cipher. According to Suetonius, his biographer, "he wrote anything he had to say in cipher, which means by so rearranging the alphabet's letters' order." Anyone who wants to interpret and understand their significance must replace letters A with D, the fourth letter of the alphabet, and the same as the remaining letters. Thus, they employed this technique to send messages secretly.

Such encryption provides a fairly easy approach for conveying any communication in a secret. To translate such a form of language, both ends of the message channel would need a book of code words, and there would be no new words that you had not previously considered. You can encrypt any message that you can conceive with the Caesar cipher. The difficulty is that, unlike a complicated code book, it is far easier to properly transmit and retain the algorithm and key in advance for everyone conversing [23–26].

As a matter of fact, advancements in cryptography and computer development were closely related. Charles Babbage was interested in encryption and came up with the Difference Engine concept, which was later used to create contemporary computers. Germans encrypted their communications with the electromechanical Enigma machine during World War II. Alan Turing, a British team leader, is renowned for leading the development of a machine that deciphered the code and helped establish some of the foundations for the first computers. With the advent of computers, cryptography grew dramatically more sophisticated, but for several more decades it remained the domain of spies and generals.

Security experts can use cryptography techniques to maintain the privacy of the data's content and verify the sender and recipient of a message's identities and the data's integrity by demonstrating that nothing has changed. This shows that the purported sender transmitted this communication.

Computer science and mathematical theory form a strong foundation for modern cryptography [14]. Computational hardness assumptions are used in the design of cryptographic algorithms, making it difficult for adversaries to defeat real-world scenarios. Although it is theoretically conceivable to compromise a well-designed system, this is not practical in reality.

Therefore, these methods are referred to as "computationally secure" if they are well-designed. Advances in computer technology and theory, such as enhanced integer factorization techniques, require constant assessment and if required, modification of these designs. The finest theoretically breakable but computationally secure techniques are far easier to deploy in reality than information-theoretically safe schemes, such as the one-time pad, which cannot be cracked even with infinite computer power.

Many legal concerns have emerged in the Information Age owing to the development of cryptography technology. Due to the possibility of using cryptography as a tool for espionage and dissident activities, several countries have classified it as a weapon and restricted or outright banned its export and usage [16–19]. The revelation of encryption keys for documents pertinent to an inquiry can be compelled by law in certain areas where the use of cryptography is allowed. Digital media cases pertaining to copyright infringement and digital rights management are other areas in which cryptography is heavily involved [20–22].

The primary concerns of cryptography prior to the early 1900s were lexicographic and linguistic concerns. Since then, the field of cryptography has expanded, and now includes a wide range of mathematical subdisciplines, including number theory, finite mathematics, statistics, information theory, computational complexity, and combinatorics. Although other engineering specialties, such as chemical or civil, simply have to deal with neutral natural forces, cryptography is a unique form of engineering because it deals with active, intelligent, and malicious resistance. Studies on the connection between quantum physics and cryptography are also ongoing. More complicated ciphers were made feasible by the advancement of digital computers and electronics, as they aided in cryptanalysis. Moreover, computers make it possible to encrypt any type of representable data [15].

Cryptography is still essential for securing communication and information while it is in transit and preventing unauthorized parties from reading it, despite its lengthy history extending back to the hieroglyphics of ancient Egypt. It uses techniques such as encrypted keys and digital signatures to encode communications into difficult-to-decipher codes that protect data privacy and secure online transactions, such as credit cards, email, and web browsing [29]. Mathematics plays a vital role in cryptography. Many researchers have used different techniques to secure a message, which will be discussed in the following.

Hiwarekar modified the Laplace Transform in [1] for encrypting purposes. The Laplace transform was subsequently applied as a cryptographic technique by Gencoglu, Hemant *et al.*, Nagalakshmi *et al.*, and Dhingra [2–5]. Saha used the Laplace–Mellon Transform for Cryptography [6].

Mohan *et al.* used a bilinear transform with probability for encryption to covertly share information. The Laplace transform, hyperbolic tangent function, and conformal mapping were also modified for the cryptography method by the same author [7, 9].

In cryptography, Nagaram *et al.* used ODE with a variable separable method, deck of cards, and employed PDF and CDF functions [8, 27, 28]. This goal of this chapter is to organize the text's system of equations and use Hamilton's theorem to disclose the suggested plain text. A secure extended greatest common divisor computation approach is efficient. Schoenmakers and Segers worked on a constant-time 2-adic algorithm by Bernstein and Yang, who modified it to operate only over integers. This results in a significantly improved method for multiparty computing, but it also presents a new issue with Bézout coefficient growth.

Many concepts are used to keep the information between the sender and receiver secret. In *Section 4.2*, the primary stream definitions employed in cryptographic analysis are explained. *Section 4.3* presents the encryption algorithm used in this study. An example of the algorithm presented in *Section 4.3* is provided. The decryption process utilizing cipher text is described, and the decryption technique is described in *Section 4.4*. Conclusions and references are presented in *Section 4.5*.

4.2 Mainstream Definition

The study of ciphertext, ciphers, and cryptosystems, with the goal of comprehending their operation and developing methods for circumventing or weakening them, is known as cryptanalysis. Figure 4.3 shows a flow chart of the cryptography technique.

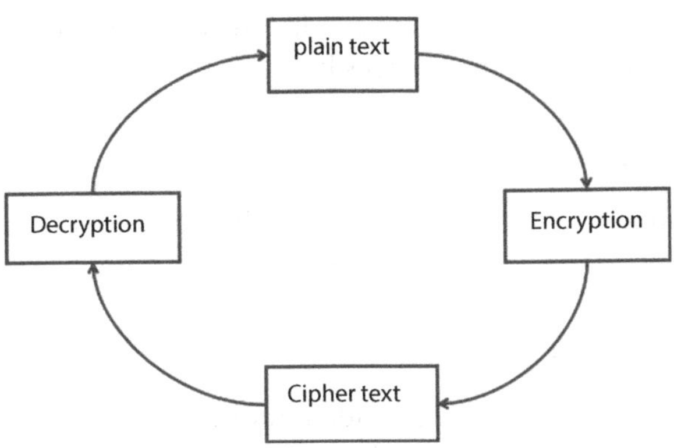

Figure 4.3 A flow chart of cryptography technique.

The cryptographic study in this work uses the procedures listed below.

4.2.1 Plain Text

Data that are not encrypted and are either utilized as an input for encryption or as an output for decryption is known as plaintext. This refers to everything that a person may directly understand. This is referred to as plaintext because it is quite common and simple. Plain text is frequently employed for a number of tasks, such as creating documents, developing software, and sending emails. Because it is portable and easy to use, it is also the recommended format for sending and storing large volumes of text data. It is frequently used for many different purposes, including composing emails, creating software, and producing paper. Because plaintext may be transformed to ciphertext and vice versa, both processes go hand in hand.

Although humans cannot interpret binary files, which are composed of 0s and 1s, they are nevertheless available to users in some way. As a result, the binary files were not classified as plaintext. In essence, it refers to the data entered into an encryption process or a cipher. Data that can be read directly by anybody are known as plain text. This information must be communicated to the recipient in confidence.

4.2.2 Cipher Text

Encrypted text, also known as ciphertext, is a string of random characters and numbers that is meaningless to others. An encryption algorithm generates ciphertext by applying this method to a plaintext message. Using decryption, the original plaintext can be obtained by reversing the ciphertext.

The term "cipher text" refers to an altered version of plain text that can only be decrypted using the sender's key.

4.2.3 Cipher

The term "cipher" describes an algorithm that converts ordinary text into ciphertext.

4.2.4 Encryption

The process of converting the provided information into a secret message is known as encryption. By employing the secret key, this prevents the unwanted parties from seeing the original information.

The act of securing information or data by employing mathematical models to jumble it so that only those with the necessary key may decode it is known as encryption at its most basic level. The data and information that organizations and consumers depend on a daily basis are protected by particular types of encryption developed by mathematicians and computer scientists. This method can be as simple or complicated as required.

4.2.5 Decryption

An encryption algorithm is used to convert plaintext into encrypted or ciphertext. Unreadable ciphertext must first be decrypted and then transformed into plaintext using a key. A procedure known as decryption cipher converts the ciphertext back into plaintext. The opposite of encryption is that of decryption. In this procedure, the secret key is used to translate the encrypted text back to its original form.

"Plaintext" is converted into "ciphertext" in the process of encryption, usually with the use of mathematical models called algorithms used in cryptography. A decryption key, string of digits, or password that is also generated by an algorithm are needed to decode the data back to the plaintext. Because many cryptographic keys are associated with secure encryption techniques, an unauthorized individual cannot simply use a computer to calculate the proper character string by testing every possible combination or estimating which one is accurate.

4.2.6 Trigonometric Functions

One of the most important mathematical analyses is trigonometric function. The angle of the right triangle can be used as the domain input value for the six basic TF, which have range-based numerical results. The $[-1, 1]$ range and domain of the TF of f(x) are the angles expressed in degrees or radians. The domains and ranges of all other functions are similar.

4.2.7 Pythagorean Theorem

Greek mathematician Pythagoras of Samos invented the Pythagorean theorem (PT). A Greek philosopher from antiquity founded a community of mathematicians who lived as monks and worked with numbers as vocations. Although the theorem was first presented by Pythagoras, evidence suggests that it was already in use a millennium before Pythagoras's time. Between the 20th and 16th centuries B.C., the Old Babylonian Period denoted the earliest evidence that has been discovered.

A fundamental relationship in Euclidean geometry between the right triangle's three sides is known as PT. According to Pythagorean theorem, this rule states that the square of the hypotenuse side of a right-angled triangle equals the sum of the squares of the other two sides. Perpendicular, Base and Hypotenuse are the names assigned to the three sides of the triangle. Because the hypotenuse lies in opposition to the 90° angle, it is the longest side in this instance. The Pythagorean theorem explains the relationship between the three sides of a triangle. The Pythagorean theorem explains the relationship between the three sides of a triangle. The following Figure 4.4 express the flow chart of the cryptography technique using trigonometry function and Pythagorean theorem.

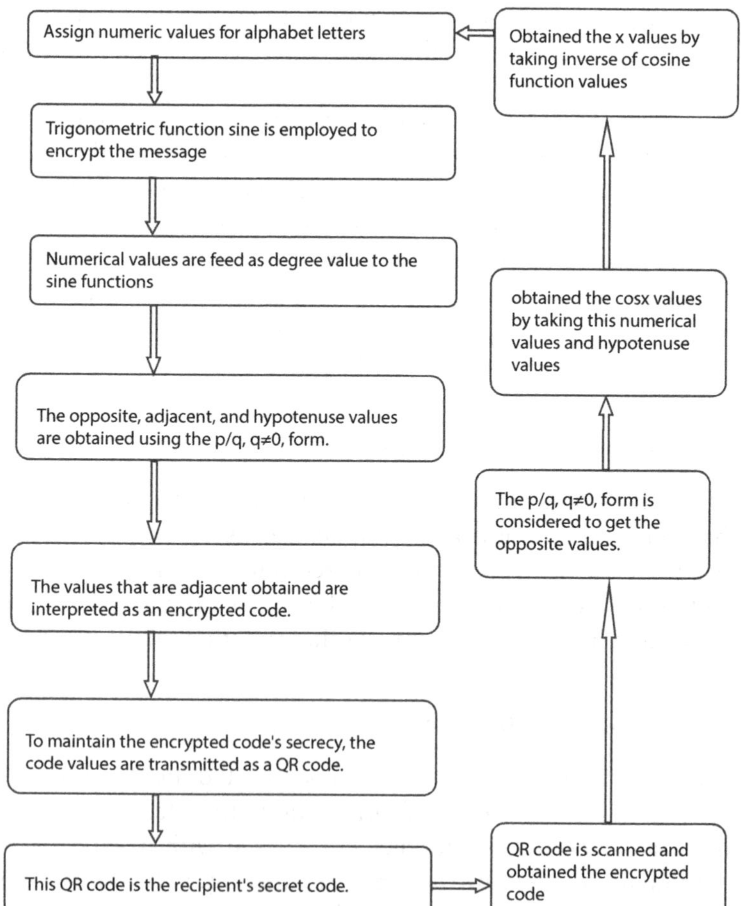

Figure 4.4 Flow chart of the cryptography technique using trigonometry function and Pythagorean theorem.

4.3 Description of the Work

Cryptography comprises two basic steps: encryption and decryption. The plaintext was encrypted throughout the encryption process and converted into ciphertext using a cipher.

Conversely, decryption converts ciphertext into plaintext using the same cipher. The main goal of this study is to use an enciphering approach to increase the security of an existing cryptosystem. The "two phases encryption model" is the proposed stronger cipher. Confusion, diffusion, and output are the three fundamental encryption algorithms included. To deliver a secure service, the user must authenticate and resource-sharing apps employ a two-stage encryption paradigm.

The following is a step-by-step process for encryption and decryption:

- In the first process, the text is converted into values that are assumed to be numerical values from A to 1, B to 2, C to 3, ...Z to 26.
- A trigonometric function was employed to encrypt the assumed numerical values. Here the 'sin' function is employed to do the process.
- The numerical values were allotted as degree values to the 'sine' function.
- The $p / q, q \neq 0$ form is considered to obtain the values of the opposite, adjacent, and hypotenuse.
- The obtained adjacent values were used as encrypted codes.
- The code values were converted into QR codes to keep the encrypted code covertly.
- The QR code is the secret code used to send the receiver.
- The numerical values were retrieved using a QR code scanner.
- The $p / q, q \neq 0$, form is considered to obtain opposite values.
- The cosx values were obtained by taking numerical values and hypotenuse values.
- The x values are obtained by taking cos^{-1} to obtain numerical values.
- The alphabet letters are retrieved from the assigned numerical values, and plain text is obtained.

4.3.1 Algorithm for Encryption

Here is an overview of the encryption procedure.

The text is translated in the first step into values that are considered numerical values, such as A to 1, B to 2, C to 3, Z to 26. The assumed numerical values were encrypted using the trigonometric function. The procedure is performed using the "sine" function. The "sine" function is assigned a degree value based on the numerical values. Opposite, adjacent, and hypotenuse values were obtained using the p / q, $q \neq 0$ form. The neighboring values obtained were interpreted as encrypted code. The code values are transmitted as QR codes to maintain the secrecy of the encrypted code. QR code is the recipient's secret code.

4.3.2 Numerical Simulation for Encryption Process

The Plain Text "MATHS" is considered to send to the receiver secretly.

The word "MATHS" is chosen to demonstrate the encryption procedure, and its corresponding parameter numerical values are assigned in Table 4.2.

The numerical values of the alphabet are taken as, 13°, 1°, 20°, 8°, and 19°.

The 'sin' function is considered to find the taken degree values as follows in Equation (4.1):

$$\begin{aligned} \sin(13^\circ) &= 0.225, \\ \sin(1^\circ) &= 0.017, \\ \sin(20^\circ) &= 0.342, \\ \sin(8^\circ) &= 0.139, \\ \sin(19^\circ) &= 0.326. \end{aligned} \tag{4.1}$$

The following values were obtained for the numerical values: 0.225, 0.017, 0.342, 0.139, and 0.326. The p/q form is constructed by assuming the denominator as 1,000, followed by $\frac{225}{1{,}000}$, $\frac{17}{1{,}000}$, $\frac{342}{1{,}000}$, $\frac{139}{1{,}000}$, and $\frac{326}{1{,}000}$.

Table 4.2 Encryption alphabet.

M	A	T	H	S
13	1	20	8	19

Figure 4.5 The QR code for the values 974.4, 999.9, 939.6, 990.3, and 945.4.

The adjacent values are calculated by the following Equation (4.2)

$$\text{adjacent} = \sqrt{\text{hypotenuse}^2 - \text{opposite}^2} \tag{4.2}$$

and were obtained as follows: 974.4, 999.9, 939.6, 990.3, and 945.4, respectively.

The encrypted codes of 974.4, 999.9, 939.6, 990.3, 945.4 is converted as QR codes which are given below to send to the receiver. Figure 4.5 shows the QR code for the encrypted data.

4.4 Algorithm for Decryption

The QR code scanner retrieves numerical numbers. It appears that the $p / q, q \neq 0$ form yields the opposite values. Numerical quantities and hypotenuse values were used to produce the cosx values. The process of obtaining the numerical values yields the x values. The alphabetic characters were extracted from the designated numerical values, yielding unformatted text.

4.4.1 Numerical Simulation for the Decryption Process

The QR code scanned and obtained the numerical values of 974.4, 999.9, 939.6, 990.3, and 945.4. The cosx values were then determined by taking the numerical and hypotenuse values as follows: $\frac{974.4}{1,000}$, $\frac{999.9}{1,000}$, $\frac{939.6}{1,000}$, $\frac{990.3}{1,000}$, and $\frac{945.4}{1,000}$, respectively. The x value is obtained by taking the inverse of the cosine as $13°$, $1°$, $20°$, $8°$, and $19°$. Thus, we assigned the assumed values of Table 4.2 to the numerical data and obtained the plain text "MATHS."

4.5 Conclusion

To safeguard electronic devices, including mobile phones, computers, cars, and lockers against hackers, security is required. Mathematical methods in cryptography are important tools for sending messages covertly, which is of interest to researchers. Trigonometry studies how angles and length ratios are related to one another. There are six types of trigonometric functions: sine, cosine, tangent, cosecant, secant, and cotangent. Unknown lengths can be computed from the established or measured angles in geometric shapes using trigonometric functions. In this study, trigonometric functions are used to encrypt the secret code, and the Pythagorean theorem for decrypting the secret code is processed and given in detail. This leads to covertly sending a message to the receiver.

References

1. Hiwarekar, A.P., New Mathematical Modeling for Cryptography. *J. Inf. Assur. Secur.*, 9, 027–033, 2014.
2. Gencoglu, M.T., Cryptanalaysis of a New Method of Cryptography using Laplace Transform Hyperbolic Functions. *Commun. Math. Appl.*, 8, 183–189, 2017.
3. Undegaonkar, H.K., Security in Communication By Using Laplace Transform and Cryptography. *Int. J. Sci. Technol. Res.*, 8, 3207–3209, 2019.
4. Nagalakshmi, G., Chandra Sekhar, A., Ravi Sankar, D., Asymmetric key Cryptography using Laplace Transform. *Int. J. Innov. Technol. Explor. Eng.*, 9, 3083–3087, 2020.
5. Dhingra, S., Savalgi, A.A., Jain, S., Laplace Transformation based Cryptographic Technique in Network Security. *Int. J. Comput. Appl.*, 136, 6–10, 2016.
6. Saha, M., Application of Laplace - Mellin Transform for Cryptography. *Raj J. Technol. Res. Innov.*, 5, 12–17, 2017.
7. Mohan, K.R., Rasappan, S., Murugesan, R., Kumaravel, S.K., Elngar, A.A., Secret Information Sharing Using Probability and Bilinear Transformation. *Proceedings of 2nd International Conference on Mathematical Modeling and Computational Science*, 2022, Ch-109.
8. Nagaram, N.B., Mohan, K.R., Kumaravel, S.K., Rasappan, S., Secret Sharing of Information using First Order ODE and Variable Separable Method, in: *Recent Trends in Computational Intelligence and Its Application*, CRC Press, London, 2022, Ch-109.

9. Mohan, K.R., Nagaram, N.B., Murugesan, R., Rasappan, S., A Cryptographic Technique Using Conformal Mapping, in: *Recent Trends in Computational Intelligence and Its Application*, pp. 519–523, CRC Press, London, 2023.
10. Cajori, F., Trigonometric Notations, in: *A History of Mathematical Notations*, vol. 2, pp. 142–179 (511–537), 1929.
11. Maor, E., *Trigonometric Delights*, Reprint ed., Princeton Univ. Press, New Jersey, 2002, 1998, ISBN 0-691-09541-8.
12. O'Connor, J.J. and Robertson, E.F., *Trigonometric functions*, University of St Andrews, Scotland, 1996, MacTutor History of Mathematics archive.
13. Weisstein, E.W., "*Tangent*" *from MathWorld*, A Wolfram Web Resource, 2006, https://mathworld.wolfram.com/Tangent.html.
14. Schoenmakers, B. and Segers, T., Secure Groups for Threshold Cryptography and Number-Theoretic Multiparty Computation. *Cyber Secur. Cryptology Mach. Learn.*, 7, 4, 56, 2023.
15. Diffie, W. and Hellman, M., New Directions in cryptography. *IEEE Trans. Inf. Theory*, IT-22, 6, 644–654, 1976.
16. Jyothi, V.E., Prasad, B.D.C.N., Mojjada, R.K., A*nalysis of Cryptography Encryption for Network Security. IOP Conf. Ser.: Mater. Sci. Eng.*, 2020, 981(2):022028, DOI 10.1088/1757-899X/981/2/022028.
17. Mohammed, A. and Varol, N., A Review paper on cryptography. *7th International Symposium on Digital Forensics and Security*, 2019, DOI: 10.1109/ISDFS.2019.8757514.
18. C. E. Shannon, Communication theory of secrecy systems, *Bell Syst. Tech. J.*, 28, 656–715, Oct. 1949.
19. Orman, H., Recent Parables in Cryptography. *IEEE Internet Comput.*, 18, 82–86, 2014.
20. Schneier, B., The Non-Security of Secrecy. *Commun. ACM*, 47, 120–120, 2004.
21. Callas, J., The Future of Cryptography. *Inf. Syst. Secur.*, 16, 15–22, 2007.
22. Massey, J.L., Cryptography—A selective survey. *Digital Commun.*, 85, 3–25, 1986.
23. Jirwan, N., Singh, A., Vijay, S., Review and Analysis of Cryptography Techniques. *Int. J. Sci. Eng. Res.*, 3, 1–6, 2013.
24. Gupta, A. and Walia, N.K., Cryptography Algorithms: A Review. *Int. J. Eng. Dev. Res.*, 2, 1667–1672, 2014.
25. Tayal, S., Gupta, N., Gupta, P., Goyal, D., Goyal, M., A Review paper on Network Security and Cryptography. *Adv. Comput. Sci. Technol.*, 10, 763–770, 2017.
26. Sharma, N., Prabhjot, Kaur, H., A Review of Information Security using Cryptography Technique. *Int. J. Adv. Res. Comput. Sci.*, 8, 323–326, 2017.

27. Mohan, K.R., Devi, R.N., Nagaram, N.B., Murugresan, R., Bharathi, T., A Cryptographic Algorithm using Fuzzy Logic and Deck of Cards. *Southeast Eur. J. Soft Comput.*, 12, 30–33, 2023.
28. Devi, R.N., Mohan, K.R., Nagaram, N.B., Novel Cryptographic Approach Based On Pdf And Cdf. *Southeast Eur. J. Soft Comput.*, 12, 34–38, 2023.
29. Singh, G., Kumar, P., Taneja, N., Kaur, G., A Research Paper on Cryptography. *Int. J. Technol. Res. Eng.*, 7, 6266–6268, 2019.

5

Exploring the Synergy of Cybersecurity and Blockchain: Strengthening Digital Defenses

Mohan Kumar Dehury[1]*, Bhabendu Kumar Mohanta[2], Manorama Patnaik[1], Biresh Kumar[1] and Purushottam Kumar[1]

[1]Amity Institute of Information Technology, Amity University, Jharkhand, Ranchi, India
[2]College of Information Technology, United Arab Emirates University, Al Ain, United Arab Emirates

Abstract

The integration of cybersecurity and blockchain technology is a promising strategy for improving digital defenses in today's unstable digital environments. Blockchain's decentralized nature, immutability, cryptographic methods, and transparency offer a strong barrier against unauthorized alterations or tampering, ensuring data integrity and preventing bad actors from modifying or tampering with sensitive information. The built-in cryptographic protocols ensure secure data transmission and storage. Blockchain technology also has the potential to transform cybersecurity in areas such as identity management and access control, allowing individuals to have more control over their personal information and reducing the risk of identity theft and illegal access. However, scaling, interoperability, and regulations remain challenging. The integration of blockchain and cybersecurity offers great promise for enhancing digital defenses, but it requires addressing the issues of scaling, interoperability, and regulation. Exploring the overlap between cybersecurity and blockchain is crucial for creating robust and secure digital ecosystems. This chapter examines the possibilities of blockchain technology and cybersecurity in enhancing digital defenses. The decentralized nature, immutability, cryptographic methods, and transparency of blockchain improve data storage, identity management, and forensics. However, scaling,

**Corresponding author*: mohankdehury@gmail.com

Subhabrata Barman, Santanu Koley and Subhankar Joardar (eds.) Next-Generation Systems and Secure Computing, (79–104) © 2025 Scrivener Publishing LLC

interoperability, and regulation issues must be addressed to ensure robust digital ecosystems.

Keywords: Cryptographic methods, digital systems, blockchain technology, blockchain network, cybersecurity

5.1 Introduction

A growing collection of documents, referred to as blocks, describes how blockchain technology is best described. Beyond the development and upkeep of an ongoing list of records, the innovation of blockchain technology is the enhancement of the security and anonymity of digital transactions based on the application of cryptographic algorithms [1–3]. A cryptographic hash or distinctive code associated with the previous block must come after the new block for a peer to add it to the blockchain. The header and body of a block are two essential components of any new block. The structure of the block header consists of information such as the version number, timestamp, nonce, hash value of the previous block, target hash bit, and Merkel root [4]. The body of the block contains all transactional details [5]. More precisely, the new block also contains transaction data and extra properties, such as a timestamp, to ensure that the information is consistent. This implies that the blockchain is resistant to data manipulation by design [6]. Timestamping and hashing processes are required before adding a new block to the chain; as a result, the data contained in the block becomes transparent to all blockchain participants.

One crucial operation within the blockchain is "mining." Broadly characterized, "mining" is often described as the digital generation or creation of new Bitcoins. However, a much more advanced procedure is involved in validating digital transactions and adding new links to the chain, that is, the distributed and digital ledger [6]. The process of granting miners the necessary rights add a new block and subsequently update the blockchain is one of the most crucial steps in the blockchain [7]. Consequently, with the addition of each new block to the chain, a fresh link is established, originating from the initial block known as the "genesis block." This process maintains an unbroken transaction record over time. The consensus agreement procedure, which is examined in sentences that follow [8], is a component of the mining operation. Digital ledger lack centralized authority; hence, a consensus procedure is necessary. As a result, fresh cryptocurrency (digital currency) is provided to miners to compensate for their efforts to secure the network [9].

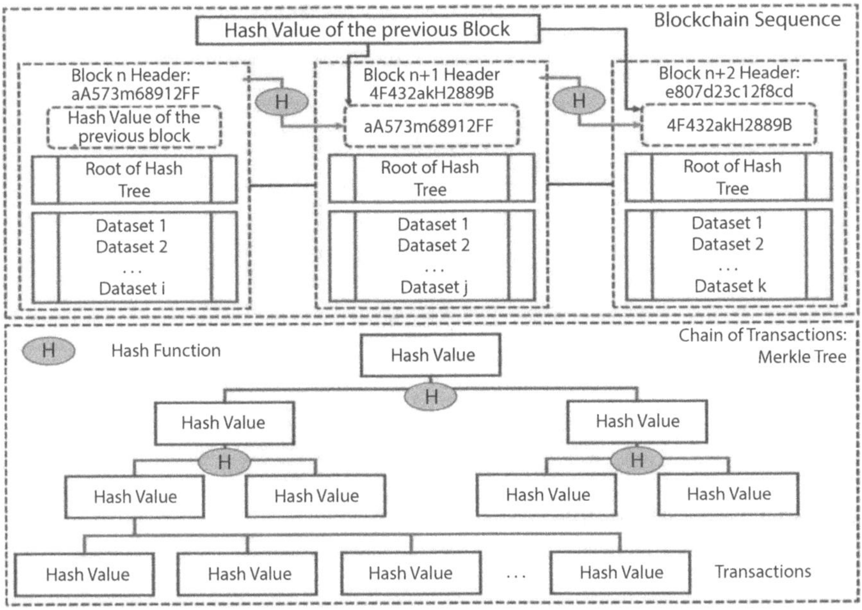

Figure 5.1 The fundamental idea behind blockchain.

The framework for exchanging data, networking features, and validating data comprise the network layer, which is necessary for node-to-node communication. Figure 5.1 presents the fundamental idea behind the blockchain. This is how the blockchain works [10]. The consensus agreement process, which is also a part of mining, is examined in the following sections. The lack of centralized authority in a digital ledger necessitates a consensus process. By following this process, new digital coins (cryptocurrencies) are provided to miners as compensation for their efforts to maintain the network's security.

5.2 Blockchain Infrastructure

Figure 5.2 illustrates the layers that make up the blockchain's infrastructure, such as the Application, Consensus, Network, Data, and Hardware layers. Numerous application situations were included, particularly in the application layer. The contract layer combines the fundamental algorithmic backend, encompassing code scripts, algorithms, and smart contracts [11].

Consensus mechanisms constitute the foundation of every blockchain used in cryptocurrencies. Figure 5.3 illustrates the consensus mechanism.

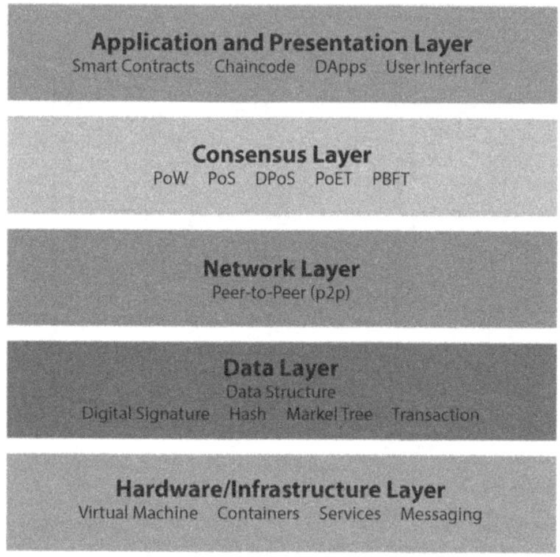

Figure 5.2 Layers of blockchain architecture.

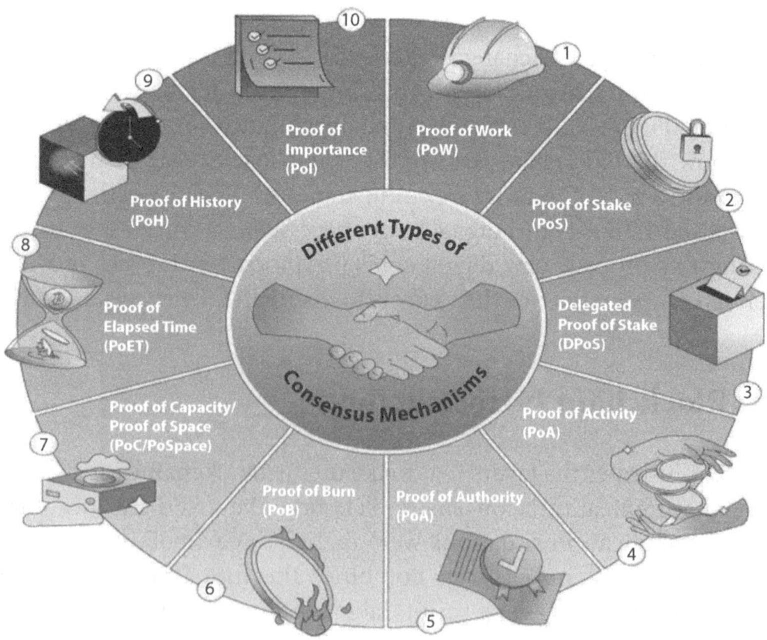

Figure 5.3 Consensus mechanism in blockchain technology [13].

In essence, consensus procedures blame blockchain's security flaws. Consensus methods are necessary to ensure unanimous agreement between every node in a blockchain network regarding a singular version of the ledger. A set of rules that makes it easier to defend networks from malicious behavior and cyberattacks can be realized as consensus mechanisms. There are various types of consensus mechanisms, which primarily vary in terms of their energy needs, the level of security they provide, and their capacity for scaling. The most popular consensus procedures are given and explained in the following paragraphs [12–17].

5.2.1 Proof of Work (PoW)

The PoW consensus algorithm was the first choice for blockchain implementation. Despite the underlying scalability difficulties, PoW is thought to be the most dependable and safe process thus far applied to blockchain. In terms of mining, PoW provides each user an equal opportunity to digitally generate a new block in the network. Consequently, the mining pools compete with each other to solve highly complex cryptographic mathematical problems. The winning miner first computes the hash number, a 64-digit hexadecimal number, granting them the authority to authenticate the transaction on the ledger and receive cryptocurrency tokens as a reward. As a result, PoW has significant running expenses because the construction and insertion of new blocks demands considerable processing resources and energy.

5.2.2 Proof of Stake (PoS)

In a PoS system, miners are required to "stake" a pre-established quantity of tokens from their account to be selected randomly as validators. The quantity of cryptocurrencies available affects miners' choices. PoS compensates the miner with transaction fees, as opposed to extra cryptocurrency, as with PoW. When comparing the PoS and PoW operating principles, the former is more ecologically friendly because it places less importance on the miner's computational resources. The PoS also exhibited a greater resistance to 51% attacks. It becomes evident that the Proof of Stake (PoS) rewards users and miners with larger quantities of tokens, potentially leading to centralization, an outcome often considered undesirable in the context of blockchain.

5.2.3 Delegated Proof of Stake (DPoS)

This process of consensus might be viewed as a revised version of the PoS. This change is related to the network voting system used to choose candidate miners. Network users are given the opportunity to cast votes for the nodes that they see as most qualified to create new blocks. By contributing their tokens to a stacking pool, voters acquire the ability to cast a ballot. The stake size that the user has placed in the stake pool determines the weight of each vote. This consensus process can be viewed as a PoS revision. The change relates to the network voting system used to choose candidate miners.

5.2.4 Proof of Activity (PoA)

This technique was developed by combining PoW and PoS mechanisms. In PoA, a pool of miners competes to use their computer resources to solve challenging mathematical problems, similar to the mining method used in PoW. Once a block has been mined, the PoS technique is used to spread information regarding the new block throughout the network. The hash is then approved by a group of validators chosen at random, who then validate the insertion of the new block. Similar to the PoS, the total amount of holdings a validator influences whether they are chosen, and the rewards are split between the validators and the miners.

5.2.5 Proof of Authority (PoA)

In this method, based on their reputation rating, validators are chosen in blockchains that use the Proof of Authority (PoA) consensus method. In PoA, validators do not employ cryptocurrency money; instead, they rely on their reputation to acquire the necessary privileges for block validation. Because the network is made aware of the validator's identity, PoA differs from the procedures previously outlined. Another benefit of the PoA method is that it requires only a small amount of computer power, which makes it an appropriate solution for private networks.

5.2.6 Proof of Burn (PoB)

The so-called Proof of Burn (PoB) is another sustainable alternative consensus mechanism for the Proof of Work (PoW). The PoB's innovation depends on the procedure of burning a specified quantity of tokens to grant the miner the required block mining rights. However, the burning process was verified. For instance, tokens are sent by miners to a predetermined address, from which they cannot be obtained or used. The likelihood of a miner getting chosen increases as the number of tokens burned increases. It is emphasized that burned coins cannot be reclaimed by their owners and sold. This technique encourages miners to remain committed to the network in the long term.

5.2.7 Proof of Capacity/Proof of Space (PoC/PoSpace)

The Proof of Capacity (PoC) is based on the use of a mining algorithm, in which the primary selection criterion is the amount of accessible space on the miner's hard drive. This is in contrast to other mining algorithms that generate recommendations based on the available processing power or the staked coins. This method is also known as Proof of Space (PoSpace). In PoC, miners produce a potential hash in advance as part of the plotting procedure. This makes it appropriate for use by individuals in a commercial way or by businesses because of the minimal need for specialized equipment. As PoSpace follows a framework that is more decentralized and requires fewer energy resources, it is a good substitute.

5.2.8 Proof of Elapsed Time (PoET)

PoET is a safe computing technique introduced by Intel in 2016 that uses SGX CPU instructions for random waiting times on permissioned blockchain platforms. A node enters standby mode once it receives its waiting time assignment in the PoET, where waiting times are distributed randomly to miners. Consequently, mining privileges are given to nodes with the shortest waiting time. Applying the randomization principle in this method guarantees equity and fairness in the selection of miners in a network.

5.2.9 Proof of History (PoH)

PoH is a blockchain method developed by Solana that embeds timestamps within a network by using a sequential-hashing verifiable delay function (VDF). This method creates a continuum of transactions, making it eco-friendly and efficient and reducing computing time and resources.

5.2.10 Proof of Importance (PoI)

The PoI is a combinatorial consensus process that can be implemented. The miners are chosen based on several factors, including network activity, the volume and size of transactions within the last 30 days, and the amount of Bitcoin invested. Each node receives an automatic score based on the aforementioned factors and is then used to choose the best miner. Unlike PoS, PoI uses additional metrics to avoid automatically rewarding wealthier users, considering their contribution to the blockchain network.

5.3 Literature Review

Many surveys have been conducted in this area because blockchain is currently a hot issue. Security has also not been overlooked, including studies on blockchain technology security concerns [17]. This provides a more in-depth review of the weaknesses and threats of blockchain technology. In addition, [17] analyzed security risks and actual attacks on blockchain networks. [18] addressed business, organizational, and operational issues while taking a fresh look at blockchain security. Accordingly, various levels of security issues have been investigated, including those involving data, smart contracts, and networking protocols. Blockchain benefits are identified and addressed for cybersecurity in terms of blockchain applications. Similar analyses of blockchain-based applications have been conducted by [9] and [19], although the latter additionally highlights privacy and security issues with blockchains. [20] examines blockchain use cases for fog-enabled IoT. Given the connection between blockchain and fog computing in Internet of Things, we investigate how cybersecurity objectives might be met. From the same perspective, [21] examined the integration of blockchain, classifying apps without a clear security focus despite underlining its necessity and identifying it as. Focusing on Industry 4.0, which is related to IoT technologies, [22] offers a thorough analysis of how blockchain systems can overcome cybersecurity obstacles. The failure of important nodes in centralized platforms is a cybersecurity concern that has been examined; however, this work does not directly analyze cybersecurity properties and techniques [23].

The elimination of miners and the fee needed for transaction validation is another innovation presented under the umbrella of Blockchain 3.0. An integrated mechanism has taken the role of the aforementioned and helps lower transaction costs [24, 25]. The primary distinction between Blockchain 2.0 and Blockchain 3.0 is the adoption of additional consensus methods and the introduction of DApps to increase the visibility and usability of smart contracts for network users [26]. The advancements of Blockchain 3.0, in comparison to earlier generations, have been mentioned thus far in the previous paragraphs. Innovative digital technologies, including AI, have not been incorporated, despite the growing adoption of blockchain in a variety of businesses and organizations. Another drawback of Blockchain 3.0 is the complexity of the consensus processes, which must be incorporated into smart contracts.

5.4 Cybersecurity Fundamentals

The basics of security are covered in this section, along with the history of cybercrime. It discusses the fundamental ideas behind potential cybersecurity remedies and reasons why cyberattacks have become more frequent. In addition, it highlights the significance of cyber security, examines cyber threats, and suggests countermeasures [27].

5.4.1 Threats, Attacks, and Vulnerabilities

The section on well-known cyberthreats, security risks, vulnerabilities, and assaults is detailed. Viruses, Trojan horses, worms, rootkits, and hackers were first considered as cyber dangers [28]. Then, explanations are provided for well-known threats such as ransomware, scareware, joke programs, and spyware. The most popular vulnerability scanning tools are subsequently listed, along with security flaws. The most prevalent attack types, including passwords and man-in-the-middle assaults [29], are fully covered. These include social engineering assaults and man-in-the-middle attacks. Suggestions, safety measures, and awareness were provided for each form of attack.

5.4.2 Network Protection

Within this segment, we delve into the specifics of the network security concerns. We initiate the discussion by first discussing the Open Systems Interconnection (OSI) model along with its layers and corresponding protocols. Subsequently, a thorough examination of the attacks targeting each layer was conducted. Following this, we provide insights into various network-protection devices and tools. Finally, we focus on wireless network security by exploring attacks on wireless networks and their corresponding security methodologies. Summarizing the outcomes of this study, we highlight the contributions made through a meticulous exploration of the aforementioned topics [30].

The technological advancements provided by the cyber security field and their shortcomings are discussed. The fundamental details of the principles of cybersecurity are provided. The discussion encompasses cybersecurity risks, threats, and attacks along with recent studies in these domains.

Additionally, topics such as network security, OSI layers, and attacks on each layer have been thoroughly addressed [31].

Given these contributions, this study offers the following benefits to scholars working in this area: one may readily receive information on the most well-known and frequent risks and attack types, one can be updated on the latest current studies in this field, and even a rookie researcher can understand the basics of cyber security [32].

5.4.3 History of Cyber Crime and Security

Various definitions of cyber security have been used to secure data in a digital environments. Data security seeks to shield digital information throughout its lifecycle from unauthorized access, modification, or dissemination [33]. Preventing unauthorized people from gaining access to, or using any physical or electronic information is known as information security to maintain the data's availability, integrity, and secrecy. Network security strives to protect the privacy, accessibility, and integrity of computer networks and data sent across communication media [34]. On the other side, cyber security is the practice of defending against harmful attacks on computers, servers, mobile devices, electronic systems, computer networks, and data. Cyber security has a considerably wider application area that spans end-to-end information flows, and data security, information security, and network security are all focused on preventing unauthorized access, use, alteration, or destruction of stored data or data in transit. Today, the phrase "cyber security" is frequently used. Cybercrime emerged several years ago. Because there were fewer machines in the digital environment back then, and attacks were less sophisticated, it was simpler to defend the digital world. However, as technology advanced, cybercriminals were able to use automated systems to perform sophisticated cyberattacks. Various devices and platforms, such as smartphones, tablets, Internet of Things (IoT) devices, cloud platforms, and social media platforms, have also been introduced to the internet [35]. Owing to all these factors, cybercrime has developed from crude jokes to complex attacks that drain trillions of dollars annually from the global economy.

In the early 1940s, computers were invented [36]. There was no Internet connection at the time, and only a few computers could be used. There were no threats or computer assaults because the computers did not share information. In the 1950s, phone phreaking first appeared. Phone phreaks attempt to sabotage phone system protocols to make free calls or lower long-distance call rates. At the time, many phone companies were unable to stop phreaking. Future computer systems could be breached using methods akin to phone phishing [37].

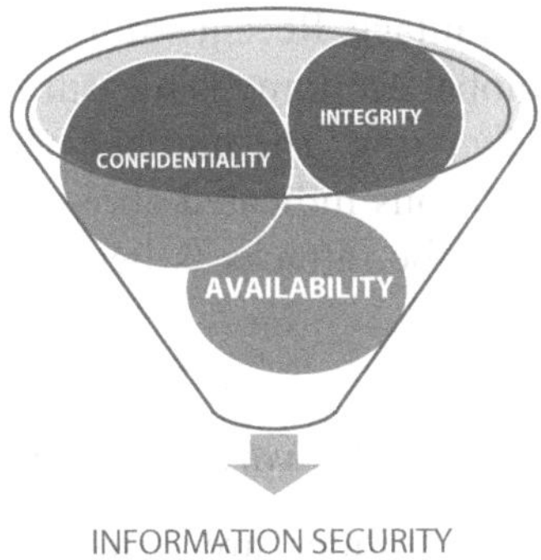

Figure 5.4 Principles of information security.

5.4.4 Principle of Information Security

Cybersecurity has three dimensions, as illustrated in Figure 5.4. The first component, commonly referred to as the "principle of information security," focuses on defending data from intruders. Confidentiality, integrity, and availability are included in this principle (CIA) [38]. The second aspect of cyber security aims to safeguard data, whether it is being processed, transported, or stored [36]. Data can be exchanged between devices, for instance, using wired, wireless, and Sneakernet networks. Therefore, when data are stored or moved between network devices and hosts, cybersecurity measures must guarantee data confidentiality, integrity, and availability (Figure 5.4). The third aspect of cyber security entails deploying extra instruments to help safeguard cyberspace, including rules and practices, new technologies, and user awareness.

5.4.5 Why Cyber Attacks are Increasing

Internet use and relevance have expanded dramatically globally in recent years. This growth has caused daily life to migrate into the digital sphere. This process was sped up by the COVID-19 (2019 Coronavirus disease) epidemic. For instance, people now make acquaintances on social media platforms, use online banking services, and schedule seminars and meetings. These factors have also contributed to the online transfer of common crimes.

Hackers are people or professional organizations that commit cybercrime. Hackers have in-depth knowledge of operating systems, have a quick writing speed, and can swiftly identify program and system flaws [39]. Cyber attackers are motivated by the creation of new attack tools and an enormous cash advantage. Recent studies have found that the cost of cyber-attacks on the global economy is measured in trillions of dollars, and that the cost is steadily rising. The number of cyber-related attacks is increasing daily, for the reasons indicated above. Reviewing the primary causes and motivators of cyber-attacks is beneficial before delving into them in more detail.

5.4.5.1 Attacks Caused by Hardware Deficiencies

Because software-based techniques are insufficient for detecting and preventing attacks connected to hardware, attacks initiated by hardware defects and errors are more challenging to stop [40]. Hardware attacks frequently use Trojan horses as their primary source. These malicious software variations consume an excessive amount of power, which causes the system to shut down and reduce performance.

In addition, stealing hardware components and buying questionable parts online provide the computer system with backdoors. It is difficult to identify hardware-related vulnerabilities owing to the interdependence of hardware components and complexity of integrated circuits. One integrated circuit change can have an impact on numerous other components and may go unnoticed for some time [40]. Consequently, it is difficult to identify and respond to cyber-attacks byemploying well-designed hardware vulnerabilities. Strategies have been proposed to stop cyberattacks caused by hardware defects and flaws. Hardware watermarking, obfuscation, and tamper-proof devices can significantly reduce the risk of such assaults [41].

5.4.5.2 Attacks Caused by Software-Based Bugs

Currently, application software flaws, mistakes, and vulnerabilities are the main causes of cyberattacks. Every day, these flaws and mistakes get worse [42, 43]. Figure 5.5 illustrates the different types of attacks that may occur in a blockchain network. The following are some of the main reasons why software is vulnerable to errors and flaws:

Software is created quickly; however, security checks are frequently insufficient throughout both the development and testing stages. This issue is worsened by the lack of understanding among developer teams regarding secure software development procedures. Another factor contributing to the increase in software-related attacks is the use of applications across many platforms and devices. For instance, overflowing a

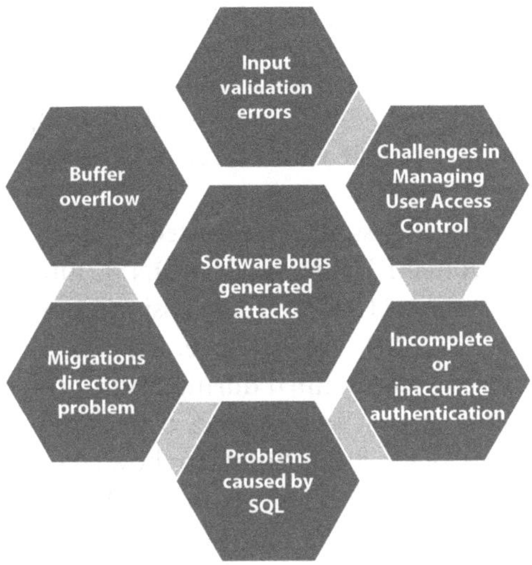

Figure 5.5 Attacks caused by software-based bugs.

buffer with data can result in lost data or unauthorized users accessing the system [44].

Databases can become overloaded by SQL assaults, which can also result in theft of credit card numbers, usernames, and passwords. Software updates are the most frequently advised approach for correcting software-related faults and flaws; however, they may not always be effective. Errors and vulnerabilities in software are not always fixed through upgrades; occasionally, new versions introduce new issues. Producing error-free program designs and requirements prior to creating code in the software development process lifecycle is the most efficient technique for reducing software-based assaults.

This makes training in a secure software development process essential for software professionals. It is inappropriate to create software hastily and attempt to address security flaws later. As a result, security threats and assaults should be considered throughout software development, and each code block should undergo both manual and automated testing. For instance, by making the Security Development Life Cycle (SDL) phase a requirement, Microsoft drastically reduced errors and vulnerabilities in the software development process. SDL was used in the development of Windows Vista, which has approximately 45% fewer flaws and faults than Windows XP, which is not designed with SDL [45].

5.4.5.3 Attacks Caused by Vulnerabilities in Computer Networks

Hackers have access to, and can change completely, data while being transferred across the internet. The use of previously developed computer network protocols and equipment without regard to security is the primary cause of such dangers [46].

Most computer network assaults are caused by flaws in network protocols, including the Domain Name System (DNS), Internet Protocol (IP), Address Resolution Protocol (ARP), Transmission Control Protocol (TCP), and Internet Protocol (TCP). For instance, the information included in packets can be exposed and modified during transport because there is no structure to control the accuracy and secrecy of packets while they are being transported over a network using IP. Similar to how attackers might establish phoney servers because DNS replies are not validated, users may connect to these phoney servers rather than to the real server. Attackers may also make a lot of request to DNS servers, which would prevent genuine users from using them [47]. In addition, attackers may be able to intercept data during transmission owing to switches, routers, and wireless access points that have been configured improperly or insufficiently. To secure data as it travels over computer networks, new protocols must be established, existing protocols must be made less vulnerable, and network devices must be

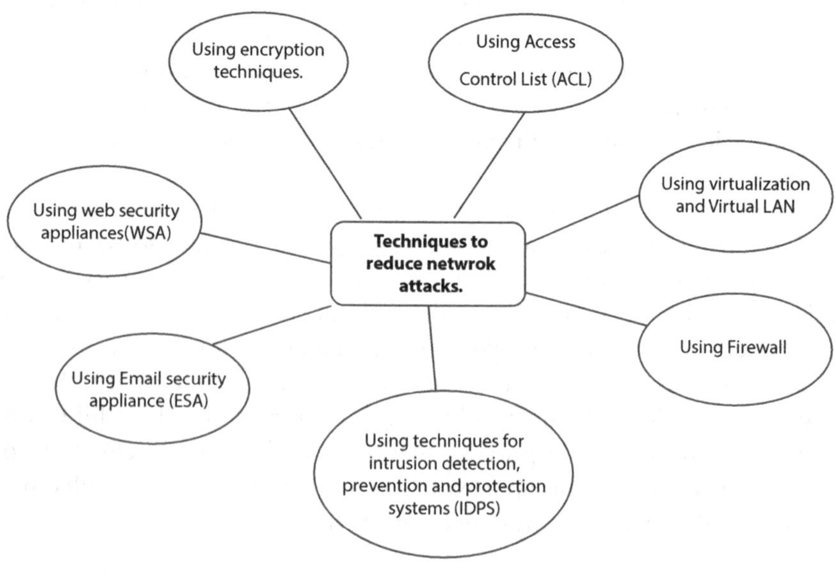

Figure 5.6 Startegies for reducing network attacks.

properly set. The following are some frequently used cybersecurity strategies for reducing network attacks, as shown in Figure 5.6.

These strategies can be used to a certain extent to safeguard data in a network setting, but they cannot offer total security. Therefore, it is essential to enhance the current methods and suggest new methods [48].

5.5 Synergies Between Blockchain and Cybersecurity

More specifically, Haber and Stornetta published interesting research on the timestamping of digital documents in 1991, when the idea of blockchain was first proposed [32]. Since then, the field of cryptography has undergone further development, giving rise to the current iteration of blockchain [49]. According to recent studies, the current industrial sector is moving towards implementing a blockchain ecosystem to increase system transparency, prevent fraud, and increase visibility [50]. Blockchain technology is not new, but is still in its infancy; therefore, there is still potential for advancement in both the methods (i.e., algorithms) and the necessary infrastructure for the seamless integration of such technologies [51]. Several blockchain-based frameworks are offered in a wide range of domains [52]. The integration of IoT technology in various fields, such as security, smart grids, and smart cities, can enhance data integrity and financial activities. However, the competitive environment for higher education institutions is becoming increasingly challenging owing to economic, political, and social changes, increasing student demand, and the rise of fraud and corruption in higher education [53]. Therefore, higher education will inevitably use blockchain technology. More specifically, several nations, such as the US and the UK, have already put such platforms in place to make it easier for staff and students to monitor academic progress and achievements [54].

The key contributions of blockchain technology to higher education were also examined in a recent study [55]. The referenced authors concentrated on addressing the challenges within the academic credentialing domain. They introduced a four-layer architecture for assessing educational credentialing frameworks integrated with the blockchain technology. Their investigation explored the utilization of blockchain as a means to enhance data management in higher education, leveraging advanced cryptographic techniques and decentralized authority within the network. Given these factors, the integration of blockchain in higher education presents the following challenges: 1. minimization of expensive academic bureaucracy; 2. delays in technology adoption; and 3. democratization and automation of higher education. In this regard, a proposed framework integrates blockchain functionalities with the goal of fostering collaboration among academia, research organizations, and industrial companies. Within this framework, the use of smart contracts enables stakeholders to generate digital portfolios showcasing their accomplishments and digitally verify the integrity of their academic profiles. A significant outcome of this study is the development of a framework for establishing a common, shared, and decentralized accreditation system for academic students. This framework facilitates the seamless recognition of academic achievements in the highly competitive global job market [44].

5.6 Applications of Blockchain and Cybersecurity

Cybersecurity uses and application domains based on objectives and content can be classified into many categories. Seven categories were identified for this study:

- IoT: The Internet of Things (IoT) is a worldwide infrastructure for the information society that connects (physical and virtual) items based on cooperating information and communication technologies to enable improved services [56]. This category includes all suggestions that mention using blockchain in connection with IoT. Smartphones, smart houses, similar equipment [62], sensors [32, 60], cars [30, 41, 60], and other resource-constrained, portable devices are examples of devices/elements.
- Cloud/distributed computing: A distributed computing system is one whose parts are spread across numerous networked computers, and coordinates its operations by sending messages to one another [50]. The on-demand distribution of computing power, database storage, applications, and other IT resources is referred to as cloud computing [44]. This can be applied to boost the storage capacity or processing power of a system or application. All types of parallel, distributed, and cloud computing systems are included in this category. Secure multiparty computation is a special instance of cloud computing used to strengthen data security by computing cryptographic procedures while maintaining the privacy of some data [40, 42, 63].

- E-commerce: It focuses on the exchange of goods through the Internet or online services. Fair commerce and fair lotteries are two frequent examples in this field [40, 56], as are the significance of user security when purchasing or trading online [35, 55, 59]. Additionally, we consider e-business use cases in this area, which are applications that have an impact on the economy but are related to business, such as using blockchain for supply chain inventory or managing human resource records.

5.7 Challenges and Considerations

Clinical analysts, healthcare providers, and individuals benefit from blockchain innovation in various ways [56]. Making a single repository for all health information, tracking customized information continuously, and granularly setting information access consent would serve research as effectively as personalized medicine [57]. To advance the understanding of infection, accelerate biomedical discovery, track the improvement of pharmaceuticals quickly, and develop customized treatment plans based on genetic characteristics, life operations, and climate, health analysts require extensive information collection [58]. The shared information structure of blockchain provides a broad spectrum of informative indices by including patients from various racial, economic, and geographic backgrounds [59]. Because blockchain collects data, it provides the best data for longitudinal studies and well-being information over the lifetime of an individual [60]. A healthcare blockchain will increase the variety of health information available by incorporating data from groups of people who are underserved by the clinical network or are typically not interested in research [61]. Blockchain's widespread information environment makes it easier for "hard-to-reach" masses to be intrigued and for the general populace to produce results that are more intelligent [62]. Another class of "intelligent" medical service provider applications that would avoid the most recent clinical studies and produce modified treatment routes would likely be made possible by a medical service blockchain. The provider of medical services and the patient would approach the same facts and participate in an amicable, educated discourse about exploration-based therapy options rather than instinct-based best-case scenarios.

A decentralized application (DApp) that supports a private blockchain network and a back-end distributed file system will implement the framework (DFS). A blockchain smart contract system for healthcare was implemented using Ethereum. With a vibrant community and sizable public DApp repository, this open-source network is currently one of the largest public blockchain networks. The platform currently uses the Ethash proof-of-work (PoW) consensus algorithm, but developers are hoping to switch to a proof-of-stake (PoS) scalability algorithm. Distributed applications should ideally be designed using a consensus technique that uses a Delegated Proof-of-Stake (DPoS) or Practical Byzantine Fault Tolerance (PBFT). The DApp can identify abnormalities, unauthorized data insertions, and missing entities by comparing DFS content with ledger records. There was a timeline for auditing the next stage. The fundamental components of smart contracts are functions, events, state variables, and modifiers, which are created using Solidity, a high-level programming language. The Remix and Kovan test network was used to test net ethers and smart contracts to pay transaction fees. Writing, compiling, and announcing are the three steps in the construction of a smart contract using Solidity programming. The Solidity real-time compiler creates a bytecode. Ethereum Wallet was used to publish smart contracts to the blockchain. Figure 5.7 illustrates the functioning of smart contracts on Ethereum, simplifying the explanation by omitting the mining process. The smart contract undergoes machine compilation into byte codes, where each byte represents an operation. Subsequently, it is uploaded to the blockchain as an EVM-1 transaction, which is confirmed by a miner in Block-1. EVM-2 retrieves

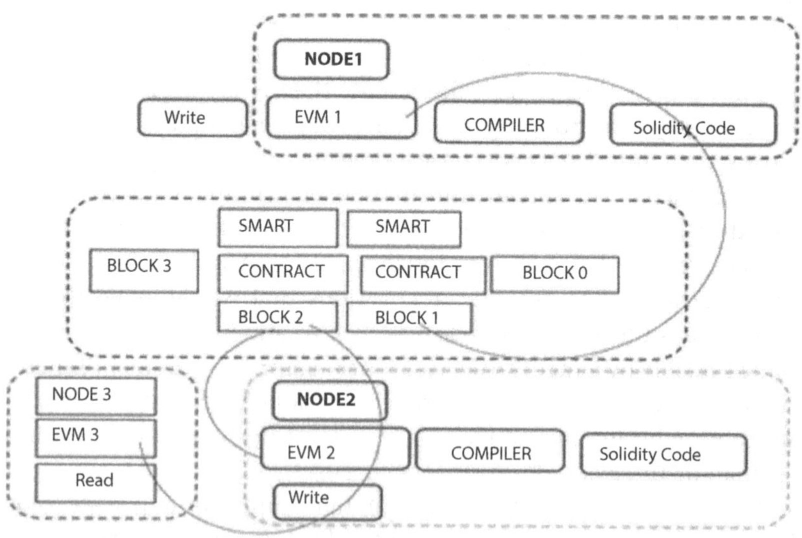

Figure 5.7 Ethereum-based smart contract system.

web-based data, incorporates it into Transaction tx, and deploys it to the blockchain upon user request through a web interface. Block-2 updates the status of transaction tx. Node 3 must synchronize up to at least Block-2 to observe the changes caused by tx when checking the states stored in the contract. Figure 5.7 outlines the smart contract framework.

5.8 Future Directions and Innovations

From versions 1.0 to 6.0, blockchain was seen through several iterations. The requirements of industries concerning the technological foundations and advancements of Industry 4.0, remain open for further development. This is attributed to the fact that the industrial objectives of earlier blockchain generations have not been sufficiently fulfilled [32]. For instance, a new generation of blockchains is required to reach the necessary level of industrial automation. Integrating cybersecurity with cutting-edge technologies, such as supply chain management, the Internet of Things (IoT), and AI, is one of Industry 4.0's critical prerequisites. Thus, the advent of the new blockchain age known as "Blockchain 4.0," in line with technological advancements, is necessary to provide businesses with improved privacy, security, transparency, and data integrity [49].

In light of this, InterValue was used to build a Blockchain 4.0 platform. InterValue with Blockchain 4.0 aims to achieve a Directed Acyclic Graph (DAG) that exhibits enhanced reliability, usability, and scalability as its central objective [50]. Several publications have explored the considerations of Blockchain 4.0 applications and their utilization across various industrial sectors, acknowledging the advancements in scalability, interoperability, and transaction rates compared with previous generations [51]. To create secure systems and provide secure network connectivity, emerging technologies such as blockchain and software-defined networking (SDN) might be leveraged [52]. As a result, advancements in the scalability, security, and transparency of blockchain networks are anticipated for use in industrial applications.

In recent decades, research has focused on critical factors, including the cost-effectiveness of this technology and the speed of transaction execution/completion, evaluated in terms of data rate. This emphasis spans the various blockchain eras outlined earlier. Energy efficiency has become one of the top demands in recent years, as mining for cryptocurrencies has grown into a global industry with businesses setting up miner farms. These "miner farms" work tirelessly to solve difficult cryptographic challenges in the hope of earning rewards. To put this into perspective, the Bitcoin community uses more energy than a nation with a population of 45 million people annually—roughly 150 terawatt hours— and this is just one example. Additionally, the annual carbon dioxide (CO2) emissions are predicted to be 65 megatons [53]. Nonetheless, the fifth blockchain age is also concerned with issues such as scalability, economic dependability, security, transparency, and secrecy.

Companies have a hard time believing that they can successfully integrate blockchain technology into their business operations models because of the economic stability and reliability of such ecosystems [63]. Relictum Pro is the first commercial application of Blockchain 5.0 that we are aware of [64]. The fundamental idea behind Relictum Pro is the development of a network that enables the configuration of numerous smart contracts for the execution of transactions, thus outperforming rival solutions in terms of security. It has become clear that research efforts have concentrated on important factors, such as the cost-effectiveness of this technology and the speed of transaction execution/completion assessed in terms of data rate, during the last decades, and through the numerous blockchain eras outlined before. Energy efficiency has become one of the top demands in recent years as mining for cryptocurrencies has grown into a global industry with businesses setting up miner farms. These miner farms work extremely hard to solve difficult cryptographic riddles with the hope of winning rewards.

5.9 Conclusion

The description above clarifies that fraudsters, data manipulators, and other people who handle personal data improperly may find the blockchain to be a nightmare. In general, a bright future can be predicted for the application of blockchain to address many elements of security and privacy based on evolving processes and pressures. In addition, the decentralized, autonomous, and trustless features of the blockchain can be used to address some of the major security issues related to the cloud. By ensuring that each party is held accountable for its specific contributions to the transaction, the blockchain eliminates disagreements. The decentralized, consensus-driven features of blockchain are anticipated to offer a more secure method as the network size increases rapidly. The decision between permissioned and permissionless blockchains is dependent on the number of participants, the value of the assets being traded or exchanged, and the significance of authenticating participants with various credentials.

This is because a blockchain network may include different types of participants [65]. Most hacking operations can be stopped or at least significantly reduced when machines can implement cryptographic protection. Numerous blockchain-related activities carried out at various levels have precisely this point of concentration. Blockchain may make it possible to verify a device's characteristics without spending money. MitM, replay, and other forms of attacks are expected to be stopped by the cryptographic verifiability capability [3]. Transactions made using blockchain technology are also very simple to audit. Blockchain may play a significant role in identifying the causes of supply chain insecurity as well as in handling and dealing with emergency scenarios such as product recalls in the event of a security vulnerability, primarily because of these and other capabilities [66].

References

1. Peng, L., Feng, W., Yan, Z., Li, Y., Zhou, X., Shimizu, S., Privacy preservation in permissionless blockchain: A survey. *Digit. Commun. Netw.*, 7, 295–307, 2021.
2. Akram, S.V., Malik, P.K., Singh, R., Anita, G., Tanwar, S., Adoption of blockchain technology in various realms: Opportunities and challenges. *Secur. Priv.*, 3, 1–23, 2020.
3. Bao, Q., Li, B., Hu, T., Sun, X., A survey of blockchain consensus safety and security: State-of-the-art, challenges, and future work. *J. Syst. Softw.*, 196, 1–25, 2023.
4. Zhang, L., Ma, Z., Ji, X., Wang, C., Blockchain: Application in the system of teaching informatization management of higher education, in: *Proceedings of the 2020 3rd International Conference on Smart BlockChain (SmartBlock)*, Zhengzhou, China, 23–25 October 2020, pp. 185–190.
5. Mourtzis, D., Angelopoulos, J., Panopoulos, N., Blockchain in engineering education: The teaching factory paradigm, in: *Proceedings of the Conference on Learning Factories (CLF)*, Graz, Austria, 1–2 July 2021, 1–6.
6. Mourtzis, D., Simulation in the design and operation of manufacturing systems: State of the art and new trends. *Int. J. Prod. Res.*, 58, 1927–1949, 2020.
7. Sasikumar, A., Subramaniyaswamy, V., Ketan, K., Indragandhi, V., Logesh, R., Ganeshsree, S., Ajith, A., Blockchain-based trust mechanism for digital twin empowered Industrial Internet of Things. *Future Gener. Comput. Syst.*, 141, 16–27, 2023.
8. Singh, S.K., Yang, L.T., Park, J.H., FusionFedBlock: Fusion of blockchain and federated learning to preserve privacy in industry 5.0. *Inf. Fusion*, 90, 233–240, 2023.

9. Ivanov, D. and Dolgui, A., OR-methods for coping with the ripple effect in supply chains during COVID-19 pandemic: Managerial insights and research implications. *Int. J. Prod. Econ.*, 232, 1–16, 2021.
10. Dolgui, A. and Ivanov, D., Ripple effect and supply chain disruption management: New trends and research directions. *Int. J. Prod. Res.*, 59, 102–109, 2021.
11. Hader, M., Tchoffa, D., Mhamedi, A., Ghodous, P., Dolgui, A., Abouabdellah, A., Applying integrated Blockchain and Big Data technologies to improve supply chain traceability and information sharing in the textile sector. *J. Ind. Inf. Integr.*, 28, 1–20, 2022.
12. Klöckner, M., Schmidt, C.G., Wagner, S.M., Building resilient post-pandemic supply chains through digital transformation, in: *Supply Chain Resilience; Springer Series in Supply Chain Management*, vol. 21, Cham, Switzerland, Springer, 211–223, 2023.
13. Huang, S., Wang, G., Yan, Y., Fang, X., Blockchain-based data management for digital twin of product. *J. Manuf. Syst.*, 54, 361–371, 2020.
14. Chen, Y., Chen, H., Zhang, Y., Han, M., Siddula, M., Cai, Z., A survey on blockchain systems: Attacks, defenses, and privacy preservation. *High-Confid. Comput.*, 2, 1–20, 2022.
15. Christen, P., Schnell, R., Ranbaduge, T., Vidanage, A., A critique and attack on blockchain-based privacy-preserving record linkage. *Inf. Syst.*, 108, 1–7, 2021.
16. Homoliak, I., Venugopalan, S., Reijsbergen, D., Hum, Q., Schumi, R., Szalachowski, P., The Security Reference Architecture for Blockchains: Toward a Standardized Model for Studying Vulnerabilities, Threats, and Defenses. *IEEE Commun. Surv. Tutor*, 23, 341–390, 2021.
17. Lin, I.-C. and Liao, T.-C., A survey of blockchain security issues and challenges. *IJ Netw. Secur.*, 19, 5, 653–659, 2017.
18. Li, X., Jiang, P., Chen, T., Luo, X., Wen, Q., A survey on the security of blockchain systems. *Future Gener. Comput. Syst.*, 107, 841–853, 2020.
19. Leng, J., Zhou, M., Zhao, J.L., Huang, Y., Bian, Y., Blockchain security: A survey of techniques and research directions. *IEEE Trans. Serv. Comput.*, 15, 4, 2490–2510, 2020.
20. Dai, F., Shi, Y., Meng, N., Wei, L., Ye, Z., From Bitcoin to cybersecurity: A comparative study of blockchain application and security issues, in: *2017 4th International Conference on Systems and Informatics (ICSAI)*, 2017, November, IEEE, pp. 975–979.
21. Mohanta, B.K., Jena, D., Panda, S.S., Sobhanayak, S., Blockchain technology: A survey on applications and security privacy challenges. *Internet Things*, 8, 1–30, 2019.
22. Nair, M.M., Tyagi, A.K., Sreenath, N., The future with industry 4.0 at the core of society 5.0: Open issues, future opportunities and challenges, in: *Proceedings of the 2021 International Conference on Computer Communication and Informatics (ICCCI)*, Coimbatore, India, 27–29 January 2021, pp. 1–7.

23. Yang, Y., Zhao, Y., Huang, H., Xiong, Z., Kang, Z., Zheng, Z., Fusing Blockchain and AI With Metaverse: A Survey. *IEEE Open J. Comput. Soc.*, 3, 122–136, 2022.
24. Cacciagrano, D., Corradini, F., Mostarda, L., Blockchain and IoT integration for society 5.0, in: *Society 5.0; Communications in Computer and Information, Science*, vol. 1477, A. Gerber and K. Hinkelmann (Eds.), Springer, Cham, Switzerland, 2021.
25. Cha, H.-S. and Im, C.-H., Performance enhancement of facial electromyogram-based facial-expression recognition for social virtual reality applications using linear discriminant analysis adaptation. *Virtual Real.*, 26, 385–398, 2022.
26. Sahu, N.K., Patnaik, M., Snigdh, I., Data analytics and its applications in brief, in: *Applications of big data in large-and small-scale systems*, pp. 115–125, IGI Global, New York, 2021.
27. Wang, F.-Y., Qin, R., Wang, X., Hu, B., Metasocieties in metaverse: Metaeconomics and metamanagement for metaenterprises and metacities. *IEEE Trans. Comput. Soc. Syst.*, 9, 2–7, 2022.
28. Xi, N., Chen, J., Gama, F., Riar, M., Hamari, J., The challenges of entering the metaverse: An experiment on the effect of extended reality on workload. *Inf. Syst. Front.*, 25, 2, 659–680, 2022.
29. Jovanovic, A. and Milosavljevic, A., Vortex metaverse platform for gamified collaborative learning. *Electronics*, 11, 317, 2022.
30. Mohapatro, M. and Snigdh, I., An experimental study of distributed denial of service and sink hole attacks on IoT based healthcare applications. *Wireless Pers. Commun.*, 121, 707–724, 2021.
31. Duan, H., Li, J., Fan, S., Lin, Z., Wu, X., Cai, W., Metaverse for social good: A university campus prototype, in: *Proceedings of the 29th ACM International Conference on Multimedia, Virtual Conference*, 20–24 October 2021, pp. 153–161.
32. Snigdh, I., Anonymity in Body Area Sensor Networks-an Insight, in: *2018 IEEE World Symposium on Communication Engineering (WSCE)*, 2018, December, IEEE, pp. 1-7.
33. Xu, M., Chen, X., Kou, G., A systematic review of blockchain. *Financ. Innov.*, 5, 1, 1–14, 2019.
34. Badruddoja, S., Dantu, R., He, Y., Upadhayay, K., Thompson, M., Making smart contracts smarter, in: *Proceedings of the 2021 IEEE International Conference on Blockchain and Cryptocurrency (ICBC)*, Sydney, Australia, 3–6 May 2021, pp. 1–3.
35. Saini, K., Roy, A., Chelliah, P.R., Patel, T., Blockchain 2.O: A smart contract, in: *Proceedings of the International Conference on Computational Performance Evaluation (ComPE)*, Shillong, India, 1–3 December 2021, pp. 524–528.
36. Ethereum Official Website. Available online: https://ethereum.org/en/ (accessed on 20 November 2022).

37. Kim, T.-H., Kumar, G., Saha, R., Rai, M.K., Buchanan, W.J., Thomas, R., Alazab, M., A privacy preserving distributed ledger framework for global human resource record management: The blockchain aspect. *IEEE Access*, 8, 96455–96467, 2020.
38. Mora, O.B., Rivera, R., Larios, V.M., Beltrán-Ramírez, J.R., Maciel, R., Ochoa, A., A use case in cybersecurity based in blockchain to deal with the security and privacy of citizens and smart cities cyberinfrastructures, in: *2018 IEEE International Smart Cities Conference (ISC2)*, IEEE, pp. 1–4, 2018.
39. Biswas, K. and Muthukkumarasamy, V., Securing smart cities using blockchain technology, in: *IEEE Intl. Conf. on High Performance Computing and Communications*, IEEE, pp. 1392–1393, 2016.
40. Sharples, M. and Domingue, J., The blockchain and kudos: A distributed system for educational record, reputation and reward, in: *European Conference on Technology Enhanced Learning*, Springer, pp. 490–496, 2016.
41. Aitzhan, N.Z. and Svetinovic, D., Security and privacy in decentralized energy trading through multi-signatures, blockchain and anonymous messaging streams. *IEEE Trans. Dependable Secure Comput.*, 15, 5, 840–852, 2018.
42. Guo, R., Shi, H., Zhao, Q., Zheng, D., Secure attribute-based signature scheme with multiple authorities for blockchain in electronic health records systems. *IEEE Access*, 6, 11676–11686, 2018.
43. Hofman, D., Shannon, C., McManus, B., Lemieux, V., Lam, K., Assadian, S., Ng, R., Building trust & protecting privacy: Analyzing evidentiary quality in a blockchain proof-of-concept for health research data consent management, in: *IEEE Intl. Conf. on Internet of Things*, IEEE, pp. 1650–1656, 2018.
44. Azaria, A., Ekblaw, A., Vieira, T., Lippman, A., Medrec: Using blockchain for medical data access and permission management, in: *2016 2nd International Conference on Open and Big Data (OBD)*, IEEE, pp. 25–30, 2016, http://dx.doi.org/10.1109/OBD.2016.11.
45. Wang, Y. and Gao, J., A regulation scheme based on the ciphertext-policy hierarchical attribute-based encryption in bitcoin system. *IEEE Access*, 6, 16267–16278, 2018.
46. Medury, S., Skjellum, A., Brooks, R.R., Yu, L., Scraaps: X. 509 certificate revocation using the blockchain-based scrybe secure provenance system, in: *Intl. Conf. on Malicious and Unwanted Software*, IEEE, pp. 145–152, 2018.
47. Xing, Q., Wang, B., Wang, X., Poster: Bgpcoin: A trustworthy blockchain-based resource management solution for BGP security, in: *ACM SIGSAC Conf. on Comp. and Comms. Security*, ACM, pp. 2591–2593, 2017.
48. Saad, M., Thai, M.T., Mohaisen, A., Poster: deterring ddos attacks on blockchain-based cryptocurrencies through mempool optimization, in: *Asia Conference on Computer and Communications Security*, ACM, pp. 809–811, 2018.
49. Rahman, M.A., Hossain, M.S., Loukas, G., Hassanain, E., Rahman, S.S., Alhamid, M.F., Guizani, M., Blockchain-based mobile edge computing

framework for secure therapy applications. *IEEE Access*, 6, 72469–72478, 2018.

50. Mohanta, B.K., Dehury, M.K., Sukhni, B.A., Mohapatra, N., Cyber Physical System: Security Challenges in Internet of Things System. *2022 Sixth International Conference on I-SMAC (IoT in Social, Mobile, Analytics and Cloud) (I-SMAC)*, Dharan, Nepal, pp. 117–122, 2022, doi: 10.1109/I-SMAC55078.2022.9987256.
51. Le, T. and Mutka, M.W., Capchain: A privacy preserving access control framework based on blockchain for pervasive environments, in: *Proceedings - 2018 IEEE International Conference on Smart Computing, SMARTCOMP 2018*, IEEE, pp. 57–64, 2018, http://dx.doi.org/10.1109/SMARTCOMP.2018.00074, arXiv:1401.0532.
52. Kosba, A., Miller, A., Shi, E., Wen, Z., Papamanthou, C., Hawk: The blockchain model of cryptography and privacy-preserving smart contracts, in: *Proceedings - 2016 IEEE Symposium on Security and Privacy, SP 2016*, pp. 839–858, 2016, http://dx.doi.org/10.1109/SP.2016.55, arXiv:1608.00771.
53. Hammi, M.T., Hammi, B., Bellot, P., Serhrouchni, A., Bubbles of trust: A decentralized blockchain-based authentication system for iot. *Comput. Secur.*, 78, 126–142, 2018.
54. Chatzopoulos, D., Gujar, S., Faltings, B., Hui, P., Privacy preserving and cost optimal mobile crowdsensing using smart contracts on blockchain, in: *IEEE Intl. Conf. on Mobile Ad Hoc and Sensor Systems*, pp. 442–450, 2018.
55. Manorama, and Snigdh, I., Principal Component Analysis in Body Sensor Networks for Secure Data Transmission. *Trends Wireless Commun. Inf. Secur. Proc. EWCIS*, 2020, 237–245, 2021.
56. Xia, Q., Sifah, E.B., Asamoah, K.O., Gao, J., Du, X., Guizani, M., Medshare: Trust-less medical data sharing among cloud service providers via blockchain. *IEEE Access*, 5, 14757–14767, 2017.
57. Khandelwal, P., Johari, R., Gaur, V., Vashisth, D., BlockChain technology based smart contract agreement on REMIX IDE, in: *Proceedings of the 8th International Conference on Signal Processing and Integrated Networks (SPIN)*, Noida, India, 26–27 August 2021, pp. 938–942.
58. Consensus Mechanisms in Blockchain: A Beginner's Guide. Crypto.com, Available online: https://crypto.com/university/consensus-mechanisms-in-blockchain (accessed on 20 November 2022).
59. Hafid, A., Hafid, A.S., Samih, M., Scaling Blockchains: A Comprehensive Survey. *IEEE Access*, 8, 125244–125262, 2020.
60. Kumar Mohanta, B., Kumar Dehury, M., Varma Kalidindi, S., Identity Management in IoT using Blockchain. *2022 13th International Conference on Computing Communication and Networking Technologies (ICCCNT)*, Kharagpur, India, pp. 1–6, 2022, doi: 10.1109/ICCCNT54827.2022.9984498.
61. Banerjee, K. and Saha, S., A Comparative Study of Smart Contracts-Based Blockchain, IGI Global, New York, 289–306, 2023.

62. Guo, C., Liu, Y., Na, M., Song, J., Dual-Layer Index for Efficient Traceability Query of Food Supply Chain Based on Blockchain. *Foods*, 12, 11, 1–27, 2023.
63. Gimenez-Aguilar, M., de Fuentes, J.M., Gonzalez-Manzano, L., Arroyo, D., Achieving cybersecurity in blockchain-based systems: A survey. *Future Gener. Comput. Syst.*, 124, 91–118, 2021.
64. Xie, S., Hong, Y., Wang, X., Shen, J., Research on Data Security Technology Based on Blockchain Technology. *2021 7th IEEE Intl Conference on Big Data Security on Cloud (BigDataSecurity).*
65. Khan, M.A. and Salah, K., IoT security: Review, blockchain solutions, and open challenges. *Future Gener. Comput. Syst.*, 2018.
66. Wang, D., Jia, Y., Dong, M., Ota, K., Liang, L., Blockchain-Integrated UAV-Assisted Mobile Edge Computing: Trajectory Planning and Resource Allocation. *IEEE Trans. Veh. Technol.*, 73, 1263–1275, 2023.

6

Protecting in the Digital Age: A Comprehensive Examination of Cybersecurity and Legal Implications

Nazeer Shaik*, **B. Hari Chandana, P. Chitralingappa and C. Sasikala**

Department of Computer Science & Engineering, Srinivasa Ramanujan Institute of Technology, Anantapur, India

Abstract

The complicated legal issues of cybersecurity were examined in this comprehensive examination. This report summarizes cybersecurity legislation and regulations in the following sections. First, the legal framework of cybersecurity is explained, emphasizing the need for enterprises and people to understand and follow law. Investigating international cybersecurity laws and jurisdictions, including cross-border cyber events and the role of extradition, international treaties, and mutual legal aid programs in fighting cybercrime. This study discusses cyber liability and accountability, including legal frameworks that define cyber incident liability, third-party liability, and the cybersecurity duty of care. Employment laws and cybersecurity, including employee obligations, data protection, workplace privacy, and employer responsibilities and liabilities in the case of a breach, were examined. The legal environment of digital commerce is demonstrated by evaluating online transactions, electronic contracts, consumer protection, online platforms, and marketplace liability. The last part of the study discusses emerging cybersecurity legal issues, emphasizing the need to update legal frameworks to match technological improvements and encourage public discussions of their moral and legal implications. This comprehensive overview of cybersecurity law equips corporations, professionals, and people with the ability to manage legal issues, ensure compliance, and promote a safe digital environment.

***Keywords*:** Legal issues, cybersecurity, laws and regulations, data protection, IPR, digital realm

**Corresponding author*: shaiknaz2020@gmail.com

Subhabrata Barman, Santanu Koley and Subhankar Joardar (eds.) Next-Generation Systems and Secure Computing, (105–136) © 2025 Scrivener Publishing LLC

6.1 Introduction

Various legal topics can emerge, including business, family, criminal, civil, and intellectual property laws.

Legal issues in the context of cyber security can cover a broad range of concerns regarding the legal framework surrounding technology use, safeguarding digital assets, protecting privacy and data, adhering to regulations, cybercrime, liability, and intellectual property rights. To address and resolve disputes or establish preventive measures, these issues necessitate an understanding of the legal landscape, pertinent laws and regulations, and application of legal principles [1].

As technology develops and cyber threats grow more complex, the field of cyber security is rapidly changing, bringing new legal challenges.

6.1.1 Introduction to Legal Issues in Cybersecurity

The book's introduction to legal issues in cyber security gives readers a basic understanding of the subject and sets the scene for the rest of the book. It draws attention to the connection between law and technology and stresses the importance of understanding the legal environment surrounding cybersecurity [2].

Because modern society is becoming increasingly dependent on technology and interconnected systems, it is imperative that we comprehend the legal landscape surrounding cybersecurity. This chapter guarantees that readers have a common understanding when they enter the following chapters by acquainting them with important legal concepts and vocabulary.

6.1.2 Importance of Understanding the Legal Landscape in Cybersecurity

It is crucial to understand the legal environment surrounding cyber security for several important reasons. Through the comprehension of relevant laws, regulations, and standards, they can guarantee adherence and reduce legal hazards linked to online activities.

The legal system provides a framework for dealing with cyber threats and making people and organizations responsible for their actions [3]. Knowing these laws gives rise to legal actions and prosecutions in the event of an incident, as well as serves as a deterrent to potential cybercriminals.

Having a solid understanding of the law also helps protect people's rights and private information. Businesses and individuals can exercise their right to privacy and take appropriate measures to safeguard personal information when aware of these regulations.

Furthermore, a secure online environment depends on the cybersecurity legislative framework. International agreements and treaties facilitate information sharing, extradition, and coordinated responses to cyber threats [4].

6.2 First-Order Heading

Cybercrime laws and regulations are imperative to address and combat illegal activities carried out via computer systems and the Internet [5]. These regulations protect people, businesses, and vital infrastructure against various online dangers. The following summarizes the main elements of cybercrime laws and regulations:

1. Unauthorized Access: Unauthorized access to computer systems, networks, or digital accounts is illegal under cybercrime law. This covers actions, such as breaking security protocols, hacking, and obtaining unauthorized access to computer resources.
2. Data Breach Regulations: Owing to legal and regulatory obligations, security measures and data protection techniques are mandatory. In the event of a data breach, these regulations frequently mandate the immediate reporting of the affected parties and regulatory bodies.
3. Identity Theft and Fraud: Theft or fraudulent use of personal data is covered by cybercrime laws. They forbid actions, such as identity theft, phishing, online fraud, and other types of fraud involving computers.
4. Online Harassment and Stalking: Cyberbullying, harassment, and stalking through digital means are prohibited by law. These legal measures seek to shield individuals from cyberbullying, threats, and psychological distress.

Because cybercrime laws and regulations differ from jurisdiction to jurisdiction, it is crucial to check local laws and legal resources for specific information and applicability.

6.2.1 Second-Order Heading

Laws against hacking and unauthorized access are essential elements of cybercrime legislation [6]. The purpose of these laws is to prevent and address illegal access to networks, digital accounts, and computers. Below is a summary of the laws pertaining to hacking and unauthorized access:

1. Definition of Unauthorized Access: Attempting to enter a computer system, network, or digital account without authorization or beyond what is permitted is known as an unauthorized access. Legal limits are established to access digital resources by law, which also define what is considered unauthorized access.
2. Prohibition of Hacking: Malicious actions taken by people with the intention of undermining or manipulating computer networks or systems are specifically targeted by hacking laws. These laws make it illegal to do things like access computer resources without authorization, get around security measures, take advantage of vulnerabilities, and hack them into systems.
3. Criminalization of Malware and Exploits: The development, dissemination, and use of viruses, malware, and other malicious software or code intended to obtain unauthorized access or damage computer systems are covered by laws. Laws may also target the creation and distribution of exploitation kits and hacking tools.
4. Protected Systems: Critical infrastructure, government networks, financial systems, and other vital services are examples of protected systems frequently defined by laws. Due to the possible impact on national security, the economy, public safety, unauthorized access, or hacking attempts targeting these systems may result in more severe penalties and negative outcomes.

To learn the precise rules and sanctions pertaining to hacking and unauthorized access in a given jurisdiction, it is crucial to refer to local laws and legal resources [7]. These regulations are essential to prevent unwanted intrusions, safeguard private data, and foster a safe online environment.

6.2.2 Data Breach Notification Requirements and Regulations

Cybersecurity laws now require data breach notification policies and procedures to safeguard people's private information and ensure transparency in the event of a data breach [8]. Organizations are frequently mandated by law, legislation, or other regulations to notify the affected parties, regulatory agencies, and others in the event of a data breach. The following laws and regulations summarize the reporting of data breaches:

1. Definition of a Data Breach: In context of the laws governing data breaches, the terms "personal data" and "data breach" are used interchangeably. A person's name, Social Security number, bank account information, email address, password, and other comparable data are examples of identifiable information, but they are not the only examples.
2. Obligation to Notify Affected Parties: Organizations are generally required to notify individuals whose personal information has been compromised or is in danger in the event of a data breach. The notice ought to describe the type of breach, compromised datasets, potential consequences of the breach, and any actions that could be taken to limit the harm.
3. Notification Timeline: Following the discovery of a data breach, regulations frequently specify precise timeframes within which organizations must notify affected individuals. The timelines could range from instant notification to a sensible amount of time that permits an examination and evaluation of the breach.
4. Notification to Regulatory Authorities: A number of data breach regulations mandate that organizations notify the appropriate regulatory bodies or data protection agencies of the breach in addition to informing the affected individuals. The purpose of this notification is to facilitate regulatory oversight, enforcement, and monitoring of data breach trends.

It is crucial to remember that different jurisdictions have different laws and requirements regarding data breach notifications. To obtain information on the particular regulations that apply to their operations, organizations should check regulatory bodies and local laws [9]. These laws are essential for encouraging accountability in the handling of personal data, transparency, and empowering the impacted parties to take the required precautions.

6.2.3 Identity Theft Laws and Countermeasures

As the issue of criminals using stolen identities to commit fraud was tolerated, legislation and preventative measures against identity theft were developed [10]. Identity theft is the use of someone's name, Social Security number, credit card number, or other private information without the person's knowledge or consent. See below for more information on identity theft and legal protection against it.

1. Identity theft is now considered a serious crime; obtaining or using someone else's personal information for deceptive or fraudulent means is illegal. The use of stolen identities for financial gain, including credit card fraud, account opening fraud, and access to financial resources, is prohibited by identity theft laws.
2. Penalties and Punishments: Identity theft laws stipulate fines and penalties for those found guilty of identity theft. Probation, fines, jailtime, and victim restitution are some examples of these sanctions. The degree of identity theft, victims' monetary losses, and any prior criminal history all affect how harshly the punishment is applied.
3. Reporting and Investigating Identity Theft: Many laws require identity theft victims to report an offense to the police or identity theft departments. Reporting an event helps initiate an inquiry and provides evidence for prosecuting criminals. Victims may be required to cooperate with the law police and submit supporting paperwork to aid the investigation.
4. Programs for Victim Assistance and Support: Identity theft laws may include provisions for these types of services. These initiatives are designed to help those who have been victims of identity theft by offering them support and resources to help them through the healing process and lessen the possible harm that theft may have caused.

To learn about precise laws and regulations pertaining to identity theft in a given jurisdiction, it is crucial to refer to local laws and regulations [11].

Identity theft laws and countermeasures are essential for preventing identity theft, helping victims, and creating a safe environment for private data.

6.2.4 Computer Fraud and Online Scams

Digital deceptive practices used to defraud people or organizations are known as computer fraud and online scams [12]. These fraudulent activities frequently cause victims to suffer financial losses or other harm by tricking on them using technology and the Internet. Below is a summary of the laws and remedies pertaining to computer fraud and online scams:

1. Definition of Computer Fraud: The deliberate use of a computer or other electronic device to trick, mislead, or defraud people is covered by laws pertaining to computer fraud. False claims, deception, fraudulent schemes, and access to computer systems for illegal ends are examples of such actions.
2. Types of Online Scams: Numerous varieties of online scams include phishing, advance fees, romance, lottery/sweepstakes, phony marketplaces, investments, and identity theft. Scammers employ a wide range of dishonest tactics to exploit victims.
3. Criminalization of Computer Fraud: Cybercrimes, including computer fraud, are now considered crimes under law and are subject to penalties. These laws are intended to discourage people from participating in fraudulent activities and to give victims legal recourse in the event that they have incurred losses or other damages.

People should be vigilant when disclosing personal information online, be aware of common online scams, and report any suspicious activity to relevant authorities [13]. Adhering to safe online practices and complying with consumer protection laws can also help reduce the likelihood of becoming victims of online scams and computer fraud.

6.3 Data Protection and Privacy Laws

Regulations pertaining to data protection and privacy are particularly crucial in the current digital age because they dictate the manner in which companies are required to handle private client data [14]. This chapter provides an overview of the basic concepts, guidelines, and legal structures pertaining to privacy and data protection laws.

1. Definition of Personal Data: Information about a specific or identifiable individual is considered personal data under the rules protecting this data. Names, addresses, phone numbers, email addresses, bank and credit card details, medical history, and other similar information fall into this category.
2. Principles of Data Protection: Information about a specific or identifiable individual is considered personal data under the rules protecting this data. Names, addresses, phone numbers, email addresses, bank and credit card details, medical history, and other similar information fall under this category.
3. Consent and Individual Rights: Before collecting, processing, or disclosing an individual's personal data, organizations typically require data privacy rules to seek the individual's informed and explicit consent. Individuals are afforded rights under these statutes, including access to their data, correction of inaccurate information, deletion of personal data, and limitations or objections to certain data-processing activities.

Individuals and organizations must comprehend data protection and privacy regulations to handle personal information responsibly, maintain trust, and comply with legislation. These regulations foster data security and transparency in data-driven environments and protect privacy [15].

6.3.1 Introduction to Data Protection and Privacy Regulations

The laws governing the use, storage, and disclosure of private consumer data by businesses are known as data protection and privacy regulations. These regulations aim to safeguard individual privacy while ensuring that personal information is handled securely and lawfully.

6.3.1.1 An Introduction to Data Protection and Privacy

1. Law Goal of Regulations: It is more crucial than ever to have laws in place to protect people's privacy and personal data in today's increasingly digital world. Their objective was to strike a balance between the demands of companies to collect and utilize data and the privacy concerns of their clientele.

2. Scope of Personal Data: Information related to an identified or identifiable individual is included in the broad definition of personal data provided by regulations. Along with more conventional identifiers, such as names and addresses, this also includes data such as IP addresses, identification numbers, geolocation information, online identifiers, and biometric data.
3. Fundamental Principles: The fundamental ideas that underpin privacy and data protection laws direct the processing of personal data. These guidelines usually consist of the following: accuracy, storage restriction, security, accountability, transparency (letting people know about data processing activities), purpose limitation (gathering data only for designated purposes), data minimization (gathering only the required information), and people's rights to access and control their data [16].
4. Consent and Lawful Basis: Many organizations need consent or a legal basis to process personal data. Consent must be voluntary, informed, and clear. Consent could be withdrawn at any time. Additionally, the interests of the data controller or a third party may justify processing personal data to fulfill a contract, comply with legal obligations, protect someone's life or health, carry out a public interest or official authority task, or pursue legal claims.

Data protection and privacy laws include the US California Consumer Privacy Act (CCPA), EU General Data Protection Regulation (GDPR), and Canadian Personal Information Protection and Electronic Documents Act (PIPEDA). To protect customer privacy, build trust, and comply with the law, businesses must understand and comply with these requirements.

6.3.2 General Data Protection Regulation (GDPR)

On 25 May 2018, the EU and EEA enacted the General Data Protection Regulation (GDPR), a comprehensive data protection and privacy law [17]. Data Protection Directive 95/46/EC was replaced by it, which also enhanced and revised the data protection laws. The following succinctly describes the General Data Protection Regulation (GDPR):

1. Scope: The GDPR will apply to the personal data of EU/EEA citizens regardless of where the processing occurs.

Businesses based outside of EU/EEA that target clients or gather information about their operations are governed by the regulation.

2. Basic Concepts: Legality, equity, transparency, purpose limitation, data minimization, accuracy, storage limitation, integrity and confidentiality, accountability, and portability are the eight guiding principles that form the foundation of the General Data Protection Regulation (GDPR).
3. Consent: Considering the GDPR, obtaining legitimate consent is a prerequisite for processing personal data. Permission may be withdrawn by individuals at any time, and consent must be freely provided, specific, informed, and unambiguous.
4. Data Subject Rights: Under the General Data Protection Regulation (GDPR), data subjects are given additional protection. The following were included: data portability, restriction of processing, access, rectification, erasure (the "right to be forgotten"), ability to process objects, and defense against automated decision-making.
5. Name a Data Protection Officer (DPO): Under the General Data Protection Regulation (GDPR), certain companies are required to name a DPO. A DPO is an impartial position that supervises data protection compliance and acts as the main point of contact for individuals subject to data protection laws.
6. Data Breach Notifications: In event of a data breach, notice requirements under the General Data Protection Regulation (GDPR) must be met. Organizations must notify the appropriate supervisory body of a breach within 72 h of becoming aware of it unless it is unlikely to harm individuals' rights and freedoms.

Many businesses worldwide have had to modify their data protection policies to comply with the GDPR requirements when handling the personal information of EU/EEA residents. This emphasizes the need to hold companies accountable for their effective data management procedures and uphold individuals' rights to privacy [18].

6.3.3 The California Consumer Privacy Act (CCPA)

It is a piece of state-level privacy legislation from California in the United States. June 2018 saw the enactment of the law, which was effective on

1 January 2020. Businesses must abide by the CCPA's regulations and the state's citizen protection when gathering and processing personal data from California's residents. A summary of the California Consumer Privacy Act (CCPA) is presented here.

1. Scope: The CCPA first applies to businesses that process a significant amount of personal data from California residents or those with a specific annual gross income.
2. Personal Information: "Individual identifiers" are broadly defined by the CCPA [19] and include names, addresses, SSNs, IP addresses, geolocation data, biometric information, and online identifiers, among others.
3. Consumer Rights: Lastly, the CCPA safeguards Californians' right to privacy in a number of ways. People have the right to know when and how their personal data are being collected, the right to see that data, the right to ask for their deletion, the right to stop data from being sold, and the right to equitable treatment in terms of price and service should they choose to exercise their right to privacy.
4. Business Obligations: Businesses are required to clearly communicate to consumers the information they collect and utilize along with the rationale behind it. They should also have policies in place to handle inquiries from clients who wish to access or delete their data. Businesses are not permitted to sell the personal information of their children without the consent of their parents.
5. Data Security and Breach Notification: To protect consumers' personal information, businesses must comply with the CCPA and implement appropriate security measures. When a data breach occurs, businesses have an obligation to notify customers of their personal information as soon as possible.

An important privacy law that has affected privacy not only in California but also around the world is the CCPA. Organizations have been compelled by their emphasis on consumer rights, accountability, and transparency to reevaluate their data-handling procedures and strengthen privacy safeguards for Californians [20].

6.3.4 Other Notable Data Protection Laws and Frameworks

There are other significant laws besides the California Consumer Privacy Act (CCPA) and the General Data Protection Regulation (GDPR) that protect personal information. The following are some examples:

1. Canada's Personal Information Protection and Electronic Documents Act (PIPEDA) governs the gathering, use, and disclosure of personal data by the private sector for business purposes. It establishes rules on how to obtain consent before collecting people's data, protecting that data, giving people access to it, and dealing with security breaches and complaints [21].
2. The United States federal law, known as the Health Insurance Portability and Accountability Act (HIPAA), was passed to guarantee the privacy of patient health records and to set minimum standards for ePHI security. Companies connected to clearinghouses, insurers, and suppliers of healthcare supplies.
3. Third, Singapore's Personal Data Protection Act (PDPA) governs how companies can utilize, distribute, and keep track of private client data. It establishes guidelines on when and how to obtain individuals' consent to use their data, gives them access to that data and maintains its accuracy and security.
4. The APP, or Australian Privacy Principles—Australia's Privacy Act of 1988—contains these privacy guidelines. The legislation governs the use of personal data by Australian public and private entities. These rules cover the acquisition, use, sharing, protection, and accessibility of data to individuals.

There are just a few of the numerous laws and guidelines pertaining to data protection that are in place worldwide. Businesses need to be aware of the rules relevant to their particular processes and industries to protect individuals' privacy and follow the law [22].

6.4 Intellectual Property Rights in Cyberspace

Intellectual property laws protect and control online IP ownership and usage. Intellectual property is also crucial. The exclusive rights of artists and innovators boost artistic creation and economic growth.

Cyberspace intellectual property rights is based on copyright. Digital copyright issues arise from unauthorized replication, distribution, and exchange of software, music, movies, and publications.

Patents are crucial for online IP. Protecting trade secrets in the digital age involves avoiding unauthorized access, theft, or exploitation of consumer data, intellectual algorithms, and company strategies.

The Internet's worldwide reach and absence of boundaries challenge cyberspace IP enforcement. Individuals and organizations must grasp their intellectual property rights and duties in cyberspace, secure their assets, and navigate the ever-changing landscape of digital rights and obligations [23].

6.5 Cybersecurity Regulations and Compliance

Cybersecurity laws address such dangers and promote effective security measures. The International Telecommunication Union and UN rules and norms aid global cybersecurity collaborations. Compliance and cybersecurity law enforcement are handled by regulatory authorities.

Compliance frameworks and standards help organizations execute effective cybersecurity practices. Examples include the NIST Cybersecurity Framework, PCI DSS for credit card firms, and ISO/IEC 27001 for information security management systems. These frameworks help firms assess cybersecurity, identify vulnerabilities, and implement solutions [24].

Organizations must follow cybersecurity requirements to safeguard resources, retain consumer trust, and prevent legal and PR issues. Frequent risk assessments, security awareness training, robust access restrictions, secure network infrastructure, incident response plans, and constant monitoring and security measure upgrades are needed [25].

6.6 Cybersecurity Incident Response and Reporting

A successful cybersecurity program must respond to and report on cybersecurity events. Organizations must respond swiftly to cybersecurity events to minimize damage and prevent further compromise.

The incident-response method has specific phases. Keep detailed records throughout the incident response to facilitate analysis, reporting, and post-event assessments [26].

For several reasons, reporting cybersecurity events is crucial. Second, incident reporting promotes cybersecurity community collaboration and information exchange, helping others strengthen their defenses and learn from their occurrence. Finally, incident reporting may help organizations evaluate their incident response systems, identify areas for improvement, and strengthen their cybersecurity.

Finally, a comprehensive cybersecurity program must record and respond to the cybersecurity issues. A well-defined incident response mechanism and timely event reporting can minimize cybersecurity risks, safeguard assets, and improve security [27].

6.7 International Laws and Jurisdiction in Cybersecurity

As cybersecurity threats are global in nature, it is imperative that their responses align with international law and jurisdiction. This chapter covers the international regulations and laws that impact cybersecurity.

1. Cybersecurity's transnational nature Due to two factors, (1) the global nature of cyber threats and attacks and (2) the cross-border nature of cyber targets, cybersecurity is a transnational issue. Due to the global nature of cybersecurity, gaps in current legal frameworks must be addressed, and enforcement efforts must be coordinated.
2. International laws and treaties: Second, various international treaties, laws, and agreements have been formulated to address cybersecurity-related matters. The United Nations Group of Governmental Experts on Developments in the Field of Information and Telecommunications in the Context of International Security and the Budapest Convention on Cybercrime are two such examples of global initiatives to combat cybercrime jointly.
3. Difficulties with Jurisdiction: The third challenge is establishing jurisdiction in cyberspace because there are no physical boundaries on the Internet. The complexity of jurisdictional issues is exacerbated by the wide variations in legal systems and cybersecurity readiness among nations.
4. Mutual Legal Assistance: Fourth, treaties and agreements pertaining to mutual legal assistance (MLATs) make it easier for cybercrime investigators and prosecutors to collaborate across international borders.

In conclusion, dealing with the transnational aspect of cyber threats requires the application of international laws and jurisdictions to cybersecurity. To combat cybercrime and promote a safe and resilient global cyberspace, efforts towards international cooperation, creation of legal frameworks, and establishment of mechanisms for mutual legal assistance are essential [28].

The transnational nature of cyberspace and difficulties in translating conventional legal principles to the digital sphere present jurisdictional challenges in cross-border cyber incidents. These are the major obstacles:

1. Attribution: It can be difficult to ascertain the real whereabouts and identities of cyberattackers. This complicates the process of determining jurisdiction by making it difficult to link specific individuals or entities to cyber-incidents.
2. Absence of Universal Jurisdiction: The main foundation of jurisdiction is territoriality, which states that a nation's laws normally apply inside its boundaries. The absence of a universal jurisdiction framework poses a challenge in determining which nation has jurisdiction to consider and prosecute cybercrimes.
3. Differing Legal Standards: Legal systems in different nations have different definitions of cybercrime, sanctions, and procedural guidelines. Simplifying legal requirements and promoting mutual comprehension between jurisdictions are essential for optimizing the jurisdictional determination process.
4. Jurisdictional Competition: Conflicts may emerge when several nations are able to assert jurisdiction over cyber incidents. Effective international collaboration requires the establishment of precise guidelines and cooperative mechanisms to resolve jurisdictional conflict.
5. Mutual Legal Assistance: Under framework of mutual legal assistance treaties (MLATs), nations can ask for and offer support in cross-border investigations and prosecutions. However, owing to issues such as varying legal requirements, resource limitations, bureaucratic procedures, and protracted response times, the efficacy of MLATs can vary.

International cooperation, the creation of shared norms and standards, and the setup of systems for information exchange and reciprocal legal aid are necessary to address these jurisdictional issues. International initiatives such as the Budapest Convention on Cybercrime provide a framework for addressing cybercrime in a cross-border setting, thereby addressing these issues and fostering international cooperation.

6.7.1 International Treaties and Co-Operation in Addressing Cybercrime

To combat cybercrime and foster international cooperation in the fight against cyber threats, international treaties and cooperation are essential [29]. The following are some significant international agreements and programs that address cybercrime:

1. The Budapest Convention on Cybercrime is a broadly ratified international agreement that aims to criminalize offenses related to the Internet, facilitate international cooperation by offering mutual legal assistance, and encourage information sharing and capacity-building.
2. Resolutions Adopted by the UN: The UN has passed a number of resolutions, highlighting the significance of global collaboration in combating cybercrime and advancing cybersecurity. To counter cyber threats, these resolutions call on member states to fortify their legal systems, promote international collaboration, and create capacity-building programs.
3. The G7 24/7 Network and CERTs: The Group of Seven (G7) nations created the G7 24/7 Network to foster cooperation among Computer Emergency Response Teams (CERTs) and to enable the real-time sharing of cyber threat intelligence. The network's objectives are to strengthen cyber resilience among member nations, share best practices, and improve incident-response capabilities.
4. United Nations Office on Drugs and Crime (UNODC): With several initiatives and programs, the UNODC contributes significantly to the fight against cybercrime. It helps member states develop their capacities, offers technical support, encourages international collaboration in the investigation and prosecution of cybercrime cases, and facilitates information and expertise sharing between nations.

6.7.2 Mutual Legal Assistance and Extradition Processes

These agreements and programs highlight the importance of international coordination and collaboration in fighting cybercrime. Their ultimate objective is to effectively address the worldwide nature of cyber threats through the development of standardized legal frameworks, enhanced protocols for exchanging information, encouragement of capacity building, and government cooperation.

The legal frameworks of extradition and mutual legal assistance, which governments employ to promote international cooperation, are advantageous for cybercrime investigations and prosecutions. The following is a summary of how mutual legal assistance and extradition operate:

1. Mutual Legal Assistance (MLA):
    - The term "mutual legal assistance" describes the official collaboration between nations in information sharing, evidence collection and exchange, and other legal support related to criminal cases.
    - MLA is essential for cross-border cybercrime investigations because it allows nations to ask for and offer help in gathering evidence, holding interviews, seizing assets, and carrying out search warrants, among other tasks.

2. Extradition:
    - If someone is facing criminal charges or is serving a sentence in one country, another country may ask for their surrender through a legal procedure called "extradition."
    - When a suspect in a cybercrime lives in or is present in a jurisdiction different from the crime scene, extradition may be requested.

3. Challenges and Considerations:
    - Issues and concerns can arise for both extradition and mutual legal assistance procedures, especially regarding cybercrime.
    - The obstacles encompass dissimilar legal frameworks, disparate evidence standards, human rights issues, political deliberations, and possible contradictions among national security concerns.

4. International Cooperation and Agreements:
   - Bilateral and international agreements between nations have improved in two areas: mutual legal assistance and tradition.
   - Agreements such as extradition and mutual legal assistance treaties (MLATs) address issues with jurisdiction, evidence sharing, and extradition requirements and create frameworks and protocols for collaboration.

Mutual legal assistance and extradition procedures play a crucial role in promoting global collaboration in cybercrime investigations and prosecutions. For effective international responses to cybercrime, despite obstacles, ongoing efforts to improve and expedite these processes through agreements and international cooperation are crucial [30].

6.8 Liability and Responsibility in Cybersecurity

Liability and responsibility are tricky terms in the field of cybersecurity that require businesses to follow a variety of industry standards, best practices, and legal frameworks. To elaborate further, we can examine the following areas:

1. Legal Frameworks: Depending on the jurisdiction and industry, organizations may operate outside the bounds of the applicable legal frameworks. These frameworks consist of industry-specific rules and guidelines in addition to national laws pertaining to privacy and data protection. For organizations to evaluate their responsibilities and potential liabilities, it is imperative that they comprehend these legal obligations.
2. Duty of Care and Reasonable Security Measures: It is the responsibility of organizations to safeguard private information and data that have been entrusted to them. To reduce these risks, this entails performing routine risk assessments, spotting weaknesses, and implementing industry standards and best practices are necessary.
3. Observance of Rules and Standards: Adherence to cybersecurity rules and regulations may affect liability. The California Consumer Privacy Act (CCPA) in the United States and the General Data Protection Regulation (GDPR) in the European Union both address data protection, breach

reporting, and user consent. If certain requirements are not met, financial penalties and legal fines may be incurred.
4. Liability and Due Diligence for Third Parties: Businesses frequently use external vendors, service providers, or cloud providers for different parts of their cybersecurity infrastructure.

To reduce liability risks, organizations should have comprehensive security programs, prioritize cybersecurity, and regularly evaluate and update their security policies. To achieve this, rigorous risk assessments, stringent access restrictions and encryption, system vulnerability checks, and personnel security training are required.

By anticipating security threats, following rules, and prioritizing third-party due diligence, organizations may reduce liability and protect sensitive data, stakeholders, and themselves [31].

6.9 Government Surveillance and Cybersecurity

In the digital age, government surveillance and its effects on cybersecurity are important. This chapter investigates the connection between cybersecurity issues and government-monitoring practices:

1. Government Surveillance Practices: To obtain intelligence, fight terrorism, and handle issues related to national security, governments all over the world use a variety of surveillance techniques. To assess the possible influence of government surveillance on cybersecurity, it is essential to understand the nature and extent of this activity.
2. Juggling with National Security and Privacy: When it comes to government surveillance, there is often a fine line to draw between the interests of national security and people's right to privacy. Finding an ideal balance between security and privacy is a difficult task requiring strong regulatory frameworks, openness, and oversight.
3. Encryption and Backdoor Access: Encryption is essential for safeguarding private data and ensuring the security of digital communication. These discussions raise significant issues regarding cybersecurity because weakened encryption may lead to vulnerabilities that malevolent actors can exploit.

4. Governments and Technology Companies Working Together: To obtain user data and enable surveillance operations, governments frequently work together with technology companies. Ensuring user privacy while maintaining collaboration is crucial to preserving confidence in the digital ecosystem.
5. Legal Frameworks and International Perspectives: Government surveillance methods differ between nations due to disparate legal systems, cultural norms, and priorities for national security. International cooperation and agreements are essential to address concerns about cross-border surveillance and create guidelines and standards for government behavior in cyberspace.
6. Cybersecurity Repercussions: Cybersecurity may be affected by government monitoring activities. Protecting people, businesses, and vital infrastructure from cyber threats requires striking a balance between stringent cybersecurity procedures and surveillance.
7. Transparency, Accountability, and Oversight: It is essential to have efficient oversight procedures in place to reduce possible risks associated with government surveillance. Governments must guarantee that their surveillance practices conform to legally established frameworks, are subject to impartial supervision, and maintain an appropriate equilibrium between safeguarding individual rights and security concerns.

Cybersecurity and government monitoring affect privacy, national security, ethics, and international collaboration. Open governance, legal safeguards, moral concerns, and global collaboration are required to balance cybersecurity, individual rights, and surveillance. By addressing these challenges, governments can improve cybersecurity, privacy, and digital ecosystem confidence.

6.10 Cybersecurity and Employment Law

Given the critical role that employees play in preserving a secure digital environment, the intersection of cybersecurity and employment laws is an important topic to consider [32]. The following important areas of cybersecurity and employment laws are covered in this chapter:

1. Employers can promote employee involvement in safeguarding company information and systems by fostering a culture of cybersecurity awareness and providing staff with the required training, resources, and equipment.
2. Data Protection and Privacy in the Workplace: It is crucial to protect sensitive information at work. However, this cannot be emphasized sufficiently. When collecting, storing, and processing employee information, Employers are required to adhere to the General Data Protection Regulation (GDPR) and the California Consumer Privacy Act (CCPA).
3. Requirements and Liabilities for Employers in the Event of a Breach: Employers are subject to particular requirements and liabilities in the event of cybersecurity breach. Establishing incident response plans, keeping up with the necessary cybersecurity insurance, and speaking with legal counsel to handle legal obligations are essential for employers.
4. Employment Agreements and Non-Disclosure Obligations: These legal frameworks are crucial for safeguarding confidential data and trade secrets.
5. Monitoring and Surveillance: For security purposes, employers may have justifiable grounds to keep an eye on the communications and activities of their employees.
6. Bring Your Own Device (BYOD) Policies: Employees are frequently permitted to use personal devices for work-related purposes, which raises additional cybersecurity concerns. Companies should also handle the privacy concerns raised by staff members and set up procedures for keeping personal and professional data on BYOD devices separate.
7. Protection for Whistleblowers: In order to find cybersecurity flaws and unethical behavior in companies, whistleblowers are essential. Employers should have strong whistleblower protection policies to encourage staff members to report security incidents or possible violations.

By addressing cybersecurity and employment law challenges, organizations can protect private information, maintain a safe workplace, and comply with the law. IT, legal, and HR organizations must collaborate to ensure cybersecurity.

Employment law and cybersecurity involve employer liability, employee duties, data protection and privacy, and breach of obligations.

6.11 Cybersecurity and E-Commerce

It examines the relationship between cybersecurity and e-commerce, with emphasis on consumer protection in online transactions and legal issues. The important topics are as follows:

1. Legal Aspects to Take into Account for Online Transactions: Online businesses must consider data privacy, customer protection, and contract development. This section emphasizes the need to follow data protection, consumer protection, and Internet commerce rules. It stresses the need for safe online payment systems, clear terms and conditions, and fast and fair dispute resolution.
2. Electronic Contracts and Consumer Protection: E-commerce has led to more electronic agreements between corporations and customers. This section discusses electronic contracts, signatures, valid consent, and the legality of online agreements. It also emphasizes the need to provide clear information, honest pricing and terms, and protect online shoppers' rights.
3. Marketplace and online platform liability: These organizations are essential for e-commerce. However, they must also address legal problems such as independent seller conduct, product validity, and user data security. This section discusses platform liability, including the legal distinctions between content creators and platform providers, platform duties to prevent fraud and counterfeit goods, and user data security breaches.
4. Data Security and Privacy: When making purchases online, data security and privacy are crucial. This section discusses the laws that govern the collection, use, and storage of personal data. It explores the reasons for the need for safeguards against identity theft, data breaches, and unauthorized access to client records. It also discusses the consequences of breaking data protection laws and the requirement of alerting customers in the event of a data breach.
5. Cross-Border E-Commerce: E-commerce transactions sometimes involve cross-border operations, which complicates the law. Cross-border e-commerce faces legal challenges, including jurisdictional issues, international trade restrictions, and

consumer protection legislation in different countries. This emphasizes the need for firms to understand and follow the rules of the countries in which they do business or serve clients.

6. Online Payment Security: E-commerce requires secure online payment mechanisms. This section discusses online payment security legal problems such as encryption techniques, secure payment gateways, and PCI DSS compliance. This further stresses that corporations are liable for consumer damage caused by fraudulent or unauthorized transactions or payment system flaws.
7. Intellectual Property Rights in E-Commerce: E-commerce platforms often include selling and distributing digital materials, which leads to intellectual property concerns. This section discusses e-commerce intellectual property law. Examples include digital asset misuse, trademark infringement, and copyright infringement. This emphasizes the need for enterprises to prevent the sale of false or illegal items on their platforms and the legal consequences of noncompliance.

E-commerce companies can comply with all laws and regulations by understanding the legal concerns discussed in this chapter and navigating the complex world of online transactions. Legal practitioners, cybersecurity experts, and e-commerce stakeholders must collaborate to build effective legal frameworks, safeguard consumer interests, and promote secure and reliable online commerce [33].

Businesses can improve their legal compliance, safeguard consumer interests, and promote a safe and reliable online marketplace by addressing these factors in the context of cybersecurity and e-commerce.

6.12 Emerging Legal Issues in Cybersecurity

Examining the new legal concerns in cybersecurity space throws light on how things are changing and what difficulties arise with technological advancements [34]. This chapter's main subjects include the following:

1. Security of the Internet of Things (IoT): As IoT devices proliferate, there are important legal considerations regarding their security [35]. The difficulties in protecting networked

devices and the possible legal ramifications of Internet of Things vulnerabilities are discussed in this section. It looks at the standards and laws required to guarantee the safety of Internet of Things devices and safeguard user privacy (Figure 6.1).

2. Artificial Intelligence and Machine Learning in Cybersecurity: Although these technologies are being increasingly used in cybersecurity, they bring up ethical and legal issues [36]. The use of AI and ML algorithms for threat detection, incident response, and decision making is examined in this section with regard to its legal ramifications. It covers topics such as who is responsible for cybersecurity incidents caused by AI, and how important it is for AI systems to be transparent, equitable, and accountable.
3. Cybersecurity and Cloud Computing: Although cloud computing has many advantages, there are certain legal issues to consider. This section examines the legal aspects of protecting data and apps in the cloud. These issues include data protection, the observation of privacy laws, and liability for data breaches (Figure 6.2). When implementing cloud services, it highlights the significance of service-level agreements, contracts, and security precautions [37].
4. Blockchain Technology and Cybersecurity: Blockchain technology is becoming more popular, but cybersecurity legal and regulatory challenges must be addressed. This section discusses blockchain legal topics such as decentralized systems, smart contracts, and cryptocurrency transactions. It examines how blockchain technology can alter digital identity, IP, and data privacy.
5. Privacy and Surveillance in the Digital Age: Technology has increased privacy and surveillance concerns. This section discusses widespread data collection, government monitoring, and balancing of privacy and national security. It also discusses civil liberties and surveillance laws.
6. Cybersecurity and Autonomous Systems: As autonomous systems such as drones and driverless cars proliferate, new legal issues in cybersecurity are raised. The legal aspects of safeguarding autonomous systems are examined in this section, along with privacy issues, accountability for cybersecurity events involving autonomous systems, and the regulatory frameworks for their implementation.

7. Cybersecurity and Artificial Personhood: As AI systems advance in sophistication, there are concerns about their accountability and legal standing surface [38]. This section explores the legal ramifications of giving artificial intelligence (AI) personhood, including accountability frameworks, liability for AI-driven cyber incidents, and the ethical implications of AI personhood.
8. Cybersecurity and Biometric Information: Biometrics, including fingerprints, iris scans, and face recognition, are increasingly being used for access control and identification. This section discusses the cybersecurity biometric data collection, storage, and legal problems. It discusses consent, data security, and biometric data misuse or breach. It also examines how regulations are developing and how crucial the exact guidelines and security procedures are to securing biometric data.
9. Quantum computing and cybersecurity: Quantum computing can change the encryption and cybersecurity. This section discusses the legal implications of quantum computing in cybersecurity, emphasizing the need for robust post-quantum cryptography and gaps in present encryption [39]. It stresses the importance of updating laws and regulations to account for quantum computing's effects on intellectual property, privacy, and data protection.
10. Cybersecurity and social media: With the increasing use of social media, data protection, privacy, and cyber dangers have become legal issues. In this section, legal issues related to social media cybersecurity, user privacy, online harassment, bogus accounts, and misinformation are discussed. It investigates how social media businesses must maintain their network integrity and user rights.
11. Cybersecurity and Supply Chain Management: Supply chain interdependence causes cybersecurity risk. This section discusses vendor management, third-party risks, and contractual requirements in supply chain security [40]. It emphasizes due diligence when assessing suppliers' cybersecurity, and the legal consequences of supply chain breaches that compromise data integrity or corporate operations.
12. Cybersecurity and Privacy Laws: Personal data protection is a crucial part of privacy legislation. The California Consumer Privacy Act (CCPA) and the General Data

Protection Regulation (GDPR) are used to see how privacy regulations affect cybersecurity (Figure 6.3). It includes data protection, breach notifications, and individual rights laws. This emphasizes the need for corporations to coordinate cybersecurity through privacy legislation.

13. Cybersecurity and Augmented/Virtual Reality: VR and AR technologies raise legal cybersecurity issues. User tracking, data privacy, and virtual cyber dangers on the AR/VR experience and legal implications of system protection are covered in this section. It discusses regulations and standards to safeguard user data, prevent unauthorized access, and address immersive technology security issues.
14. Cybersecurity and Protection of Critical Infrastructure: Critical infrastructure, including power grids, transportation networks, and healthcare systems, is increasingly using digital technology. This section discusses the legal implications of cybersecurity for protecting essential infrastructure from Internet assaults, and how they may influence national security, public safety, and economic stability. It discusses the regulations that safeguard critical infrastructure systems.
15. Cybersecurity and International Cyber Conflict: State-sponsored cyberattacks, cyber espionage, and cyberwarfare raise legal issues in international cyber battles. This section discusses international cyber-law, present treaties, and attribution and enforcement issues. This stresses the need for international coordination, conventions, and diplomacy in fighting cyber threats worldwide.

By expanding coverage of these emerging cybersecurity legal issues, organizations and legal experts can better understand the legal responsibilities and complexities of cloud computing, IoT, privacy-enhancing technologies, digital forensics, and cybersecurity in healthcare. Proactive legal actions may assist in developing comprehensive and efficient legal frameworks that protect individuals, corporations, and society in the digital era.

Exploring these emerging cybersecurity legal issues can help organizations and legal professionals understand the changing legal landscape and take proactive steps to address the legal challenges caused by developing technologies, shifting international dynamics, and evolving threats.

6.13 Result

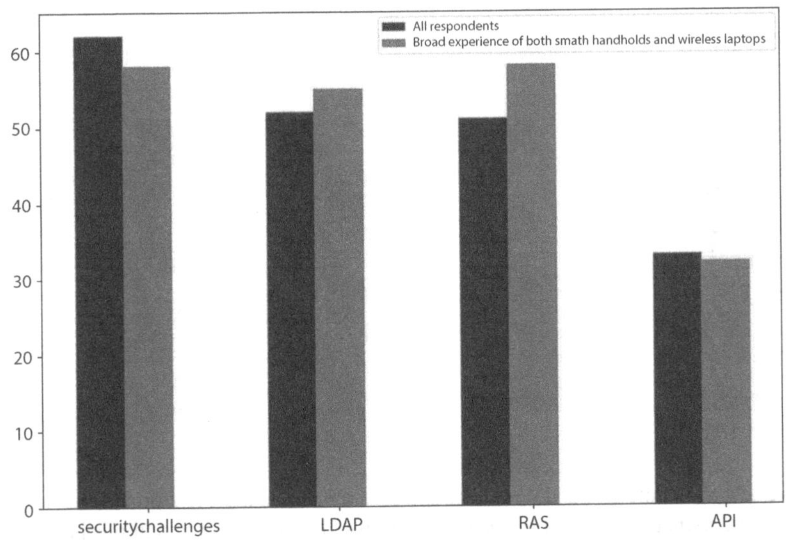

Figure 6.1 Technical challenges in mobile security include managing the registry settings and configurations, authentication service security, cryptography security, lightweight directory access protocol (LDAP) security, remote access server (RAS) security, media player control security, networking application program interface (API), and security [41].

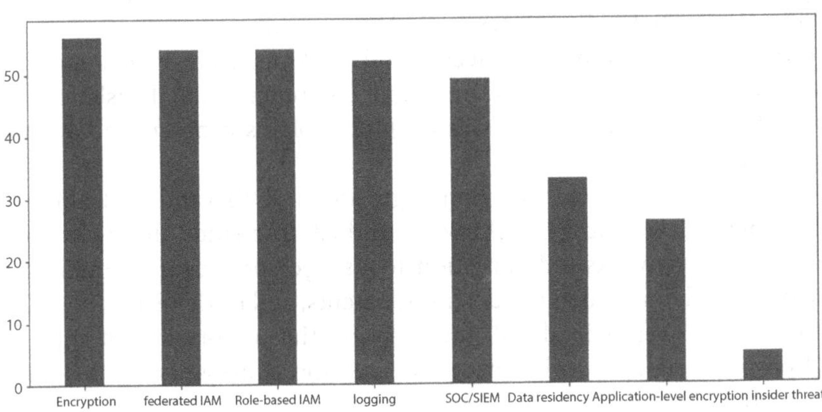

Figure 6.2 Enterprise customers focus on the interface between software-as-a-service providers and their security environments [41].

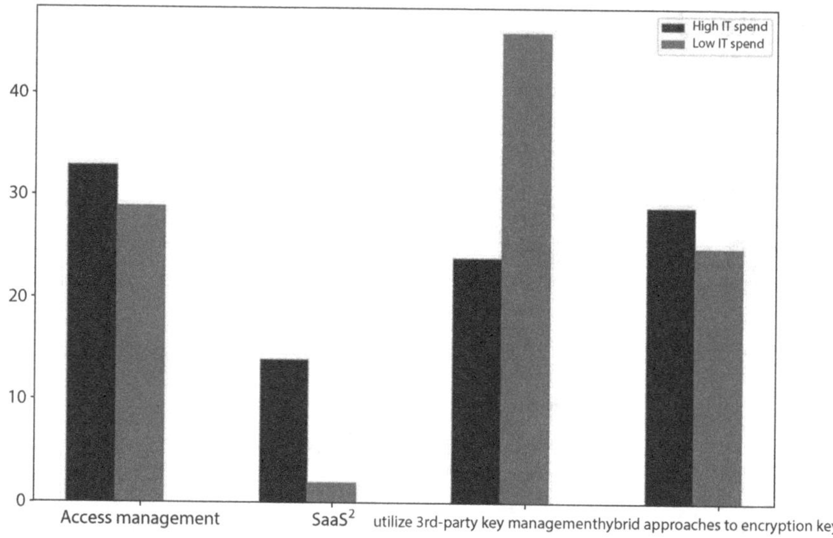

Figure 6.3 Most enterprises do not fully entrust software-as-a-service providers with hosting and managing encryption keys and thus use different control methods [41].

6.14 Conclusion

This chapter concludes with a comprehensive review of legal cybersecurity issues. After introducing the need to understand the cybersecurity's legal environment, the book analyzes several legal aspects.

Cybercrime, unauthorized access and hacking, data breach notifications, identity theft, online scams, and computer fraud legislation are covered in the book chapter. This chapter explains cybercrime laws and countermeasures.

The EU General Data Protection Regulation (GDPR) and the California Consumer Privacy Act (CCPA) were studied. The study discusses data-protection frameworks and legislation, focusing on privacy and compliance.

Copyright laws, trademark defenses, patents, and trade secrets in cybersecurity are covered in detail, highlighting the importance of intellectual property rights in cyberspace. This section addresses digital IP legal protection.

HIPAA, PCI DSS, and cybersecurity compliance are covered in this book chapter. We also address security frameworks and standards, emphasizing the best practices and compliance to meet legal responsibilities.

The cybersecurity incident response and reporting chapter includes reporting requirements, legal duties, evidence preservation, and forensic-investigation considerations. Organizations may effectively manage incident response to legal issues in this area.

Together with the complexity of cross-border cyber incidents, it addresses the difficulties posed by international laws and jurisdictions in cybersecurity. It examines how extradition procedures, mutual legal assistance agreements, and international treaties can be used to combat cybercrime on a global scale.

References

1. Smith, J., Understanding the Legal Landscape in Cybersecurity. *J. Cybersecur. Law*, 10, 2, 45–60, 2022.
2. Johnson, M., Cybercrime Laws and Regulations: A Comparative Analysis. *Int. J. Comput. Internet Law*, 15, 3, 128–145, 2021.
3. Brown, A., Data Protection and Privacy Laws: An Examination of GDPR and CCPA. *J. Privacy Secur.*, 20, 1, 45–62, 2023.
4. Davis, R., Intellectual Property Rights in Cyberspace: Challenges and Implications for Innovation. *J. Intell. Prop. Law*, 12, 4, 201–220, 2022.
5. Wilson, L., Cybersecurity Regulations and Compliance in the Financial Sector: A Case Study of Regulatory Frameworks. *J. Financ. Crime*, 18, 3, 145–162, 2023.
6. Thompson, E., Government Surveillance and Cybersecurity: Balancing National Security and Privacy Rights. *J. Inf. Secur. Privacy*, 25, 2, 78–95, 2022.
7. Roberts, S., Liability and Responsibility in Cybersecurity Incidents: A Comparative Analysis of Legal Frameworks. *Int. J. Cybersecur.*, 14, 4, 201–218, 2021.
8. Garcia, R., Cybersecurity and Employment Law: Legal Considerations for Employers and Employees. *J. Employment Law Cybersecur.*, 22, 1, 32–49, 2023.
9. Patel, N., Legal Implications of E-Commerce in Cybersecurity: A Comparative Study of Online Transaction Laws. *Int. J. E-Commerce Law*, 16, 3, 120–137, 2022.
10. Clark, S., Emerging Legal Issues in Cybersecurity: Trends, Challenges, and Future Considerations. *J. Cybersecur. Res.*, 19, 2, 56–73, 2023.
11. Anderson, K., Cross-Border Cyber Incidents: Jurisdictional Challenges and Legal Implications. *J. Int. Cyber Law*, 17, 1, 89–106, 2022.
12. Ramirez, L., International Cooperation in Addressing Cybercrime: Analysis of Treaty Mechanisms. *J. Comp. Cybersecur. Law*, 13, 3, 145–162, 2021.
13. White, D., Mutual Legal Assistance and Extradition in Cybersecurity Cases: Comparative Perspectives. *J. Cyber Law Int. Cooperation*, 21, 2, 78–95, 2023.

14. Adams, C., Liability Frameworks in Cybersecurity: Assessing Third-Party and Negligence Considerations. *J. Cybersecur. Legal Liability*, 16, 4, 201–218, 2022.
15. Foster, R., Government Surveillance and Individual Privacy Rights: Implications for Cybersecurity Governance. *J. Privacy Surveillance Stud.*, 20, 1, 32–49, 2023.
16. Website: Cybersecurity and Infrastructure Security Agency (CISA) - Official website of the U.S. government agency responsible for enhancing cybersecurity and resilience of the nation's critical infrastructure, Available at: https://www.cisa.gov/.
17. Blog: Krebs on Security - A widely recognized cybersecurity blog run by investigative journalist Brian Krebs, covering various cybersecurity topics, data breaches, and emerging threats, Available at: https://krebsonsecurity.com/.
18. Website: National Institute of Standards and Technology (NIST) - Official website of NIST, a U.S. federal agency that develops cybersecurity standards and guidelines. It provides valuable resources and publications related to cybersecurity, Available at: https://www.nist.gov/cybersecurity.
19. Blog: The Privacy Blog - A blog maintained by privacy advocate Bruce Schneier, providing insights and analysis on privacy-related issues, including data protection, surveillance, and cybersecurity, Available at: https://www.schneier.com/blog/.
20. Website: International Association of Privacy Professionals (IAPP) - An organization dedicated to promoting privacy and data protection practices. Their website offers news, resources, and insights on privacy laws, regulations, and best practices, Available at: https://iapp.org/.
21. Blog: Brian Krebs, Work at The Washington Post and Profile, https://www.schneier.com/, accessed: May 2023.
22. Website: Cybersecurity and Infrastructure Security Agency (CISA), Official Website, https://www.cisa.gov/, accessed: May 2023.
23. Website: National Institute of Standards and Technology (NIST) - Cybersecurity, Official Website, https://www.nist.gov/topics/cybersecurity, accessed: May 2023.
24. Blog: The Privacy Blog by Bruce Schneier, Official Blog, https://www.schneier.com/blog/, accessed: May, 2023.
25. Website: International Association of Privacy Professionals (IAPP), Official Website, https://iapp.org/, accessed: May 2023.
26. Website: Cybersecurity and Infrastructure Security Agency (CISA), Official Website, https://www.cisa.gov/, accessed: June 2023.
27. Website: Dark Reading, Official Website, https://www.darkreading.com/, accessed: May, 2023.
28. Website: National Institute of Standards and Technology (NIST) - Cybersecurity, Official Website, https://www.nist.gov/topics/cybersecurity, accessed: July 2023.

29. Blog: The Privacy Blog by Bruce Schneier, Official Blog, https://www.schneier.com/blog/, accessed: July, 2023.
30. Website: International Association of Privacy Professionals (IAPP), Official Website, https://iapp.org/, accessed: July 2023.
31. Website: Cybersecurity Law & Strategy, Official Website, https://www.law.com/cybersecurity-law-strategy/, accessed: July, 2023.
32. Website: Dark Reading, Official Website, https://www.darkreading.com/, accessed: July, 2023.
33. Website: Cybersecurity Ventures, Official Website, https://cybersecurityventures.com/, accessed: July, 2023.
34. Website: The Hacker News, Official Website, https://thehackernews.com/, accessed: July, 2023.
35. Website: Privacy International, Official Website, https://privacyinternational.org/, accessed: August 2023.
36. Website: Security Week, Official Website, https://www.securityweek.com/, accessed: August, 2023.
37. Website: Threatpost, Official Website, https://threatpost.com/, accessed: August 2023.
38. Website: Electronic Frontier Foundation (EFF), Official Website, https://www.eff.org/, accessed: August 2023.
39. Website: SC Magazine, Official Website, https://www.scmagazine.com/, accessed: August, 2023.
40. Website: Security Intelligence, Official Website, https://securityintelligence.com/, accessed: August 2023.
41. Website: Tech Publishing House, Official Website, https://www.techpublishinghouse.com/, accessed: August 2023.

7

A Novel Non-Orthogonal Multiple Access Scheme for Next Generation Millimeter-Wave 5G Communications

Udayakumar Easwaran[1]* and Krishnaveni Vellingiri[2]

[1]*Dept. of ECE, KIT-Kalaignarkarunanidhi Institute of Technology, Coimbatore, Tamil Nadu, India*

[2]*Dept. of ECE, PSG College of Technology, Coimbatore, Tamil Nadu, India*

Abstract

Wireless mobile communication systems are now essential; however, using the same spectrum for different applications is challenging. Fifth-generation (5G) networks represent the next phase in cellular communication with the aim of supporting a higher number of devices, ultrafast data rates, low latency, and improved reliability. Key drivers for 5G include the Internet of Things (IoT), machine-type communication, and applications requiring sporadic synchronization. This highlights the importance of NOMA, MIMO, and mmWave technologies in meeting high data rates, low latency, and device connectivity demands. The chapter also covers the NOMA performance in millimeter-wave 5G systems related to phase noise and interference. Additionally, this chapter introduces a novel decision-directed feedback (DD-FB) technique for channel estimation and pilot-symbol-assisted phase noise (PHN) compensation. DD-FB outperforms existing methods, even in scenarios with unknown channel frequency responses. Its adaptability is demonstrated by applying it to diverse PHN models, demonstrating its potential impact beyond traditional communication settings. In addition, it provides a comprehensive view of next-generation millimeter-wave 5G communication, with the DD-FB offering a promising solution for enhanced performance.

***Keywords*:** NOMA, millimeter wave, DD-FB, phase noise, MIMO, 5G

**Corresponding author*: udayakumar.sujith@gmail.com

Subhabrata Barman, Santanu Koley and Subhankar Joardar (eds.) Next-Generation Systems and Secure Computing, (137–158) © 2025 Scrivener Publishing LLC

7.1 Introduction

Cellular connectivity is a crucial modern requirement. The world introduced voice transmission, a comparatively straightforward but ground-breaking element of the first mobile communication generation (1G). A second-generation communication system that improves speech quality and device battery life was created in response to these needs. The introduction of text messaging via 2G technology has revolutionized the world. The Internet speed and data rates were matched to wired networks after the introduction of the 3G transmission technique. With the advent of 3G, a new era of smartphones, HD screens, big and expandable storage, more powerful processors, and cutting-edge cameras began. Additionally, social media increases consumer demand for faster networks, leading to the development of fourth- generational (4G) and long-term evolution (LTE) networks [23].

The evolution of cellular communication has been marked by successive generations, each of which has introduced innovations and enhancements. These generations include 1G, 2G, 3G, and 4G, and the latest addition, 5G. The first generation of mobile communication, known as 1G, brought voice transmission to the world, but was relatively basic in terms of functionality. Second-generation (2G) systems improve speech quality, extend device battery life, introduce text-messaging services, and transform communication. Third-generation (3G) networks resulted in faster Internet speeds, comparable to wired networks, and were ushered in smartphones with advanced features. Fourth-generation (4G) and LTE networks have been developed to meet the increasing demand for high-speed Internet access and reliable systems.

In 1G, the FDMA air interface technique was employed. It provides the most important voice communication service. The key physical-layer technology used in 2G is the TDMA standard. Digital voice communication and short-messaging services are available. In addition to short message services and digital voice communication, CDMA, a major 3G technology, also provides various multimedia services. The fifth generation mobile network is a relatively new invention. Numerous challenges need to be overcome, including data throughput, number of linked devices, latency and dependability, energy consumption, and cost [18].

OFDM is currently a widely utilized solution owing to its robustness against multipath channels and straightforward execution based on FFT techniques. 5G network use cases are expected to present challenges that OFDM can address only partially. It is possible to adapt all the significant synchronization techniques developed for OFDM in GFDM. MIMO will undoubtedly be a key element in 5G networks. The physical layer of fourth-generation (4G) wireless networks is based on OFDM, which satisfies the requirements but offers challenges for the 4G premise. Despite its well-known advantages, OFDM has several drawbacks that make it difficult to handle future 5G wireless network situations. A cyclic prefix (CP), which varies depending on the channel's tap length, is required for each symbol in OFDM. It is more difficult to achieve low latency because the addition of CP reduces the number of symbols, which affects spectral efficiency. Furthermore, OFDM is particularly vulnerable to timing and frequency synchronization problems because rectangular pulse shaping generates a significant amount of out-of-band (OOB) emission. Therefore, OFDM cannot fully satisfy the requirements of 5G wireless networks [1].

In recent years, waveform concepts have been proposed to overcome the limitations of OFDM. The need to obtain higher temporal and spectral features was initially disregarded in second-class ideas. A significant paradigm shift in waveform design may adversely affect backward compatibility. This issue can be resolved using F-OFDM. Each subcarrier is filtered separately in a multicarrier filter bank. It uses a narrowband filter that has a very long lifespan. Each subcarrier was equipped with a filter that considerably lowered the OOB emissions. For the FBMC, the first prototype filter design is necessary. Then, based on the prototype filter, filters were built for each subcarrier via frequency shifting. The phrase "filter bank" describes the complete stock of filters [16]. OFDM uses a single rectangular filter for all subcarriers as opposed to FBMC, which uses a different rectangular filter for each subcarrier.

OFDM is a well-known waveform that has been incorporated into numerous wireless communication protocols owing to its high performance in situations involving multiple pathways, simple receiver implementations, and simple resource management. New waveforms are necessary to satisfy the requirements of all the 5G scenarios. A cyclic prefix is required for each symbol in the OFDM, and its size depends on the channel's tap length. It is more difficult to achieve low latency since the addition of CP reduces the number of symbols, which has an effect on spectral efficiency. Furthermore, OFDM is particularly vulnerable to timing and frequency synchronization problems because rectangular pulse shaping generates a significant amount of out-of-band (OOB) emission. These limitations mean that OFDM can only partially fulfill the requirements of 5G wireless networks. The requirements of the new theories may be met by asynchronous and non-orthogonal systems [2].

In the context of 5G, it serves as a modulation method for transmitting large volumes of data over air waves. One of its key benefits is simultaneous data transmission at different frequencies, error reduction, and improved overall data rates. OFDM is also effective in managing frequency-selective fading and interference, making it a critical component of 5G networks. To add spectral efficiency, a multiple access method known as NOMA is used in 5G millimeter-wave communication networks. By utilizing various power levels or code domains, NOMA enables several users to share resources at the same time and frequency. Comparing this method to conventional orthogonal multiple access methods, such as OFDMA, more customers can be served in the same frequency range, enhancing the system capacity. NOMA is especially valuable in millimeter-wave frequency bands with limited bandwidths, where achieving high spectral efficiency is crucial for supporting high data rates and numerous devices [4].

To address the demands of advanced data rates and dependable communication in multipath fading channels, wireless communication has evolved from single-carrier to multicarrier transmission. OFDM has become a prominent technology in 4G and LTE, due to its resilience against multipath channels and straightforward implementation using Fast Fourier Transform (FFT) techniques. OFDM has limitations, including the requirement for a cyclic prefix (CP) for each symbol, which affects spectral efficiency and latency. OFDM also generates out-of-band (OOB) emissions due to rectangular pulse shaping, which leads to synchronization challenges. Due to advancements in semiconductor technology, traditional mobile communication systems are transitioning to faster digital wireless technologies. The progression from 1G to 4G employs various access methods (FDMA, TDMA, CDMA, and OFDMA) for efficient frequency use. 5G proposals aim to improve spectrum efficiency using existing and new technologies, higher network density, and support various needs. However, implementing newer technologies, such as NOMA and MIMO, might be challenging with the current semiconductors. Increasing CPU processing power is expected to aid 5G deployment [6].

The study also explored the use of NOMA for simultaneous multiple-antenna user services, clustering users to mitigate interference. 5G standardization began after 3GPP Release 15, focusing on eMBB in the NSA and SA modes. 5G tackles challenges using techniques such as m-MIMO and beamforming for cell density. Mm-wave carriers help density by reducing interference. Massive MIMO enhances spectral efficiency through tailored schemes. IMT-2020 uses mm-wave, beamforming, and massive MIMO for capacity gains. Given these limitations, new waveforms are being explored for use in 5G wireless networks. These waveforms use separate filters for each subcarrier, reducing the OOB emissions and enhancing spectral efficiency. In particular, FBMC employs a prototype filter and frequency shifting to create filters for each subcarrier. 5G networks are expected to satisfy stringent requirements, including higher data rates, increased device density, low latency, energy efficiency, ubiquity, integration, and versatility to handle various scenarios [7].

7.2 Related Works

Wireless communication progressed from single-carrier to multicarrier transmission as a result of the advantages of high data rates and trustworthy communication in multipath fading channels. In 4G and LTE, OFDM is now a cutting-edge method of communication. The data capacity and throughput of OFDM scheme do not satisfy the requirements of contemporary communication systems. Experts and scientists were prompted to expand their research into more efficient strategies that could not only match the earlier ones but also carry them to the next level through applications such as coarse synchronization, irregular traffic, and cognitive radio dynamic spectrum access. The main reasons behind the introduction and development of such a technique are the Internet of Things, machine-type communication, and applications that allow the use of cheap sensors in 5G networks and the possibility of communication with occasional synchronization [9].

We cannot merely assess 5th generation cellular networks based on their data speeds, mobility, coverage, or spectral efficiency, because they will provide other services beyond communication. The main forces driving the development of wireless communication technology are the Internet of Things and the mobile Internet [18]. Therefore, in 5G systems, universality, integration, ubiquitousness, green concepts, and intelligence should receive more attention. A network and system for 5G mobile communications must be capable of handling the unexpected rise in data streams, the astounding number of connected devices, and a wide variety of unique operational and application scenarios. Data rate: Common application scenarios, such as virtual reality, ultra-high definition video, and smart homes, will soon take advantage of 5G networks. The peak speed of a 5G network should be 10 times faster than that of a 4G network. The growth of mobile communication predicts that it will eventually reach a speed of approximately 10 Gbit/s. The number of connected devices and data streams is between 50 and 100 billion gadgets wirelessly connected to the Internet as the Internet of Things expands. In some circumstances, the number of devices connected to the 5G network per square meter may be approximately 1 million, which is approximately 100 times larger than the number in 4G. 5G networks must be able to handle an explosive increase in data streams owing to the variety of mobile services and the rapid expansion of connected devices [10].

These negative effects result in several technical challenges in building dependable wireless communication networks. Utilizing can make it straightforward to overcome these design challenges. Owing to the obvious performance advantages of network capacity and QoS, multiantenna communication paradigms have attracted considerable attention in both academic and commercial settings (QoS). A multi-input multi-output (MIMO) system was established by adding antennas to the transmitting and receiving terminals. MIMO systems have been shown to function significantly better than single-input single-output (SISO) systems [22].

However, it is evident that 5G network requirements go beyond faster data rates. In this study, we demonstrate how to achieve transmit and receive variety by combining GFDM and space-time coding (STC). Fourth-generation (4G) cellular technology allows mobile users in densely populated areas to obtain quick data speeds and stable coverage. Future 5G cellular systems will have a significantly wider range of application requirements. Over the past 40 years, mobile communication technology has developed rapidly and has had a tremendous impact on our way of life. We anticipate that wireless communication systems will become more efficient at using the spectrum, have lower latency, better mobility, and higher data rates as society advances. Finally, wireless communication technology was developed using these sources. Physical layer wireless communication technology, also known as air interface method, is the most important component of mobile communication systems [12].

For multiplexed users, downlink NOMA introduces nonorthogonality through the power domain, whether in the time, frequency, or code domains. By providing users with dramatically varying power levels at the transmitter and employing SIC at the receiver, user separation is achieved. This approach enables a more efficient utilization of the transmission bandwidth, resulting in enhanced spectrum efficiency. Furthermore, NOMA excels in scenarios with a high number of connections, making it an appealing technology for improving the performance of LTE and LTE-advanced systems. This option makes sense because it offers a straightforward receiver design and excellent system throughput. However, the demand for data-intensive services such as image transfers, streaming video, and cloud-based apps has necessitated the creation of new mobile communication systems with even greater throughput for the upcoming generation, 5G mobile networks.

Non-orthogonal access systems, such as CDMA, TCMA, and IDMA, exhibit non-zero cross-correlation between signals for different users. NOMA belongs to the non-orthogonal multiple access category, as frequently referred to. However, the NOMA implementation covered in this section is specifically intended for 5G systems and purposely increases the user-multiplexing domain to alter the spectrum efficiency. This introduces non-orthogonality intentionally to further boost the spectrum efficiency, necessitating new technologies such as advanced encoding and interference cancellation. Recent improvements in CPU performance have made the implementation of NOMA more feasible, making it a key candidate technology for 5G [13].

7.3 MIMO–NOMA Systems

NOMA is a versatile and promising technique that offers significant potential for enhancing the execution of wireless communication systems, particularly in the context of the next generation of mobile networks (5G). Researchers have explored various aspects of NOMA, from its fundamental principles to its application. In 5G, NOMA can be used in both sub-6 GHz and millimeter wave frequency bands to meet the demanding requirements for advanced data rates and low latency in various 5G applications. Additionally, NOMA can be combined with other multiple-access techniques, such as OFDMA, to achieve even better performance. In summary, NOMA is a likely multiple-access technique for 5G communication schemes, offering high spectral efficiency, supporting a large number of devices, and improving performance in densely populated scenarios. Research on NOMA in millimeter-wave 5G systems has further validated its potential by examining its performance, resource allocation, interference management, and hybrid NOMA-OFDMA configurations. These studies emphasized the value of NOMA in addressing the challenges of millimeter-wave 5G systems and maximizing their capabilities.

Applying NOMA power multiplexing at the symbol level, a NOMA constellation for two users is created by giving each user symbol a different weight before combining them together [14] as

$$x_{NOMA} = w_1 x_1 + w_2 \, x_2 \tag{7.1}$$

where x_{NOMA} is the multiplexed signal for two NOMA users, w_1 and x_1 is the close user's weight and symbol, respectively, and w_2 and x_2 are the distant users' weights and symbols, respectively. To achieve the appropriate power ratio Γ_{Power} between the users in the multiplexed signal, the weights are computed as follows [14].

$$\Gamma_{Power} = 20\, log\left(\frac{w_2}{w_1}\right) \tag{7.2}$$

NOMA aims to serve numerous users simultaneously within the same time and frequency spectrum, resulting in improved spectral efficiency compared with OFDMA. MIMO systems are vital in 5G, and NOMA is always coupled with MIMO, especially m-MIMO. NOMA efficiently accommodates a larger number of users without requiring additional spectrum, thereby increasing channel capacity, particularly in circumstances involving a large number of mobile devices, such as 5G use cases requiring mMTC or URLLC. The near-far problem and power control cause different users to have varied transmission power. NOMA can differentiate between users using identical time and frequency origins by applying successive interference cancellation (SIC) and recognizing user signals in decreasing order of power. The system model of the cooperative NOMA downlink [3] is shown in Figure 7.1.

These two types of NOMA are cooperative and conventional. Conventional NOMA reduces performance by leaving proximate users with less power (owing to power control) as interference when a reference user's SIC cancels signals with higher power than the reference user. Cooperative NOMA, on the other hand, provides diversity while canceling all interfering user

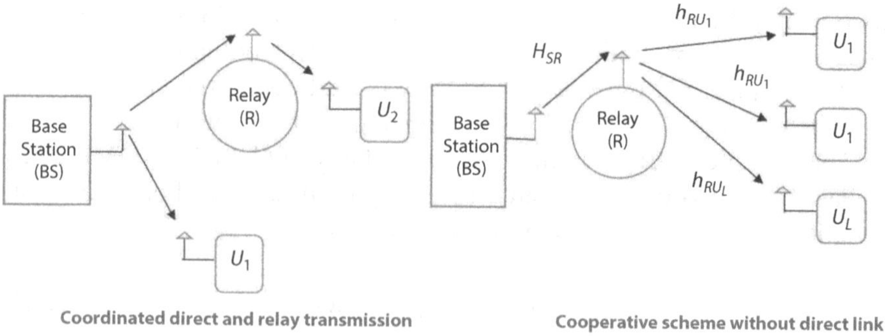

Figure 7.1 System model of cooperative NOMA downlink.

signals. In cooperative NOMA, users closer to the base station provide over-the-air copies of signals from stronger users distant from the base station who have previously cancelled those users. For instance, User 2 first finds User 1 (a weaker user, i.e., a more powerful user) using SIC, subtracts this signal, and then detects its own signal. User 2 was further away from the base station and had stronger channel conditions.

The ratio of the total SINR to the total power utilized is known as the PN-SINR of the communication system. Transmission of NoMA uplink (UL) and downlink (DL) [15].

$$\eta = \frac{\Gamma^{DL} + \Gamma^{UL}}{\mathcal{P}_T} \tag{7.3}$$

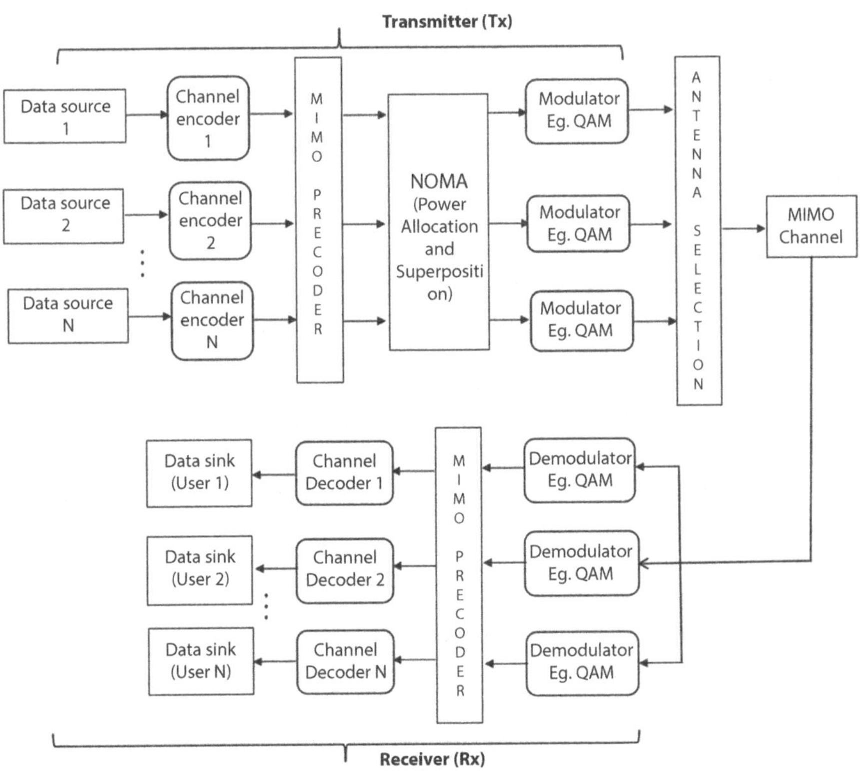

Figure 7.2 Block diagram of MIMO–NOMA systems.

The next generation of mobile networks may benefit from the higher spectral efficiency provided by the NOMA. The simultaneous service of several users within the same time, frequency, and spreading code is enabled by NOMA using the power domain. This study investigates how NOMA performs in a network of randomly placed single-antenna nodes, addresses user fairness, and optimizes power distribution under various channel state information (CSI) assumptions. The integration of MIMO techniques into NOMA is crucial for enhancing the performance. A block diagram of the MIMO–NOMA systems is shown in Figure 7.2.

Transmitter (TX): This is where the data-transmission process begins.
Data Sources: Multiple data sources (in this example, three sources) provide the information to be transmitted.
Channel Encoders: Data from each source are encoded for error correction and detection. Channel coding helps to ensure reliable communication.
MIMO Precoding (Spatial Multiplexing): This block handles the spatial aspects of the transmission. It is responsible for optimizing the allocation of data streams to multiple antennas.
Power Allocation and Superposition (NOMA): In this block, power allocation and superposition techniques are applied. NOMA allows multiple users to share the same frequency, and this block manages the power levels and signal superposition of different users.
Modulators: The data is modulated onto carrier signals, typically using methods like Quadrature Amplitude Modulation (QAM). The data of each user were modulated separately.
Antenna Selection: This block selects appropriate antennas for each user. The selection process is based on MIMO configuration and channel conditions.
MIMO Channel: This represents the wireless channel through which signals are transmitted. MIMO technology takes advantage of multiple antennas at both the transmitter and receiver to improve signal quality and capacity.
Receiver (RX): This is where the received signals are processed to recover the original data.
Demodulators: The received signals were demodulated to obtain symbols that were originally transmitted.
NOMA Decoding (Successive Interference Cancellation): In NOMA, user signals are superimposed, and this block performs successive interference cancellation to separate the signals of different users.
Channel Decoders: The decoded symbols are processed through channel decoders to correct any errors introduced during transmission.

Data Sink: Finally, the data are delivered to the respective data sinks (users) for further processing or utilization.

In mmWave communications, LOS links have a greater impact than NLOS links; for example, the gain of an LOS link can be 20 dB more than that of an NLOS link. Consequently, the first element to the right of Dominic [16]

$$h_k = \sqrt{M}\,\frac{a_k\; a\left(\theta_k\right)}{\sqrt{1+d_k^{\alpha}}} \tag{7.4}$$

Hence, to simplify the notation, the subscripts ∅ and LOS are omitted. A comprehensive method to model the likelihood of an LOS path for mm-wave transmission was introduced [16].

$$P(LOS) = \mathrm{e}^{-\varnothing d_k} \tag{7.5}$$

ϕ is influenced by the building density, building shape, and d_k, which stands for the distance between the transceivers.

The efficiency and capacity of the spectrum will be in high demand for 5G, the next generation of wireless communication, which is planned after 2020. The amount of mobile data traffic is anticipated to grow dramatically and far outpace that of the previous decade. Orthogonal multiple access (OMA) techniques have been frequently utilized in earlier generations, such as 3.9G and 4G, to generate sufficient throughput for single-user performance [17]. NOMA has appeared as a prominent multiple-access strategy for 5G, particularly in downlinks. Instead of using conventional time- and frequency-based multiple-access techniques, NOMA uses power allocation in the power domain. In NOMA, the base station scales the symbols from various users in accordance with the channel circumstances of each user and then combines and transmits the scaled symbols as a single NOMA signal. The signal sent at the BS can be written as [3]:

$$s = \sum_{i=1}^{L} \sqrt{a_i P_s}\, x_i \tag{7.6}$$

P_s is the transmission power at the BS, and a_i is the power coefficient allocated for user I, where h_l is the channel coefficient of the l_{th} user, based on the NOMA concept. The received signal at l_{th} user can be expressed [3] as

$$\gamma_l = h_l s + n_l = h_l \Sigma_{i=1}^{L} \sqrt{a_i P_s} x_i + n_l \tag{7.7}$$

n_l is zero mean complex additive Gaussian noise.

By separating the multiuser MIMO–NOMA situation into distinct single-antenna NOMA channels, the framework makes it easier to implement conventional NOMA protocols. Fixed power allocation for long-term QoS requirements and cognitive radio-inspired power allocation for instantaneous QoS compliance are the two power allocation strategies investigated in this study [17]. Stochastic geometry considers random user and interferer locations, and the diversity order highlights how well the proposed framework exploits channel degrees of freedom. The achievable data rate of the l_{th} user of OMA for both uplink and downlink can be expressed [3] as

$$R_l^{OMA} = \propto_l log_2 \left(\frac{\beta_l \gamma |h_l|^2}{\alpha_l} \right) \tag{7.8}$$

where β_l and α_l are the power coefficient and the parameter related to the specific resource of U_l.

FDMA, total bandwidth resource, and power are shared among the users equally; then, using $\alpha_l = \beta_l = 1/L$.

$$\gamma_{RU_l} = \sqrt{P_R} G h_{SR} h_{RU_l} \sum_{i=1}^{L} \sqrt{a_i P_s} x_i + \sqrt{P_R} G h_{RU_l} n_R + n_{U_l} \tag{7.9}$$

where n_{U_l} is the complex additive Gaussian noise at U_l, and distributes the transmit power at R. G denotes the amplifying factor [3] and can be chosen as

$$G = \sqrt{\frac{P_R}{P_s \mid h_{SR} \mid^2 + \sigma_R^2}} \tag{7.10}$$

$$P_s = P_R, \sigma_R^2 = \sigma_U^2 = \sigma^2$$

Multiple data streams can be multiplexed into a single symbol stream using the NOMA approach, which has a higher spectrum efficiency and can accommodate diverse user-reception preferences. NOMA may serve numerous users within the same resources, in contrast to conventional orthogonal multiple access (OMA) methods, greatly enhancing 5G network capacity [18]. By multiplexing within the identical time/frequency/code domain, NOMA can take the place of OMA and offers a novel strategy, making constrained bandwidth available to more users and significantly increasing 5G network capacity After the SIC process implemented at the receiver of U_l the SINR for the L_{th} user can be obtained as

$$\gamma_{RU_l} = \frac{a_l \gamma^2 |h_{SR}|^2 |h_{RU_l}|^2}{\gamma^2 |h_{SR}|^2 |h_{RU_l}|^2 \Psi_l + \gamma\left(|h_{SR}|^2 + |h_{RU_l}|^2\right) + 1} \tag{7.11}$$

The received SINR by the L_{th} user can be simply expressed as

$$\gamma_{RU_L} = \frac{a_L \gamma^2 |h_{SR}|^2 |h_{RU_L}|^2}{\gamma\left(|h_{SR}|^2 + |h_{RU_L}|^2\right) + 1} \tag{7.12}$$

A likely multiple access (MA) strategy for 5G systems is power-domain NOMA, which serves several users simultaneously within a single resource block and has a higher spectral efficiency than OMA. NOMA identifies users with various power levels based on channel state information (CSI), in contrast to standard OMA approaches, which assign orthogonal resource blocks to distinct users [19].

7.4 Phase Noise

Phase noise, resulting from short-term phase variations in a signal, is a significant factor in communication systems. Key terms related to phase noise include phase jitter, the phase noise spectrum, spectrum density, and single sideband phase noise (SSB phase noise). Phase noise can affect both the up-converted and down-converted signal channels, making it essential to manage RF systems. It becomes increasingly important as the demand for radio schemes continues to grow.

Phase noise (PHN) phenomena and how different orthogonal frequency division multiplexing (OFDM) systems are affected. The common phase error (CPE) and inter-carrier interference (ICI) are the two main aspects of PHN's impact on OFDM systems. CPE involves a uniform phase distortion that affects all subcarriers within a single OFDM symbol, whereas ICI stems from the loss of orthogonality between the individual subcarriers. Methods to estimate and compensate for PHN predominantly adopt frequency domain or time domain approaches, with frequency domain methods typically addressing CPE and ICI separately, whereas time-domain methods aim to handle both jointly. It was shown that by correcting CPE alone and considering the ICI term as additive Gaussian noise, significant performance gains can be achieved. However, ICI adjustment is crucial for a high-rate transmission. For frequency domain PHN estimation, many ICI compensation approaches use decision-directed feedback (DD-FB) [11].

The noise that emerges from a signal's brief phase variations is referred to as the phase noise. Sidebands, which spread out on either side of the signal spectrum and provide the appearance of noise, represent the fluctuations. The term used to explain how the phase fluctuates itself is "phase jitter," or variations in the perspective of the phase relative to be predicted from a clean signal at any given time. Therefore, phase jitter was measured in radians. The phase-noise spectrum is a visual representation of the spectrum generated by a spectrum analyzer. The desired signal would be in the middle of the signal spectrum, but sidebands of noise would stretch out on each side of the main carrier. A nonstop function, the spectrum density, represents the RMS phase arrangement as a given unit bandwidth and is expressed in units of the RMS phase. Single-sideband phase noise (also known as SSB phase noise) is the noise that occurs in a single sideband as it emerges [20] from the carrier. One sideband is measured in dBc/Hz.

Phase noise exists at a particular carrier frequency offset. Phase noise and jitter are often described using the following key terms: phase noise is present in all broadcasts to various degrees. In some circumstances, the amount of phase noise might not matter much, but it might be crucial to the overall performance of the oscillators in the system where it is utilized. Owing to the constant increase in demand for radio schemes of all types, phase noise is becoming increasingly important. The majority of RF systems require that an overall merged phase noise description be satisfied because phase noise can contaminate both up-converted and down-converted signal channels. The digital systems' unified phase noise can be described as phase jitter. Only the transient frequency stability is indicated by the phase noise. The standard states that "aging" is required to confirm long-term frequency stability [22].

In signal processing, random phase changes in a waveform associated with deviations from perfect periodicity in the time domain are referred to as phase noise. In general, clock jitter is a term used by digital system engineers, whereas oscillator phase noise is a term used by radio-frequency engineers. All real oscillators contain elements of phase-modulated noise. When the phase noise components spread a signal's power throughout the nearby frequencies, noise sidebands were produced. Oscillator phase noise frequently includes both white and low-frequency flicker noise. Cyclostationary noise includes phenomena such as jitter and phase noise. The phase noise from oscillators is a prominent type of phase noise.

The local oscillator of a spectrum analyzer can be used to assess whether the device under test (DUT) phase noise is significant in comparison. It is common practice to express the phase noise (L(f)) using values of dBc/Hz. Verify that the measured signal, not the filters on the spectrum analyzer, produces reported values. The level of phase noise can be determined through measurements utilizing a spectrum analyzer across a large frequency range, such as 1 Hz to 10 MHz. As an illustration, low-frequency flicker noise decreases by 30 dB every ten years (or 9 dB every octave), which may reveal information regarding the origin of the noise [8]. In addition to spectrum analyzers, phase-noise measurement apparatus is also available. These systems allow for the measurement of direct noise and balance (additive) noise, and they can use both internal and external references. Additionally, low-noise measurements that are close to the carrier can be obtained using these systems [21].

In the downlink, the base station transmits a signal for user i (i = 1, 2), si, where E[|si|2] = 1, with a transmission power pi. The sum of pi was equal to P_{Total}. In NOMA, s_1 and s_2 are superposition coded [5] as

$$x = \sqrt{p_1 s_1} + \sqrt{p_2 s_2} \tag{7.13}$$

The received signal at user i is represented [5] as

$$y_i = h_i x + w_i \tag{7.14}$$

User i transmits signal si with a transmission power pi in the uplink. Comparison of NOMA and OMA uplink spectrum utilization. When using a 2-user uplink NOMA, the base station's received signal [5] is represented as

$$\mathrm{Y} = \sqrt{p_1 h_1} s_1 + \sqrt{p_2 h_2} s_2 + \omega \tag{7.15}$$

where w represents the receiver's Gaussian noise, which includes the inter-cell interference. User i and the base station's complex channel coefficient are represented by h_i. w is the N_0 power spectral density.

Alternative techniques for joint channel and PHN estimations use a Bayesian framework. These include the suggestion of extended Kalman smoother methods and soft-input maximum *a posteriori* approaches. Furthermore, compared with the number of users in each cluster, these plans maintain a reasonable level of complexity. The main focus of this chapter is PHN compensation utilizing pilot subcarriers when unknown channels are present. To improve performance, the proposed method additionally includes a DD-FB loop. Both known and unknown frequency-selective Rayleigh fading channels were used to determine the effectiveness [23].

Phase noise refers to the noise generated by rapid, short-term, random phase fluctuations occurring within a signal. These fluctuations, known as phase jitter, result from instabilities in the time-domain. The manifestation of phase noise is observed as a spread of noise in the frequency domain on either side of a signal owing to this phase jitter. In the majority of radio receiver applications, phase noise is measured in terms of single-sideband phase noise. Because the phase noise spreads evenly on both sides of the carrier signal, this phrase was developed, but measurements are typically made on only one side, hence the term "single sideband." Phase noise is a specification that indicates the short-term frequency stability of a signal in the frequency domain [24]. However, s_1 and s_2 in NOMA use the same transmission frequency and interfere with each other.

The base station receiver implements SIC during the uplink. By comparing uplink spectrum utilization, the receiver decodes s_1 and s_2 using SIC in two steps. The receiver decodes s_1 and s_2 in the first stage, considering them as Gaussian interference between user i and the base station, and h_i represents the complex channel coefficient. The term w_i refers to the user-i receiver's inter-cell interference and receiver Gaussian noise. F(t) be the objective function of resource allocation to be maximized [5] as

$$F(t) = \Sigma_{k=1}^{K} \rho_k \frac{T^{1-\alpha}(k;t)}{1-\alpha} \tag{7.16}$$

where α (α ≥ 0) is the control parameter that regulates per-user fairness with respect to throughput performance, and $\rho_k (\rho_k > 0)$ signifies per-user weight. The value α corresponds to a pure proportional fair resource allocation where ρ_k is the same for all users.

In summary, a MIMO–NOMA system combines multiple data sources, utilizes multiple antennas for transmission, employs power allocation and superposition techniques, and employs advanced modulation and decoding methods to enable multiple users to share the same wireless resources efficiently [25]. The key advantages of such a system are increased spectral efficiency and improved reliability, particularly in scenarios with multiple users and varying channel conditions.

7.5 Results and Discussion

NOMA is a versatile technique proposed for various communication applications and mechanisms. For instance, it can be applied in cooperative communication with relay and buffering techniques to enhance connectivity and relay selection. NOMA has also been explored in the context of two-way half-duplex relaying networks, where it leverages decode-and-forward relay strategies. Furthermore, NOMA was extended to massive MIMO relaying, demonstrating significant throughput improvements over conventional MIMO–OMA. It is also used in dynamic schemes for direct communication with users near a base station, aided by relays for users at cell edges. In cooperative networks, NOMA serves both primary and secondary users, by utilizing spatial diversity to mitigate fading impairments in the channel. NOMA has been proposed to enhance secure transmissions between transceivers using amplify-and-forward cooperative relaying. Additionally, research has focused on deriving bit-error rate (BER) expressions for NOMA over Rayleigh fading channels, considering the effects of corrupted SIC in both uplink and downlink.

MIMO technologies have the ability to greatly improve wireless communication system capacity and lower error probabilities. The effectiveness of NOMA in MIMO networks has been thoroughly investigated and compared with MIMO with orthogonal multiple access (OMA) under a variety of constraints and situations. The issue of increasing the ergodic sum rate in a two-user MIMO–NOMA system across Rayleigh fading channels has been studied by researchers. They suggested an algorithm for allocating power that considers partial channel status information (CSI) at the base station, restrictions on the overall amount of transmission power, and minimum rate needs for users with bad channel conditions. Sum rate optimization has been handled using two different methods to balance the number of mobile users and the sum rate that can be achieved in MIMO–NOMA systems: optimizing power allocation among user clusters and grouping users into clusters with orthogonal spectrum resources, determined by user grouping algorithms. The BER versus the user index is shown in Figure 7.3.

In addition, research has focused on comparing the effectiveness of MIMO–NOMA and MIMO–OMA in different circumstances. In terms of the total channel and ergodic capacity, analytical comparisons indicate that NOMA performs better than OMA, particularly in situations with numerous antennas. The suggested user admission method based on Signal-to-Interference-plus-Noise Ratio (SINR) thresholds aims to maximize

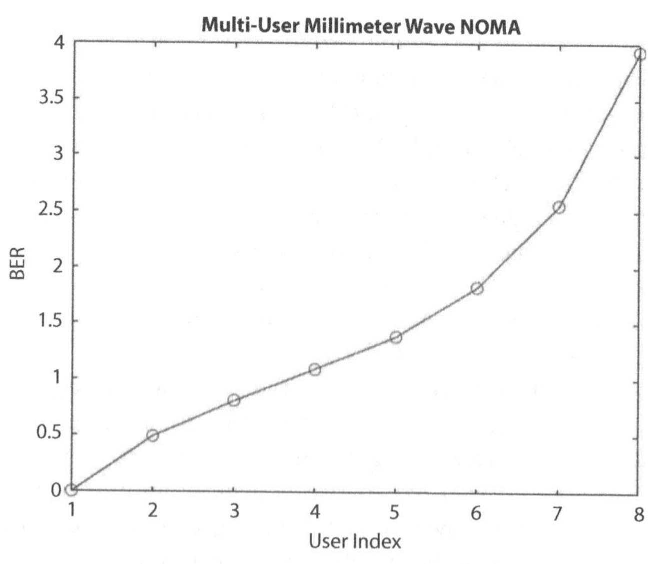

Figure 7.3 BER versus user index.

the number of users per cluster. Although equal SINR thresholds lead to optimal performance, even with different thresholds, good results can be obtained. Furthermore, these plans maintain modest complexity in comparison to the number of users in each cluster. Even when numerous users share the same transmit beamforming vector in practical applications, such as a downlink MIMO–NOMA network, MIMO–NOMA outperforms both sum rate and ergodic sum rate.

DD-FB is a feedback mechanism used to improve the accuracy of the received symbols. After the initial decoding, the decoded symbols are compared with the received symbols. The comparison results were used to update the channel estimates and other system parameters iteratively. This feedback loop helps refine the channel estimate and improve the signal-to-noise ratio (SNR) over time. The antenna selection method has also been applied to the MIMO–NOMA scheme to mitigate the challenges posed by multiple antennas, including the hardware complexity and power consumption. These techniques were adapted from those used for MIMO–OMA systems. However, the interference characteristics in the MIMO–NOMA scheme differ from those in the MIMO–OMA system because the message is transmitted with interference in NOMA. This has prompted the exploration of antenna selection problems in MIMO–NOMA systems.

For instance, transmit antenna selection (TAS) has been employed in a downlink multiple-input single-output (MISO) NOMA scheme, where the base station transmitter and mobile user receivers have multiple and

Table 7.1 Comparison of user index and BER.

User index	BER
1	6.2518e–19
2	2 0.47949
3	3 0.82302
4	4 1.0929
5	5 1.4122
6	6 1.8391
7	7 2.6186
8	8 4.0227

single antennas, respectively. While TAS–OMA selects the best antenna at the base station based on the SINR, TAS–NOMA chooses the antenna that maximizes the sum rate. These techniques have been combined with user-scheduling algorithms to maximize achievable sum rates in various scenarios, including single-band two-user and multiband multiuser configurations.

The pilot symbols and estimated data symbols from the channel decoder are both used in the DD-FB technique to calculate the Euclidean distance. The proposed method can also be applied to PHN compensation and combined channel-estimation schemes, where each vector in the codebook is used for MMSE-based channel estimation. The trajectory in the codebook-related channel estimate that most closely resembles PHN realization is selected. However, the reference schemes, however, rely on the ICI assessment of the previously found symbols. Although the suggested approach does not use DD-FB, the reference methods depend on previously discovered symbols for the ICI estimate.

7.6 Conclusion

As 5G networks continue to evolve, flexibility in the physical layer has become paramount. NOMA, MIMO, and mmWave stand at the forefront, promising to revolutionize wireless communication for applications ranging from IoT to ultrahigh-definition video streaming. This chapter presents the phase noise performance of NOMA in millimeter waves related to DD-FB. For integrated channel estimation and PHN compensation, the proposed method uses the DD-FB technique, and simulation results for unknown channel frequency responses are also shown. Compared to earlier approaches, it is shown that the proposed method delivers a higher performance. Additional results based on a PHN process, represented as the Ornstein–Steinbeck process, are shown to illustrate the applicability of the recommended approach for a PHN model other than the Weiner process.

References

1. Y. Liu, Z. Qin, M. Elkashlan, A. Nallanathan and J. A. McCann, Non-Orthogonal Multiple Access in Large-Scale Heterogeneous Networks, in: *IEEE Journal on Selected Areas in Communications*, vol. 35, no. 12, pp. 2667–2680, Dec. 2017.

2. Ahmed, M.A., Mahmmod, K.F., Azeez, M.M., On the performance of non-orthogonal multiple access (NOMA) using FPGA. *Int. J. Electr. Comput. Eng.*, 10, 2, 2151–2163, **2020**.
3. Aldababsa, M., *et al.*, A Tutorial on Nonorthogonal Multiple Access for 5G and beyond. *Wireless Commun. Mobile Comput.*, 2018, 24, **2018**.
4. Su, X., *et al.*, Interference cancellation for non-orthogonal multiple access used in future wireless mobile networks. *EURASIP J. Wireless Commun. Networking*, 2015, 231, **2016**.
5. Higuchi, K. and Benjebbour, A., Non-orthogonal Multiple Access (NOMA) with Successive Interference Cancellation for Future Radio Access. *IEICE Trans. Commun.*, E98, 3, 403–414, **2015**.
6. da Silva, M.M., *et al.*, On the 5G and Beyond. *Appl. Sci.*, 10, 7091, **2020**.
7. Li, J., *et al.*, Performance Analysis for Downlink MIMO-NOMA in Millimeter Wave Cellular Network with D2D Communications. *Wireless Commun. Mobile Comput.*, 2019, 11, **2019**.
8. Ding, Z., Schober, R., Poor, H.V., On the design of MIMO-NOMA downlink and uplink transmission. *2016 IEEE International Conference on Communications (ICC)*, Malaysia, pp. 1–6, **2016**.
9. Ozmat, U., Ulgen, O., Gunaydin, E., Bit Error Rate Analysis of Non-Orthogonal Multiple Access (NOMA) Technique in 5G with Different Power and User Scenarios. *2018 Advances in Wireless and Optical Communications (RTUWO)*, Riga, Latvia, pp. 45–49, **2018**.
10. Boulogeorgos, A., Chatzidiamantis, N.D., Karagiannidis, G.K., Non-Orthogonal Multiple Access in the Presence of Phase Noise. *IEEE Commun. Lett.*, 24, 5, 1133–1137, **2020**.
11. Negusse, S., Zetterberg, P., Händel, P., Phase-Noise Mitigation in OFDM by Best Match Trajectories. *IEEE Trans. Commun.*, 63, 5, 1712–1725, **2015**.
12. Dai, L., Wang, B., Yuan, Y., Han, S., Chih-lin, I., Wang, Z., Non-orthogonal multiple access for 5G: solutions, challenges, opportunities, and future research trends. *IEEE Commun. Mag.*, 53, 9, 74–81, **2015**.
13. Hussain, M. and Rasheed, H., Nonorthogonal Multiple Access for Next-Generation Mobile Networks: A Technical Aspect for Research Direction. *Wireless Commun. Mobile Comput.*, 2020, 1–17, **2020**.
14. Altabas, J.A., *et al.*, Nonorthogonal Multiple Access and Carrierless Amplitude Phase Modulation for Flexible Multiuser Provisioning in 5G Mobile Networks. *J. Lightwave Technol.*, 35, 24, 5456–5463, **2017**.
15. Singh, K., Wang, K., Biswas, S., Ding, Z., Khan, F.A., Ratnarajah, T., Resource Optimization in Full Duplex Non-Orthogonal Multiple Access Systems. *IEEE Trans. Wireless Commun.*, 18, 9, 4312–4325, **2019**.
16. Ding, Z., Fan, P., Poor, H.V., Random Beamforming in Millimeter-Wave NOMA Networks. *IEEE Access*, 5, 7667–7681, **2017**.
17. Udayakumar, E. and Krishnaveni, V., Interference and phase noise in millimeter wave MIMO-NOMA and OFDM systems for beyond 5G networks,

in: *Security and Privacy Schemes for Dense 6G Wireless Communication Networks*, pp. 349 –370, IET, United Kingdom, **2023**.

18. Easwaran, U. and Krishnaveni, V., Analysis of Phase Noise Issues in Millimeter Wave Systems for 5G Communications. *Wireless Pers. Commun.*, 126, 1601–1619, **2022**.
19. Udayakumar, E., Krishnaveni, V., Analysis of various Interference in Millimeter- Wave Communication Systems: A Survey. *Procd. of 10th IEEE International Conference on Computing, Communication and Networking Technologies*, pp. 1–5, **2019**.
20. Udayakumar, E. and Krishnaveni, V., A Review on Interference Management in Millimeter-Wave MIMO Systems for Future 5G Networks, in: *Innovations in Electrical and Electronics Engineering. Lecture Notes in Electrical Engineering*, Saini, H., Srinivas, T., Vinod Kumar, D., Chandragupta Mauryan, K. (Eds.), vol. 626, pp. 715–721, **2019**.
21. Chung, M. and LiuEdfors, L.O., Phase-Noise Compensation for OFDM Systems Exploiting Coherence Bandwidth: Modeling, Algorithms, and Analysis. *IEEE Trans. Wireless Commun.*, 21, 5, 3040–3056, **2022**.
22. Iradier, E., *et al.*, Advanced NOMA-Based RRM Schemes for Broadcasting in 5G mmWave Frequency Bands. *IEEE Trans. Broadcast.*, 68, 1, 143–155, **2022**.
23. Chauhan, A., Ghosh, S., Jaiswal, A., RIS Partition-Assisted Non-Orthogonal Multiple Access (NOMA) and Quadrature-NOMA With Imperfect SIC. *IEEE Trans. Wireless Commun.*, 22, 7, 4371–4386, **2023**.
24. Perdana, R.H.Y., Nguyen, T.-V., Pramitarini, Y., Shim, K., An, B., Deep Learning-based Spectral Efficiency Maximization in Massive MIMO-NOMA Systems with STAR-RIS. *2023 International Conference on Artificial Intelligence in Information and Communication (ICAIIC)*, Bali, Indonesia, pp. 644–649, **2023**.
25. Hancco, J., Quispe, A., Hilario-Tacuri, A., Analysis of bit error rate in NOMA network for M-users over AWGN channel. *2022 IEEE International Conference on Electronics, Electrical Engineering and Computing*, Lima, Peru, pp. 1–4, **2022**.

8

Generation of Key Predistribution Scheme Applying Quasi-Symmetric Designs and Bent Functions in the Wireless Sensor Network

Debashis Ghosh

Department of Mathematics, School of Engineering (SoE), UPES, Bidholi, Dehradun, Uttarakhand, India

Abstract

Due to various restrictions in wireless sensor networks (*WSN*), the unilateral pair-up, and the security of self-configured and infrastructure-free communication among the nodes, key predistribution techniques have lately become a leading research area. Across all other best practices, the implementation of a combinatorial tool provides a premier foundation for key distribution within terminals. The purpose of this study is to design a key distribution technique by utilizing a combinatorial design to effectively address not only the operational performance but also the security needs of the network. In our scheme, we use the attributes of triangle-free quasi-symmetric 2-designs (*TFQSD*) in key allocation across sensor nodes to minimize the storage capacity. The scheme is represented by a block graph known to be the strongly regular graph connected to *TFQSD*. The confidentiality of the designed network is investigated by analyzing the parameters of the graph based on Bent Boolean functions.

***Keywords*:** Key predistribution scheme, wireless sensor node, quasi-symmetric 2-designs, strongly regular graph, bent function, symmetric key cryptography

Email: debashis.ghosh@ddn.upes.ac.in

Subhabrata Barman, Santanu Koley and Subhankar Joardar (eds.) Next-Generation Systems and Secure Computing, (159–186) © 2025 Scrivener Publishing LLC

8.1 Introduction

8.1.1 Motivation

In the past few decades, the connections between mathematics and computer science have proven essential for the continuous development in both areas; mainly combinatorics and graph theory both require finite components that computers, by nature, manipulate. The key goal of combinatorial design theory's approach, to diverse computer problems, is to solve the computational complications involved in selecting, adopting, and describing a framework for minimum complexity. One notable aspect is the distribution of the key across the nodes in the aforementioned network, in prior instances. Here, under many constraints, one must manipulate the transmission of information through some security protocol among the nodes. Various parts of the wireless sensor network (*WSN*) include a large number of nodes, overhead communication, energy consumption, and collaborative processing among nodes optimized to be implemented by a class of combinatorial objects, such as covering array, Latin square, group divisible designs, graph designs, and balanced incomplete block designs (*BIBDs*). Because of the aforementioned factors, *WSNs* continue to draw research interest on a global scale. The notion of micro-sensing together with wireless connectivity among nodes generates the framework for an extensive variety of applications associated with military surveillance, residential, environment monitoring, healthcare, and other industrial applications. An enormous number of sensors are placed immediately at hostile locations where experiments are failing to execute, and they can considerably increase the volume and precision of scientific assessments in physical processes.

It is impractical for a large network to store all the keys securely at one end. Rather, the distribution of the key among nodes leads to the design symmetric key generation system; such a scheme was initiated by *Blom* [2 (*a*)]. Then, to reduce the storage capacity, *Mitchell and Piper* [1 (*g*)] introduced the key distribution center using a finite incidence structure and coined the key distribution pattern to minimize the storage space. These ultra-small autonomous devices equipped with short-range radio communication are not eligible for Diffie-Hellman, RSA, elliptic curve cryptography, or any other public key-based schemes [1 (q), (t), (w), 2 (b)]. For resistance to eavesdropping, we need to achieve a strong key agreement protocol, keeping in mind that storage capacity with limited bandwidth and energy differs from a block cipher system. Stream cipher possesses a quite favorable cryptosystem for having a fast encryption rate and a simple architecture with lesser complexity. Among all others, RC5 and A5 stream ciphers are generated by a 128-length LFSR with an 11-variable Boolean function. Boolean functions are preferred to design secure communication in this environment. The linear feedback shift registers, in stream cipher, use the Boolean function as a building block for the generation of a pseudo-random number sequence. This area of research has developed a lot in recent times through a series of works [1 (h), (e), 3 (a), (d), 5 (b)].

The vulnerability of cryptosystems to linear attacks can be mitigated by employing combiner functions that consist of Boolean functions with strong nonlinearity. Bent functions are a class of Boolean functions characterized by their high nonlinearity and autocorrelation, generating them is an enormous challenge. The aforementioned characteristics render bent functions highly beneficial in the development of cryptographic primitives, which are crucial for ensuring safe transmission in *WSN*s. The above features resist linear and differential attacks while communicating between nodes in *WSN*s. Among others, the transeunt triangle is employed as a tool for transforming a Boolean function into an algebraic normal form (*ANF*) to facilitate the determination of its characteristics. The balancedness property has also the capability to build a keystream that ensures the security of transmitted information in the *WSN*, along with both confidentiality and integrity of the message.

With the above, this article approaches developing a key predistribution (*KPD*) protocol using the eminent combinatorial design, triangle-free quasi-symmetric 2-designs, from its existing parameters for better and secure communication in the presence of the limitations in *WSN*s and analyzes the security aspect mathematically of the *KPD* scheme (*KPS*) using bent Boolean functions.

The expansion of *WSN* has been applied to both civilian and military operations. We are mainly interested in distributed ad hoc sensor networks, which are made up of a bunch of cheap sensor devices that have limited power, processing speed, data storage, and other features. Due to the aforementioned limitations and the extensive array of delicate applications, the matter of security has become a formidable concern for sensors in networks [1 (v)]. Traditional pairwise key setup methods that depend on complicated math operations related to large numbers are not useful and cannot even be feasible [1 (h)]. Hence, a mechanism has been proposed to provide secure interactions between nodes that transmit sensors and the subsequent transmission of messages to the ground station. This mechanism is commonly referred to as a *KPS*. During the past two decades and more, a series of scientific endeavors have focused on *KPS* for *WSN*s, and plenty of methods have been presented, taking into consideration various aspects. Three types of *KPD* approaches have been identified by researchers to address the issue of key setup before installation by assigning keys to sensor nodes: probabilistic [1 (j), (n), 2 (c)], deterministic [1 (c), (f), (i), (o), 2 (a), (d), (e), (f), 4], and hybrid [1 (d), (h)]. In this reference, we introduce a novel technique for WSN *KPD* that is reliable.

KPD framework allows you to designate the key ring to the corresponding nodes, based on prior deployment arrangements. These structures are mostly about finding a balance between the competing needs of using as little memory as possible, making sure that the network is always connected, and protecting against attackers who might break into nodes and get the stored keys. The aforementioned plan is composed of three distinct steps, namely, *KPD*, shared key identification, and establishing a path for cryptographic keys. Each sensing element is primarily equipped with a certain amount of keys that allocate a distinct key identification. Once the dispersed sensor nodes are deployed, the shared-key verification phase is initiated. During this phase, any pair of nodes inside the wireless communication range engage in a data swap by their respective lists of key identifiers. The purpose of this exchange is to identify and establish common keys between the nodes. In the event that there exists a shared collection of keys, individuals have the ability to select a specific set of values for the purpose of cryptographic conversation. The process of path-key implementation occurs when a duo terminal is unable to possess a shared key. The series of nodes is then unitedly coalesced into a path. To build a secure communication channel between node S_j and node S_i, it is necessary for node S_i to identify a path connecting with its neighbors. This path must satisfy the condition that any two adjacent nodes inside the area of the radio spectrum have a similar key. Hence, communications originating from node S_i may be sent safely to node S_j.

This study focuses on a novel KPS that utilizes combinatorial designs. The seminal research conducted by Campete and Yerner [1 (u)] presents a deterministic pairwise *KPS* that relies on symmetric designs together with generalized quadrangles. Efficient key allocation techniques may be achieved with *BIBDs*. Additionally, it was determined that the use of the combinatorial strategy yields enhanced connection by reducing key-chain dimensions. Further research in this regard may be observed [1 (k), (s), 2 (d), (f)].

In contrast, combinatorial design theory pertains to the organization of a collection of elements according to a predetermined set of principles. The constraints of design theory stipulated these guidelines [1 (j), (l), 3 (d)]. The analysis of these characteristics is conducted to examine designs. In the context of implementation within this domain, each node does not need to store the keys of all subsequent nodes. Consequently, the storehouse demand for the network's components is diminished.

The notion of the Internet of Things (IoT) is visible on everything likewise electronic gadgets, computers, digital machinery, and moving objects that are interconnected, accessible, operated, and sensed via the wide and dynamic structure of the Internet in the future. *WSN* scheme plays a substantial part in this aspect of the IoT that increases an extensive scope of applications through sensing and disseminating various information about our surroundings. During such communication, data need authenticity and scalability. Among all others, one of the most important applications is remote healthcare support, namely, chronic obstructive pulmonary disease. The device which detects it is fully automation-controlled by the *WSN* feature. The device sensed the data about the pulmonary condition, ventilation, and oxygen inhale-exhale with others, over a while. Acquiring the proper data and receiving it with authentication become a challenging task for medical practitioners. To avoid such issues, mutual authentication and secure transmission of data by a key agreement protocol in *WSN* are essential [1 (e), (i), (m), (u)]. Otherwise, from either end, the eavesdropper can temper the data and promote other attacks.

Our focus lies on the collection of parameters pertaining to triangle-free quasi-symmetric designs and their corresponding block graph having nice properties to establish a highly nonlinear Boolean function toward security.

The succeeding portions of this article are organized in the following sequential pattern: The second part of this study is all about the math behind it and shows how combinatorial design and the model of key distribution are related. Additionally, a study of prior literature pertaining to the *KPS* scheme is conducted. In section 8.3, we provide our proposed approach, which incorporates pertinent stages utilizing a quasi-symmetric design. In the subsequent part, we shall discuss the security concerns. Last, in section 8.5, the paper concludes by discussing future goals.

8.2 Background

In the year 1930, the topic of combinatorial design was first used in the planning of statistical studies. Then, a significant portion of significant progress in the field of design theory may be observed to their inspired by applications in coding theory and communication. Additionally, with close connections to geometry, algebra, number theory, and graph theory, combinatorial design approaches have been applied in a broad spectrum of other fields, including cryptography, Boolean functions, and authentication codes. For more information on various applications of combinatorial designs, one can refer to [3 (a), (b), 5 (a)].

8.2.1 Quasi-Symmetric 2-Design

Wireless communication opens up an extensive range of practical applications for combinatorial objects. Among all others, *BIBD* is the favorable incidence structure in this field.

8.2.1.1 Definition [3 (c)]

A finite incidence structure is a triplet $\Delta = (\chi, \mathcal{B}, \iota)$ where χ and $\mathcal{B}$ are non-empty finite sets and $\iota \subseteq \chi \times \mathcal{B}$. The sets χ and B are called the point set and the block set of Δ, respectively, and their elements are called points and blocks. ι is called the incidence relation between ϕ and B, provided $(\phi, \mathcal{B}) \in I$, we will say that point ϕ and block B in $\mathcal{B}$ are incident.

For a given incidence structure $\Delta = (\chi, \Lambda)$, counting in two ways gives the following equations:

$$\Sigma_{\phi\in\chi}\left(\tau_{\phi}\right) = \Sigma_{B\in\mathcal{B}}|B|$$

First, fix ϕ and count in two ways $(\psi, \mathcal{B})$ with $\psi \neq \phi$ and $\psi, \phi \in \mathcal{B}$, which gives another equation

$$\Sigma_{\substack{\psi\neq\phi \\ \psi\in\chi}} \mu(\phi,\psi) = \Sigma_{\substack{B\in B \\ \phi\in B}} (|B| - \zeta_{\phi}).$$

8.2.1.2 Definition [3 (e)]

Let $\Delta = (\chi, \mathcal{B}, \iota)$ be an incidence structure. The complementary incidence structure of Δ is $\Delta' = (\mathscr{B}, \chi, \iota')$ where $(\phi, \mathcal{B}) \in \iota'$ if and only if $(\phi, \mathcal{B}) \notin \iota$.

8.2.1.3 Definition [3 (e)]

Let $\Delta = (\chi, \mathcal{B}, \iota)$ be an incidence structure. The dual of an incidence structure is $\Delta = (\chi, \mathcal{B}, \iota^*)$, where $(\mathcal{B}, \phi) \in \iota^*$ if and only if $(\phi, \mathrm{B}) \in \iota$.

8.2.1.4 Definition [3 (d)]

An incidence structure $\Delta = (\chi, \mathscr{B})$ is called a $\tau - (\upsilon, \kappa, \mu)$ design if every τ-subset of χ occurs in exactly μ blocks, for $|\chi| = \upsilon$ and $|\mathscr{B}| = \rho$. The integers υ, κ, and μ are called the parameters of the τ-designs.

8.2.1.5 *Remark [3 (b)]*

For a τ – (υ, κ, μ) design, if $\tau = \kappa$ and $\mu = 1$, then it is to be known as a complete design.

8.2.1.6 *Remark [3 (b)]*

Now, a complete design is known to be a trivial design.

To be able to preclude these degenerative situations, we always assume the following:

$\upsilon > \kappa > \tau \geq 1$ and $\mu \geq 1$. Thus, the 2-design could be defined as follows.

8.2.1.7 *Definition [3 (b)]*

A design is an incidence structure (χ, $\mathscr{B}$), where $\mathscr{B}$ is the collection of equal length subset, where entries are taken from χ, known to be block, denoted by $\boldsymbol{B}$. The members of χ are regarded as varieties. BIBDs 2–(υ, ρ, τ, κ, μ) or 2-design meets the specified criteria:

i. $|\chi| = \upsilon$, $|\boldsymbol{B}| = \rho$.
ii. Every subset in $\mathscr{B}$ consists of precisely κ different varieties.
iii. Every variety in χ appears in τ Blocks.
iv. Every 2-subset of varieties in χ is inclusively Belongs to μ Check font members of $\mathscr{B}$.

8.2.1.8 *Lemma [1 (p)]*

The necessary condition that the parameters of a 2-design be satisfied are

$$\mu(\upsilon - 1) \equiv 0\left(mod\ (\kappa - 1)\right) \text{and}\ \upsilon\sigma \equiv 0\ (mod\ \kappa).$$

The above obvious prerequisites for the presence of a 2-design have been established to in addition serve as sufficient criteria with $\kappa = 3, 4,$ and 5, for every μ excluding $\upsilon = 15$, $\kappa = 5$, $\mu = 2$. Simultaneously, Wilson [1 (t)] showed that those necessary conditions are asymptotically sufficient. A few years later, Teirlinck [5 (d)] verified that significant τ-designs exist for every given value of τ, even when rendition blocks are included.

8.2.1.9 Example [1 (j)]

The well-known example of a ρ, 2 – (υ, κ, μ) design is 2 – ($n^2 + n + 1$, n + 1, 1) with $n \geq 2$. In particular, for n = 2, it is known as the Fano plane. Here each block contains 3 points that are in the same line or in a circle. The design can be represented by Figure 8.1.

8.2.1.10 Example

The complement of the design explained in *Example 2.9* is also a 2-design having parametric representation 2 – (7, 4, 2).

A BIBD (υ, ρ, σ, κ, μ) design having υ points like $p_1, p_2, p_3, \ldots, p_v$ and ρ blocks like $B_1, B_2, B_3, \ldots, B_\rho$ are represented of the given entity that is expressed through the utilization of an incidence matrix M = (m_{ij}) having dimension υ x b with entries 0 and 1, where m_{ij} = 1, if the ith variety belongs to the jth block, and 0 otherwise.

The particular incidence matrix M of Example 2.9 of the above Fano Plane is given by

$$M = \begin{pmatrix} 1 & 0 & 1 & 0 & 0 & 0 & 1 \\ 1 & 1 & 0 & 1 & 0 & 0 & 0 \\ 1 & 0 & 0 & 0 & 1 & 1 & 0 \\ 0 & 1 & 1 & 0 & 1 & 0 & 0 \\ 0 & 1 & 0 & 0 & 0 & 1 & 1 \\ 0 & 0 & 1 & 1 & 0 & 1 & 0 \\ 0 & 0 & 0 & 1 & 1 & 0 & 1 \end{pmatrix}$$

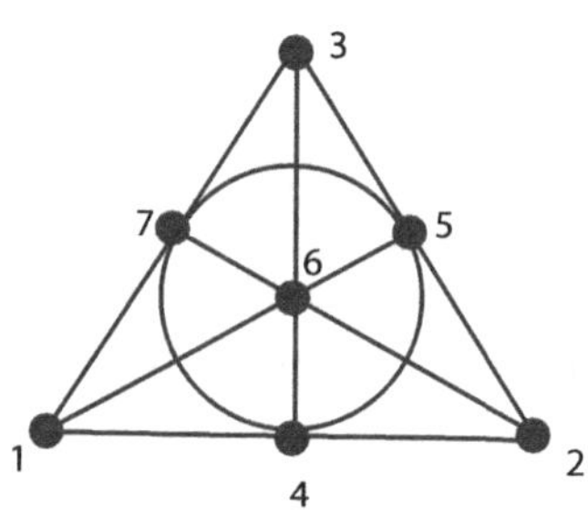

Figure 8.1 (7, 3, 1) Balanced incomplete block design.

8.2.1.11 Lemma [3 (d)]

The incidence matrix M of 2 – (υ, κ, μ) design satisfies

i. $MM^t = (\sigma - \mu)I + \mu J$

ii. $|MM^t| = (\sigma - \mu)^{(v-1)}\sigma\kappa$

8.2.1.12 Theorem (Fisher's Inequality) [1 (j)]

If a nontrivial 2 - (υ, ρ, σ, κ, μ) be exists with $2 \le \kappa < \upsilon$, then the number of blocks ρ must be greater than equal to the number of points υ.

8.2.1.13 Definition [3 (d)]

A 2 – (υ, κ, μ) design is called symmetric if $\upsilon = \rho$.

8.2.1.14 Result [3 (b)]

The following are equivalent for a 2 – (υ, κ, μ) design,

i. Δ is symmetric.
ii. $\sigma = \kappa$.
iii. Any two blocks intersect in μ points.
iv. The dual Δ^* of Δ is a 2-design.

Thus, any 2-design is said to be a symmetric design, if any two blocks meet a common number of points. This definition can be extended to define a new design.

For, every $0 \le \phi < \kappa$, ϕ is called a block intersection number if there exists B, $B' \in \boldsymbol{\mathcal{B}}$ such that $|B \cap B'| = \phi$. A symmetric design is a design such that $\rho = \mu_0 = \upsilon$ and $\sigma = \mu_1 = \kappa$ and any 2 blocks intersect in μ points. A subtle modification to the aforementioned concept would result in a broader scope that encompasses all symmetric designs. The inequality $\rho \ge \upsilon$ established in Fisher's work moves toward generalization. The intersection numbers are denoted as ϕ and ψ, with the assumption that $0 \le \phi < \psi < \kappa$. In this analysis, we will examine an ideal quasi-symmetric design, namely one in which both intersection numbers are positive and unequal i.e. both the intersection numbers are positive and not equal. An instance of quasi-symmetric design may be described as a symmetric design that incorporates supplementary blocks, which cross either at μ places or not at all. On the other hand, let Δ be a multiple of a 2 – (v, κ, μ) symmetric design. Then Δ is a quasi-symmetric 2-design with $\phi = \mu$ and $\psi = \kappa$ too [1 (k)]. To access comprehensive information about design theory, we recommend referring to [3 (e)].

8.2.1.15 *Definition [3 (e)]*

A 2 – (v, κ, μ) design is said to be a quasi-symmetric design if any two blocks from $\mathscr{B}$ intersect at two different numbers ϕ or ψ, with $\phi \neq \psi$.

Thus, the parameters (v, ρ, σ, κ, μ, ϕ, ψ) are considered to be the standard parameter of the QSD. The following are a few important examples to understand this design and its parameters.

8.2.1.16 *Example*

A 2 – (v, κ, 1) design having a number of blocks greater than the number of points would be a quasi-symmetric design, where any two blocks meet at either 0 or 1.

8.2.1.17 *Example [3 (e)]*

A multiple class of a symmetric 2 – (v, κ, μ) design Δ will be a quasi-symmetric 2-design having $\phi = \mu$ and $\psi = \kappa$.

8.2.1.18 *Example [3 (b)]*

The Witt 3 – (22, 6, 1) design which is the extension of PG(2, 4) is also a quasi-symmetric design having intersection numbers 0 and 2.

8.2.1.19 *Theorem [1 (a)]*

Let Δ be a quasi-symmetric 2 – (v, κ, μ) design with intersection numbers ϕ and ψ. Then,

i. $\psi - \phi$ divides $\kappa - \phi$ and $\sigma - \mu$.
ii. $\kappa\,(\sigma - 1)(\phi + \psi - 1) + \phi\ and (1 - \rho) = \kappa(\kappa - 1)(\mu - 1)$.
iii. if $\phi = 0$, then $(\sigma - 1)(\psi - 1) = (\kappa - 1)(\mu - 1)$.
iv. if Δ has no repeated blocks, then $\rho \leq \frac{v}{2}$.

v. if $\phi = 0$, then $\rho \leq \frac{\upsilon(\upsilon-1)}{k}$.
vi. if $\mu > 1$ and $\phi < \mu$.

Classification of the quasi-symmetric 2-designs is still a difficult open problem. A family of quasi-symmetric 2-designs is classified into various combinatorial designs. A list of classifications has been made with the help of the difference in the intersection number $z = \phi - \psi$ [1 (j), (p), (r)].

8.2.1.20 *Theorem*

For proper quasi-symmetric designs with non-zero intersection numbers ϕ, ψ, and $\mu > 1$,

i. A quasi-symmetric design with $z = \psi - \phi$ and $v \geq 2\kappa$. If $\phi \geq 1 + z + z^3$, then $\mu < \phi + 1 + z + z^3$. For a quasi-symmetric design with the difference of intersection number 1, the design has its parameters $\upsilon = \frac{(1+p)(2+p)}{2}$, $\rho = \frac{(2+m)(3+m)}{2}, \sigma = m+3, \kappa = m+1, \mu = 2, \phi = 1, \psi = 2$, and $m = 2, 3, \ldots$ or complement of one of these design or Δ is a design with parameters $\upsilon = 5$, $\rho = 10$, $\sigma = 6$, $\kappa = 3$, $\mu = 3$, $\phi = 1$, and $\psi = 2$.
ii. If the difference in the intersection numbers is 4, then there will only be finite numbers of quasi-symmetric design, provided that $3 < \phi < 68$. Still, many parameters of the design are needed to identify the existence or not of the design, and others are open to verify the parameters.

8.2.1.21 *Example*

To keep things simple, we take into account a specific design component:

$\upsilon = 22$
$\kappa = 6$
$\mu = 5$
$\sigma = 21$
$\rho = 77$

with ϕ = 0 and ψ = 2 being the number of common elements between two blocks. The computer search result displays the blocks as

$\mathcal{A}$ = {αςϖϱεϵ, αςζηξA, αςBCDE, αςFGHI, αςJKLM, αϖζBFI, αϖηCGK, αϖξDHL, αϖAEIM, αϱζCHM, αϱηBIL, αϱξEFK, αϱADGJ, αεζDIK, αεηEHJ, αεξBGM, αεACFL, αϵζEGL, αϵηDFM, αϵξCIJ, ςϖηBHM, αϵABHK, ςϖζCIL, ςϖηBHM, ςϖξEGJ, ςϖADFK, ςϱζBGK, ςϱηCFJ, ςϱξDIM, ςϱAEFL, ςεζEFM, ςεηDGL, ςεξCHK, ςεABIJ, ςϵζDHJ, ςϵηEIK, ςϵξBFL, ςϵACGM, ϖϱζηDE, ϖϱξABC, ϖϱFGLM, ϖϱHIJK, ϖεζAGH, ϖεηξFI, ϖεBEKL, ϖεCDJM, ϖϵζξKM, ϖϵηAJL, ϖϵBDGI, ϖϵCEFH, ϱεηAKM, ϱεζξJL, ϱεBDFH, ϱεCEGI, ϱϵζAFI, ϱϵBEJM, ϱϵCDKL, εϵζηBC, ϱϵηξGH, εϵξADE, εϵFGJK, εϵHILM, ζηFHKL, ζηGIJM, ζξBEHI, ζξCDFG, ζABDLM, ζACEJK, ηξCELM, ηABEFG, ηξBDJK, ηACDHI, ξAFHJM, ξAGIKL, BCKIKM, BCGHJL, DEFIJL, DEGHKM }

8.2.2 Strongly Regular Graph

The graphical representation is one of the modest ways to simplify the quasi-symmetric designs. The most recommended block graph Γ is the strongly regular graph. Here, vertices of Γ are represented by the blocks of the design. Two vertices of the graph are considered close if they have a common set of ψ connectors. The attributes (v, a, c, and d) of Γ are associated with the parameters of quasi-symmetric designs. Specifically, v represents the number of vertices, a represents the degree, c represents the number of adjacent vertices, and d represents the number of adjacency vertices that are nonadjacent [1 (s)]. Here, we are not considering the case of triviality neither the null graph nor the complete graph.

$$a = \frac{\kappa\ (\sigma - 1) + \phi\ (1 - \rho)}{(\psi - \phi)},$$

$$c = a + \mu_1\ \mu_2 + \mu_1 + \mu_2,$$

$$d = a + \mu_1\ \mu_2,$$

$$\mu_1 = \frac{\sigma - \mu - \kappa + \phi}{\psi - \phi},$$

$$\mu_2 = \frac{\phi - \kappa}{\psi - \phi}.$$

The (0, 1) adjacency matrix N of the strongly regular graph Γ is defined with parameters (υ, a, c, and d) and satisfies the following equation:

$$NJ = aJ$$
$$N^2 = aI + cA + d(J - I - N).$$

The integral values of a, c, d, and J denote the matrix of the same order of A with all 1s.

8.2.2.1 Lemma [3 (b)]

The complementary graph $\{\bar{\Gamma}\}$ of $\Gamma(\upsilon$, a, c, d) is also a strongly regular graph having parameters ($\bar{\upsilon}, \bar{a}, \bar{c}$, and $\bar{d}$), where $\bar{a} = \upsilon - 1 - a$, $\bar{c} = \upsilon - 2a + d - 2$, and $\bar{d} = \upsilon - 2a + c$.

The two matrices incidence and adjacency of the design are denoted by M and N, respectively. Subsequently, with these elements, a matrix denoted as P may be constructed as

$$P = \begin{pmatrix} 0 & M \\ M' & N \end{pmatrix}$$

A strongly regular graph Γ would be regarded as triangle-free if and only if the value of c vanishes, indicating that the graph does not include any cycles of length three. A design that exhibits quasi-symmetry is said to be "triangle-free" if its counterpart, denoted as $\bar{\Gamma}$, does not include any triangles. Alternatively, this may be expressed as the design having no three mutually disjoint blocks.

8.2.2.2 Theorem [3 (e)]

Let Δ be a quasi-symmetric design ($\upsilon, \rho, \sigma, \kappa$, and μ) with block intersections ϕ and ψ (ϕ ≠ ψ). Let M and N be the incidence matrix and adjacency matrix of the design Δ. Let j_υ and 0_ρ be row vectors of all 1s and 0s, respectively. Then, P will represent a strongly regular graph iff Δ has parameters $\upsilon = (\psi^2 + 3\psi + 1), \rho = (\psi^2 + 2\psi - 1)(\psi^2 + 3\psi + 1), \sigma = (\psi + 1)(\psi^2 + 2\psi - 1)$, $\kappa = \psi(\psi + 1), \mu = \psi(\psi + 1) - 1, \phi = 0, \psi$. Furthermore, the merely strongly regular graph P that comes out is sometimes referred to as "negative

Latin square graphs" $NL_{\psi}(\psi^2+3\psi)$ with parameters $((\psi^2+3\psi)^2,$ $\psi(\psi^2+3\psi+1), 0,$ and $\psi(\psi+1))$.

8.2.2.3 *Example*

Consider the design Δ with parameters (υ, κ, μ, ρ, and σ) = (22, 6, 5, 77, and 21) is a quasi-symmetric design as in Example 2.21. Its corresponding parameter of the strongly regular graph is $\rho = (\psi^2+3\psi)^2 = 100$, $a = \psi(\psi^2+3\psi+1) = 22$, $\sigma = 0$, $d = \psi(\psi+1) = 6$. Since it contains no cycle of length 3, To avoid such issues, this line graph additionally serves as an example of a triangle-free strongly regular graph. The corresponding diagram is given in Figure 8.2.

8.2.2.4 *Theorem [1 (b)]*

For any triangle-free quasi-symmetric design, Δ the following hold good,

i. ψ divides κ;
ii. let $\kappa = m\psi$, then $2 \le m \le (\psi + 1)$;
iii. m = 2 if and only if Δ is a Hadamard 3-design;
iv. for a fixed ψ, there are only finitely many triangle-free quasi-symmetric designs Δ with ψ as the positive block intersection number.

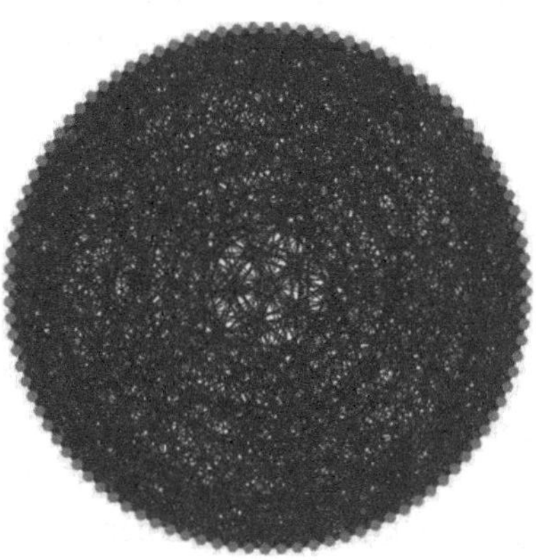

Figure 8.2 Figure of tf-SRG.

8.2.3 Background of Key Predistribution Scheme

Prior to the sensor network implementation, the *KPD* system, which depends on combinatorial designs, decides the number of selected keys that are set to the key chain. The aforementioned study domain has gained prominence as a result of the organization of items inside finite sets into subsets that adhere to diverse features. Eschenauer and Gligor [2 (c)] proposed the fundamental random *KPD* method in 2002. In this proposed framework, setting up a shared key across both nodes will occur exclusively if they possess a certain quantity of shared keys. Every node receives a key ring with k number of keys picked at arbitrary from an extensive collection S. These keys are made through a process called "key derivation." If two entities next to each other have no fewer than one shared key after the launch phase, they will make a safe connection and then figure out their session secret key. This session's hidden key comes from the shared key which has already been mentioned. If two nodes next to each other do not share keys, they need to set up secure paths made up of reliable connections that go in order. The aforementioned methodology exhibits characteristics of both CPU and energy efficiency but necessitates a substantial allocation of memory space for the storage of the key ring. Furthermore, in the event the network nodes undergo gradual corruption, it is possible for the attacker to potentially get access to a significant portion or the entirety of the global key pool. Consequently, a significant quantity of linkages will be affected.

In 2004, Camtepe and Yener proposed a deterministic method *KPD* structure, which utilized projective planes, generalized quadrangles, and symmetric BIBDs. They conducted an analysis of the scheme's security and interconnectivity aspects, including scalability and durability. At that juncture, Lee and Stinson (2004) separately employed the notion of transversal design for *KPD* in *WSN* [2 (d)]. Through the analysis and use of the architecture put out by Lee and Stinson, scholars are afforded the opportunity to make alterations to the needs for robustness, connection, and storage of the *KPS*. The authors also explain how the robustness of the system may be enhanced by integrating a transversal design with Blom's approach [2 (a)] in 1984 for constructing *KPDs*, which they refer to as a "multiple space scheme."

Chakrabarti *et al.* [1 (h)] proposed another technique that involves the random selection of a certain number of blocks, denoted as ϕ which are subsequently combined to create a novel node. The blocks have been selected in a manner that ensures the absence of an internode connection. In certain instances, because of random selection, it was inevitable for internode communication to arise. The researchers made adjustments to their network by incorporating the MOVE function, which aimed to enhance the level of connectedness among various pairings of nodes. The operation denoted as MOVE enhances connectivity by facilitating the exchange of blocks between a maximum-connected pair and a zero-linked pair.

Subsequently, a range of combinatorial entities was employed in the development of KPDs to enhance both performance and security in load distribution. Notably, partially *BIBD* and Reed-Solomon codes were proposed by Ruj and Roy in 2007 [4], while Dong *et al.* suggested the utilization of orthogonal arrays and 3-designs in 2008, among other contributions. In addition to these strategies, it is crucial to establish interconnected networks to minimize the number of hops and mitigate the possible dangers associated with node capture. Random techniques alone cannot provide the desired level of network connectivity. Deterministic protocols are chosen for security applications in networks to guarantee a high level of connectedness.

8.2.4 Bent Functions

We are interested in a family of strongly regular graphs associated with a special type of Boolean function. The study focuses on Boolean functions that exclusively embrace input from constant weight arrays earlier for various aspects [3 (a)].

F_2^n denotes n copies of F_2, which represents a vector space over the finite field having two elements. The Hamming weight of any member $u = (u_1, u_2, \cdots, u_n) \in F_2^n$ denoted by $w_H(u)$ defines the cardinality of its support set $\{i = 1,\dots,n \mid u_i = 1\}$. $(u \cdot v)$ denotes the inner product between two vectors u, v in F_{2^n}, for instance, their usual inner product defined by $u \cdot v = \Sigma_{i=1}^n u_i v_i$ (calculated in F_2). Given some basis of the n-dimensional vector space F_{2^n} over F_2, there is a natural bijective F_2-linear mapping from F_{2^n} to the Galois field F_{2^n}.

Functions from F_{2^n} to F_2 are known to be the Boolean functions in n variables.

On generalization, for any prime and prime power number q,

$$\phi = exp(i\frac{2\pi}{q})$$

is the q-th root of unity in C, for $i = \sqrt{-1}$.

Then, a function from F_{q^n} of n tuples to F_q presented by

$$\mathfrak{F}(w) = \frac{1}{\sqrt{q^n}} \sum_{\psi \in F_{q^n}} \phi^{(f(\psi)-w.\psi)} \quad w \in F_{q^n},$$

where $\mathfrak{F}(w)$ signifies the Fourier transformation of f(ψ). The case of multivariate representation of affine Boolean function over F_{q^n} is in the form of

$$a_1\psi_1 + \ldots + a_n\psi_n + \zeta \ (modulo\ q),$$

where $a \in F_{q^n}$ and $\zeta \in \mathrm{F}_q$.

Multiple univariate visualizations, known as trace or polynomial representations, can be used to describe Boolean functions. These formats are not necessarily unique and rely on the identification among the vector space F_q^n and the field F_{q^n}. Every Boolean function may be expressed uniquely as a polynomial in a single variable ψ, where ψ belongs to the field F_q^n, in the following form: We also have the trace function

$$Tr_1^n(a\psi) = \psi + \psi^2 + \psi^{2^2} + \ldots + \psi^{2^{n-1}}$$

which gives the elementary member of the corresponding field F_{q^n}. Thus, with the help of a bivariate representation of the trace function, we may design a bent function when n is even. Such could be identified as $F_{q^{n/2}} \times F_{q^{n/2}}$.

8.2.4.1 *Definition [1 (t)]*

The Walsh-Hadamard transform of a Boolean function f of n variables is an integer-valued function on F_{q^n} is given by

$$\mathrm{W}_f(y) = \Sigma_{x \in F_{q^n}} (-1)^{<x,y> \oplus f(x)}, \text{ for any } y \in F_q^n$$

This transformation helps a Boolean function to determine uniquely. For further implementation of the Boolean function, we consider our field of the element from F_{2^n}.

8.2.4.2 *Definition [3 (b)]*

The *nonlinearity* of a Boolean function f in n variable, denoted by N_f, is defined to be the Hamming distance from the function to the set of all affine functions

$$N_f = \min_{a \in F_{2^n}, b \in F_{2^n}} dist(f, l_{a,b}).$$

where $l_{a,b} = \langle a, x \rangle \oplus b$ is an affine function.

A Boolean function in n variables is referred to as maximal nonlinear when the parameter N_f achieves its maximum value. For an even n, the maximal nonlinearity of the function is attained at $2^{(n-1)} - 2^{\left(n/2\right)-1}$. Still, the fact is open for odd n.

A class of Boolean functions that attained the maximal possible nonlinearity for an even number of variables is known to be the *Bent* function. This class of mathematical objects is represented by Hadamard matrices, block schemes, a set of subspaces of a Boolean cube, strongly regular graphs, and bent rectangles [5 (c)]. It is known that there are exactly $88{,}965{,}425{,}430{,}528 \equiv 2^{32.3}$ and $2^9 \times 1938878696600280670034880102 40$ bent functions in two, four, six, and eight variables, respectively. This class of functions reveals some of the best-known cryptographic properties to prevent the amplification of attacks.

8.2.5 Association Between Key Allocation Employing Quasi-Symmetric Designs

After determining the network dimension (ρ) and the number of keys per node (κ), the central authority selects a regular, consistent structure with a rank κ, denoted as (X, $\mathcal{A}$) which consists of precisely ρ blocks. The key-ring space is denoted as (X, $\mathcal{A}$) in the design. The keyring space serves as a KPD strategy for a network consisting of ρ nodes.

The sensor nodes that belong to this are indicated by $\upsilon_1, \upsilon_2, \upsilon_3, \ldots, \upsilon_\rho$. Let

$$X = \{x_i \mid 1 \le i \le \upsilon\}$$

and let

$$\mathcal{A} = \{A_j | 1 \leq j \leq \rho\}.$$

The elements in set X that are denoted by the symbol υ can be paired with a set of υ keys using a one-to-one correspondence. This correspondence is established as follows: A key, represented as K_i, is selected randomly and uniformly from a designated key space, where $1 \leq i \leq \upsilon$, say S (e.g. $S = \{0, 1\}^{256}$).

Then, for each $j, 1 \leq j \leq \rho$, the sensor node υ_j receives the set of κ keys

$$\{K_i : i \in A_j\}.$$

In this context, it can be observed that each point ϕ_i serves as a key selector for K_j, while each block A_j is responsible for identifying the key set that is allocated to the node υ_j. The aforementioned technique has a resemblance to the Eschenauer-Gligor scheme described in [2 (c)], whereby the key-ring space is defined as the subset of all κ-subsets derived from the set X. The model's version is characterized by the absence of three mutually disconnected blocks, meaning that the complement of the block graph does not contain any triangles. This feature effectively decreases the storage cost of the network in question. Hence, Table 8.1 provided below illustrates the relationship between the design and KPS. Table 8.1 shows the framework between quasi-symmetric design with key allocation parameters.

The effectiveness of a sensor network can be explained by the following two aspects:

Table 8.1 Parameter allocation between quasi-symmetric designs and key space generation.

Quasi-symmetric designs		**Key allocation**
Point set	→	Key space *S*
Block	→	key ring
# Blocks (*B*)	→	# key chain or # key ring, # Nodes
# points in a block	→	# K_i in key chain
# Blocks that a point is in	→	# Key chains that a key is in
Two Blocks adjacent for *y* points in common	→	Two nodes communicate for *y* keys are common

i. The connectivity probability, denoted by $p_{connect}$, is a measure of the likelihood that a link exists between any two sensor nodes. It is defined as the chance that a pair of sensor nodes have a specific number of common keys, denoted as ψ. The measurement of the sensor network's efficacy is determined by this.

ii. The probability of failure, denoted as P(fail(1)), is defined as the likelihood that a sensor node is identified as a compromised node, resulting in the discontinuation of all keys possessed by that node within the sensor network. Then, the probability of a failing network is given by

$$fail(1) = \frac{The\ lost\ connectives}{The\ connectives\ remains},$$

where N denotes network size.

Two nodes possess a minimum of ψ shared keys, and they utilize all of these shared keys to calculate their bilateral key. This calculation is accomplished using a suitable key derivation mechanism.

8.3 Our Proposed Scheme

The distribution of keys among the sensor nodes has been achieved by the implementation of a combinatorial design termed a quasi-symmetric 2-design. This design is a small extension of a symmetric design. Consider a combinatorial design (X, $\boldsymbol{B}$) where X is a set of cardinality v and $\mathcal{B}$ is a collection of blocks. Each block B' in $\mathcal{B}$ contains κ pieces from X. A design is referred to as a 2 – (v, κ, μ) design if every pair of elements from the set X appears in exactly μ blocks and each element of X belongs to σ number of blocks. In addition to that, if any distinct blocks meet at one of two unique positions, denoted as ϕ and ψ, then the design is referred to as a quasi-symmetric 2-design. In this study, we examine the quasi-symmetric design characterized by a nontrivial overlapping number, specifically where the variable ψ is greater than ϕ and both variables are more than or equal to zero.

8.3.1 Network Generation

8.3.1.1 Lemma

Let (ϕ, B) be a nonflag of a triangle-free Δ and suppose $\alpha(\phi, B)$ is the number of blocks on ϕ not meeting B. Then,

$$\alpha(\phi, B) = \sigma - m\mu,$$

for any integer m, its value is restricted by $2 \leq m \leq \psi + 1$.

8.3.1.2 Theorem

Let Δ be a quasi-symmetric design with block intersection numbers 0 and ψ. Suppose Δ has no three mutually disjoint blocks. Then, the parameters of Δ can be expressed as follows:

$$\upsilon = \psi(\psi^2 + 3\psi + 1), \qquad \rho = (\psi^2 + 2\psi - 1)(\psi^2 + 3\psi + 1),$$
$$\sigma = (\psi + 1)(\psi^2 + 2\psi - 1), \quad \kappa = \psi(\psi + 1), \quad \mu = \psi^2 + \psi - 1.$$

8.3.1.3 Remark

The above Δ becomes a triangle-free quasi-symmetric 2-design. With the help of this design, we can construct a *KPD* scheme.

Let us consider a sensor network of ρ nodes, resulting in ρ key chains. The maximum capacity of each key chain is limited to κ, with the keys being selected from a pool denoted as X. Given that each key is present in r blocks. The connection between the nodes is established when there is an exact match of ψ keys; otherwise, no key chain is initiated.

8.3.2 Algorithm of the Proposed Key Predistribution Protocol

Require: Choose ψ an integer ≥ 2

Step 1. Calculate $\upsilon = \psi(\psi^2 + 3\psi + 1)$.
Step 2. Calculate $\kappa = \psi(\psi+1)$.
Step 3. Calculate $\rho = (\psi^2 + 2\psi - 1)(\psi^2 + 3\psi + 1)$.
Step 4. Establish $\sigma = \upsilon - 1$ and $\mu = \kappa - 1$.
Step 5. Calculate μ_1 and μ_2.
Step 6. Compute $a = -2 + \rho + \mu_1\mu_2$.

Step 7. Compute $c = a + \mu_1 + \mu_2 + \mu_1\mu_2$.
Step 8. Generate a connection across both nodes, given that they possess ψ a few shared keys.

8.3.3 Calculation of Storage Overhead of the Proposed Scheme

In the context of the suggested method involving triangle-free quasi-symmetric design, which utilizes a highly regular graph of uniform rank κ, it is necessary to equip each node with a key ring that corresponds to a specific block from the design. Therefore, it can be observed that every node is initially populated with a total of $\psi(\psi + 1)$ keys. The amount of memory needed to hold keys may be calculated as l. $\psi(\psi + 1)$, where l represents the size of the key.

8.3.4 Measurement of Network Scalability of the Proposed Scheme

The overall amount of potential key rings in the context of the triangle-free quasi-symmetric design-based scheme may be expressed as $\rho = (\psi^2 + 2\psi - 1)(\psi^2 + 3\psi + 1)$. This value represents the upper limit of supported nodes. We could not be able to increase by increasing the scalability of the network by introducing more nodes randomly, then it will overflow the upper bound of the network scalability limit.

8.3.5 Session Key Sharing Scheme of the Proposed Methodology

In the context of quasi-symmetric design sketching, it is shown that each key is utilized in precisely $\psi(\psi^2 + 3\psi + 1)$ key rings out of the total $(\psi^2 + 2\psi - 1)$ $(\psi^2 + 3\psi + 1)$ potential key rings. Let us imagine two nodes, denoted as ϕ_1 and ϕ_2, that are picked in a random manner. Node ϕ_1 is initially equipped with a key ring A_{ϕ_1} containing ψ $(\psi + 1)$ distinct keys, whereas node ϕ_2 is also equipped with a key ring A_{ϕ_2} with the same number of keys. These two nodes may either lack a shared key or possess a certain amount of common keys, denoted as ψ. Consequently, the adjacency of nodes is contingent upon the presence of a shared set of ψ keys. In the context of strongly regular graphs, it is observed that two nearby nodes possess precisely c shared neighbors. Once more, the symbol $\bar{\Gamma}$ is used to denote triangle-free quasi-symmetric designs with the aforementioned parameters. It is worth noting that these designs also give rise to a negative

Latin square graph, in which two adjacent nodes do not have any common neighbors. This is due to the fact that a triangle-free highly regular graph does not include any cycles of length 3. In contrast, it can be shown that two nonadjacent nodes possess a total of ψ (ψ^2 + 4 ψ + 2) common neighbors. These resources will aid in the construction of the key path.

Every key is present in (υ – 2) additional key rings. It is observed that the occurrence of each pair of keys is exclusively confined to ($\psi^2 + \psi - 1$) blocks. Consequently, the blocks encompassing ψ + 1 distinct keys of A_{ϕ_1} are entirely separate from one another. Consequently, every node is associated with precisely one key among a total of $\psi^3 + 3\psi^2 + \psi - 2$ nodes, out of the $\psi^3 + 3\psi^2 + \psi - 1$ alternative nodes available. Hence, the overall amount of links formed for a given node may be expressed as ψ (ψ + 1).

Let $p_{connect}$ be the chance that two nodes share precisely ψ keys in order to establish a safe connection.

$$p_{connect} = \frac{\psi(\psi+1)}{\rho}.$$

8.3.6 Resiliency Against Random Node Compromise of the Proposed Scheme

The issue of security in WSNs is of significant importance. The security issues present in WSNs arise from a range of constraints, such as limited storage capacity, low processing power, a high volume of network nodes, and their utility in such communication technology. In this study, we have conducted an evaluation of a novel scheme with regard to its ability to withstand node collusion and selective node capture attacks. However, the concept of resilience is in conflict with the likelihood of key sharing. This is due to the fact that when many blocks are affected, a greater number of keys are shared across the nodes in the event of a block breach. A node is considered compromised when it is actively implicated in node collusion, such as when it is seized by an external attacker or reprogrammed to inflict impairment upon the altogether network. Mathematically, the computation of failing the distribution of data among the nodes that are not in compromised mode may be computed as

fail(1) = The number of links discontinued because of s number of nodes that are compromised /(((N-s) (N-s-1))/2)

Table 8.2 Comparison data for the resiliency of the proposed network.

ψ	ρ	υ	κ	s	$p_{connect}$	fail(1)
4	667	116	20	7	0.2121	0.00064
5	1394	205	30	11	0.2386	0.00034
6	2585	330	42	16	0.2615	0.00020
7	4402	497	56	27	0.3456	0.00015
8	7031	712	72	37	0.3809	0.00011
9	8941	799	94	42	0.4460	0.00010

In the event of selective node acquisition beatings, the attacker gains control of nodes whose encryption keys are not yet compromised. During the phase of shared key discovery, only node identities are transmitted, while key identifiers are not exchanged. Therefore, the attacker is unable to determine which key IDs are included within each node at any given point. Therefore, the attacker is unable to get any information through the utilization of this technique.

Table 8.2 presents a compilation of probability values $p_{connect}$ and fail (1) of our scheme.

8.4 Conclusion

In this article, we may summarize that every key management strategy possesses both advantages and disadvantages. This study presents a novel and scalable key predistribution strategy for WSNs. In this study, we employ the triangle-free quasi-symmetric design for the purpose of enhancing resilience, marking the first instance of its utilization. Our study demonstrates that by employing a fundamental mapping technique from quasi-symmetric designs to a key predistribution strategy, it is possible to obtain a significant enhancement in network scalability while simultaneously improving the likelihood of key-sharing. The suggested proposal gives the idea of an improved quasi-symmetric design–based architecture that introduces a novel key management technique with the advantages of high network scalability and a favorable key-sharing probability. Analytical computations were performed to demonstrate that our technique effectively improves network scalability while maintaining strong overall performance. In further research, we intend to further investigate the analysis of our parameter selection to include a class of rectified combinatorial design in order to provide values that offer the optimal balance. Moreover, this investigation offers several opportunities to effectively utilize the limited resources of WSNs and enhance network usage securely.

References

1. (Journal articles) (a) Baartmans, A. and Shrikhande, M.S., Designs with no three mutually disjoint blocks. *Discrete Math.*, 40, 129–139, **1982**.
 (b) Blondeau, C. and Nyberg, K., Perfect nonlinear functions and cryptography. *Finite Fields Appl.*, 32, 120–147, **2015**.
 (c) Carlet, C., Meaux, P., Rotella, Y., Boolean functions with restricted input and their robustness; application to the flip cipher. *IACR Trans. Symm. Crypto.*, 3, 192–227, **2017**.
 (d) Carlet, C. and Mesnager, S., Combinatorial design of key distribution mechanisms for wireless sensor networks. *Int. J. Inf. Coding Th.*, 1, 133–148, **2010**.
 (e) Ding, C. and Tang, C., Combinatorial t-designs from special functions. *Crypto. Comm.*, 12, 5, 1011–1033, **2020**.
 (f) Ding, C. and Li, C., Infinite families of 2-designs and 3-designs from linear codes. *Discrete Math.*, 340, 2415–2431, **2017**.
 (g) Mitchell, C.J. and Piper, F.C., Key storage in secure networks. *Discrete Appl. Math*, 21, 215–228, **1988**.
 (h) Chakrabarti, D., Maitra, S., Roy, B.K., A key pre-distribution scheme for wireless sensor networks merging blocks in combinatorial design. *Int. J. Inf. Sec.*, 5, 2, 105–114, **2006**.
 (i) Ghosh, D. and Pal, J., New Approach of Deterministic Key Predistribution Scheme Using Triangle Free Quasi Symmetric Designs. *Appl. Appl. Math*, 14, 1, 188–198, **2019**.
 (j) Ghosh, D. and Dey, L.K., On some parametric classification of Quasi-Symmetric 2-Designs. *Tamkang J. Math*, 46, 3, 269–280, **2015**.
 (k) Liu, D. and Ning, P., Establishing pairwise keys in distributed sensor networks. *Comput. Commun. Secur.*, 52–61, **2003**.
 (l) Hanani, H., Balanced incomplete block designs and related designs. *Discrete Math.*, 11, 255–369, **1975**.
 (m) Dong, J.W., Pei, D.Y., Wang, X.L., A class of key pre-distribution schemes based on orthogonal arrays. *J. Comput. Sci. Tech.*, 23, 5, 825–831, **2008**.
 (n) Xue, K., Ma, C., Hong, P., Ding, R., A temporal-credential-based mutual authentication and key agreement scheme for wireless sensor networks. *J. Netw. Comput. Appl.*, 36, 1, 316–323, **2013**.

(o) Das, M.L., Two-factor user authentication in wireless sensor networks. *IEEE Trans. Wireless Commun.*, 8, 3, 1086–1090, **2009**.
(p) Shrikhande, M.S., A survey of some problems in combinatorial designs — A matrix approach. *Linear Algebra Appl.*, 79, 215–247, **1986**.
(q) Olsen, J., Scholtz, R., Welch, L., Bent-function sequences. *IEEE Trans. Inform. Theory*, 28, 6, 858–864, **1982**.
(r) Pawale, R.M., Quasi-symmetric designs with a fixed difference of block intersection numbers. *J. Combin. Des.*, 15, 1, 49–60, **2007**.
(s) Kavut, S., Maitra, S., Tang, D., Construction and search of balanced boolean functions on even number of variables towards excellent auto correlation profile. *Des. Codes Cryptogr.*, 87, 2-3, 261–276, 2019.
(t) Mitra, S., Mukhopadhyay, S., Dutta, R., A group-based deterministic key pre-distribution scheme for wireless sensor network. *Int. J. @ Wireless Mob. Compt.*, 7, 5, 435–447, **2014**.
(u) Camtepe, S.A. and Yener, B., Combinatorial design of key distribution mechanisms for wireless sensor networks. *ACM Trans. Netw.*, 15, 2, 346–358, **2007**.
(v) Du, W., Deny, J., Han, Y.S., Varshney, P., Katz, J., Khalili, A., A pairwise key pre-distribution scheme for wireless sensor networks. *ACM Trans. Inf. Syst. Sec.*, 8, 2, 228–258, **2005**.
(w) Zhou, Y., Fany, Y., Zhany, Y., Security wireless sensor networks: A survey. *IEEE Commun. Surv. Tut.*, 10, 1–4, 6–28, **2008**.

2. (Conference proceedings) (a) Blom, R., *Proceeding of EUROCRYPT*, pp. 335–338, **1984**.
(b) Blundo, C., Santis, A.D., Herzberg, A., Kutten, A., Vaccaro, U., Yung, M., Perfectly-secure key distribution for dynamic conference. *740*, 471–486, **1992**.
(c) Eschenauer, L. and Gligor, V.B., *Proceedings of the 9th ACM Conference on Computer and Communications Security*, Washington, DC, USA, pp. 41–47, **2002**.
(d) Lee, J. and Stinson, D.R., *Proc. 11th International Workshop, SAC*, pp. 294–307, **2004**.
(e) Di Pietro, R., Mancini, L.V., Mei, A., Panconesi, A., *Proc. of the 2nd ACM SASN workshop*, pp. 53–58, **2004**.
(f) Shafiei, H., Mehdizadeh, A., Khonsari, A., OuldKhaoua, M., *Proc of the IEEE "GLOBECOM"*, **2008**.

3. (Books) (a) Carlet, C., Cambridge Univ. Press, Cambridge, U.K., **2021**.
(b) Colbourn, C.J. and Dinitz, J.H., *Chap: Quasi-symmetric Designs*, 2nd, M.S. Shrikhande (Ed.), pp. 578–582, CRC Press, New York, USA, **2010**.
(c) Shrikhande, M.S. and Sane, S.S., *London Math. Soc. Lecture Notes 164*, Cambridge University Press, **1991**.
(d) Wilson, R.M., pp. 19–49, Academic Press, New York, **1984**.
(e) Cameron, P.J. and Van Lint, J.H., *London Math. Soc. Lecture Note Series*, Cambridge University Press, vol. 43, **1980**.

4. (Edited Books) Ruj, S. and Roy, B., *ISPA, Lecture Notes in Computer Science*, Springer, vol. 4742, pp. 431–445, **2007**.
5. (Website) (a) Knuth, D.E., The art of computer programming, **2020**, Vol.4–Pre-fascicle 8A. Available at https://www-cs-faculty.stanford.edu/~knuth/fasc8a.ps.gz.
(b) Papaioannou, M., Karageorgou, M., Mantas, G., Sucasas, V., Essop, I., Rodriguez, J., Lymberopoulos, D., *Transaction on Emerging Telecommunication Technology*, Wiley, **2020**, Online, https://doi.org/10.1002/ett.4049.
(c) Tokareva, N.N., Generalizations of bent functions. A survey. *J. Appl. Ind. Math.*, 5, 1, 110–129, **2011**. Available also on Cryptology ePrint Archive, report 2011/111.
(d) Teirlinck L., Non-trivial t–designs without repeated blocks exist for all t, Discrete Math, 65, 301–311, 1985.

9

Enhanced Security Measures Within the ITS Infrastructure Through the Application of Machine Learning Algorithms for Anomaly Detection

Shiplu Das[1]*, Soumi De[2], Ananya Ghosh[2], Sovraj Dey[2] and Tania Bhattacharjee[2]

[1]*Department of Computer Science and Engineering, Adamas University, West Bengal, India*
[2]*Department of Computer Science and Engineering, Brainware University, West Bengal, India*

Abstract
Intelligent Transportation Systems (ITSs) have been advancing in recent years, improving traffic management, vehicular accidents, congested roads, etc. This study proposes the open nature of ITS as a wireless technology, considering its security and privacy challenges. Scalability, privacy, computational cost, communication overhead, latency, and other types of security assaults have all been considered when categorizing security and privacy methods in ITS and their limits. This collaborative approach, based on group feedback, is advantageous for creating a transport system for the future. In this study, using techniques such as Machine Learning, Traffic simulation, and Anonymization, the work of ITS is enhanced. This poll has identified several issues with intelligent transport systems and has suggested crowd-intelligent remedies. This study explored the application of machine-learning algorithms for anomaly detection in ITS to detect and mitigate potential security breaches and abnormal activities. By analyzing vast amounts of data collected from various ITS components, machine learning algorithms can identify patterns and anomalies that may indicate potential security threats. This study discusses the benefits of using machine-learning algorithms for anomaly detection, including their ability to adapt and learn from new data, detect

**Corresponding author*: shiplud63@gmail.com

Subhabrata Barman, Santanu Koley and Subhankar Joardar (eds.) Next-Generation Systems and Secure Computing, (187–204) © 2025 Scrivener Publishing LLC

unknown or emerging threats, and provide real-time insights. This highlights the importance of feature selection and data preprocessing techniques to improve the accuracy and efficiency of anomaly detection algorithms.

Keywords: Intelligent transport system, machine learning, security and privacy

9.1 Introduction

In recent years, rapid advancements in technology have revolutionized the way we live and interact with the world. One area that has benefited greatly from these technological developments is transportation. The emergence of Intelligent Transportation Systems (ITSs) has transformed the traditional concept of transportation into smart and efficient networks of interconnected vehicles, infrastructure, and users. Intelligent Transportation Systems encompass a wide range of technologies including connected vehicles, smart traffic management systems, advanced driver assistance systems, and real-time data analytics. These systems aim to enhance the safety, efficiency, and sustainability of transportation networks, while also improving the overall user experience. However, as ITS continues to evolve and expand, ensuring security, privacy, and trust has become a critical concern. With the integration of various technologies and collection of massive amounts of sensitive data, the vulnerabilities and risks associated with cybersecurity and privacy breaches have become more prominent. Securing ITS infrastructure and data is of utmost importance to protect against potential threats such as hacking attempts, unauthorized access, data manipulation, and disruption of services. Breaches in the ITS ecosystem can have severe consequences ranging from safety hazards to financial losses and compromised user privacy. Therefore, robust security measures must be implemented to safeguard the integrity and confidentiality of a system. Privacy is another significant aspect that must be addressed in the context of ITS. As intelligent transportation systems gather vast amounts of data about individuals' travel patterns, location information, and personal preferences, concerns regarding misuse and unauthorized access to this sensitive information arise. Safeguarding user privacy is essential to building and maintaining public trust in these systems, as individuals need reassurance that their personal data are protected and used responsibly. Moreover, ensuring trust is crucial for the successful adoption and acceptance of intelligent transportation systems. Trust involves establishing confidence in the reliability, dependability, and ethical use of the technologies deployed in the ITS. Users must trust that the system will provide accurate information, make sound decisions, and prioritize their safety and privacy. To address these challenges, researchers, policymakers, and industry professionals are actively developing and implementing robust security frameworks, privacy-enhancing technologies, and trust-building mechanisms. These efforts involve the adoption of encryption techniques, authentication protocols, secure communication channels, and anonymization methods to protect the data and prevent unauthorized access. Additionally, legal and regulatory frameworks are being developed to ensure compliance with privacy laws and establish guidelines for the responsible use of personal data. Information and communication technologies are being integrated into transportation infrastructure, cars, and user devices through the development of intelligent transportation systems (ITSs), which are disruptive technologies. By enabling real-time data collection, analysis, and decision-making, the main objective is to improve the effectiveness, well-being, and maintainability of transportation systems. These systems employ technological methods such as automation, big data, communication networks, and sensors to improve traffic flow, reduce congestion, increase road safety, and provide users with individualized services. The evolution and implementation of intelligent transportation systems have many advantages; however, they also pose serious security, privacy, and trust issues. This study includes all relevant issues regarding safety, privacy, and faith when creating intelligent transportation systems. It discusses the difficulties, solutions, and ideal procedures that apply to both technical and practical aspects of ITS. To provide a thorough understanding of the topic, the study will provide insights from previously published literature, case studies, business practices, and scholarly research.

This study aims to contribute to the creation of tough and dependable ITS ecosystems that can unleash the full potential of intelligent transportation while protecting the interests of users and stakeholders by addressing the security, privacy, and trust concerns in the field. The goals of this research document are:

- To pinpoint cyber threats, unapproved entry, and system flaws, which are security concerns and liability for intelligent transportation systems.
- To investigate privacy issues raised by gathering, archiving, and inspecting private and delicate information in intelligent transportation systems.
- To discuss the value of trust in relation to intelligent transportation, particularly trust in dependability, honesty, and parties involved in the system.

- To suggest methods and recommended procedures for guaranteeing the safety, seclusion, and dependability of intelligent transportation systems.
- To address safety, privacy, and faith in intelligent transportation, reports or records will be scrutinized and will focus on successful implementations, lessons discovered, and industry-government cooperation.
- To investigate new developments in the field, including quantum-safe encryption, artificial intelligence, and blockchain technologies, and their possible effects on safety, privacy, and faith.

9.2 Literature Review

The study [1] explained how cyber security can be implemented to protect separate vehicles and public transport in ITS. This study describes the application of technology to progress avenue transportation, where information is obtained from sensors and apparatus in cars. It also proposes that ITS requires wireless communication between vehicles and road infrastructure. The author also provides an overview of ITS security issues where countermeasures are only powerful tools to overcome the security reaches of ITS, although the viability of countermeasures is not estimated precisely. Sheng *et al.* [2] focuses on internal ITS research based on comparison and analysis. The author represents advanced ITS technology, such as GPS, DSRC, wireless networks, radio wave beacons, roadside camera recognition, and probe vehicles, to design an integrated model that is more efficient in solving existing transportation issues worldwide. This study also states that the new integrated model or new intelligent vehicle can make major advances over VICS services based on smart way technology by offering traffic information, location, and surrounding information to the driver. Juan *et al.* [3] proposed how sensors can be integrated with Transportation Infrastructure to achieve an efficient and viable ITS. The author explained that ITS largely depends on accurately accessing, collecting, and processing data from the environment using sensing technology, which is classified into two categories. They stated that sensors are important components used for data collection during V2V communication, and the in-vehicle sensor collects data from vehicle conditions. Urban sensing technology collects data regarding traffic conditions, which are then sent to a traffic management system for processing and relevant actions. In addition, in this study, the author described some key sensors such as road sensors—LADAR, CMOS images, intrusive and non-intrusive sensors. The difficulty faced by the proposed model is the monitoring of the sensing device's range on the road. To overcome these issues, data fusion techniques with AI have been used to allow vehicles to address their current state. Besma *et al.* [4] analyzed the qualitative risk regarding threat and TVRA methodology in ITS and they focused on ETSI ITS communication architecture which supports wired and wireless communication between two vehicles. The author demonstrated a VANET system that is used to ensure the safety of the driver and to ensure the privacy of the V2V and V2I communication protocols. It proposed different vulnerabilities such as attack-targeting authentication and attack-targeting availability. To protect ITS entities from cyber-attacks, this study proposed machine learning techniques where data are most important to secure connected vehicles. Julie *et al.* [5] investigated different ITS security issues and provided different solutions regarding secure ITS. In this study, some selective threat vectors such as DDoS attacks, system gaming and theft, physical attacks, VANET attacks, and wired and wireless network attacks against ITS were evaluated. To identify security-related issues, biometrics can be used as an authentication technique, network segmentation using firewalls, anti-phishing, encryption algorithms, and BDS. Sakti *et al.* [6] investigated Blockchain based secure IoT communication that protects 5G-connected ITS from several threats. The author intends to build a blockchain-based IoT-enabled 5G ITS that protects security breaches and maintains the privacy of users by enabling nodes to communicate with each other. The proposed model utilizes a consortium blockchain and IPoRto to provide secure data communication on an edge-based transport system. Pedada *et al.* [7] presented an overview of V2X communication systems that amplify the connectivity between vehicles and access points using wireless technology and cellular networks such as LTE and 5G. In this study, a variety of attacks were explored in the V2X system. To secure V2X environment-two-factor authentication, CRL compression and public-key cryptography are used in the proposed model. Zhaojun *et al.* [8] exhibited a trust management model using the VANET system to fill the research gaps in ITS and reviewed innominate authentication methods applied by pseudonymity techniques. The author introduced high-quality security approaches, such as availability, confidentiality, authentication, and integrity, for securing V2I and V2X channel systems. Rathin *et al.* [9] introduced crowd intelligence techniques in ITS which uses artificial intelligence to extract information from crowd-source for decision making. The author focused on creating an automatic vehicle and parking system, although this is still under open research. In this study, intelligent crowd methods, such as travel demand prediction, optimum route prediction, missing data modeling, crowd-sensing, and dynamic topology of vehicular networks, have been discussed for transportation layers that require reinforcement learning, game theory, SVM, and neuro-fuzzy approaches. Manak *et al.* [10] proposed a cloudlet that supported V2V and V2I communication in ITS using edge-infrastructure which provides assurance about protection and authentic message exchanging among vehicles and provides important use cases like accident/ice threat warning. This study demonstrated that running vehicles are connected to nearby cloudlets. In this study, the AB-ITS model is presented along with the concept of application of the proposed solution to the AWS IoT platform.

9.2.1 Development of Intelligent Transportation

This study presents notable contributions to the field of intelligent transportation systems (ITS) by addressing the key aspects that drive its advancement. By focusing on the technological, societal, and environmental dimensions, this study aims to foster a comprehensive understanding of the contributions required for the successful development of intelligent transportation.

- Integration of Advanced Technologies: This study [11] emphasizes the significance of incorporating cutting-edge technology into intelligent transportation systems, including sensor networks, communication systems, data analytics, and automation. To obtain the best system performance and efficiency, the necessity of smooth interchange among different technologies it emphasized.
- Infrastructure Development: This study highlights the importance of creating strong infrastructure to enable intelligent transportation systems, including the implementation of linked car infrastructure, smart traffic control systems, and intelligent transportation networks. It investigates how improving infrastructure might improve traffic flow, lessen congestion, and boost the overall transportation effectiveness.
- Artificial Intelligence and Machine Learning: The development of intelligent transport has benefited from the use of machine learning (ML) and artificial intelligence (AI) approaches [12, 13], as acknowledged in this study. It examines how AI and ML are used in traffic prediction, route

optimization, intelligent traffic light control, and autonomous vehicle systems.

- Enhanced Safety: The importance of intelligent transportation systems in enhancing traffic safety is emphasized in this study. It investigates how cutting-edge driver monitoring, real-time driver assistance, and collision avoidance systems can improve safety by identifying and reducing possible risks on the road.
- Accessibility and Mobility: The study emphasized the role that intelligent transport systems play in fostering accessibility and mobility for all people, including the elderly and

Table 9.1 Different functions and services of ITS.

Functions of ITS	Services
Services for public transport	• Management of public transport • Details while traveling
Commercial vehicle administration	• Clearance of customs • Occurrence and reaction to risky items • Shipping • Managing the fleet effectively • Safety
Travel administration	• Traffic monitoring • Route direction • Level crossing on a railway • Management of incidents • Speed alerts
Travel demand control	• Before traveling, information • Advance reservations
Emergency planning	• Crisis automobiles • Response to disasters and evacuation • Allocation for law enforcement • Distribution of emergency services
Services for electronic payments	• Electronic payment of tolls • Electronic payment for parking • Automated fare collection
Advanced vehicle safety and control	• Prevention of side collisions and rear collisions • Safety • Roadway automation system

those with impairments. It emphasizes the significance of inclusive transport systems that meet a range of mobility needs and facilitate hassle-free travel.

- Improved User Experience: This report acknowledges the role of intelligent transport systems in improving user experience in general. To provide users with convenience and happiness, it investigates the integration of user-centric features such as tailored trip suggestions, timely information updates, and seamless multimodal transit options.
- Sustainable Transportation: The article acknowledges how intelligent transport systems help the environment by lowering carbon emissions and support.
- Environmentally friendly transport options. To reduce the environmental impact of transportation, this study investigates the integration of electric vehicles, shared mobility services, and environmentally appropriate routing. Table 9.1 represents the different functions and services of ITS.

9.2.2 Security Threats in ITS

Cybersecurity Attacks: Intelligent transport systems, among other systems and businesses, are seriously threatened by cybersecurity assaults [14]. These systems are vulnerable to attacks by hostile actors because of their interconnectedness, dependence on data interchange, and the existence of communication networks. Typical cyber-attacks that could harm intelligent transportation systems include the following:

- Malware and Ransomware: Systems may become infected by hostile software, which would jeopardize their security and functionality. A malware called ransomware encrypts data and requests a price in exchange for its release, interrupting activities, and costing money.
- Denial-of-Service (DoS) Attacks: These attacks are designed to flood the target system with too much traffic, preventing it from responding to valid requests. A DoS attack can interfere with communication networks, traffic control, or the interconnection between vehicles and infrastructure in the context of intelligent transportation systems.
- Spoofing and Man-in-the-Middle Attacks: Spoofing entails pretending to be a trustworthy organization to obtain access or change data without authorization. Man-in-the-Middle

attacks occur when an attacker eavesdrops on two parties' conversations and changes them, perhaps obtaining access to data or injecting harmful content.

- Remote Exploitation and Hacking: Intelligent transport systems depend on a variety of software parts and interfaces that hackers can take advantage of. Utilizing system flaws to gain unauthorized access to or control private data is known as remote exploitation.

Unauthorized Access and Data Breaches: Unauthorized people may be able to access crucial systems or data if authentication processes are frail or access managements are insufficient [15]. Confidential information may be exposed as a result of data breaches, endangering user privacy and opening the door for additional assaults. Physical Infrastructure Vulnerabilities: When discussing the physical components of intelligent transportation systems, the term "physical infrastructure vulnerabilities" refers to the flaws that they may include. Hostile actors may take advantage of these weaknesses to jeopardize the infrastructure's honesty, vacancy, and safety. Insider Threats: Security concerns from inside users with permission to access systems, networks, or data are known as insider threats. Insider threats in the context of intelligent transportation systems can be people working for transportation companies, services, or tech companies who abuse their power to jeopardize the security and reliability of the system.

9.2.3 Privacy Concerns in ITS

The ITS uses a variety of sensors, cameras, and communication devices to collect information on vehicles, drivers, and passengers. Location, speed, travel habits, and even personally identifiable information (PII), such as license plate numbers or driver identification, may be included in these data. Such data are collected in large quantities, raising questions regarding surveillance and possible unauthorized access. Real-time data processing is essential for an efficient and responsive transportation management. To allow features such as traffic monitoring, incident detection, and dynamic routing, ITS systems must analyze and interpret data in real-time [16]. The large amounts of data produced by ITS must be efficiently managed, stored, and processed. To manage the growing amount of data and provide accessibility and scalability, a solid data storage infrastructure should be established. The infrastructure should include servers, databases, and cloud-based platforms. To prevent data loss, adequate data backup and disaster-recovery techniques are necessary. Generalization entails swapping specific values with broader ones. For instance, age ranges may be used instead of actual ages or larger regions in place of precise geographic coordinates. Suppression is the process of eliminating details or complete records that can be used to identify specific individuals. Pseudonymization substitutes pseudonyms or aliases for personally identifiable information. Using a different key or mapping table, the original data can be connected to pseudonyms to enable data analysis while preserving anonymity. Depending on whether it is necessary to recover the original data, pseudonymization can be reversible or irreversible. Each record in a dataset must be indistinguishable from at least K-1 other records to be K-anonymous. To accomplish anonymity inside the groups, similar records were grouped together based on a combination of quasi-identifiers (attributes that may be used to identify specific individuals). By ensuring that each cluster of related records has at least L different values for sensitive variables, L-diversity improves upon k-anonymity [17]. By ensuring that sensitive information is not unduly concentrated within a group of comparable records, attribute exposure is prevented. The distribution of sensitive attribute values within each group is considered by the l-diversity extension measure, known as t-closeness. It seeks to guarantee that there are no appreciable differences in the distribution of sensitive attribute values throughout a group.

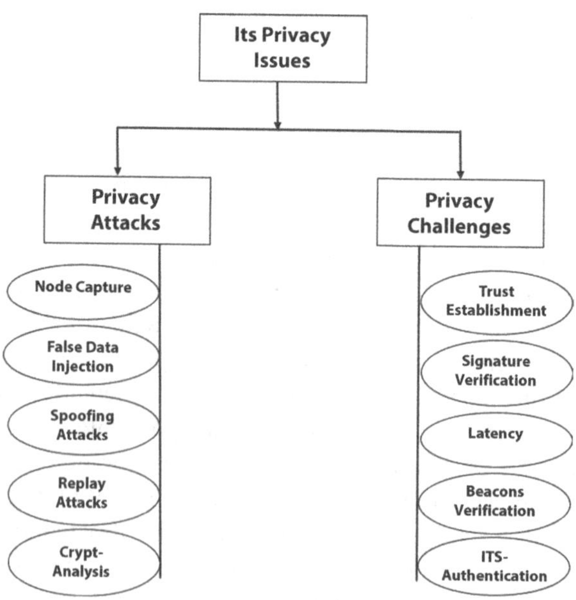

Figure 9.1 Privacy attacks and privacy challenges.

Data masking involves removing sensitive information and replacing it with fictitious or jumbled data while maintaining the statistical properties of the original data. Character encoding, tokenization, and encryption methods, such as format-preserving encryption and token-based encryption, are examples of common techniques [18, 19]. A mathematical approach called differential privacy offers privacy assurance for data analysis. To ensure that the presence or absence of a specific individual's data has no appreciable impact on the analysis results, controlled noise or randomization is introduced. While preserving the general correctness of aggregated data, differential privacy seeks to safeguard the privacy of each individual. Figure 9.1 presents the privacy attacks and privacy challenges.

9.3 Proposed Work

Intelligent transportation systems (ITSs) have emerged as a transformative force in the transportation industry, leveraging advanced technologies to create a smart and efficient network of interconnected vehicles, infrastructure, and users. As the ITS continues to evolve, it is crucial to address the challenges associated with security, privacy, and trust. Machine learning algorithms play a vital role in enhancing the security and privacy of ITS, enabling trustworthy and reliable transportation systems. Machine learning algorithms have revolutionized the analysis and interpretation of data, providing valuable insights and enabling intelligent decision making. In the context of ITS, these algorithms can be leveraged to detect and mitigate security threats, protect user privacy, and establish trust within a system. One significant aspect of securing an ITS is the detection and prevention of cyber threats. Machine-learning algorithms can be trained to identify patterns and anomalies in real-time data, enabling the system to promptly detect and respond to potential security breaches. By analyzing network traffic, user behavior, and system logs, these algorithms can identify abnormal activities, such as intrusion attempts, malware attacks, or unauthorized access, and trigger appropriate security measures to mitigate risks.

Moreover, machine-learning algorithms can contribute to preserving user privacy within an ITS ecosystem. With the vast amount of data collected from vehicles, infrastructure, and users, protecting individual privacy has become paramount. Privacy-preserving techniques, such as differential privacy and secure multiparty computation, can be integrated with machine learning algorithms to ensure that personal data are anonymized and aggregated while maintaining the integrity of the system's analytics and decision-making capabilities. Building trust in ITS requires not only robust security and privacy measures but also reliable and transparent decision-making processes. Machine-learning algorithms can aid in building trust by providing explainable and interpretable models. By utilizing interpretable machine learning algorithms such as decision trees or rule-based models, the system can provide insights into how decisions are made, making it easier for users to understand and trust the system's recommendations.

Machine learning algorithms can contribute to the continuous improvement of security, privacy, and trust in ITS. Through the analysis of historical data and real-time monitoring, these algorithms can identify emerging patterns, trends, and vulnerabilities, allowing system administrators to proactively address potential risks and enhance their overall security posture.

Machine-learning algorithms play a pivotal role in ITS by enabling the system to process and interpret diverse data sources, including vehicle sensor data, traffic patterns, and user behavior [20]. These algorithms can learn from historical data, detect patterns, and make accurate predictions, allowing for real-time traffic management, dynamic route planning, and proactive decision making. By leveraging the power of machine learning, ITS can enhance safety measures, optimize traffic flow, and reduce travel time, resulting in improved overall transportation efficiency. Depending on particular requirements and applications, different algorithms and techniques are employed in the development of intelligent transportation systems (ITS). A few ITS algorithms that are frequently used and traffic signal control, dynamic route planning, and autonomous vehicle control are all excellent candidates for optimization using RL algorithms such as Q-learning, deep Q-learning, or proximal policy optimization (PPO). Figure 9.2 represents the security measures within the ITS infrastructure using the ML algorithm. Complex and dynamic transport scenarios are well-suited for RL because they enable systems to learn and adapt based on feedback from the environment. To produce precise forecasts, ML algorithms can examine previous data, sensor inputs, and other relevant factors. Natural selection serves as the inspiration for population-based search algorithms, such as Dijkstra's algorithm, A* algorithm, and GA [21, 22]. It is frequently used to optimize fleet management, vehicle routing, and route planning in transportation systems. Combinatorial optimization problems can be handled by GAs by iteratively evolving and selecting optimal solutions. CV algorithms are crucial for tasks such as vehicle detection, licence plate recognition, and pedestrian detection in intelligent transportation systems that depend on video or image data. These algorithms include object detection, tracking, and classification techniques such as Haar cascades, Histogram of Oriented Gradients (HOG), and

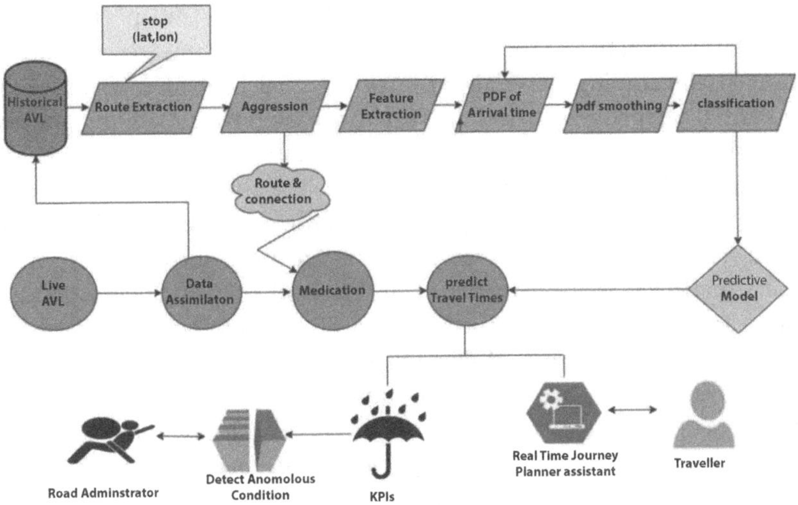

Figure 9.2 Security measures within the ITS infrastructure through ML algorithm.

Convolutional Neural Networks (CNNs). The acceleration, braking, and steering of autonomous cars can be managed using control methods, such as proportional-integral-derivative (PID) controllers, Model Predictive Control (MPC), and Reinforcement Learning algorithms. The performance of transport networks is simulated and evaluated using microscopic or macroscale traffic flow simulation models such as the Intelligent Driver Model (IDM) or Cell Transmission Model (CTM) [23]. To effectively address various aspects of the transportation domain, it frequently integrates several algorithms and methodologies. Furthermore, the development of intelligent transportation systems may involve new algorithms or variants brought about by continuing research and breakthroughs in the field.

9.4 Methodology Analysis and Discussion

This section presents an analysis of the results obtained from the application of machine learning algorithms for anomaly detection in enhancing security measures within the Intelligent Transportation Systems (ITS) infrastructure. The objective of this analysis was to evaluate the effectiveness of these algorithms in identifying and mitigating security breaches in real time, thereby protecting critical transportation assets and ensuring user safety. The purpose of this analysis was to evaluate the effectiveness of enhanced security measures within an Intelligent Transportation System (ITS) infrastructure using machine learning algorithms for anomaly detection. By leveraging these algorithms, the goal is to identify and mitigate potential security breaches in real-time, thereby enhancing the overall security and protection of critical transportation assets.

Table 9.2 shows the current situation, the most likely scenario in the future, and how the public perceives factors connected to ICT, ITS, and road transport in the research region. It has been shown that in the present situation, 55% of drivers utilize ICT, and 64% of drivers say they are open to embracing new, cutting-edge ITS technologies. The use of ICT (26%) in travel, the use of existing ITS (21%), and the adoption of new and advanced ITS (19%) were all quite low. The use of ICT to influence travel decisions before a journey (39%), ITS to influence travel decisions before a journey (24%), ITS to influence travel decisions during a journey (15%), ITS to influence travel behavior during a journey (15%), and IT'S to influence travel patterns (13%) by road users is also currently very sparse.

Table 9.2 The public perceives factors connected to ICT, ITS, and road transport.

Parameters	**(%) of people**	**Perception index for likely success**	**Standard deviation (SD)**
Use of ICT	55 80	0.74	0.14
Use of ICT in transportation related decisions	26 55	0.76	0.11
Use of current ITS in travel	21 70	0.72	0.11
Adoption of new and advanced ITS technology	19 80	0.73	0.13
Use of ICT and change in travel decisions before the journey	39 60	0.79	0.18
Use of ITS change in travel decision before the journey	24 54	0.68	0.12
Use of ITS change of travel decision during the journey	15 65	0.64	0.12
Use of ITS and change of travel behaviour during the journey	15 66	0.67	0.10

These results suggest that although a sizable portion of 215 road users use ICT and are willing to adopt ITS, only a small portion of road users currently use and adopt these technologies in their travel requirements, travel-related decision-making, and changes in travel patterns and behavior. In other words, there is not much usage of travel-related technologies. In addition, only approximately one-third of the respondents now agree that ITS helps reduce traffic, accidents, and travel time.

The view of road users, in contrast, differs with regard to the future usage of ICT and ITS. Most road users (80%) said that they would like to utilize ICT more generally, and 55% said that they would like to use it to make transportation decisions. Similarly, although approximately two-thirds (70%) of road users will not utilize ITS in its current condition, more than 75% of road users are eager to embrace and adopt new and upgraded ITS technology in the future. Additionally, around 60% of road users want to utilize ITS to alter their pre- and post-trip travel decisions, as well as their on-the-road behavior. Additionally, PI research revealed that both ICT and ITS are anticipated to have a major impact on road transport. While people would want to embrace and implement present ITS technologies (PI = 0.72), they believe that future and improved ITS technologies will be more widely adopted in the field of road transport (PI = 0.80 and 0.74). The high perception indices of ITS use in relation to important travel characteristics suggest that ITS is likely to have a significant impact on changing travel decisions before (PI = 0.73), during (PI = 0.64), and after the trip (PI = 0.67). However, ITS did not have a significant impact on altering travel behavior (PI = 0.45). Table 9.3 displays the results of the significance test. A test of significance (t test) was performed to determine the link between the employment of ITS in its present and improved forms, and different aspects of how road users travel. However, there was no statistically significant correlation between the use of ITS (using both current and advanced technologies) and travel behavior ($p > 0.05$ for 0.05). This shows that even if they want to continue accepting and using the present ITS technology, road users are eager to accept and adapt to new and sophisticated ITS technology. The application of enhanced security measures through the utilization of machine learning algorithms for anomaly detection is a significant step towards safeguarding the Intelligent Transportation System infrastructure. By effectively identifying and responding to potential security breaches, this application ensures the protection of critical transportation assets, enhances user safety, and establishes a robust security framework in the ITS environment. Through continuous monitoring, evaluation, and adaptation, the application provides a proactive approach to address security challenges and mitigate emerging threats in the ever-evolving transportation landscape.

Table 9.3 T index values and p-values of transportation variable.

Transportation variables	t-Test results (T index values and p-values at α ≤0.05), *1 tailed and ** 2 tailed	
	Use of recent ITS technology	**Use of advanced ITS technology**
Acceptance and adoption of ITS	(14.003)	(20.16)
	0.00000021*	0.00000003*
	0.00000026*	0.00000005**
Travel decisions before journey	(9.27)	(22.2)
	0.0000079*	0.00000001*
	0.0000151**	0.00000003**
Travel decisions during the journey	(5.71)	(17.83)
	0.00022*	0.00000004*
	0.00034**	0.0000008**
Travel behavior during the journey	(7.23)	(18.79)
	0.000039*	0.00000001*
	0.000088**	0.00000002**
Travel pattern	(1.59)	(1.93)
	0.069*	0.062*
	0.111**	0.123**

9.5 Conclusion

The development of intelligent transportation systems (ITSs) has the potential to significantly improve the effectiveness, security, and sustainability of transportation networks. However, the broad use of ITS also causes important problems with regard to security, privacy, and trust. Cyberattacks, unauthorized access, and system failures are just a few of the hazards that pose security risks to intelligent transportation systems. It is essential to implement strong intrusion detection and prevention systems, secure communication and authentication mechanisms, and secure design and development practices to reduce these risks. Trust is essential for successful adoption of advanced transport solutions. To build and sustain trust in an ITS, it is essential to use trustworthiness evaluation, trust models, reputation systems, and accountability mechanisms. Utilizing blockchain and distributed ledger technologies for secure and decentralized data sharing, utilizing AI and machine learning for advanced analytics and decision-making, exploring quantum-safe cryptography for long-term security, addressing data ownership and sovereignty concerns, and considering ethical and legal considerations are some future directions and emerging trends in the development of intelligent transportation systems. Large volumes of data are produced by the ITS from a variety of sources, including sensors, cameras, and linked devices. Our future aim is to work on a vast dataset and include User Experience and Human–Machine Interaction.

References

1. Valentini, E.P., Meneguette, R.I., Alsuhaim, A., An attacks detection mechanism for intelligent transport system, in: *2020 IEEE International Conference on Big Data (Big Data)*, pp. 2453–2461, IEEE, December, 2020.
2. An, S.-h., Lee, B.-H., Shin, D.-R., A survey on intelligent Transportation Systems. *2011 third International Conference on computational intelligence, communication and networks.*
3. Guerrero-Ibanez, J., Zeadally, S., Contreas Castillo, J., sensor Technologies for Intelligent transportation System. *Sensors*, 18, 4, 1212, 2018.
4. Zeddini, B., Maachaoui, M., Inedjaren, Y., Security threats in intelligent transportation systems and their risk levels. *Risks*, 10, 5, 91, 2022.
5. Harvey, J. and Kumar, S., A survey of intelligent transportation systems security: challenges and solutions, in: *2020 IEEE 6th Intl Conference on Big Data Security on Cloud (Big Data Security), IEEE Intl Conference on High Performance and Smart Computing, (HPSC) and IEEE Intl Conference on Intelligent Data and Security (IDS)*, IEEE, pp. 263–268, 2020, May.
6. Kumaresh, S., Towards Blockchain-Based Secure IoT Communication for 5G Enabled Intelligent Transportation System, *Int. J. Comput. Netw. Appl. (IJCNA)*, 10, 1, January–February, 2023.
7. Saraswathi, P., Rajkumar, G., Rao, P.M., Intelligent transport system using IoT-V2X: communication technologies, security issues, challenges and countermeasures, 2022.
8. Lu, Z., Qu, G., Liu, Z., A survey on recent advances in vehicular network security, trust, and privacy. *IEEE Trans. Intell. Transp. Syst.*, 20, 2, 760–776, 2018.
9. Chandra Shit, R., Crowd intelligence for sustainable futuristic intelligent transportation system: a review. *IET Intel. Transport Syst.*, 14, 6, 480–494, 2020, https://doi.org/10.1049/iet-its.2019.0321.

10. Gupta, M., Benson, J., Patwa, F., Sandhu, R., Secure V2V and V2I communication in intelligent transportation using cloudlets. *IEEE Trans. Serv. Comput.*, 15, 4, 1912–1925, 2020.
11. Xiang, Z., Li, C., Chen, L., Pan, B., Chen, D., Zhang, L., Efficiency of Risk Classification and Insurance Market Regulation through the Integration of Advanced Technology. *World Eng. Appl. Sci. J.*, *14*, 2023, 3986–3992, 2023.
12. Gangwani, D. and Gangwani, P., Applications of machine learning and artificial intelligence in intelligent transportation system: A review. *Applications of Artificial Intelligence and Machine Learning: Select Proceedings of ICAAAIML 2020*, pp. 203–216, 2021.
13. Gaur, L. and Sahoo, B.M., Introduction to Explainable AI and Intelligent Transportation, in: *Explainable Artificial Intelligence for Intelligent Transportation Systems: Ethics and Applications*, pp. 1–25, Springer International Publishing, Cham, 2022.
14. Kelarestaghi, K.B., Heaslip, K., Khalilikhah, M., Fuentes, A., Fessmann, V., Intelligent transportation system security: hacked message signs. *SAE Int. J. Transp. Cybersecur. Privacy*, *1*, 11-01-02-0004, 75–90, 2018.
15. Mather, T., Cloud Security and Privacy: An Enterprise Perspective on Risks and Compliance, O'Reilly Media, 2009, ISBN-13, 978-0596802769.
16. Peres, R.S., Rocha, A.D., Leitao, P., Barata, J., IDARTS–Towards intelligent data analysis and real-time supervision for industry 4.0. *Comput. Ind.*, *101*, 138–146, 2018.
17. Gangarde, R., Sharma, A., Pawar, A., Joshi, R., Gonge, S., Privacy preservation in online social networks using multiple-graph-properties-based clustering to ensure k-anonymity, l-diversity, and t-closeness. *Electronics*, *10*, 22, 2877, 2021.
18. Kapil, G., Agrawal, A., Attaallah, A., Algarni, A., Kumar, R., Khan, R.A., Attribute based honey encryption algorithm for securing big data: Hadoop distributed file system perspective. *PeerJ Comput. Sci.*, *6*, e259, 2020.
19. Crowe, M., Pandy, S., Lott, D., Mott, S., Is Payment Tokenization Ready for Primetime? *Jun*, *11*, 1–51, 2015.
20. Ali, E.S., Hasan, M.K., Hassan, R., Saeed, R.A., Hassan, M.B., Islam, S., Bevinakoppa, S., Machine learning technologies for secure vehicular communication in internet of vehicles: recent advances and applications. *Secur. Commun. Netw.*, *2021*, 1–23, 2021.
21. Rajan, C., Geetha, K., Priya, C.R., Sasikala, R., Investigation on bio-inspired population based metaheuristic algorithms for optimization problems in ad hoc networks. *Int. J. Math. Comput. Phys. Electr. Comput. Eng.*, *9*, 3, 163–170, 2015.
22. Hussein, A., Mostafa, H., Badrel-din, M., Sultan, O., Khamis, A., Metaheuristic optimization approach to mobile robot path planning, in: *2012, international conference on engineering and technology (ICET)*, IEEE, pp. 1–6, October 2012.
23. Jin, Y., Yao, Z., Han, J., Hu, L., Jiang, Y., Variable Cell Transmission Model for Mixed Traffic Flow with Connected Automated Vehicles and Human-Driven Vehicles. *J. Adv. Transp.*, *2022*, 2022.

10

The Impact of Distributed Ledger in IoT: A Comprehensive Overview

Rick Hore, Rishav Dan, Abhijit Sarkar and Sabyasachi Samanta*

Haldia Institute of Technology, Haldia, WB, India

Abstract

Distributed Ledger Technology (DLT) is an option to bolster the safety of networks and devices connected to the Internet of Things (IoT). DLT offers a safe and tamper-proof method for storing and exchanging data, which may assist in the prevention of cyber-attacks on Internet of Things devices. A safe method of authenticating devices is one way that DLT can be used to increase the security of the Internet of Things. When a piece of hardware joins a network, it may utilize DLT to demonstrate its true identity to the network. This makes it far more difficult for unauthorized devices to connect to the network and launch attacks. Another way that Distributed Ledger Technology may be used to enhance the security of the Internet of Things is by offering a safe mechanism to store data. The use of DLT allows the creation of a distributed database that can be accessed by all devices connected to the network. This database can store sensitive data, including user passwords and financial information. Because they are dispersed, the database makes it difficult for potential attackers to access the data or make changes to it. DLT may also be used to increase the security of the Internet of Things by offering a safe method for devices to interact with one another. Devices can interact with one another using a secure message system that may be created with the help of a DLT. This helps prevent attackers from listening to conversations between devices or meddling with those communications in any way. DLT has the potential to be a very helpful tool for enhancing the safety of IoT networks and devices. DLT may assist in safeguarding Internet of Things devices from cyber-attacks by offering a method for storing and exchanging data that is both secure and impossible to alter. Here in this chapter, we introduce the use of DLT to enhance the security of the IoT environment by offering safe appliances to store facts. In addition,

**Corresponding author*: sabyasachi.smnt@gmail.com

Subhabrata Barman, Santanu Koley and Subhankar Joardar (eds.) Next-Generation Systems and Secure Computing, (205–228) © 2025 Scrivener Publishing LLC

we have discussed an overall overview og DLT, IoT, IoT-powered DLT, and IoT-based security systems, which are emerging in day virtual security.

Keywords: Internet of Things (IoT), distributed ledger technology (DLT), IoT security, blockchain, automation

10.1 Introduction

10.1.1 Distributed Ledger System

One type of digital database, known as a distributed ledger system, is dispersed over a number of nodes or other network members. It enables the safe storage and administration of data, communications, or any other type of digital information on a vast scale. A distributed ledger system relies on consensus to validate and record new transactions or data inputs. This ensured that the ledger was accurate and reliable. Blockchain is perhaps the most well-known use of distributed ledgers. The data in a blockchain are structured into blocks, and each block can be thought of as containing a collection of transactions or information. A chain of blocks is created when these blocks are connected to one another via the use of a cryptographic hash. Each node in the network maintains a copy of the whole blockchain and validates new transactions using a consensus method as proof of work or claim. A blockchain is a distributed ledger that records transactions in a distributed ledger. A distributed ledger system is characterized by its

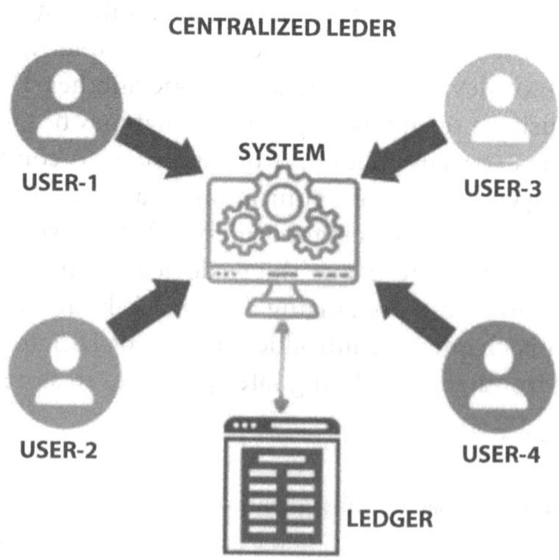

Figure 10.1 Centralized ledger system [4].

lack of centralized control, which ensures that no one organization may exert authority over the entire database. Instead, the duty to maintain the ledger and arrive at a consensus is shared among a number of stakeholders. Because it takes the majority or a significant amount of the computer power of the network to edit or alter the data stored in the ledgers, this method of implementing distributed memory provides a higher level of security [16]. The centralized ledger system is shown in Figure 10.1. Figure 10.2 represents the distributed ledger system.

10.1.2 Use of Distributed Ledger Together with IoT

Distributed ledger technology is often connected to blockchain and has the potential to transform the Internet of Things by overcoming major obstacles such as security, scalability, dependability, and data integrity. This is one of the reasons why DLT are commonly associated with blockchain.

- **Safety and Reliability:** The Internet of Things may benefit from the decentralized and immutable ledger offered by DLT.
- **Data integrity and source:** A trustworthy record of the data collected by Internet of Things devices can be maintained using DLT assuring both consistency and transparency.
- **Smart contracts and automation:** Smart contracts are often supported by DLT systems. These are pre-specified contracts that are automatically executed after they have been created.

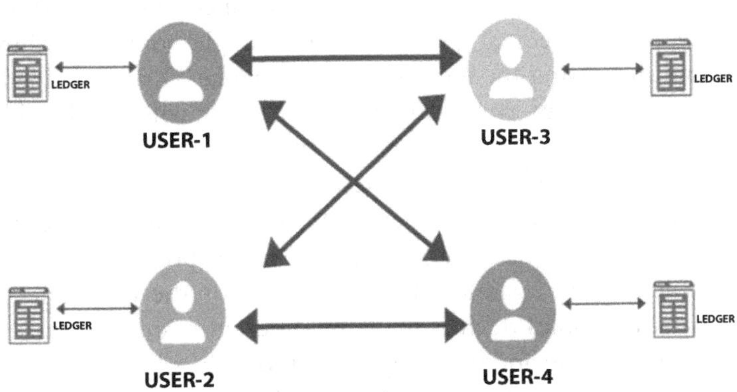

Figure 10.2 Distributed ledger system [6].

- **Scalability and performance interaction:** The scalability and interoperability of the IoT ecosystem may be improved with the help of a DLT.
- **Data economy and ownership:** IoT device owners can have more control over their data and receive direct money because of the DLT's capabilities.

10.1.3 Advantages of IoT-Powered DLT

- **Security:** IoT-powered distributed ledger technology offers improved network security for IoT systems using cryptographic techniques and decentralized consensus methods. The integrity of the records is ensured while also providing authentication and encryption, which in turn reduces the likelihood of cyberattacks and unwanted access.
- **Trust and Transparency:** The development of an immutable and auditable record of transactions and information exchanges is one way to add transparency to IoT networks. Since they can verify the legitimacy and integrity of the information, folks are more likely to consider what is being said.
- **Data Integrity:** The recording of transactions on a distributed ledger is how DLT assures that the information collected by IoT devices is accurate. Because each transaction is displayed and confirmed by more than one node, it is impossible to manipulate or alter the statistics, which ensures that the information is accurate and reliable.
- **Decentralization and Resilience:** IoT-powered distributed ledger technology eliminates the need for centralized authority, thereby reducing the number of single points of failure and increasing the community's resilience. Distributed ledger technology ensures that no one entity will ever be able to control the entire network, which contributes to the increased stability of the system as a whole.
- **Interoperability:** Interoperability between different Internet of Things devices and systems is made possible by DLT which offers a standardized protocol for the exchange of data. It enables devices made by different manufacturers to communicate and work together smoothly, which paves the way for the development of unified IoT ecosystems.

➢ **Automation and Efficiency:** Intelligent contracts that enable automatic interactions and transactions between Internet of Things devices are routinely supported by DLT systems. Because of this automation, the need for middlemen and guide interventions is reduced, which results in increased efficiency and reduced costs [17].

10.1.4 Disadvantages of IoT-Powered DLT

➢ **Scalability:** When dealing with many Internet of Things devices and high transaction volumes, Distributed Ledger Technology, particularly blockchain-based systems might run into scalability challenges. Both the throughput and processing speed of the network may be hindered by consensus procedures and statistical replication that occur across a few nodes.

➢ **Resource Intensive:** Systems that are enabled by IoT and DLT may have a resource-in-depth approach to computing

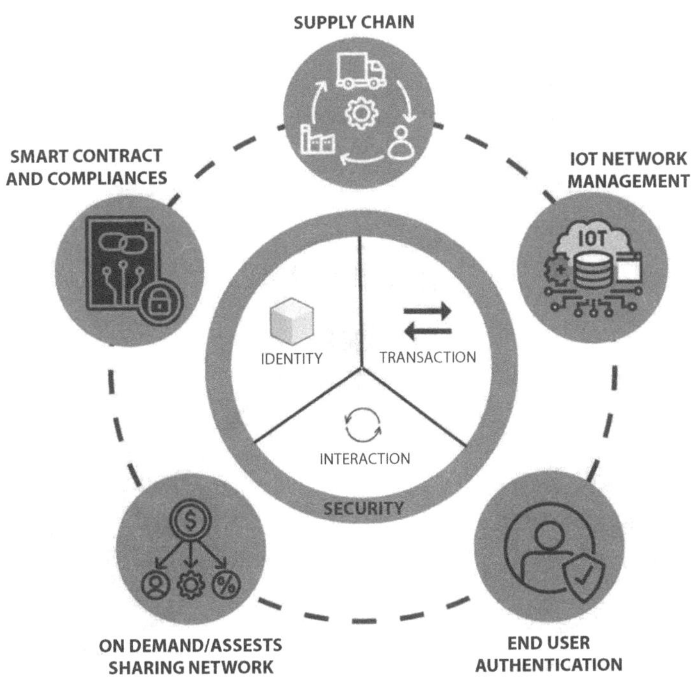

Figure 10.3 Use cases of distributed ledger in IoT [8].

electricity, storage space, and power consumption. It consumes considerable computing power to run consensus algorithms and cryptographic procedures, which might be problematic for Internet of Things devices that are limited in their available resources.

- **Complexity:** It may be difficult to implement and manage DLT systems driven by the internet of things. Blockchain technology, cryptography, consensus processes, and the integration of IoT devices are all required areas of expertise. It is possible that the intricacy of the technology may further hinder its acceptance and execution.
- **Cost:** There may be significant costs involved in the installation of IoT-powered DLT structures as well as their ongoing maintenance. It is possible that the infrastructure, processing resources, and safety measures necessary for allocated ledgers would result in expensive costs, particularly for the installation of the Internet of Things on a smaller scale.

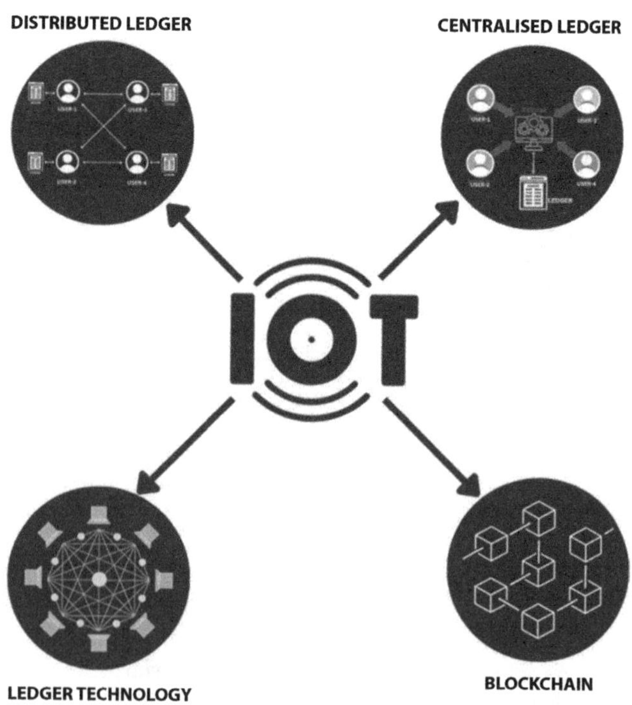

Figure 10.4 IoT system with other implementations [8].

- **Regulatory and Legal Challenges:** Regulatory and criminal risks are posed by the use of DLT in the IoT. Navigating the legal landscape may be challenging because the requirements for data ownership, privacy, and compliance can vary significantly among businesses and regions.
- **Lack of Standardization:** Interoperability and cooperation among unusual systems and structures may be hindered if the established protocols and frameworks for IoT-powered DLT are lost. Fragmentation and compatibility concerns may arise because of the lack of industry-wide standards.

While distributed ledger technology, driven by the Internet of Things (IoT), provides several advantages, it is imperative that issues related to scalability, useable resource restrictions, complexity, and standardization be resolved to realize its full potential in IoT ecosystems. Figure 10.3 pronounces the use cases of distributed ledgers in IoT. Figure 10.4 portrays the IoT system. Figure 10.5 appearances the disadvantages of DLD in IoT [18].

Section 10.2 represents recent related work on distributed ledger technology and the Internet of Things (IoT). *Section 10.3* signifies the potentiality of

Figure 10.5 Determinants of DLT in IoT [8].

both systems. *Section 10.4* denotes the recent habits of DLT and IoT systems. *Section 10.5* represents the opportunities and challenges of integrating DLT with IoT. *Section 10.6* signifies the future of DLT in IoT ecosystems. Finally, *Section 10.7* draws a conclusion regarding the current challenges.

10.2 Related Work

Although blockchain is still a fairly young technology, it has already been the focus of a significant number of studies that have applications in a wide variety of industries.

Kumar *et al.* [1] has provided a comprehensive discussion from both a technical and a social point of view. The authors covered a variety of themes pertaining to the Internet of Things, including essential application fields, architecture, and critical obstacles. Additionally, the study sheds light on previously published literature and illustrates how it has contributed to various aspects of the Internet of Things. In addition, the significance of big data and its analysis in relation to the Internet of Things has been highlighted.

Rawlins *et al.* [2] suggested a machine-learning strategy using a multi-arm bandit that was built for auditing on constrained devices. This approach overcomes these challenges and allows them to be fixed. This approach was evaluated in a reinforcement learning environment that simulated the generation of an IOTA ledger using a decision tree. This technique was shown to be secure against assaults based on impulse manipulation using regret analysis and testing. The approach also maintains energy efficiency. Although the IOTA protocol was an early leader in the field of lightweight distributed ledgers, it is reasonable to anticipate that future blockchain protocols would adopt strategies similar to those discussed in this study.

Dolenc *et al.* [3] provided a variety of criteria for the assessment of a distributed ledger ecosystem, which does not just concentrate on the technology elements of potentially useful solutions. In addition, they consider the decentralized application development viewpoint and long-term viability of its usage. The authors presented a quick review of some alternative distributed ledger ecosystems that may be used for the development and implementation of decentralized apps for business and IoT. Ethereum, Hyperledger, HederaHashgraph, EOS, Corda, IOTA, and Multichain are the distributed ledger systems and networks that have been examined.

To encourage investigations on state-of-the-art research and to enable one to contribute to developing the convergence of blockchain and IoT,

Farahani *et al.* [4] offered a comprehensive reference architecture together with the basics, current developments, promises, and problems.

Panda *et al.* [5] presented readers with an in-depth introduction of distributed ledger technology (DLT) as well as some of the current solutions that are available to address the security needs of IoT systems that utilize DLT. This study also draws attention to the many difficulties associated with integrating DLT with Internet of Things.

Red *et al.* [6] compared current distributed ledger systems with an eye toward deployable sensor and IoT use cases. In this study, the author proposed a set of criteria for classifying distributed ledger implementations in the context of the Internet of Things and sensors. Limitations in the size, weight, and power of IoT devices are considered when evaluating technical methods and performance. The feasibility and safety of consensus and smart contracts, if applicable, were also evaluated. The readiness of distributed ledgers for corporate interoperability will be assessed considering their sensors' and Internet of Things' usability.

Atlam *et al.* [7] explored the common ground between DLTs and the Internet of Things. It began with a brief introduction to DLT, focusing on its essential features, advantages, and potential pitfalls. The authors also discussed a centralized IoT system and its shortcomings. The advantages of combining blockchain with IoT are outlined. The benefits and drawbacks of combining blockchain technology with the Internet of Things are examined.

In the context of the IOTA Foundation's DAG-based system, Cullen *et al.* [8] analyzed a frequent assault scenario called parasite chain attack, which seeks to undermine the immutability and irreversibility of the ledger. The authors analyzed the weaknesses of IOTA's main Tip Selection process under this attack using a Markov chain model and proposed an update to the algorithm to increase the resistance of the ledger.

Singh *et al.* [9] presented a framework for a secure, distributed P2P infrastructure to manage electronic stamps and property registration, as well as an interface for authenticating documents. The suggested efficient consensus approach saves CPU calculation power and network traffic, while reducing the cost of broadcasting a new block by more than half. A cloud server architecture and online interface for verifying property registration deed is also suggested to guarantee that persons in distant regions with limited resources may participate and reap these advantages.

Abdulrahman *et al.* [10] conducted a comprehensive evaluation of the current research on the subject, including both academic and commercial studies. It is divided into various application domains, such as authentication, access control, and data integrity. In conclusion, the authors highlighted open research issues and possible future paths for the application of blockchain and DLTs in the context of Internet of Things (IoT) security. This survey report is a helpful resource for academics and practitioners interested in understanding current state-of-the-art research in this significant area of Internet of Things (IoT) security.

An experimental study of IOTA was conducted on a variety of Internet of Things platforms, and Elsts *et al.* [11] presented their findings. The authors demonstrated that even if the communication overhead required to join the IOTA network can be greatly reduced by applying a proxy-based architecture, the computational cost is still very high. This is the case even though communication overhead may be significantly reduced. The authors concluded that IOTA is not yet suitable for Internet of Things devices powered by batteries.

To provide quick and scalable IoT data integrity verification using resource-constrained IoT GWs, Cherupally *et al.* [12] presented a lightweight and scalable distributed ledger for IoT (LSDI) based on a directed acyclic graph. Pruning and Clustering are two of the LSDI's central approaches, both of which are aimed at lowering the computational overhead of IoT GWs by dividing a huge P2P network into many smaller P2P networks. By effectively regulating the storage and processing overhead of IoT GWs, the proof-of-concept implementation evaluation results demonstrate that the proposed LSDI system achieves high transaction throughput and scalability.

Pinto *et al.* [13] examined research on tried-and-true applications. To evaluate the 39 existing programs, the authors developed a user-centric taxonomy. No clear patterns have yet emerged in people-focused DLT-IoT designs, which the authors have found to be in their infancy. The ethereum is the most popular DLT. Insufficient attention was paid to suitable technologies such as IOTA and ideas such as Self-Sovereign Identity (SSI). The authors found a heightened focus on privacy-protecting and edge-computing methods and identified three research avenues for further exploration.

Hernández *et al.* [14] explained the planning, implementation, and testing of a proof-of-concept system that use distributed ledger technology (DLT) smart contracts to choose edge nodes for offloading computing activities in an effective manner. In particular, the authors maximize offloading of compute under dynamic connection options by incorporating network performance indicators into smart contracts on a hyper ledger blockchain. The suggested technique is sufficiently flexible to be used with networks of varying topologies and connection types. The findings demonstrate a broad range of potential industrial applications of blockchain smart contracts.

Dahiya *et al.* [15] highlighted the integration of blockchain technology with Internet of Things (IoT), cloud computing, and social media, as well as the concerns and obstacles associated with this integration. In addition, the authors also provided a selection of the most significant research works completed in each field.

10.3 The Potential of DTL in IoT Application

Distributed ledger technology (DLT), which is often associated with the development of blockchain, has substantial potential in Internet of Things (IoT) packages. The combination of distributed ledger technology with IoT has the potential to improve several aspects of business operations, including security, scalability, transparency, and interoperability [19]. The following is a list of some of the most important ways in which DLT may benefit IoT programs:

i. **Security and Trust:** DLT offers a distributed and immutable ledger that can keep information and devices connected to the internet of things stable. DLT safeguards against tampering or fraud by using cryptographic methods and consensus algorithms. It also guarantees that information is not accessed by unauthorized parties and prevents its integrity from being compromised. This makes it possible to verify and authenticate the identities of devices in a safe manner, making it possible for IoT stakeholders to have faith in the connected devices.

ii. **Data Integrity and Provenance:** The Internet of Things creates huge volumes of information, and it is essential to ensure the integrity of the information and its origin. The DLT can generate an immutable record of all transactions and data exchanges, which enables a transparent and auditable chain of events to be created. This feature is most helpful in the management of the delivery chain, where it is possible to record on the ledger the tracking of the beginning location, movement, and current state of items.

iii. **Interoperability and Standardization:** IoT ecosystems often consist of several devices, platforms, and protocols that can interact with one another seamlessly. The DLT has the potential to set up a standardized environment on which Internet of Things devices may connect, compute statistics, and carry out transactions across a variety of networks. DLT helps decrease the complexity of integration while also promoting interoperability. This is achieved by providing a decentralized and uniform infrastructure.

iv. **Scalability and Decentralization:** When it comes to scalability, traditional centralized Internet of Things designs have a tough time keeping up with the demands of managing a wide array of devices and transactions. Distributed ledger technology (DLT) presents a distributed and decentralized method that makes it possible to scale infrastructure. DLT can cope with a huge number of Internet of Things devices because of its peer-to-peer networks and consensus processes, while preserving the performance and reliability of the devices.

v. **Smart Contracts and Automation:** In Internet of Things (IoT) projects, the execution of smart contracts may be facilitated by DLT. Smart contracts are agreements that can execute themselves and automate processes depending only on the set conditions. IoT devices can independently cause and carry out activities, such as paying bills, owing to the incorporation of smart contracts in the DLT. This eliminates the need for middlemen. This function helps reduce overhead costs while streamlining the business methods. Figure 10.6 depicts the overall view of the distributed ledger system.

vi. **Micropayments and Monetization:** Devices connected to the Internet of Things can create and share records, which may be useful in a variety of settings. DLT makes it possible

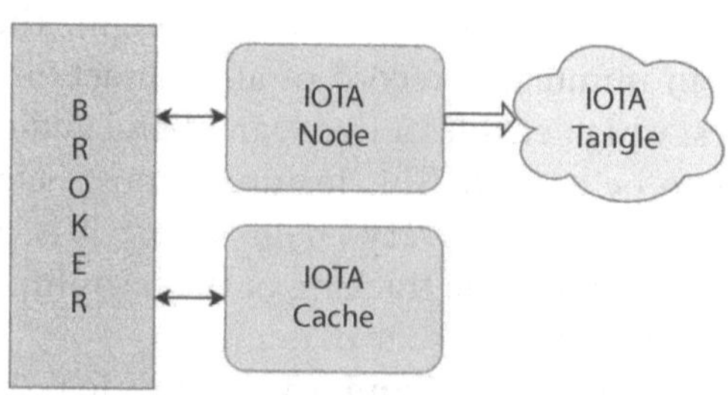

Figure 10.6 Components of a DLT area: an arrow indicates the MQTT-based communication interface, while a thick arrow indicates the IOTA interface [17].

to make micropayments using cryptocurrencies or tokens, which enables Internet of Things devices to instantly monetize the information or services they provide. This feature makes it possible for new types of business models to emerge, such as those in which connected devices may engage in peer-to-peer transactions with one another and provide economic incentives inside IoT networks. Figure 10.7 represents the centralized ledger system.

vii. **Privacy and Data Ownership:** DLT offers the opportunity to customize IoT packages in terms of their level of privacy and the data they carry. The DLT enables decentralized storage and control, which means that sensitive data do not have to be kept on centrally located servers. Users can preserve custody and control over their statistics, making it possible for them to provide limited access to certain people while still protecting their privacy.

The combination of distributed ledger technology with the Internet of Things, when taken as a whole, provides several benefits, the most notable of which are increased security, information integrity, interoperability, automation, and monetization options. Nevertheless, it is essential to consider the scalability, energy consumption, and implementation constraints associated with DLT in IoT. These technologies are still developing, and genuine worldwide deployments must be thoroughly considered to avoid potential issues [22, 23].

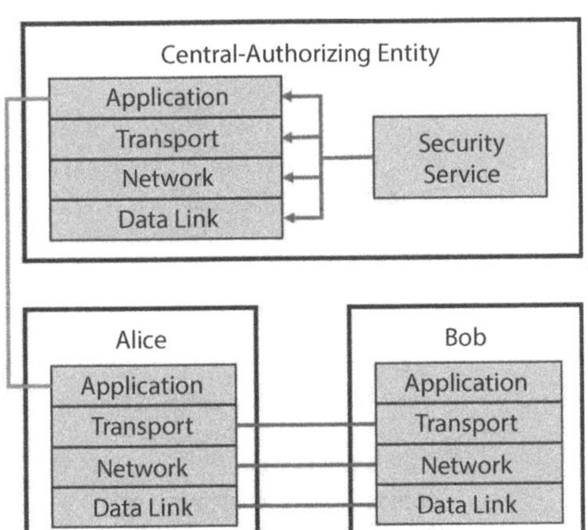

Figure 10.7 Centralized ledger system in networking [18].

10.4 Current Use Cases of IoT and DLT

The combination of the Internet of Things with Distributed Ledger Technology is already being researched or put into practice in several real-world applications worldwide. Figure 10.8 shows the current use cases of IoT and DLT systems [20]. The following are a few instances that really stick out:

i. **Supply Chain Management:** Controlling the supply chain entails keeping track of and checking the transit of products through several different organizations. With the help of integrating IoT devices, distributed ledger technology (DLT) can enhance the transparency, traceability, and performance of supply chains. These improvements can reveal the location, circumstances, and validity of products across the entire supply chain. This combination makes it possible for every transaction to include both safe and auditable information, which helps reduce instances of fraud, counterfeiting, and inefficiency.

ii. **Energy Management:** IoT devices, such as smart meters, can gather real-time power usage information from residential and commercial properties, as well as from government agencies and electrical networks. By incorporating DLT, this information can be safely stored and exchanged among many stakeholders, which enables higher power management efficiency, billing accuracy, and grid optimization. Peer-to-peer energy purchasing and selling may also be made easier with

Figure 10.8 Current use cases of IoT and DLT [28].

the help of DLT. Under this model, individuals or organizations buy and sell power directly from one another, thereby reducing their dependency on centralized energy suppliers.

iii. **Autonomous Vehicles and Transportation:** Sensors and other devices enabled by the Internet of Things are essential components of autonomous cars and intelligent transportation infrastructure. DLT has the potential to improve the safety and dependability of the data collected from these devices, thereby ensuring the authenticity of the data collected from automobiles, as well as monitoring and communication. It has the potential to provide continuous over-the-air software upgrades, decentralized car-to-car communication, and streamlining processes such as coverage claims and possession verification.

iv. **Healthcare and Medical Devices:** IoT devices are becoming more prevalent in the healthcare industry, where they are utilized to monitor patient health, collect important symptoms, and modify medical systems. The integration of distributed ledger technology improves the security of patient data, the confidentiality of patient information, and the interoperability of medical devices. This can lead to automated bill and claim processing, promote steady communication of clinical data across healthcare carriers, and provide tamper-evidence audit trails for pharmaceutical supply chains.

v. **Agriculture and Food Safety:** In agricultural contexts, Internet of Things sensors may provide information about soil conditions, weather patterns, crop growth, and animal health. The Internet of Things (IoT) and distributed ledger technology (DLT) work together to provide farmers with the ability to store and distribute data on agricultural yields, supply chain techniques, and food safety certifications. This integration has the potential to promote transparency within the food supply chain, better traceability to determine the origin of contaminated products and provide customers with more information about the food they consume.

vi. **Smart Homes and Energy Grids:** It is possible to establish decentralized power grids using DLT by integrating IoT devices found in smart homes with other smart technologies, such as thermostats, lighting control systems, and appliances. This integration enables efficient energy intake, peer-to-peer buying and selling of energy, and coordination among many intelligent devices, in a manner that is both reliable and autonomous. It is possible to assist in optimizing energy consumption, thus reducing expenditures and increasing the power grid's resistance to disruption.

These are just a few instances of how the Internet of Things and distributed ledger technology might be used to address real-world challenging scenarios in a variety of business sectors. We anticipate that more innovative use cases will emerge in the future as technology develops and matures. This is something that we can look forward to.

10.5 Opportunities and Challenges of Integrating DLT with IoT

The integration of DLT with IoT opens the door to several opportunities that might result in more desired functionality and advanced operations. However, it presents several issues that need to be resolved [21]. The following is a list of opportunities and problems associated with the integration of DLT and IoT:

10.5.1 Opportunities

i. **Security and Trust:** IoT applications may benefit from a decentralized and tamper-resistant ledger that uses distributed ledger technology (DLT) provides. This improves both the protection and acceptability. This makes it possible to verify the identification of secure tools, ensure the integrity of data, and authenticate users, thereby protecting the integrity of transactions and interactions between IoT devices.

ii. **Data Integrity and Provenance:** Using DLT, Internet of Things (IoT) networks may have an immutable and transparent record of all transactions and information exchanges. This feature improves the integrity, provenance, and auditability of information, providing stakeholders with a source of information that can be relied on and verified.

iii. **Interoperability and Standardization:** DLT has the potential to make it easier for a wide variety of IoT devices, systems, and protocols to work together. DLT makes it possible for diverse Internet of Things structures to seamlessly integrate and collaborate with one another by providing a common platform for communication and data exchange. This reduces complexity and makes it possible to market standardized interactions.

iv. **Automation and Smart Contracts:** The execution of smart contracts, which automate procedures largely depending on predetermined circumstances, is made possible by distributed ledger technology (DLT). This function enables autonomous interactions between IoT devices, which may then be used to initiate motions and transactions without the need for any type of middleman. Operations are streamlined, expenses are reduced, and efficiency is improved.

v. **Monetization and Micropayments:** Micropayments may be made using DLT utilizing cryptocurrencies or tokens, opening up the possibility for Internet of Things devices to directly monetize the information or services they provide. This facilitates the development of new business models and financial incentives inside IoT ecosystems, which in turn encourages the sharing of data and creation of new value.

10.5.2 Challenges

i. **Scalability:** When integrating DLT with IoT, new computational and storage space requirements are introduced, which may have an impact on scalability. To meet the ever-increasing demand, a DLT network must find a way to accommodate an increasing number of Internet of Things devices and transactions without sacrificing either its capacity or speed.

ii. **Energy Consumption:** It is possible for DLT networks to use a significant amount of power, particularly those that are built on consensus processes such as evidence of paintings. This presents challenging circumstances in power-constrained IoT systems, where it is essential to maximize the efficiency in terms of energy usage. To have a successful integration with the IoT, it is essential to develop electricity-efficient DLT protocols.

iii. **Latency and Speed:** Processing statistics and making decisions in real time or very close to real time are often requirements for IoT products. The consensus processes used in DLT networks may add delay, which may influence time-sensitive Internet of Things systems that depend on instantaneous response.

iv. **Standardization and Governance:** The ecosystems of both DLT and the internet of things include several parties, protocols, and needs. The process of establishing common criteria, protocols, and governance frameworks for the integration of DLT with IoT involves cooperation and coordination among various groups.

v. **Cost and Complexity:** It is possible to implement DLT in IoT packages to incur extra charges, which may include infrastructure setup and maintenance fees, as well as transaction fees. In addition, the integration of DLT and IoT systems, as well as the management of the complex relationships between the two, may require the use of specialized expertise and resources.

vi. **Privacy and Regulation:** Because of the open and unchangeable nature of DLT, there is an increased cause for concern over privacy and compliance with legislation, which includes the legal requirements governing statistical safety and privacy. To ensure compliance and protect consumer statistics, it is essential for Internet of Things apps to find a middle ground between openness and confidentiality.

To find solutions to these challenging problems, it is necessary for stakeholders in the generating industry, policymakers, and researchers to continuously conduct research and development and work together. The maturation of this period will bring forth breakthroughs in scalability, power performance, and interoperability, all of which will play a wider role in maximizing the benefits of combining DLT with IoT [24, 25].

10.6 The Future of DLT in IoT Ecosystems

The future use of distributed ledger technology (DLT) in Internet of Things ecosystems offers a great deal of potential for the transformation of many different sectors and the facilitation of creative packaging [13]. The following is a list of important factors that point to the capacity future of DLT in IoT:

i. **Enhanced Security and Privacy:** DLT has the potential to significantly improve the security and confidentiality of IoT ecosystems. As the number of devices connected to the

Internet of Things (IoT) continues to rise, it is becoming increasingly important to protect the confidentiality of data and to lock down communication channels. IoT devices may be shielded against unwanted access, tampering, and data breaches using the decentralized and tamper-resistant characteristics of DLT, which can also provide comprehensive safety measures [8].

ii. **Interoperability and Standardization:** DLT can handle interoperability demanding circumstances that arise as a result of the proliferation of different IoT devices, platforms, and protocols. These situations arise because of the proliferation of diverse IoT devices. The DLT has the potential to provide smooth interoperability among a wide variety of IoT structures by providing a standardized platform for the communication and exchange of records. Standardization initiatives and protocols created on top of distributed ledger technology (DLT) may further improve interoperability, which is important when considering more environmentally friendly and scalable Internet of Things ecosystems [26].

iii. **Data Monetization and Ownership:** Distributed ledger technology (DLT) may provide owners of IoT tools with the ability to maintain ownership and control over their statistics while also providing avenues for monetization of their data. IoT devices can safely share data with trusted third parties and receive immediate compensation via micropayments because distributed ledger technology (DLT) is both transparent and auditable. This not only gives individuals more control over their data but also makes it possible for new business models to emerge. In addition, it encourages the exchange of data [27].

iv. **Decentralized Autonomous IoT Networks:** The development of decentralized, self-sufficient IoT networks may be facilitated using the DLT. These networks can function without the need for major authorities, making it possible for Internet of Things devices to communicate and conduct business with one another in real time using smart contracts. These kinds of networks may simplify business processes, reduce expenses and enable consumers to make more informed decisions about Internet of Things devices.

v. **Edge Computing and DLT Integration:** Edge computing, which entails processing facts closer to the supplier rather than dependent entirely on centralized cloud infrastructures, meshes perfectly with the allocated nature of the DLT. Edge computing entails processing statistics closer to supply than traditional cloud computing. Integrating DLT with edge computing may enable the creation of IoT structures that are scalable and efficient. This is because statistics can be processed, proved, and stored at the edge of the network while still maintaining the benefits of the security and transparency provided by the DLT [28].

vi. **Energy Efficiency and Sustainability:** Future innovations will concentrate on boosting the energy performance of distributed ledger technology (DLT) networks, because power consumption is a challenge shared by both DLT and IoT architectures. Consensus procedures, such as proof-of-stake, are being investigated to minimize the amount of energy required while maintaining the integrity of the network. DLT, when combined with energy-efficient Internet of Things devices and renewable power sources, has the potential to contribute to a more sustainable Internet of Things ecosystem.

vii. **AI and Machine Learning Integration:** To provide improved data analytics and decision making in IoT systems, DLT may be combined with AI and device-studying algorithms. IoT systems can provide priceless insights, automate strategies, and improve operations in real time when they combine the trustworthiness and transparency of DLT with the data-processing abilities of AI.

Although the future of distributed ledger technology (DLT) in Internet of Things (IoT) ecosystems seems bright, it is necessary to address difficulties such as scalability, strong performance, standardization, and regulatory compliance. Understanding the ability of DLT to shape the future of IoT may require ongoing study, development, and cooperation among industry stakeholders, policymakers, and technical experts [29]. This is due to the potential significance of this topic.

10.7 Conclusion

Both of these techniques will interact subtly to shape the ledgers of the future. Emerging hybrid solutions combine the openness of the distributed ledger with the security of the centralized ledger. Wider adoption is also facilitated by research on energy-efficient protocols, enhanced cryptography, and consensus procedures. The ideal answer ultimately relies on the unique requirements and limitations of each application. There is little doubt that the ledger revolution is still in its early stages and will significantly alter how information will be recorded, validated, and shared in the years to come.

The combination of distributed ledger technology (DLT) with Internet of Things architecture has significant potential to revolutionize the way people interact with technology. DLT offers answers to a wide variety of problems associated with the Internet of Things, including those pertaining to security, interoperability, transparency, and the facilitation of trustworthy transactions. As the Internet of Things becomes more pervasive, there will be more chances to integrate DLT. This will result in improved solutions, greater transparency, and an ecosystem that is better suited for the exchange of data and assets. Finally, distributed ledger technology has the potential to profoundly affect the IoT landscape. It enhances security, privacy, decentralization, and automation while also improving transparency, scalability, and trust. However, the successful integration of DLT into IoT ecosystems requires addressing the technical challenges and regulatory considerations.

References

1. Kumar, S., Tiwari, P., Zymbler, M., Internet of Things is a revolutionary approach for future technology enhancement: a review. *J. Big Data*, 6, 1, 2019, Springer Science and Business Media LLC. https://doi.org/10.1186/s40537-019-0268-2.
2. Rawlins, C.C. and Jagannathan, S., An Intelligent Distributed Ledger Construction Algorithm for IoT. *IEEE Access*, 10, 10838–10851, 2022, Institute of Electrical and Electronics Engineers (IEEE). https://doi.org/10.1109/access.2022.3146343.
3. Dolenc, D., Turk, J., Pustisek, M., Distributed Ledger Technologies for IoT and Business DApps, in: *2020 International Conference on Broadband Communications for Next Generation Networks and Multimedia Applications (CoBCom)*, IEEE, 2020, https://doi.org/10.1109/cobcom49975.2020.9174188.
4. Farahani, B., Firouzi, F., Luecking, M., The convergence of IoT and distributed ledger technologies (DLT): Opportunities, challenges, and solutions. *J. Network Comput. Appl.*, 177, 102936, 2021, Elsevier BV. https://doi.org/10.1016/j.jnca.2020.102936.
5. Panda, S.S., Mohanta, B.K., Dey, M.R., Satapathy, U., Jena, D., Distributed Ledger Technology for Securing IoT, in: *2020 11th International Conference on Computing, Communication and Networking Technologies (ICCCNT)*, IEEE, 2020, https://doi.org/10.1109/icccnt49239.2020.9225333.

6. Red, V.A., Practical comparison of distributed ledger technologies for IoT, in: *SPIE Proceedings*, Hall, R.D., Blowers, M., Williams, J. (Eds.), SPIE, 2017, https://doi.org/10.1117/12.2262793.
7. Atlam, H.F. and Wills, G.B., Intersections between IoT and distributed ledger. *Adv. Comput.*, 73–113, 2019, Elsevier. https://doi.org/10.1016/bs.adcom.2018.12.001.
8. Cullen, A., Ferraro, P., King, C., Shorten, R., On the Resilience of DAG-Based Distributed Ledgers in IoT Applications. *IEEE Internet Things J.*, 7, 8, 7112–7122, 2020, Institute of Electrical and Electronics Engineers (IEEE). https://doi.org/10.1109/jiot.2020.2983401.
9. Singh, N. and Vardhan, M., Distributed Ledger Technology based Property Transaction System with Support for IoT Devices. *Int. J. Cloud Appl. Comput.*, 9, 2, 60–78, 2019, IGI Global. https://doi.org/10.4018/ijcac.2019040104.
10. Abdulrahman, S. and Useng, M., Blockchain and Distributed Ledger Technologies for IoT Security: A Survey paper. *Mesopotamian J. Comput. Sci.*, 5–8, 2022, Mesopotamian Academic Press. https://doi.org/10.58496/mjcsc/2022/006.
11. Elsts, A., Mitskas, E., Oikonomou, G., Distributed Ledger Technology and the Internet of Things, in: *Proceedings of the 1st Workshop on Blockchain-enabled Networked Sensor Systems. SenSys '18: The 16th ACM Conference on Embedded Networked Sensor Systems*, ACM, 2018, https://doi.org/10.1145/3282278.3282280.
12. Cherupally, S.R., Boga, S., Podili, P., Kataoka, K., Lightweight and Scalable DAG based distributed ledger for verifying IoT data integrity, in: *2021 International Conference on Information Networking (ICOIN)*, IEEE, 2021, https://doi.org/10.1109/icoin50884.2021.9334000.
13. Pinto, F., Ferreira da Silva, C., Moro, S., People-centered distributed ledger technology-IoT architectures: A systematic literature review. *Telematics Inf.*, 70, 101812, 2022, Elsevier BV. https://doi.org/10.1016/j.tele.2022.101812.
14. Hernández, D.M., Queralta, J.P., Westerlund, T., Distributed Ledger Technologies for Managing Heterogenous Computing Systems at the Edge (Version 3), 2022, arXiv. https://doi.org/10.48550/ARXIV.2210.10572.
15. Dahiya, A., Gupta, B.B., Alhalabi, W., Ulrichd, K., A comprehensive analysis of blockchain and its applications in intelligent systems based on IoT, cloud and social media. *Int. J. Intell. Syst.*, 37, 12, 11037–11077, 2022, Hindawi Limited. https://doi.org/10.1002/int.23032.
16. Denis, N., Laurent, M., Chabridon, S., Integrating Usage Control into Distributed Ledger Technology for Internet of Things Privacy. *IEEE Internet Things J.*, 1–1, 2023, Institute of Electrical and Electronics Engineers (IEEE). https://doi.org/10.1109/jiot.2023.3283300.
17. Chiti, F. and Gandini, G., Distributed Ledger as a Service: A Web 3.0-Oriented Architecture. *J. Sens. Actuator Netw.*, 12, 4, 57, 2023, MDPI AG. https://doi.org/10.3390/jsan12040057.

18. Han, R., Shapiro, G., Gramoli, V., Xu, X., On the performance of distributed ledgers for Internet of Things. *Internet Things*, 10, 100087, 2020, Elsevier BV. https://doi.org/10.1016/j.iot.2019.100087.
19. Xu, R., Lan, Q., Pokhrel, S.R., Li, G., A Knowledge Graph based Survey on Distributed Ledger Technology for IoT Verticals. *ACM Comput. Surv.*, 2023, Association for Computing Machinery (ACM). https://doi.org/10.1145/3609503.
20. Xie, Q., Dong, F., Feng, X., HLOChain: A Hierarchical Blockchain Framework with Lightweight Consensus and Optimized Storage for IoT, in: *Security and Communication Networks*, vol. 2023, Cui, J. (Ed.), pp. 1–14, Hindawi Limited, 2023, https://doi.org/10.1155/2023/3412200.
21. Sadique, K.M., Rahmani, R., Johannesson, P., DIdM-EIoTD: Distributed Identity Management for Edge Internet of Things (IoT) Devices. *Sensors*, 23, 8, 4046, 2023, MDPI AG. https://doi.org/10.3390/s23084046.
22. Cullen, A., Ferraro, P., Sanders, W., Vigneri, L., Shorten, R., Access Control for Distributed Ledgers in the Internet of Things: A Networking Approach. *IEEE Internet Things J.*, 9, 3, 2277–2292, 2022, Institute of Electrical and Electronics Engineers (IEEE). https://doi.org/10.1109/jiot.2021.3096129.
23. Soltani, R., Zaman, M., Joshi, R., Sampalli, S., Distributed Ledger Technologies and Their Applications: A Review. *Appl. Sci.*, 12, 15, 7898, 2022, MDPI AGhttps://doi.org/10.3390/app12157898.
24. Ahsan, T., Zeeshan khan, F., Iqbal, Z., Ahmed, M., Alroobaea, R., Baqasah, A.M., Ali, I., Raza, M.A., IoT Devices, User Authentication, and Data Management in a Secure, Validated Manner through the Blockchain System, in: *Wireless Communications and Mobile Computing*, vol. 2022, Sur, S.N. (Ed.), pp. 1–13, Hindawi Limited, 2022, https://doi.org/10.1155/2022/8570064.
25. Pathak, S., Jhawar, A., Sharma, M., Kohli, A., Improvised Security of IoT Through Blockchain. *SSRN Electron. J.*, 2022, Elsevier BV. https://doi.org/10.2139/ssrn.4027047.
26. Anthony Jnr, B., Distributed Ledger and Decentralised Technology Adoption for Smart Digital Transition in Collaborative Enterprise. *Enterp. Inf. Syst.*, 17, 4, 2021, Informa UK Limited. https://doi.org/10.1080/17517575.2021.198949.
27. Fan, C., *Performance Analysis and Design of an IoT-Friendly DAG-based Distributed Ledger System*, University of Alberta Libraries, 2019, https://doi.org/10.7939/R3-21YJ-3545.
28. Alam, T., Blockchain-Based Internet of Things: Review, Current Trends, Applications, and Future Challenges. *Computers*, 12, 1, 6, 2022, MDPI AG. https://doi.org/10.3390/computers12010006.
29. Zheng, X., Sun, S., Mukkamala, R.R., Vatrapu, R., Ordieres-Meré, J., Accelerating Health Data Sharing: A Solution Based on the Internet of Things and Distributed Ledger Technologies. *J. Med. Internet Res.*, 21, 6, e13583, 2019, JMIR Publications Inc. https://doi.org/10.2196/13583.

11

A Cryptographic Technique Using Chemicals and Graphs

Kala Raja Mohan[1]*, Nagadevi Bala Nagaram[2], R. Narmada Devi[2], Regan Murugesan[2] and Subashini Chandrasekar[3]

[1]*Department of Mathematics, Panimalar Engineering College, Poonamallee, Chennai, India*

[2]*Department of Mathematics, Vel Tech Rangarajan Dr. Sagunthala R&D Institute of Science and Technology, Avadi, Chennai, India*

[3]*Department of Chemistry, Rajalakshmi Institute of Technology, Poonamalee, Chennai, India*

Abstract

In early days, each and every process involved many tedious processes. In particular, communication takes a lot of time. In order to communicate information from one person to another, postal communication was used. This method of communication takes nearly a week for the information to reach the receiver. In case of emergency, thanthi mode of communication was carried out. People faced many difficulties to communicate. Travel also was a very difficult procedure. To move from one place to another, people have to spend hours or days together. To invite for any function or to share any happy moments like birth of a child, people used to travel many hours.

The invention of internet has set a path to overcome all these difficulties. Mobile and Laptop are providing a tremendous help in overcoming such difficulties. Many user-friendly applications are available nowadays to make people finish their work at ease. The application named 'maps' has provided with a healthy way of transport, wherein people can reach the unknown destination also without any difficulty. With regards to communication, many user-friendly applications like whatsapp, facebook, twitter etc are available. These applications makes people to share their information to lakhs or crores of people in no time with the help of internet.

These user friendly applications takes access to all information available in mobile or laptop. This creates a chance of the data being shared in our device to

**Corresponding author*: kalamohan24@yahoo.co.in

Subhabrata Barman, Santanu Koley and Subhankar Joardar (eds.) Next-Generation Systems and Secure Computing, (229–238) © 2025 Scrivener Publishing LLC

be hacked by unknown people. To secure our personalized information is very much essential in this world of internet. Though many cryptographic techniques are available. many researchers still involves themselves in finding various secured information sharing methods.

Chemicals play an important role in our day to day life. There exists 118 chemicals which are presented in periodic table. Each chemical element are provided individual symbol and atomic number. They are classified as alkali metals. alkaline earth metals, transition metals. Metalloids, non metals, halogens, noble gases, lanthanides, actinides and non metals based on their properties. Mendeley in the year 1869 made his efforts in organizing these element in the form of a periodic table.

Graphs are the pictorial representation of any data. Bar graphs, pie chart, line graph are few examples of graphs. Graphs which are used to model the relationship between objects are done using nodes and edges. The study of such graphs is known as graph theory. It find its application in many fields of research. It provide itself comfortable in many practical real time applications too. Directed and undirected graphs are the two types of graphs referred in general. Weighted graphs also exists which provides numerical weight to each edge. Google maps, web search engines, traffic lights, airline scheduling are few practical applications of graph theory.

This chapter proposes a cryptographic algorithm making use of chemicals together with graphs. Both the encryption and decryption algorithm are to be validated with a help of an example sentence. Being a novel secured information sharing algorithm, this algorithm ensures a secured method for information sharing between the sender and the receiver.

***Keywords*:** Cryptography, encryption, decryption, chemicals, graphs

11.1 Introduction

In this world of the Internet, the use of mobile devices, laptops, and other such electronic devices is inevitable. All such devices come with an option to save all passwords in the devices themselves in all applications. There is a possibility of hacking individuals' personal data. Hiding information from trespassers essential. The major part of hiding information is handled by the various logic of cryptography. Various cryptographic techniques that use mathematical concepts are described below.

Hiwarekar introduced two techniques for cryptography making use of Hyperbolic functions together with Laplace Transform in 2013 and 2014 [1, 4]. In 2019, Undegaonkar introduced a cryptographic method using Laplace Transform for secret-sharing of information [2]. In 2013, Sujatha discussed the cryptography method in Laplace Transforms [3]. Sedeeg *et al.* in 2016 made use of the Aboodth transform in their cryptographic technique [5]. In 2016, Dhingra *et al.* framed a network security algorithm using Laplace transform [6], which involved Gencoglu finding a cryptographic method that makes use of hyperbolic functions [7]. Saha presented a method of cryptography involving Mellin–Laplace Transform in the year 2017 [8]. Jayanthi and Srinivas introduced a Laplace cryptographic method making use of mathematical modeling in the year 2019 [9]. In 2020, Nagalakshmi *et al.* utilized a Laplace Transform involving an asymmetric key for cryptographic studies [10]. In 2022, Meenakshi *et al.* incorporated an encryption algorithm from graphs and their network [11]. Mohan *et al.* in 2022 and 2023 introduced two different techniques involving Bilinear transformation, Probability, hyperbolic functions and Laplace transform, conformal mapping [12–14]. Nagaram *et al.* used ordinary differential equations to introduce a cryptography technique in 2023 [15].

In *Section 11.2*, the standard definitions used of in this crypto analysis are described. A detailed explanation of the periodic table is provided in *Section 11.3*. The coding tables described in this study are presented in *Section 11.4*. *Section 11.5* represents the algorithm applied for encryption. The encryption algorithm explained in *Section 11.5* is demonstrated with an example in *Section 11.6*. *Section 11.7* depicts the algorithm applied for decryption. Using the cipher text obtained in *Section 11.7*, the decryption process is explained in *Section 11.8*. *Section 11.9* is about the conclusion followed by the references.

11.2 Standard Definitions

Cryptographic analysis uses the following standard positions in this chapter.

- ➢ Information in readable form is termed plain text.
- ➢ The message obtained in the encrypted form using the specified algorithm is cipher text.
- ➢ The transformation of plain text to cipher text occurs in the cipher.
- ➢ The method by which plain text is converted into ciphertext is encryption.
- ➢ The method of converting ciphertext into plain text is decryption.
- ➢ The tabular representation of assigning numbers to letters and symbols required for the cryptographic process is a coding table.
- ➢ The arrangement of all the chemical elements in the table is periodic.

11.3 Periodic Table

Mendeleev created a period table in 1896. This is an arrangement of elements based on their properties. The elements are placed in the form of rows and columns. The row-wise elements are called the periods. Column-wise elements are known as groups. The positions of the elements are fixed based on their atomic numbers. There were four partitions in the table terms as blocks. Chemical elements of the same characteristics were placed in each block. Chemicals are divided into metals, semi-metals, and non-metals. Semi-metals fall between the other two types. The metals are on the left side of the periodic table. The non-metals are placed on the upper right. Each box is marked with a symbol and its atomic number. There are 118 elements in the table.

11.4 Coding Table with Chemical Elements

Based on a periodic table, a cryptographic algorithm was proposed. For this purpose, two types of coding tables were formed. In total, 118 elements were split into two tables. Elements with odd atomic numbers were placed in the first table. Elements with even atomic numbers were placed in the second coding table. There are 59 elements in each table. To these elements, capital letters from A to Z, small letters from a to z, space, #, $, @, ., %, ! are assigned. Thus, two coding tables representing the same letters and symbols with different chemical elements were formed.

Table 11.1 First coding table with odd atomic numbers.

1;H;A	**3;Li;B**	**5;B;C**	**7;N;D**	**9;F;E**	**11;Na;F**	**13;Al;G**	**15;P;H**
17;Cl;I	19;K;J	21;Sc;K	23;V;L	25;Mn;M	27;Co;N	29;Cu;O	31;Ga;P
33;As;Q	35;Br;R	37;Rb;S	39;Y;T	41;Nb;U	43;Tc;V	45;Rh;W	47;Ag;X
49;In;Y	51;Sb;Z	53;I;a	55;Cs;b	57;La;c	59;Pr;d	61;Pm;e	63;Eu;f
65;Tb;g	67;Ho;h	69;Tm;i	71;Lu;j	73;Ta;k	75;Re;l	77;Ir;m	79;Au;n
81;Tl;o	83;Bi:p	85;At;q	87;Fr;r	89;Ac;s	91;Pa;t	93;Np;u	95;Am;v
97;Bk;w	99;Es;x	101;Md;y	103;Lr;z	105;Db; (space)	107;Bb;#	109;Mt;$	111;Rg;@
113;Nh;.	115;Mc;%	117;Ts;!					

Table 11.2 Second coding table with even atomic numbers.

2;He;A	4;Be;B	6;C;C	8;O;D	10;Ne;E	12;Mg;F	14;Si;G	156;S;H
18;Ar;I	20;Ca;J	22;Ti;K	24;Cr;L	26;Fe;M	28;Ni;N	30;Zn;O	32;Ge;P
34;Se;Q	36;Kr;R	38;Sr;S	40;Zr;T	42;Mo;U	44;Ru;V	46;Pd;W	48;Cd;X
50;Sn;Y	52;Te;Z	54;Xe;a	56;Ba;b	58;Cs;c	60;Nd;d	62;Sm;e	64;Gd;f
66;Dy;g	68;Er;h	70;Yb;i	72;Hf;j	74;W;k	76;Os;l	78;Pt;m	80;Hg;n
82;Pb;o	84;Po:p	86;Rn;q	88;Ra;r	90;Th;s	92;U;t	94;Pu;u	96;Cm;v
98;Cf;w	100;Fm;x	102;No;y	104;Rf;z	106;Sg; (space)	108;Hs;#	110;Ds;$	112;Cn;@
114;Fl;.	116;Lv;%	118;Og;!					

11.5 Encryption Algorithm

This section describes the steps involved in the encryption process.

- The plain text to be converted into ciphertext was first provided with its position.
- The odd and even positions are split into two sets of tables.
- The chemical and its atomic number corresponding to the alphabets or symbols in odd positions in the text are referred to in the first coding table.
- Similar to odd-number positions, the alphabets or symbols in even-number positions and their corresponding elements with their atomic numbers are noted from the second coding table.
- Using the atomic number and its chemical element, a directed graph is formed, which is shared as an encrypted image.

11.6 Encryption Process—Example

In this section, the encryption process discussed here is illustration of the sentence "All is Well!" is presented.

The exclamatory sentence "All is Well!" and their equivalent values from the coding table are listed in Table 11.3.

From the table obtained, two tables of odd= and even-position alphabets or symbols are formed. For each of the table contents, the corresponding chemical and atomic numbers from coding Tables 11.1 and 11.2 were obtained.

Table 11.3 Positions of the plain text.

Alphabet	A	l	l		i	s		W	e	l	l	!
Position	1	2	3	4	5	6	7	8	9	10	11	12

Table 11.4 Odd positions with its chemical and atomic numbers.

Alphabet	A	l	i		e	l
Position	1	3	5	7	9	11
Chemical	H	Re	Tm	Db	Pm	Re
Atomic no.	1	75	69	105	61	75

Table 11.5 Even positions with its chemical and atomic numbers.

Alphabet	l		s	W	l	!
Position	2	4	6	8	10	12
Chemical	Os	Sg	Th	Pd	Os	Og
Atomic no.	76	106	90	46	76	118

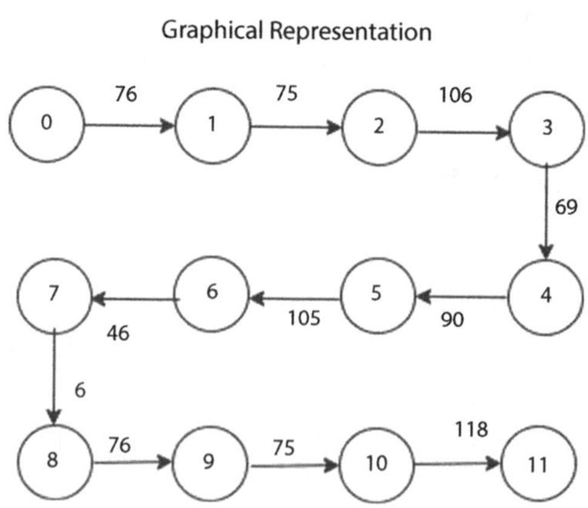

Figure 11.1 Encrypted image.

The obtained values are listed in Tables 11.4, 11.5. The directed graph shown in Figure 11.1 is shared as an encrypted image.

11.7 Algorithm for Decryption

The various steps involved in the decryption process are as follows:

- The atomic numbers obtained from the encrypted image were arranged in order.
- Alternate odd- and even-position atomic numbers are separated.
- The table with the first set of numbers was compared with the first coding table and the corresponding chemical, assigned alphabets, or symbols were obtained. The position of each element is fixed in increasing order of odd numbers starting from 1.
- The process is repeated for even numbers, with positioning numbers starting from 2 in increasing order of even numbers.
- Combining both tables, the positions are represented in increasing order, and its corresponding alphabets are arranged in the same order, which provides the plain text.

11.8 Decryption Process-Example

From Figure 11.1, which is obtained as an encrypted message, a set of atomic numbers is obtained. The odd position numbers are combined into a table, and the second number from the pairs is combined into another table. These two tables are referred to in the corresponding coding tables. The chemical equivalent to the atomic number, its corresponding alphabet,

Table 11.6 Plain text obtained from first coding table.

Atomic no.	1	75	69	105	61	75
Chemical	H	Re	Tm	Db	Pm	Re
Position	1	3	5	7	9	11
Alphabet	A	l	i		e	l

Table 11.7 Plain text obtained from second coding table.

Atomic no.	76	106	90	46	76	118
Chemical	Os	Sg	Th	Pd	Os	Og
Position	2	4	6	8	10	12
Alphabet	l		s	W	l	!

Table 11.8 Combining positions to form plain text.

Position	1	2	3	4	5	6	7	8	9	10	11	12
Alphabet	A	l	L		i	s		W	e	l	l	!

or symbols are obtained as in Tables 11.6, 11.7. The position numbers are odd numbers for the first table and even numbers for the second table.

By arranging the positions obtained in both tables with their corresponding alphabets and symbols, the plain text was obtained, as shown in Table 11.8.

11.9 Conclusion

A new cryptographic algorithm employing a periodic table and a directed graph is introduced in this chapter. Because the algorithm involves chemicals in the encryption and decryption processes, it is difficult to identify a secretly shared message. In addition, two different representations are provided for the set of alphabets and symbols to be used in plain text. The procedure for both the encryption and decryption processes has been presented. In addition, both encryption and decryption process has been illustrated with an example sentence "All is Well!"

References

1. Hiwarekar, A.P., A new method of Cryptography using Laplace transform of Hyperbolic functions. *Int. J. Math. Arch.*, 4, 208–213, 2013.
2. Hemant, K. and Undegaonkar, K., Security in Communication By Using Laplace Transform and Cryptography. *Int. J. Sci. Technol. Res.*, 8, 3207–3209, 2019.

3. Sujatha, S., Application of Laplace Transforms in Cryptography. *Int. J. Math. Arch.*, 4, 67–71, 2013.
4. Hiwarekar, A.P., New mathematical modeling for cryptography. *J. Inf. Assur. Secur.*, 9, 027–033, 2014.
5. Sedeeg, A.K.H., Abdelrahim Mahgoub, M.M., Saif Saeed, M.A., An Application of the New Integral "Aboodh Transform" in Cryptography. *Pure Appl. Math. J.*, 5, 151–154, 2016.
6. Dhingra, S., Savalgi, A.A., Jain, S., Laplace Transformation based Cryptographic Technique in Network Security. *Int. J. Comput. Appl.*, 136, 6–10, 2016.
7. Tuncay Gencoglu, M., Cryptanalaysis of a New Method of Cryptography using Laplace Transform Hyperbolic Functions. *Commun. Math. Appl.*, 8, 183–189, 2017.
8. Saha, M., Application of Laplace – Mellin Transform for Cryptography. *Raj J. Technol. Res. Innov.*, 5, 12–17, 2017.
9. Jayanthi, C.H. and Srinivas, V., Mathematical Modelling for Cryptography using Laplace Transform. *Int. J. Math. Trends Technol.*, 65, 10–15, 2019.
10. Nagalakshmi, G., Chandra Sekhar, A., Ravi Sankar, D., Asymmetric key Cryptography using Laplace Transform. *Int. J. Innov. Technol. Explor. Eng.*, 9, 3083–3087, 2020.
11. Meenakshi, A., Senbagamalar, J., Neel Armstrong, A., Encryption on Graph Networks. *Proceedings of 2nd International Conference on Mathematical Modeling and Computational Science*, pp. 123–130, 2022.
12. Mohan, K.R., Rasappan, S., Murugesan, R., Kumaravel, S.K., Elngar, A.A., Secret Information Sharing Using Probability and Bilinear Transformation. *Proceedings of 2nd International Conference on Mathematical Modeling and Computational Science*, pp. 115–122, 2022.
13. Mohan, K.R., Rasappan, S., Kumaravel, S.K., Secured Information Sharing Using Laplace Transform and hyperbolic Tangent Function. *AIP Conference Proceedings*, vol. 2516, pp. 1–7, 2022.
14. Mohan, K.R., Nagaram, N.B., Murugesan, R., Rasappan, S., A Cryptographic Technique Using Conformal Mapping, in: *Recent Trends in Computational Intelligence and its Applications*, pp. 519–523, CRC Press, Taylor and Francis Group, New York, 2023.
15. Nagaram, N.B., Mohan, K.R., Kumaravel, S.K., Rasappan, S., Secret Information Sharing Using First Order ODE and Variable Separable Method, in: *Recent Trends in Computational Intelligence and its Applications*, pp. 515–518, CRC Press, Taylor and Francis Group, New York, 2023.

12

Federated Learning: A Secure Distributed Machine Learning Approach for IoT Technology

Rituparna Saha[1] and Amit Biswas[2*]

[1]*Department of Computer Science & Engineering, Haldia Institute of Technology, MAKAUT, West Bengal, India*

[2]*Department of Agricultural Engineering, Haldia Institute of Technology, MAKAUT, West Bengal, India*

Abstract

The network of interconnected devices, referred to as the Internet of Things (IoT), generates a large amount of data. In this context, the concept of edge computing, which leverages the growing computational ability of IoT devices, performs the processing and storage of local data in the edge network. However, this results in various challenges such as data privacy issues due to the transfer of raw sensitive data from IoT devices, communication latency issues due to the limited bandwidth of IoT devices, and energy efficiency issues due to resource-constrained IoT devices with limited battery power. Federated learning (FL) addresses these challenges by enabling IoT devices to collaboratively learn a single global model without transferring local data to a central server. Multiple IoT devices or clients, distributed across different regions, participated in the training process. Initially, a global model was created using a centralized server. Then, a set of client devices is selected based on their device status and configured using the global model sent by the server. In the next step, the training process was performed using local data, and the global model was updated. When the local training process is completed, the client devices send the updated model parameters to the centralized server. After receiving all the local updates, the centralized server performs the global aggregation process and updates the global model. Therefore, FL is advantageous over the centralized training approach owing to its privacy preservation of sensitive data, dealing with non-independent and identically distributed data, reducing

**Corresponding author*: amitmbiswas@gmail.com

Subhabrata Barman, Santanu Koley and Subhankar Joardar (eds.) Next-Generation Systems and Secure Computing, (239–256) © 2025 Scrivener Publishing LLC

communication overhead, and ensuring scalability and fault tolerance. Owing to these positive aspects, the FL is adopted by the various application domains, such as healthcare and mobile applications, where data privacy and security are essential. Although FL has different advantages, it faces different challenges owing to data variation across IoT devices, limited resources across IoT devices, and privacy and security issues during communication between centralized servers and clients. In this chapter, we briefly introduce the FL, discuss the different key challenges associated with the FL, and discuss the current research and future studies relevant to the challenges of the FL. In addition, various application domains of FL are discussed in the present chapter.

Keywords: Federated learning, internet of things, machine learning, privacy, security

12.1 Introduction

The proliferation of IoT devices generates a large amount of data every day in a modern distributed network. This growth will continue to increase as 5G networks continue to connect more devices [2]. However, the increasing computation capability of IoT devices, coupled with the concern of privacy risks, is favored to push the storage and computation of data at the edge of the network. On the other hand, in centralized machine learning all user data are stored in centralized server in order to train a comprehensive ML model. Therefore, the efficiency of the ML model depends on the computational power of the centralized server [76]. However, centralized training faces privacy and security challenges owing to the sharing of personal data from the end nodes to the centralized server. This introduced the concept of *edge computing*.

In the distributed computing paradigm [80], edge computing involves the processing of data near data sources, such as devices, edge servers, or gateways [1, 77]. Thus, proximity to data sources enables real-time decision-making, reduces latency, and mitigates privacy security risks [72, 73]. In addition, edge computing reduces network congestion and the demand for a high-bandwidth connection status across end devices [75]. Furthermore, the scalability of edge computing can be easily increased by adding more edge devices [74]. Edge computing may be used in various domains, such as healthcare, smart cities, and agriculture. Distributed machine learning is the concept of training ML models across different nodes or devices distributed across a network [3]. However, this involves the distribution of data across multiple devices, which may be a potential issue for sensitive data. This led to the invention of FL [4].

12.1.1 Overview of Federated Learning

In 2016, McMahan *et al.* [5] first introduced the concept of FL and proposed a federated averaging (FedAvg) algorithm. FedAvg is a distributed learning technique in which a set of nodes or client devices collaboratively train a machine learning model without transferring their local dataset to the central server [78, 79]. In the following section, we discuss the different steps of FL following the Federated Averaging algorithm proposed by McMahan *et al.* [5]

a) **Client Selection:** The centralized server selects a set of clients based on their device status [5].
b) **Configuration:** Selected clients download the global model from the centralized server and configure themselves [5].
c) **Local Training and Update:** Each client device locally performs a training operation on its local dataset and updates the global model. For example, ran SGD on local data [5].
d) **Aggregation:** The centralized server performs the aggregation operation after collecting locally updated model parameters from all selected client devices and updates the global model [5].

12.1.2 Differences Between Distributed Learning and Federated Learning

Distributed learning is a centralized training process where training data is collected from different sources and stored on the centralized server to train the model. On the other hand, federated learning is a decentralized training process where models are trained locally into the local devices and the updated model parameters are transferred to the centralized server to aggregate the model updates and build a global model [6]. Therefore, compared to the federated learning approach, the distributed learning approach faces privacy issues and communication overhead challenges due to the transfer of raw data from source to centralized server [16]. Google's Gboard is an example of federated learning, where the keyboard on the device learns the training pattern without sending the sensitive information.

12.1.3 Main Advantages of FL

The FL is privacy secured. Here the training data needs not to be shared across other nodes; it remains local [4, 6].

The FL reduces communication overhead. The FL does not need communication between nodes. The FL needs communication between nodes and a centralized server to transfer the locally updated model parameter [7].

12.1.4 Core Challenges of FL

12.1.4.1 Communication Overhead

Communication is a critical problem in a federated network. At each round of FL, the set of selected IoT devices have to communicate with the centralized server—a) to configure themselves to download the global model and b) to upload the updated model parameters using the local dataset [13]. Here, the first type of communication is downlink communication, i.e., from server to client, and the second type of communication is uplink communication, i.e., from client to server [14]. However, due to the higher performance of the server node than the resource-constrained client node, uplink communication suffers from communication overhead than downlink communication. Therefore, it necessitates building up a communication-efficient FL framework that helps the resource-constraint client devices to complete the training process.

12.1.4.2 System Heterogeneity

In the federated network, each client device has a variation of resources in terms of bandwidth, battery energy, and computation power [19]. Additionally, they are having variability in hardware (CPU and memory) and network connectivity (2G, 3G, 4G, and 5G). These system-related variations cause a sudden drop out of an active client at a given iteration due to network connectivity or energy consumption [22]. It may affect the global aggregation time at each communication round as well as the federated learning time. Therefore, it necessitates building up a robust FL framework to handle the dropout of clients during training time [23].

12.1.4.3 Heterogeneous Data

Client devices generate non-independent and identically distributed data based on the user's interaction [16, 17]. For example, in the context of next-word prediction, each different mobile phone user has different usage of language. Its consequences increase in FL convergence time.

12.1.4.4 *Privacy and Security Risks*

Indeed, FL secures privacy by adopting collaborative learning across client devices without sharing the sensitive data, but it still suffers from the risk of exposing local information for the sharing of model parameters [8]. To address this challenge, FL is adopting different methods such as secure multiparty computation (SMC), differential privacy, and secure aggregation techniques [70, 71]. Again, the FL faces different security threats, such as model inversion attacks, poisoning attacks, and inference attacks [72].

12.2 Categorization of FL

12.2.1 Data Partitioning

There are three different approaches to implement FL: Horizontal FL, Vertical FL, and Federated Transfer Learning.

12.2.1.1 *Horizontal FL*

In horizontal FL, each client device consists of different data samples but similar feature space, or each device consists of a subset of the sample dataset whereas the features are the same [9]. For example, in a healthcare scenario, the FL model can be implemented across the different hospitals having the same feature lists (e.g., patient age, blood pressure, medical history) of different patients without sharing their private data. Therefore, horizontal FL is used in situations where we need to aggregate data from different resources with the same feature lists but with different instances. The main advantage of this method is that it increases the user sample size.

12.2.1.2 *Vertical FL*

In vertical FL, each client device has data related to a different feature set but of the same data instance. In other words, in vertical FL, each device consists of different aspects of information of the same data instance [10]. For example, one bank may loan-related information of one customer, and another bank may have information related to income and spending habits. In this case, vertical FL will allow learning a model collaboratively across these banks without sharing their own local data. The main advantage of this method is that it increases feature dimension [11].

12.2.1.3 Federated Transfer Learning

It is a combination of two techniques: federated learning and transfer learning. In transfer learning, the model is trained over one task and used to predict another related task. Thus, the source task and the target task are different. Federated transfer learning is used in the cases where the users and the feature list do not overlap. For example, there are two types of institutions: one is e-commerce in India, and another is social application in the United States. Now these two different institutions would have two different client lists based on their geo-locations and also have different lists of user features due to different working objectives of the institutions [31, 32]. This results in a small overlap between the datasets. In this case, federated transfer learning is effective to use. In addition, the main advantage of this method is that it increases both user sample size and feature dimension [33].

12.3 Data Availability

The FL can be classified into two classes based on the availability of data and the number of clients available: cross-silo FL and cross-device FL.

12.3.1 Cross-Silo FL

In this case, small-scale numbers of clients, such as 2–100 devices, usually participate during the training process. Cross-silo FL is mainly used to train a ML model within an organization or within groups of organizations. Here, horizontal and vertical FL are used for data partitioning.

12.3.2 Cross-Device FL

In this case, a large number of clients with similar domains participate during the training process. Here, the selection procedure mainly happens in a random way.

12.4 Federated Learning Training Approaches

There are two types of approaches for FL training: asynchronous FL and synchronous FL. In synchronous FL, performance and data privacy are retained by selecting a fixed number of clients at each epoch. Existing studies in synchronous FL focus on reducing training time without considering the straggler device. However, asynchronous FL focuses on convex loss and does not consider client drop out problems [40].

12.5 Key Research Directions Related to FL

Federated learning is an active research topic. There are different research directions on various aspects of this technology. In the following, we discuss some of the key research directions related to federated learning.

12.5.1 Privacy and Security

The collaborative learning approach of FL across a huge number of clients and transferring model parameters from each client device to a centralized server at each communication round makes FL vulnerable to various attacks [8, 12, 21, 23]. In the following, we have discussed different threats and attacks possible in FL.

a) **Poisoning:** Poisoning attacks mainly occur during the FL training. Poisoning attacks can be of two types, data poisoning and model poisoning attacks [71]. In data poisoning attacks, the attacker targets the training dataset across client devices and manipulates the dataset or poisons the dataset with malicious data, which would degrade the model training accuracy [30]. On the other hand, in model poisoning attacks, attackers directly target the global model. In general, a malicious attacker first manipulates the local model parameters, which consequences the manipulation in the global model.
b) **Inference:** Inference attacks also occur during the FL process by malicious clients or centralized servers. It is as severe as poisoning attacks [71].
c) **Backdoor Attack:** Backdoor attacks are not as transparent as poisoning and inference attacks [71]. Backdoor attacks mainly target the actual model without making an impact on the accuracy. Therefore, the severity of the backdoor attack is higher than poisoning and inference attacks.

12.5.2 Communication Overhead

In FL participating edge devices such as IoT devices, mobile devices often suffer from communication bottlenecks due to unreliable network connections [28, 29, 39]. Existing works follow two types of approaches to address this challenge: a) reducing the number of bits of client updates; b) reducing the number of communication rounds between the clients and centralized server [22].

Many of the existing works follow the first approach. Konecny *et al.* [4] proposed a data compression approach to compress the client updates. However, the limitation of this technique is that it suffers from information loss, which may impact the training accuracy and convergence time. On the other hand, some of the existing studies follow the second approach to address the communication overhead problem. Wang *et al.* [24] proposed CMFL to dynamically identify the irrelevant updates and exclude them, whereas Lin *et al.* [41] introduced the deep gradient compression technique to reduce communication bottlenecks.

12.5.3 Data Heterogeneity

The FL also suffers from statistical challenges due to the presence of non-IID local data across client devices, which means data heterogeneity in local data distributions across clients [18, 49]. The FL uses a stochastic gradient descent algorithm for the training of deep learning models [42–47]. The presence of non-IID data degrades the performance of FL due to the weight divergence of local models [15, 34, 36, 38]. Smith *et al.* [20] proposed a multitask learning framework named MOCHA. Again, Zhao *et al.* [48] followed earth mover's distance (EMD) to calculate the weight divergence and proposed a strategy to improve FL training on non-IID data.

12.6 Application Areas of FL

There are wide ranges of applications across various domains and industries where FL can be used for generating collaborative learning models while preserving data privacy and security [52]. In the following, we have discussed some of the important use cases [25].

12.6.1 Healthcare

The FL can be useful for hospitals and medical organizations through developing an AI model to perform various tasks such as diagnosing disease, drug discovery, etc. [26, 27, 51]. In the following, we have discussed some key applications of FL in healthcare.

12.6.1.1 Predictive Model

The FL can be used to develop an accurate and general predictive model for various clinical purposes by aggregating the patients' clinical data from different hospitals without sharing the personal data [53].

12.6.1.2 Personalized Medicine

A personalized treatment plan for an individual patient can be generated by analyzing data from different sources without sharing its personal data [50].

12.6.1.3 Drug Discovery

The FL can be used to discover new drugs by pharmaceutical companies through analyzing large amounts of patient data from different locations while maintaining privacy [53, 57].

12.6.1.4 Disease Prediction

The FL can assist doctors to predict disease in an early stage through analyzing various healthcare data [54].

12.6.1.5 Medical Image Analysis

The FL can be used to improve medical image analysis from X-rays, MRI scans, etc., through training an AI model with aggregating data from different hospitals without sharing the medical images [55].

12.6.1.6 Remote Patient Monitoring

The FL can be used to improve remote patient monitoring systems by continuously updating the AI model used to analyze patient data from wearable devices [54, 56].

12.6.1.7 Healthcare Fraud Detection

The FL can be used to detect fraud claims by analyzing the billing patterns [67, 68].

12.6.2 Agriculture

12.6.2.1 Crop Yield Prediction

The FL can be used to predict crop yield by aggregating various agronomical data, such as weather condition, soil quality, and crop type, from different farms without transferring the actual data [59].

12.6.2.2 Disease Prediction

Early detection of crop disease is essential for preventing crop loss. The FL can be used to build a generalized ML model for detecting disease or pests in individual crops through analyzing the field images [35]. The FL enables the aggregation of information from different fields at different locations without sharing their data [37].

12.6.2.3 Precision Agriculture

Precision agriculture uses real-time data such as weather data, irrigation, fertilizer, and pesticides for crop health management [59]. The FL can improve precision agriculture and build a generalized model through gathering information from different fields from different locations without sharing data.

12.6.2.4 Soil Health Monitoring

Soil health management is another essential process for increasing crop yield. Soil quality changes in various regions. The FL can be used to build a generalized model to analyze the soil quality through gathering soil information from different regions. The generalized model will be useful for the farmers for soil health management.

12.6.2.5 Crop Variety Recommendation

Crop growth depends on agronomical parameters such as weather data and the soil type of the region [58]. Therefore, crop variety changes with the varying region. FL can be used to build a crop variety recommendation system analyzing the different regional data. This system will be useful to the farmers for crop selection.

12.6.2.6 *Supply Chain Optimization*

The FL can be used to build an optimized supply chain for efficient distribution of fresh foods and reduce food waste. To build up the generalized AI model, FL may analyze data from various farmers, food suppliers, retailers, and consumers.

12.6.3 Smart City

The FL can be used for various applications in smart cities.

12.6.3.1 *Traffic Management*

The FL can be used to improve traffic management through analyzing real-time data from different devices, such as traffic cameras, GPS devices, across the different locations in the city while preserving data privacy [63].

12.6.3.2 *Public Transportation*

The FL can be used to build a model to optimize public transportation services through analyzing data from different public transport services such as buses, taxis, trains, and metros. The trained model can be used to predict the optimum route and arrival time [63].

12.6.3.3 *Air Quality Monitoring*

The FL can be used to build a model for air quality prediction through analyzing air quality sensor data from different locations in the city. It can be used to monitor pollution levels and improve public health in the city [36].

12.6.3.4 *Waste Management*

The FL can be used to improve waste collection systems through analyzing data from sensors integrated in waste bins. It will be helpful to generate the waste collection route based on the waste generation pattern [69].

12.6.3.5 *Security*

The FL can be used to improve security and surveillance of the city by analyzing the images from CCTV footage across the city. It will be useful to track unusual activities across the city while preserving the privacy of the citizens [61, 64–66].

12.6.3.6 Urban Planning

The FL can be used for city planning through analyzing data related to the city. It will be helpful for planning new transportation routes, buildings, power supply cables, and water supply lines [60, 62].

12.7 Conclusion

FL is a collaborative learning model that trains the machine learning model across the end devices without sharing their personal data. This chapter aims to provide an overview of FL, how does it works, and also discusses different categorizations of FL based on data partitioning, data availability, and FL training approaches. Besides, we also point out different challenges and research directions related to FL. Moreover, we also elaborate on the usage of FL in some of the application areas in different domains, such as agriculture, healthcare, and smart cities.

References

1. Yu R., Li P., Toward resource-efficient federated learning in mobile edge computing. *IEEE Netw.*, 35, 1, 148–55, 2021 Feb 16.
2. Poushter, J., *et al.*, Smartphone ownership and internet usage continues to climb in emerging economies. *Pew Res. Center*, 22, 1–44, 2016.
3. Bonawitz, K., Kairouz, P., McMahan, B., and Ramage, D., Federated learning and privacy: Building privacy-preserving systems for machine learning and data science on decentralized data. *Queue*, 19, 5, 87–114, 2021.
4. Konečny, J., McMahan, H.B., Yu, F.X., Richtárik, P., Suresh, A.T., Bacon, D., Federated learning: Strategies for improving communication efficiency. arXiv preprint arXiv:1610.05492, 2016.
5. McMahan, H.B., Moore, E., Ramage, D., Hampson, S., *et al.*, Communication-efficient learning of deep networks from decentralized data. arXiv preprint arXiv:1602.05629, 2016.
6. Samarakoon, S., Bennis, M., Saady, W., Debbah, M., Distributed federated learning for ultra-reliable low-latency vehicular communications. arXiv preprint arXiv:1807.08127, 2018.
7. Nishio, T. and Yonetani, R., Client selection for federated learning with het-erogeneous resources in mobile edge. arXiv preprint arXiv:1804.08333, 2018.

8. Kim, H., Park, J., Bennis, M., Kim, S.L., On-device federated learning via blockchain and its latency analysis. arXiv preprint arXiv:1808.03949, 2018.
9. Yang, Q., Liu, Y., Chen, T., Tong, Y., Federated machine learning: Concept and applications. *ACM Trans. Intell. Syst. Technol. (TIST)*, 10, 1–19, 2019c.
10. Zhang, C., Xie, Y., Bai, H., Yu, B., Li, W., Gao, Y., A survey on federated learning. *Knowledge-Based Syst.*, 216, 106775, 2021.
11. Briggs, C., Fan, Z., Andras, P., A review of privacy preserving federated learning for private iot analytics. arXiv preprint arXiv:2004.11794, 2020b.
12. Lyu, L., Yu, H., Yang, Q., Threats to federated learning: A survey. arXiv preprint arXiv:2003.02133, 2020.
13. Sahu, A.K., Li, T., Sanjabi, M., Zaheer, M., Talwalkar, A., Smith, V., On the convergence of federated optimization in heterogeneous networks. arXiv:1812.06127, 2018, CoRR abs/1812.06127. URL: http://arxiv.org/abs/1812.06127.
14. Sattler, F., Müller, K. R., and Samek, W., Clustered federated learning: Model-agnostic distributed multitask optimization under privacy constraints. *IEEE Trans. Neural Netw. Learn. Syst.*, 32, 8, 3710–3722, 2020.
15. Sattler, F., Wiedemann, S., Müller, K.R., Samek, W., Robust and communication-efficient federated learning from non-iid data. *IEEE Trans. Neural Netw. Learn. Syst.*, 31, 3400–3413, 2019.
16. Singh, I., Zhou, H., Yang, K., Ding, M., Lin, B., Xie, P., Differentially-private federated neural architecture search. arXiv preprint arXiv:2006.10559, 2020.
17. Wang, H., Kaplan, Z., Niu, D., Li, B., Optimizing federated learning on non-iid data with reinforcement learning, in: *IEEE INFOCOM 2020-IEEE Conference on Computer Communications*, IEEE, pp. 1698–1707, 2020 Jul 6.
18. Alkaabi, S., Gregory, M., and Li, S., Multi-Access Edge Computing Handover Strategies, Management, and Challenges: A Review. *IEEE Access*, 2024.
19. Wang, H., Yurochkin, M., Sun, Y., Papailiopoulos, D., Khazaeni, Y., Federated learning with matched averaging, in: *International Conference on Learning Representations*, 2020b.
20. Smith, V., Chiang, C.K., Sanjabi, M., Talwalkar, A.S., Federated multi-task learning. *Advances in Neural Information Processing Systems*, pp. 4427–4437, 2017.
21. Bagdasaryan, E., Veit, A., Hua, Y., Estrin, D., Shmatikov, V., How to backdoor federated learning. arXiv preprint arXiv:1807.00459, 2018.
22. Dogdu, U., 2G/3G/4G/5G signals demodulation with MATLAB using RTL-SDR 2832U and USRP B210 (Master's thesis, U. Dogdu), 2024.
23. Niu, Z., Dong, H., Qin, A. K., Gu, T., Flrce: Resource-efficient federated learning with early-stopping strategy. *IEEE Trans. Mobile Comput.*, 2024.
24. Wang, L., Wang, W., Li, B., CMFL: Mitigating Communication Overhead for Federated Learning. *2019 IEEE 39th International Conference on Distributed Computing Systems (ICDCS)*, pp. 954–964, Dallas, TX, USA, 2019, doi: 10.1109/ICDCS.2019.00099.

25. Li, L., Fan, Y., Tse, M., and Lin, K. Y., A review of applications in federated learning. Computers & Industrial Engineering. 2020 Nov 1;149:106854.
26. Rieke, N., Hancox, J., Li, W., Milletari, F., Roth, H.R., Albarqouni, S., Bakas, S., Galtier, M.N., Landman, B.A., Maier-Hein, K., Ourselin, S., The future of digital health with federated learning. *npj Digital Med.*, 3, 1, 119, 2020 Sep 14.
27. Maleki Varnosfaderani, S., Forouzanfar, M., The role of AI in hospitals and clinics: transforming healthcare in the 21st century. *Bioengineering*, 11, 4, 337, 2024.
28. Li, T., Sahu, A.K., Talwalkar, A., Smith, V., Federated learning: Challenges, methods, and future directions. *IEEE Signal Process Mag.*, 37, 3, 50–60, 2020 May 1.
29. Bonawitz, K., Eichner, H., Grieskamp, W., Huba, D., Ingerman, A., Ivanov, V., Kiddon, C., Konečný, J., Mazzocchi, S., McMahan, B., Van Overveldt, T., Towards federated learning at scale: System design, in: *Proceedings of machine learning and systems*, vol. 1, pp. 374–88, 2019 Apr 15.
30. Kairouz, P., McMahan, H.B., Avent, B., Bellet, A., Bennis, M., Bhagoji, A.N., Bonawitz, K., Charles, Z., Cormode, G., Cummings, R., D'Oliveira, R.G., Advances and open problems in federated learning. *Found. Trends® Mach. Learn.*, 14, 1–2, 1–210, 2021 Jun 22.
31. Khan, L.U., Saad, W., Han, Z., Hossain, E., Hong, C.S., Federated learning for internet of things: Recent advances, taxonomy, and open challenges. *IEEE Commun. Surv. Tutor.*, 23, 3, 1759–99, 2021 Jun 18.
32. Li, Q., Wen, Z., Wu, Z., Hu, S., Wang, N., Li, Y., He, B., A survey on federated learning systems: Vision, hype and reality for data privacy and protection. *IEEE Trans. Knowl. Data Eng.*, 35, 4, 3347–3366, 2021.
33. Ruan, Y., Zhang, X., Joe-Wong, C., How valuable is your data? optimizing client recruitment in federated learning. *IEEE/ACM Trans. Netw.*, 2024.
34. Zhu, H., Xu, J., Liu, S., Jin, Y., Federated learning on non-IID data: A survey. *Neurocomputing*, 465, 371–90, 2021 Nov 20.
35. Zhan, Y., Zhang, J., Hong, Z., Wu, L., Li, P., Guo, S., A survey of incentive mechanism design for federated learning. *IEEE Trans. Emerging Top. Comput.*, 10, 2, 1035–44, 2021 Mar 3.
36. Ma, X., Zhu, J., Lin, Z., Chen, S., Qin, Y., A state-of-the-art survey on solving non-IID data in Federated Learning. *Future Gener. Comput. Syst.*, 135, 244–58, 2022 Oct 1.
37. Aggarwal, M., Khullar, V., Goyal, N., Prola, T. A., Resource-efficient federated learning over IoAT for rice leaf disease classification. *Comput. Electron. Agric.*, 221, 109001, 2024.
38. Briggs, C., Fan, Z., Andras, P., Federated learning with hierarchical clustering of local updates to improve training on non-IID data, in: *2020 International Joint Conference on Neural Networks (IJCNN)*, IEEE, pp. 1–9, 2020 Jul 19.

39. Chen, Y., Ning, Y., Slawski, M., Rangwala, H., Asynchronous online federated learning for edge devices with non-iid data, in: *2020 IEEE International Conference on Big Data (Big Data)*, IEEE, pp. 15–24, 2020 Dec 10.
40. Shoham, N., Avidor, T., Keren, A., Israel, N., Benditkis, D., Mor-Yosef, L., Zeitak, I., Overcoming forgetting in federated learning on non-iid data. arXiv preprint arXiv:1910.07796, 2019 Oct 17.
41. Lin, Y., Han, S., Mao, H., Wang, Y., Dally, W.J., Deep gradient compression: Reducing the communication bandwidth for distributed training. arXiv preprint arXiv:1712.01887, 2017.
42. Duchi, J., Hazan, E., Singer, Y., Adaptive subgradient methods for online learning and stochastic optimization. *J. Mach. Learn. Res.*, 12, Jul, 2121–2159, 2011.
43. Tieleman, T. and Hinton, G., Divide the gradient by a running average of its recent magnitude. coursera: Neural networks for machine learning. tech. rep., Technical Report, Available online: https://zh. coursera. org/learn/neuralnetworks/lecture/YQHki/rmsprop-divide-the-gradient-by-a-running-average-ofits-recent-magnitude (accessed on 21 April 2017).
44. Kinga, D. and Adam, J.B., A method for stochastic optimization, in: *International Conference on Learning Representations (ICLR)*, 2015.
45. Bottou, L., Large-scale machine learning with stochastic gradient descent, in: *Proceedings of COMPSTAT'2010*, pp. 177–186, Springer, 2010.
46. Rakhlin, A., Shamir, O., Sridharan, K., Making gradient descent optimal for strongly convex stochastic optimization. arXiv preprint arXiv:1109.5647. Vancouver Convention Center, 2011.
47. Dean, J., Corrado, G., Monga, R., Chen, K., Devin, M., Mao, M., Senior, A., Tucker, P., Yang, K., Le, Q. V. *et al.*, Large scale distributed deep networks. in: *Advances in Neural Information Processing Systems*, vol. 25, pp. 1223–1231, 2012.
48. Zhao, Y., Li, M., Lai, L., Suda, N., Civin, D., Chandra, V., Federated learning with non-iid data. arXiv preprint arXiv:1806.00582, 2018 Jun 2.
49. Shao, J., Sun, Y., Li, S., Zhang, J., Dres-fl: Dropout-resilient secure federated learning for non-iid clients via secret data sharing. *Adv. Neural Inf. Process. Syst.*, 35, 10533–45, 2022 Dec 6.
50. Nguyen, D.C., Pham, Q.V., Pathirana, P.N., Ding, M., Seneviratne, A., Lin, Z., Dobre, O., Hwang, W.J., Federated learning for smart healthcare: A survey. *ACM Comput. Surv. (CSUR)*, 55, 3, 1–37, 2022 Feb 3.
51. Antunes, R.S., André da Costa, C., Küderle, A., Yari, I.A., Eskofier, B., Federated learning for healthcare: Systematic review and architecture proposal. *ACM Trans. Intell. Syst. Technol. (TIST)*, 13, 4, 1–23, 2022 May 4.
52. Joshi, M., Pal, A., Sankarasubbu, M., Federated learning for healthcare domain-pipeline, applications and challenges. *ACM Trans. Comput. Healthcare*, 3, 4, 1–36, 2022 Nov 3.
53. Singh, S., Rathore, S., Alfarraj, O., Tolba, A., Yoon, B., A framework for privacy-preservation of IoT healthcare data using Federated Learning and blockchain technology. *Future Gener. Comput. Syst.*, 129, 380–8, 2022 Apr 1.

54. Rahman, A., Hossain, M.S., Muhammad, G., Kundu, D., Debnath, T., Rahman, M., Khan, M.S., Tiwari, P., Band, S.S., Federated learning-based AI approaches in smart healthcare: concepts, taxonomies, challenges and open issues. *Cluster Comput.*, 26, 4, 2271–311, 2023 Aug.
55. Patel, V. A., Bhattacharya, P., Tanwar, S., Gupta, R., Sharma, G., Bokoro, P. N., and Sharma, R., Adoption of federated learning for healthcare informatics: Emerging applications and future directions. *IEEE Access*, 10, 90792–90826, 2022.
56. Ali, M., Naeem, F., Tariq, M., Kaddoum, G., Federated learning for privacy preservation in smart healthcare systems: A comprehensive survey. *IEEE J. Biomed. Health. Inf.*, 27, 2, 778–89, 2022 Jun 13.
57. Arikumar, K.S., Prathiba, S.B., Alazab, M., Gadekallu, T.R., Pandya, S., Khan, J.M., Moorthy, R.S., FL-PMI: Federated learning-based person movement identification through wearable devices in smart healthcare systems. *Sensors*, 22, 4, 1377, 2022 Feb 11.
58. Friha, O., Ferrag, M.A., Shu, L., Maglaras, L., Choo, K.K., Nafaa, M., FELIDS: Federated learning-based intrusion detection system for agricultural Internet of Things. *J. Parallel Distrib. Comput.*, 165, 17–31, 2022 Jul 1.
59. Manoj, T., Makkithaya, K., Narendra, V.G., A federated learning-based crop yield prediction for agricultural production risk management, in: *2022 IEEE Delhi Section Conference (DELCON)*, IEEE, pp. 1–7, 2022 Feb 11.
60. Boobalan, P., Ramu, S.P., Pham, Q.V., Dev, K., Pandya, S., Maddikunta, P.K., Gadekallu, T.R., Huynh-The, T., Fusion of federated learning and industrial Internet of Things: A survey. *Comput. Netw.*, 212, 109048, 2022 Jul 20.
61. Saraswat, D., Verma, A., Bhattacharya, P., Tanwar, S., Sharma, G., Bokoro, P.N., Sharma, R., Blockchain-based federated learning in UAVs beyond 5G networks: A solution taxonomy and future directions. *IEEE Access*, 10, 33154–82, 2022 Mar 21.
62. Patros, P., Ooi, M., Huang, V., Mayo, M., Anderson, C., Burroughs, S., Baughman, M., Almurshed, O., Rana, O., Chard, R., Chard, K., Rural ai: Serverless-powered federated learning for remote applications. *IEEE Internet Comput.*, 27, 2, 28–34, 2022 Sep 30.
63. Al-Huthaifi, R., Li, T., Huang, W., Gu, J., Li, C, Federated learning in smart cities: Privacy and security survey. Information Sciences, 632, 833–857, 2023.
64. Issa, W., Moustafa, N., Turnbull, B., Sohrabi, N., Tari, Z., Blockchain-based federated learning for securing internet of things: A comprehensive survey. *ACM Comput. Surv.*, 55, 9, 1–43, 2023 Jan 13.
65. Ferrag, M.A., Friha, O., Hamouda, D., Maglaras, L., Janicke, H., Edge-IIoTset: A new comprehensive realistic cyber security dataset of IoT and IIoT applications for centralized and federated learning. *IEEE Access*, 10, 40281–306, 2022 Apr 8.
66. Gosselin, R., Vieu, L., Loukil, F., Benoit, A., Privacy and security in federated learning: A survey. *Appl. Sci.*, 12, 19, 9901, 2022 Oct 1.

67. Li, H., Li, C., Wang, J., Yang, A., Ma, Z., Zhang, Z., Hua, D., Review on security of federated learning and its application in healthcare. *Future Gener. Comput. Syst.*, 144, 271–90, 2023 Jul 1.
68. Xu, Z., Guo, Y., Chakraborty, C., Hua, Q., Chen, S., Yu, K., A simple federated learning-based scheme for security enhancement over Internet of Medical Things. *IEEE J. Biomed. Health. Inf.*, 27, 2, 652–63, 2022 Jun 30.
69. Blanco-Justicia, A., Domingo-Ferrer, J., Martínez, S., Sánchez, D., Flanagan, A., Tan, K.E., Achieving security and privacy in federated learning systems: Survey, research challenges and future directions. *Eng. Appl. Artif. Intell.*, 106, 104468, 2021 Nov 1.
70. Nguyen, D.C., Ding, M., Pham, Q.V., Pathirana, P.N., Le, L.B., Seneviratne, A., Li, J., Niyato, D., Poor, H.V., Federated learning meets blockchain in edge computing: Opportunities and challenges. *IEEE Internet Things J.*, 8, 16, 12806–25, 2021 Apr 13.
71. Mothukuri, V., Parizi, R.M., Pouriyeh, S., Huang, Y., Dehghantanha, A., Srivastava, G., A survey on security and privacy of federated learning. *Future Gener. Comput. Syst.*, 115, 619–40, 2021 Feb 1.
72. Mothukuri, V., Khare, P., Parizi, R.M., Pouriyeh, S., Dehghantanha, A., Srivastava, G., Federated-learning-based anomaly detection for IoT security attacks. *IEEE Internet Things J.*, 9, 4, 2545–54, 2021 May 5.
73. Abreha, H.G., Hayajneh, M., Serhani, M.A., Federated learning in edge computing: a systematic survey. *Sensors*, 22, 2, 450, 2022 Jan 7.
74. Wang, X., Han, Y., Wang, C., Zhao, Q., Chen, X., Chen, M., In-edge ai: Intelligentizing mobile edge computing, caching and communication by federated learning. *IEEE Netw.*, 33, 5, 156–65, 2019 Jul 24.
75. Baidya, T. and Moh, S., Comprehensive survey on resource allocation for edge-computing-enabled metaverse. *Comput. Sci. Rev.*, 54, 100680, 2024.
76. Ye, D., Yu, R., Pan, M., Han, Z., Federated learning in vehicular edge computing: A selective model aggregation approach. *IEEE Access*, 8, 23920–35, 2020 Jan 22.
77. Brecko, A., Kajati, E., Koziorek, J., Zolotova, I., Federated learning for edge computing: A survey. *Appl. Sci.*, 12, 18, 9124, 2022 Sep 11.
78. Saha, R., Misra, S., Deb, P.K., FogFL: Fog-Assisted Federated Learning for Resource-Constrained IoT Devices. *IEEE Internet Things J.*, 8, 10, 8456–8463, May15, 2021, doi: 10.1109/JIOT.2020.3046509.
79. Saha, R., Misra, S., Chakraborty, A., Chatterjee, C., Deb, P.K., Data-Centric Client Selection for Federated Learning Over Distributed Edge Networks. *IEEE Trans. Parallel Distrib. Syst.*, 34, 2, 675–686, 1 Feb. 2023, doi: 10.1109/TPDS.2022.3217271.
80. Saha, R., Chakraborty, A., Misra, S., Das, S.K., Chatterjee, C., DLSense: Distributed Learning-Based Smart Virtual Sensing for Precision Agriculture. *IEEE Sens. J.*, 21, 16, 17556–17563, Aug.15, 2021, doi: 10.1109/JSEN.2020.3048593.

13

Security Analysis for Mobile Crowdsensing Scheme by Predicting Vehicle Mobility Using Deep Learning Algorithm

Monojit Manna[1*], Arpan Adhikary[1,2] and Sima Das[2,3]

[1]*RCC Institute of Information Technology, Beleghata, Kolkata, India*
[2]*Bengal College of Engineering and Technology, Durgapur, India*
[3]*Haldia Institute of Technology, Haldia Purba Medinipur, India*

Abstract

Mobile crowdsensing (MCS) systems are designed to improve multimedia service quality and encourage safe sensing in Internet of Things applications such as medical and traffic monitoring. Currently, mobile vehicles are used in metropolitan areas to perform data sensing and collection tasks for mobility and universality. In this study, we focused on large-scale dynamic and heterogeneous networks. To fulfil the necessary data in the future era within a few minutes, systems must handle security concerns, including jamming, spoofing, and fake sensing attacks during both the sensing and information exchange phases. To configure the maximum data optimization problem and budget, we map the requirements of the vehicle. The implementation of the program is essentially designed to generate a realistic online platform where real-time automobiles appear to be moving continuously. We examined safe mobile crowdsensing and outlined applications for deep learning (DL) techniques. The data center has the authority to immediately select a set of vehicles. Mobile vehicles (DLMV) will be used in a deep-learning-based plan to gather sensing data from an urban environment. This study suggests an offline technique based on deep learning to predict mobility in the future. To solve an NP-complete problem with a limited budget, we suggest a greedy strategy that applies an online algorithm step to a subset of cars. The improvement in the performance of these DL-based methods over traditional security schemes highlights the problems that must be fixed for the implementation of workable solutions. In addition to demonstrating the effectiveness of our proposed approach, the

**Corresponding author*: monojit.rcciit@gmail.com

Subhabrata Barman, Santanu Koley and Subhankar Joardar (eds.) Next-Generation Systems and Secure Computing, (257–276) © 2025 Scrivener Publishing LLC

experiment's outcome validates DLMV's applicability and increases the amount of sensing data collected when compared to alternative methods.

Keywords: Mobile crowdsensing, data collecting, vehicle recruiting, deep learning, sensing coverage

13.1 Introduction

Large-scale monitoring can be achieved by recruiting mobile users via mobile crowdsensing. In a distributed manner, the mobile nodes gather environmental information and perform sensing tasks. Recent times have seen the reconciliation of mobile vehicles for the purpose of cloud sensing due to their connectedness, mobility, and ubiquity. Various integrated communication functions develop into an intelligence function that is gradually being developed by the vehicle. Vehicles are equipped with various communication resources and large storage systems so that they can transmit and store more data than mobile devices. Participants chosen through an MCS platform keep track of the environment's properties and send sensing reports to MCS servers, which then extract pertinent data from the report [1]. Moreover, vehicles in urban cities are more ubiquitous and highly dynamic moving, covering more sensing fields than smartphones with less time duration than mobile nodes. Selfish independent people who manage mobile devices might launch insider-assault MCS systems depending on security and privacy [32], which are crucial given the prevalence of faked sensing assaults and privacy issues. Due to their vulnerability to security risks, 3G/4G, WiFi, and vehicular ad-hoc networks (VANETs), the cloud sensing cost decreases by recruiting smaller participants in a multitude of application perspectives like environmental monitoring energy management and network storage when vehicle-based mobile crowdsensing is applied.

Numerous sensing devices have been permitted in cities and placed across urban environments in various cities. Sensing devices typically rely on data center for data analysis and storage because they are unable to process this type of data locally due to resource and energy consumption limitations; the sensing data will be gathered by the data center. After collecting data, real-time decisons are made. Under a limited budget data center, selecting a subset of vehicles that can collect the best data; hence, the biggest challenge for the data center is to improve the quality of crowdsensing and recruit more mobile vehicles under a limited budget. The basic metric of crowdsensing quality depends on the collected data, because a large amount of data can provide fine sensing quality. One of the biggest obstacles to using mobile vehicles for data collection is their extremely dynamic movements.

The center can only anticipate the current location of the mobile device, and it cannot predict the future location of the vehicle. Thus, it is facing a compound challenge to recruit vehicles to gather as much sensor data as possible within allocated budget and time constraints. Alternatively, the mobility of mobile vehicles provides opportunities for data collection. As the mobility of a vehicle can be predicted over several regions, it is feasible to gather the most data with a very small footprint. It is imperative to put into practice a novel method for gathering information method mobile vehicles. Maximum data will be gathered based on suitable vehicle data collection in order to gather the most sensor data possible within the allotted budget and time constraints [2]. The present researcher is unable to make any reliable predictions in many of the studies. Due to its lack of knowledge on precise road prediction, the mobility forecasting solution will address the issue promptly. Currently, in academia and industry, people are growing interested in deep learning, and it will be applied widely in different kinds of jobs. Mobile vehicles are always in motion, and their orientation varies depending on the time of day. The use of deep learning algorithms makes it simple to embrace the new situation. Based on the estimated vehicle location, we can suggest a deep learning system to collect vehicle sensing data [3]. To collect sensing data, recruited vehicles gather sensory data that help to reduce traffic safety problems. The summary is as follows: A deep learning-based plan using a mobile vehicle DMLV technique can be suggested to gather the most sensing data possible. In the proposal of deep learning, we first estimate vehicle mobility for an offline algorithm over a minimum of ten to twelve minutes in the future. In contrast to traditional security measures, DL-based approaches [2, 18] are presented, showing how deep learning techniques can protect data privacy, expedite malware detection, enhance authentication precision, reduce the frequency of faked sensing attacks, and thwart jamming attacks in transfers of sensing data. Finally, we can use a greedy algorithm to retrieve a subset of vehicle sensing data with a limited budget. In a limited budget vehicle location, time period, and sensing data can be considered to maximize data collection within budget constraints.

13.2 Related Work

13.2.1 Crowdsensing Through Mobile Node

In traditional sensing technology, it is impossible to achieve fine-grained, large-scale urban sensing. This is crucial for managing society and cities. Conventional sensing technology has a number of shortcomings, including limited time and spatial coverage, high installation and maintenance costs, and a lack of scalability. The growing ubiquity of intelligent gadgets has made it necessary for recruiters to gather crowdsensing data and monitor the surroundings in order to facilitate speedy development [4]. Mobile users (participants), base stations (BSs), access points (APs), and an MCS server make up mobile crowdsensing systems, all of which are susceptible to assaults and security issues. Malicious MCS attackers try to compromise the MCS service level, bring down the MCS system, or steal sensitive information. Additionally, MCS systems are susceptible to insider assaults initiated by vindictive mobile users. Smart attackers determine their attack strategy and pose more serious dangers to MCS systems using machine learning techniques and smart radio equipment used in social networks, healthcare, catering recommendations, and traffic monitoring. In order to ensure the accuracy and security of several MCS applications, both foreign attacks and self-centered consumers of mobile devices can launch covert and malicious attacks on mobile crowdsensing technologies.

Currently, many researchers are introducing various mobile crowdsensing applications. Opportunistic networking is widely used by mobile users; the consumer selection problem is described as the minimal cost set cover problem, which has been shown to be NP-hard. In view of worker context, many researchers address the maximum utilization problem and propose an online context-aware hierarchical algorithm. This is based on a deep study of social networking and worker recruitment problems in mobile crowdsensing. Moreover, many hybrid task allocations have been proposed for recruiting opportunistic and participatory workers that are useful only for more Android smartphones; those schemes are not efficient and do not utilize vehicles properly. They are ineffective for mobile sensing applications and are only taken into consideration for instantaneous sensing [5]. The researchers suggest using cars to carry out activities related to crowd sensing. Numerous studies have suggested employing opportunistic communication to gather sensing data from mobile cars; the outcomes of the experiments indicate that the vehicles can complete approximately 80% of the sensory information collection tasks in a single day. Their study, however, does not take into account the prediction of vehicle mobility. They suggested a distributed car rating system based on users' preferences and recruited the optimal group of automobiles under the required parameters using game theory [25–27]. To ascertain whether stop signs or traffic lights are present at every intersection, it employs people to detect and identify traffic signals using GPS data gathered from moving vehicles. Numerous alternative solutions to the vehicle recruitment problem use greedy approximation algorithms. To attain efficient quality within a limited budget, the algorithm combines the vehicle trajectory approach with high-quality mobile crowd sensing; additionally, mobility prediction is suggested. The goal is to achieve maximum coverage by recruiting participants within a limited budget. They also used two different approaches: the genetic and greedy algorithms to fulfill the demands of the mobile crowdsensing application.

13.2.2 Vehicle Trajectory Prediction

In recent days, many researchers are predicting vehicle mobility in mobile networks. They use an artificial neural network with an undetectable layer to forecast a vehicle's movement. The neural network predicts the frame that follows in a time span of several seconds in real time, using the vehicle's position and speed as input and output. The result of that evaluation will be predicted by the trajectory of the algorithm which will reduce the mobility prediction error. It will also be predicted by the use of a partitioning filter [6, 7]. The partitioned filter will predict the accuracy which only holds for several seconds. A customizable architecture based on DNN is suggested and employs DNN training on mobile devices to protect data privacy for predicting population flow in cities by adopting deep learning technology. This method uses a local NN platform to extract features and a cloud server-based NN to use the extracted features to train the specified MCS job. To perform different types of tasks, a sequence-to-sequence search model can be utilized. Although this approach cannot predict vehicle movement, using a variety of convolutional neural networks can predict population flow in real-time. Human transportation and mobility models from multiple sources of data on human mobility and urban transportation networks suggest a deep RNN architecture and learn how to predict human flow, both inflow and outflow, in various urban areas.

13.3 System Model

Three categories of entities are present in the system model: mobile vehicles, data centers, and sensing devices.

13.3.1 Opportunistic Communication Approach for Smart Cities

In smart cities, numerous mobile vehicles are traversing the route. Mobile vehicles are initialized to fetch sensing data in order to gather it. By using an opportunistic communication approach, the selected vehicles that are still driving along their route gather sensory information from adjacent sensing devices. Collected sensing data can be sent to the data center and used there to get the reward [8].

13.3.2 Efficient Data Center Strategies for Sensory Data Collection

The responsibility of a data center is recruiting mobile devices. The job of these mobile devices is to gather sensory data and complete the data-collecting assignment on a tight budget (Figure 13.2).

13.3.3 Optimizing Surrounding Data Sensing in Smart Cities

The sensing devices will be established in the smart cities to help with sensing and collecting surrounding data [17].

13.4 Model of Threat in Mobile Crowdsensing

Mobile users (participants), base stations (BSs), access points (APs), and MCS servers are constituents of mobile crowdsensing systems and are susceptible to security issues and assaults. Malicious attackers in MCS seek to steal confidential information, crash the MCS system, or lower the quality of MCS services. MCS systems are also susceptible to insider assaults, which are initiated by self-serving mobile users to obtain more money and secrets at a lower risk of private data leaking and sensing expenses. Astute attackers select the attack strategy and present more serious risks to MCS systems by utilizing machine-learning techniques and smart radio equipment. The mobile users recruited by an MCS platform keep an eye on the surrounding features and provide sensing reports to MCS servers via AP/BS. MCS servers take relevant data from sensing reports to offer multimedia services such as social networks, healthcare, traffic monitoring, and catering recommendations. To ensure the accuracy and security of several MCS applications, mobile crowdsensing systems need to handle sneaky and insider attacks carried out by malevolent attackers as well as self-serving mobile users. (Figure 13.3) The following is a quick overview of the various important categories of MCS threats.

13.4.1 Spoofing

A spoofer impersonates a different mobile device, BS, or AP, to gain unauthorized access to the MCS system. In addition, the spoofer may conduct DoS and man-in-the-middle attacks against an AP or BS.

13.4.2 Sybil

To alter the sensing results produced by the majority-based MCS server, a Sybil user submits sensing reports to the server via APs or BSs with a large number of distinct user identities.

13.4.3 Privacy Leakage

Cloud-based MCS servers are required to safeguard user privacy, particularly regarding their whereabouts and personal data. The theft of sensing data during transmissions or from cloud resources by rogue users who are interested in private information greatly deters other mobile users from participating in MCS duties [10].

13.4.4 Faked Sensing Attacks

To save effort and preserve privacy, narcissistic mobile users occasionally provide MCS servers with fabricated or undervalued sensing information.

Malware: Malware, which includes worms, viruses, and spy tools, poses a major risk to MCS in the form of financial loss, privacy breaches, and deterioration of network performance. Malware can affect mobile users through limited power and processing capabilities.

13.4.5 Jamming

To stop the continuous transmission of sensing data and payments between mobile users and MCS servers, the jammer injects replay or bogus signals. A clever jammer can freely adjust its frequency and jamming power based on the state of communication.

13.4.6 DoS

DoS attackers typically use flooding attacks to try and stop MCS services by using all the resources on MCS servers.

13.4.7 Advanced Persistent Threat (APT)

APT attackers use cunning, continuous, targeted, and sophisticated attacks to collect personal data from mobile devices or MCS servers over an extended period, resulting in privacy breaches in MCS networks.

Table 13.1 An overview of DL-based MCS security techniques.

Reputable MCS methods	DL strategies	Approaches
Protection of privacy	Techniques for safeguarding privacy anonymization of data categorization of images using privacy restrictions	CNN [12] DNN DNN
Authentication	Network traffic analysis for spoofing detection User authentication through regular activities	DNN [12] SAE
Intrusion detection	Detecting malware while offloading detection of cyberattacks CPU allocation for APT detection	DQN SAE
Fake countermeasures to detecting for sensing	Identifying erroneous data injection Sensing accuracy-based payment policy	DQN [12] DBN

13.4.8 Smart Attacks

Using universal software radio peripherals (USRPs) or smart radio devices, an attacker can leverage machine learning techniques to probe the defense policy and select the appropriate attack strategy to target radio signals between mobile devices and access points (APs) or base stations [13, 14] (Table 13.1).

13.5 DL-Based Authentication

The purpose of authentication is to confirm the identity of mobile users participating in MCS tasks, prevent spoofing and Sybil attacks, and safeguard their privacy. Based on a test threshold established by the specified radio channel model and network model, the PHY-layer authentication system creates a hypothesis test to compare the radio channel replies of the transmitter being tested to the channel record of the claimed node. Nevertheless, it is difficult to determine the test threshold in time-variant MCS systems with a large number of mobile and heterogeneous devices. Therefore, a test threshold is not necessary when developing a DNN-based authentication method. To identify mobile users using the DNN approach, this authentication scheme records the distinctive physical characteristics of Wi-Fi signals during everyday activities. The resulting DNN abstractions were then used to build a support vector machine (SVM) that can detect spoofing assaults. More precisely, from the amplitude and phase of the channel responses of WiFi signals, the system extracts six time-domain parameters, including the maximum, minimum, and spectrogram energy, percentile frequency component, and spectrogram energy difference. Three features in the frequency domain—skewness, human physiological traits including body form, height, and weight, as well as behavioral traits like mobile users' gait patterns—can be high-level abstracted using a three-layer DNN based on an autoencoder. The simulation results indicate that under normal conditions, the DNN-based authentication scheme's performance can reliably detect spoofing attempts. For instance, the scheme's average accuracy in an office setting with seven users was 91.2%, with a standard variation of 3.67%. Unfortunately, this authentication strategy is difficult to implement in real-world MCS systems because it depends on a laborious and time-consuming feature and attribute selection process.

A neural network (NN) with several layers of sparse autoencoders is used by a spoofing detection system to expedite the MCS authentication process by capturing features. By analyzing the network traffic, the first layer extracts first-order features, and the subsequent layers use the patterns found in the first-order features to extract features that correlate to those patterns. A total of 256 neurons constitute the first hidden layer in the SAE, 128 neurons constitute the second secret layer, and 64 neurons constitute the third hidden layer. The 3-hidden-layer SAEbased authentication technique distinguishes between flooding, injection, and spoofing attackers by accurately and equitably classifying legitimate mobile users through the application of the parametric rectified linear unit (ReLU) activation function. For instance, the SAE-based authentication technique achieves a spoofing effect.

13.6 Dl-Based Privacy Protection

For effective MCS systems, privacy security for transmitting and storing sensing information on cloud servers is crucial. Data anonymization techniques, such as k-anonymity, l-diversity, and t-closeness, shield sensitive information in the database that MCS uses and offers anonymous quasi-identifiers. Due to the challenges of identifying quasi-identifiers and sensitive features, sensing reports cannot be secured by such typical data anonymization systems because they contain high-dimensional data streams, such as photos and videos. For effective MCS systems, privacy security for transmitting and storing sensing information in cloud servers is crucial. Data anonymization techniques like k-anonymity, l-diversity, and t-closeness shield sensitive information in the database that MCS uses and offer anonymous quasi-identifiers. Due to the challenges of identifying the quasi-identifiers and sensitive features, the sensing reports cannot be secured by such typical data anonymization systems because they contain high-dimensional data streams, such as photos and videos [33].

However, because the feature extraction network (FEN) relies on locally trained NNs, attackers can anticipate the composition and weights of the NN in an MSC system. To preserve the anonymity of MCS users, a pool of pre-trained NNs allows FEN derivation from different pre-trained NNs. In addition, it is challenging for attackers to find and replicate the channel-selection procedure, which includes choosing the output and intermediate channels.

The Siamese network was used in the CNN-based distributed architecture developed in. It is frequently employed in verification applications to enhance the accuracy of the sensing task and data privacy cost function and employs a CNN to enhance the MCS servers' image classification accuracy. In this system, MCS tasks, such as emotion detection, are performed in concert by an image classifier at the MCS server and a feature extractor at the mobile device. Mobile devices implement only convolutional layers, which results in a large reduction in memory overhead. This, in turn, lowers the MCS power consumption and model setup time. This framework enhances the functionality of the mobile device by eliminating unwanted data from the derived features. For example, the CNN-based framework with a Siamese network's face recognition accuracy was 2.6% and 94.5% less accurate than the framework without a Siamese network; however, the accuracy of emotion detection only decreased by 20%.In dynamic MCS networks, this may not be ideal and may even fail to balance privacy protection with sensing accuracy. As a result, the mediator can employ deep learning methods, such as CNN [15, 16], to determine the ideal threshold, enhancing user privacy and sensing accuracy.

13.7 False Sensing Countermeasures Based on DL

In dynamic secure mobile crowdsensing games [28], autonomous mobile users' fictitious sensing motive is suppressed using a DQN-based secure MCS system, as suggested in. Within this framework, mobile users in the areas of interest are notified by the server after it has decided its payment policy. Every mobile device selects the amount of sensing effort it will perform based on the payment policy and the state of its battery, and it is paid based on the MCS server's evaluation of sensing quality. Given a system state and payment strategy in the current time slot of a dynamic game [23, 24], the MCS payment process can be defined as a Markov decision process because it is independent of past states and actions. To obtain the best MCS policy for mobile users who might launch fake sensing attacks, the MCS server can use reinforcement learning (RL) techniques such as Q-learning. It can also use a deep CNN, which consists of two convolutional (Conv) layers and two fully connected (FC) layers, to compress the state space of the RL and speed up the learning process. The SGD approach, which samples a subset of summand functions, updates the CNN parameters at every iteration to reduce the computational expense [29].

Because the proposed method's CNN shrinks the state space and speeds up the learning process, it performs better than the benchmark non-DL technique in terms of sensing quality, fake sensing rate, and MCS server utility. For example, the DQN-based MCS payment system is 50.0% faster than the Q-learning-based strategy, requiring only 2,000 time slots to suppress the fake sensing rate to 10%. Compared to the Q-learning-based scheme, the proposed payment plan enhances the MCS server's usefulness and sensing quality by 96.0% and 31.5%, respectively, after 200 time slots.

13.8 Dl-Based Detection of Intrusion

Cloud-based intrusion detection [21, 22], with its high processing rates, robust security services, and large malware database, can be used in MCS systems to identify malware on mobile devices with limited power, computational capacity, and wireless bandwidth. The MCS system analyzes traces or logs and assesses the runtime behavior of programs by utilizing learning techniques such as random forest classifiers and Bayesian networks.

The accuracy of malware detection depends on various factors and qualities. Consequently, numerous current approaches, including the framework outlined in, have prolonged the detection latency when applied to extensive networks. Using an RNN to capture domain- and content-based malware characteristics and decide whether to halt dynamic detection depending on network behavior, an RNN-based malware detection system was created in. The malware detection process involves extracting features, building an RNN, training it, and classifying it according to domain and content features, including the originating node's IP address, the types of files it contains, and its byte count. An RNN is capable of accurately classifying messages and analyzing hidden functionalities of malware communications, such as information leakage and malware infection spread, particularly when processing natural languages. Because of the great flexibility of RNN, the simulation results demonstrate that this scheme, when compared to the benchmark system without deep learning, saves detection resources and speeds up the response. With a 65.1% faster analysis time than statistics-based malware detection [19, 20], RNN-based malware detection performs better and requires more than half as many MCS servers for an effective MCS dynamic analysis [30, 31].

In addition, MCS systems can use deep learning to optimize offloading policies and resource allocation to detect APT assaults without having to know about the radio channel model or APP trace generation model used for malware detection. For example, a cloud-based mobile virus detection technique, as suggested in, uses a DQN to ascertain a mobile device's offloading rate. More specifically, the offloading rate is selected based on the offloading strategy's quality function, as well as the present state, which includes the radio bandwidth and offloading rates from the past. The CNN, which consists of two Conv layers and two FC layers, estimates the Q-function. The SGD method updates the CNN parameters using minibatch and experience-replay techniques to minimize the mean-squared error of the goal values. The outcomes of the simulation indicate that the CNN is used in the DQN-based strategy to condense the state space and speed up learning, which enhances malware (Table 13.2). DL improves the detection accuracy and decreases the detection time compared with the RL-based benchmark system. In comparison with the Q-learning-based scheme, the DQN-based scheme, for example, improves detection accuracy by 24.5%, decreases detection delay by 32.3%, and boosts mobile device utility by 30.8%.

Table 13.2 A summary of the most well-liked deep learning frameworks for mobile devices.

Name	**Company**	**Android**	**Ios**	**cpu**	**time**	**characteristics**
Tensorflow lite	Google	☒	☒	☐	2017	Portable, cross-platform, quick
Core ML2	Apple	☐	☒	☒	2018	Quantification of weight and batch forecasting
SNPE	Qualcomm	☒	☐	☒	2018	Executes any depth model, but hardware severely restricts this.
MACE	Xiaomi	☒	☐	☒	2018	Compiler-level optimisation, heterogeneous acceleration, and support for multiple framework model transformations

13.9 The DLMV Approach's Design

In various cities, in an effort to gather sensory data, a large number of mobile cars are traveling down roadways with a tight budget data center trend. The high value only applies to recent data; users want to know the PM or city temperature in real time 2.7. This work objective is to with a limited budget recruiting mobile devices which sensing the mobile data there must arise some problem that is considered as MDLB problem. In this study, we proposed a deep learning algorithm (DLMV) that will be presented for effective data collection methods. Sensing devices are distributed and separated into several regions within cities that are divided into multiple regions. As soon as the recruit vehicle leaves the area where the sensing devices are located, all the sensor information can be collected

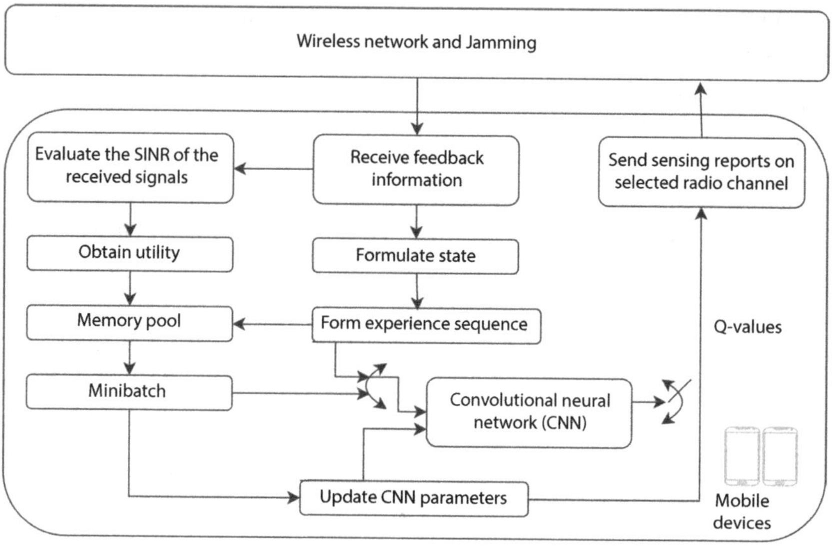

Figure 13.1 Threats to mobile crowdsensing systems during information exchange and data sensing [12].

(Figure 13.1). It is crucial to forecast vehicle motion for the approaching (next) time period to collect the most recent maximum sensing information [9]. When recruiting cars with a restricted budget, the greedy method is used by deep-learning vehicles, which are initially trained to forecast the vehicle trajectory. The DLMV divides online and offline hiring into two groups.

13.9.1 Offline Training

The data center forecasts that the information from the sensors that the duration for sensing data will be divided into numerous data slots and is aware of the past vehicle trajectories into the center map (Figure 13.4). Offline training of sensing data predictions for the following time slot offerings.

Algorithm Offline

Instructional Data: R
1. Divide Ri into Rl+1 ~ l+t and Rl−t+1~l i.
2. For the Rl−t+1~l i and Rl+1~l+t batch, do
3: Transfer Rl−t+1~l i to Ht.

4: Interpret Ht and acquire Ye
5: Use the provided equation to calculate the loss (loss = −1 n × w n i=
1 w j=1 ri,j × log(yi,j)).
6: Revise the RNN model
7: End For
8: For each Rl–t+1~l i do
9: Compute Yi using RNN model
10: End for
11: R = NULL
12: For each vi do
13: R = R ∪ Yi
14: End for
Output: R'

13.9.2 Online Recruitment

[sliding window Wt to each vehicle vi's historical trajectory Ri. There are n automobiles in all, and each vehicle has w sliding windows. The two-dimensional cross-entropy function and the loss function are minimised in order to train the historical vehicle trajectory (Figure 13.5).]

Algorithm

Online Vehicle Recruitment Input: G, S, V, R ,C, B
1: Initialize V = null ,V C= null, costv= 0
2: While cost v < B do
3: maxV S= 0, maxv= 0
4: For each v in set V – V do

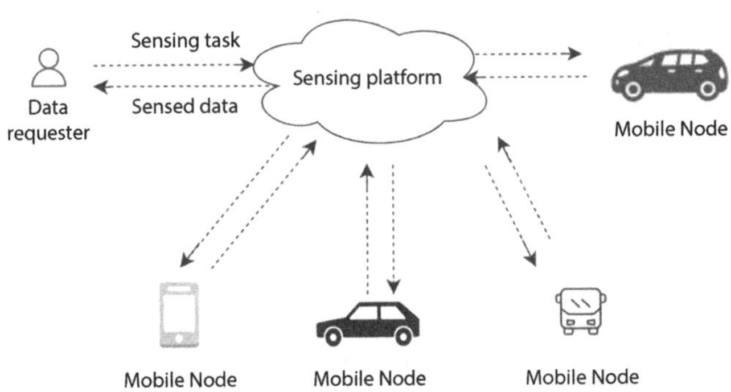

Figure 13.2 Mechanism for pre-contracting incentives [11].

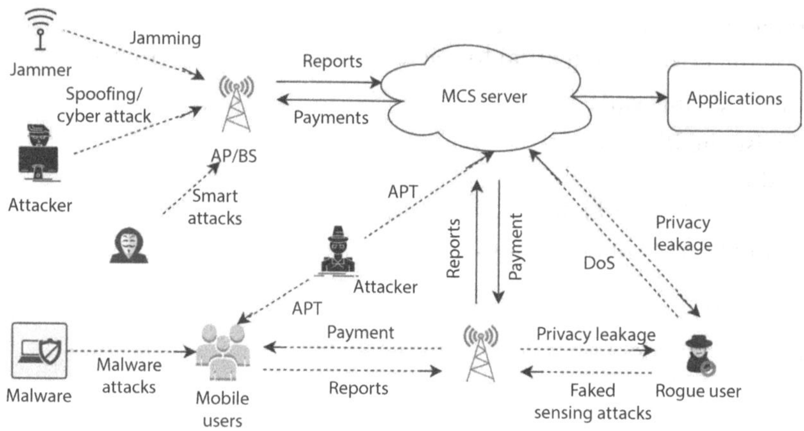

Figure 13.3 Threats to mobile crowdsensing systems during information exchange and data sensing [12].

5: V C = V ∪v
6: Compute V S for V C using Eq. (13.4)
7: If V S > maxV S then
8: maxV S = V S
9: max v = v
10: End if
11: End for
12: V = V ∪maxv
13: cost v = cost v + c max
14: End while
Output: The recruited vehicles V'

13.10 Experimental Result

	ID	Latitude	Longitude	Day	Hour	Minute	Duration	RemainingTime	Resources	Coverage	OnPeakHours	GridNumber	Ligitimacy
0	1	45.442142	-75.303369	1	4	13	40	40	9	91	0	131380	1
1	1	45.442154	-75.304366	1	4	23	40	30	9	91	0	131380	1
2	1	45.442104	-75.303963	1	4	33	40	20	9	91	0	121996	1
3	1	45.441868	-75.303577	1	4	43	40	10	9	91	0	121996	1
4	2	45.447727	-75.147722	2	15	49	30	30	5	47	0	140784	1

Figure 13.4 Experimental result according to dataset.

```
Evaluated Random ForestClassifier ( ) model
              precision    recall  f1-score   support

           0       1.00      0.97      0.98       379
           1       0.99      1.00      1.00      2518

    accuracy                           1.00      2897
   macro avg       1.00      0.98      0.99      2897
weighted avg       1.00      1.00      1.00      2897
```

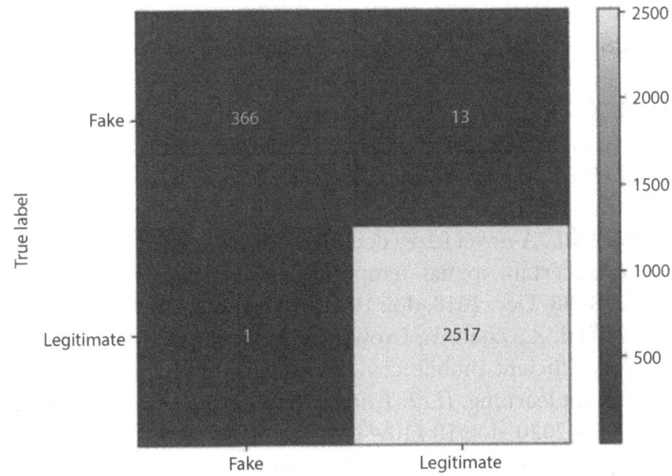

Figure 13.5 Result analysis.

13.11 Conclusion

Based on the deep learning approach used in this study, our goal in the urban IoT challenge is a vehicle-based crowdsensing problem. Here, we present a deep learning algorithm-based mobile vehicle solution for effective data collection, DL-based authentication, privacy protection, fake sensing countermeasures, intrusion detection, and anti-jamming transmissions for multimedia services in IoT applications, as well as attack models in MCS systems in a limited budget to maximize the sensing data from all moving vehicles. The data centers choose a subset of moving cars on the road, and the sensing devices collect data that are dispersed across large areas inside the cities. The security performance of MCS systems and QoE-based multimedia services can be enhanced using DL-based security approaches. There are several crucial paths for DL-based MCS security research in the future that can predict movement. Consequently, we have an opportunity to forecast the quantity of coverage generated by sensors. The matrix road data, sensing device data, and vehicle information were preprocessed into a vehicle trajectory. The RNN approach encodes the vehicle trajectory as input and output as per predicting the location of a future time period as per the recruitment we can recruit the vehicle devices, and the security approaches based on DL show promise for enhancing the security performance of MCS systems in the near future.

References

1. Pradhan, M., Johnsen, F.T., Tortonesi, M., Delaitre, S., Leveraging crowdsourcing and crowdsensing data for HADR operations in a smart city environment. *IEEE Internet Things Mag.*, 2, 2, 26–31, Jun. 2019, doi: 10.1109/IOTM.001.1900013.
2. Chen, W., *et al.*, A novel fuzzy deep-learning approach to traffic flow prediction with uncertain spatial–temporal data features. *Future Gener. Comput. Syst.*, 89, 78–88, Dec. 2018, doi: 10.1016/j.future.2018. 06.021.
3. Liu, C.H., Dai, Z., Zhao, Y., Crowcroft, J., Wu, D.O., Leung, K., Distributed and energy-efficient mobile crowdsensing with charging stations by deep reinforcement learning. *IEEE Trans. Mob. Comput. Eearly Access*, 20, 1, 130–146, Aug. 30, 2020, doi: 10.1109/TMC.2019.2938509.
4. van Wyk, F., Wang, Y., Khojandi, A., Masoud, N., Real-time sensor anomaly detection and identification in automated vehicles. *IEEE Trans. Intell. Transp. Syst.*, 21, 3, 1264–1276, Mar. 2020, doi: 10. 1109/TITS.2019.2906038.
5. Philip, B.V., Alpcan, T., Jin, J., Palaniswami, M., Distributed real-time IoT for autonomous vehicles. *IEEE Trans. Ind. Informat.*, 15, 2, 1131–1140, Feb. 2019, doi: 10.1109/TII.2018.2877217.
6. Zhu, Y., Wu, Y., Li, B., Trajectory improves data delivery in urban vehicular networks. *IEEE Trans. Parallel Distrib. Syst.*, 25, 4, 1089–1100, Apr. 2014, doi: 10.1109/TPDS.2013.118.
7. Lin, Z., Lai, Y., Gao, X., Li, G., Wang, T., Huang, G., Data gathering in urban vehicular network based on daily movement patterns, in: *Proc. 11th Int. Conf. Comput. Sci. Edu. (ICCSE)*, Aug. 2016, pp. 641–646, 2019, doi: 10.1109/ICCSE.2016.7581655.
8. Jiang, B., Huang, G., Wang, T., Gui, J., Zhu, X., Trust based energy efficient data collection with unmanned aerial vehicle in edge network. *Trans. Emerg. Telecommun. Technol.*, 33, 6, e3942, Mar. 2020, doi: 10.1002/ett.3942.
9. Ren, Y., Zeng, Z., Wang, T., Zhang, S., Zhi, G., A trust-based minimum cost and quality aware data collection scheme in P2P network. *Peer Peer Netw. Appl.*, 13, 1–24, Mar. 2020, doi: 10.1007/s12083-020- 00898-2.
10. Luo, T., Huang, J., Kanhere, S.S., Zhang, J., Das, S.K., Improving IoT data quality in mobile crowd sensing: A cross validation approach. *IEEE Internet Things J.*, 6, 3, 5651–5664, Jun. 2019, doi: 10. 1109/JIOT.2019.2904704.

11. Yi, D., Li, J., Tang, C., Lin, Z., Han, Y., & Qiu, R. (2022). Task Offloading in Wireless Powered Mobile Crowd Sensing: A Matching-Based Approach. Electronics, 11, 15, 2377.
12. Xiao, L., Jiang, D., Xu, D., An, N., Secure mobile crowdsensing with deep learning, 2018. arXiv preprint arXiv:1801.07379.
13. Truong, N.B., Lee, G.M., Um, T.-W., Mackay, M., Trust evaluation mechanism for user recruitment in mobile crowd-sensing in the Internet of Things. *IEEE Trans. Inf. Forensics Secur.*, 14, 10, 2705–2719, Oct. 2019, doi: 10.1109/TIFS.2019.2903659.
14. Siegel, J.E., Erb, D.C., Sarma, S.E., A survey of the connected vehicle landscape—Architectures, enabling technologies, applications, and development areas. *IEEE Trans. Intell. Transp. Syst.*, 19, 8, 2391–2406, Aug. 2018, doi: 10.1109/TITS.2017.2749459.
15. Ghane, S., Jolfaei, A., Kulik, L., Ramamohanarao, K., Puthal, D., Preserving privacy in the Internet of connected vehicles. *IEEE Trans. Intell. Transp. Syst.*, 22, 8, 5018–5027, Jan. 15, 2020, doi: 10.1109/tits. 2020.2964410.
16. Xu, Y., Ren, J., Zhang, Y., Zhang, C., Shen, B., Zhang, Y., Blockchain empowered arbitrable data auditing scheme for network storage as a service. *IEEE Trans. Serv. Comput.*, 13, 2, 289–300, Apr. 2020, doi: 10.1109/TSC.2019.2953033.
17. Liu, Q., Tian, Y., Wu, J., Peng, T., Wang, G., Enabling verifiable and dynamic ranked search over outsourced data. *IEEE Trans. Serv. Comput.*, 15, 1, 69–82, Jun. 11, 2019, doi: 10.1109/TSC.2019.2922177.
18. Hasan, M.M., Sohag, M.H.A., Ali, M.E., Ahmad, M., Estimation of the most effective rhythm for human identification using EEG signal., in: *2016 9th International Conference on Electrical and Computer Engineering (ICECE)*, pp. 90–93, IEEE, December, 2016.
19. Dietterich, T.G., Approximate statistical tests for comparing supervised classification learning algorithms. *Neural Comput.*, 10, 7, 1895–1923, 1998.
20. Suykens, J.A.K. and Vandewalle, J., Least squares support vector machine classifiers. *Neural Process. Lett.*, 9, 3, 293–300, 1999.
21. Liao, Y. and Vemuri, V.R., Use of k-nearest neighbor classifier for intrusion detection. *Comput. Secur.*, 21, 5, 439–448, 2002.
22. Garrett, D., Peterson, D.A., Anderson, C.W., Thaut, M.H., Comparison of linear, nonlinear, and feature selection methods for EEG signal classification. *IEEE Trans. Neural Syst. Rehabil. Eng.*, 11, 2, 141–144, 2003.
23. Bhattacharyya, S., Khasnobish, A., Chatterjee, S., Konar, A., Tibarewala, D.N., Performance analysis of LDA, QDA and KNN algorithms in left-right limb movement classification from EEG data, in: *2010 International Conference on Systems in Medicine and Biology*, pp. 126–131, IEEE, 2010.
24. Shakir, M. and Sharma, S., Adolescents under stress: The Blue Whale game challenge. *Res. Rev. J.*, 3, 7, 379–386, 2018.
25. Bavelier, D., Green, C.S., Han, D.H., Renshaw, P.F., Merzenich, M.M., Gentile, D.A., Brains on video games., *Nat. Rev. Neurosci.*, 12, 12, 763–768, 2011.

26. Zhou, Z., Zhou, H., Zhu, H., Working memory, executive function and impulsivity in Internet-addictive disorders: a comparison with pathological gambling. *Acta Neuropsychiatrica*, 28, 2, 92–100, 2016.
27. McMahan, T., Parberry, I., Parsons, T.D., Evaluating Electroencephalography Engagement Indices During Video Game Play. In FDG., June, 2015.
28. McMahan, T., Parberry, I., Parsons, T.D., Modality specific assessment of video game player's experience using the Emotiv. *Entertain. Comput.*, 7, 1–6. elsevier, 2015.
29. Das, S., Ghosh, L., Saha, S., Analyzing gaming effects on cognitive load using artificial intelligent tools. in: *2020 IEEE International Conference on Electronics, Computing and Communication Technologies (CONECCT)*, pp. 1–6, IEEE, July, 2020.
30. Alsheikh, M., Jiao, Y., Niyato, D., *et al.*, The accuracy-privacy trade-off of mobile crowdsensing. *IEEE Commun. Mag.*, 55, 6, 132–139, Jun. 2017.
31. Liu, Z., Li, Z., Wu, K., Li, M., Urban traffic prediction from mobility data using deep learning. *IEEE Netw.*, 32, 4, 40–46, Jul. 2018.
32. Yang, K., Zhang, K., Ren, J., *et al.*, Security and privacy in mobile crowdsourcing networks: Challenges and opportunities. *IEEE Commun. Mag.*, 53, 8, 75–81, Aug. 2015.
33. Tao, X., Dong, L., Li, Y., *et al.*, Real-time personalized content catering via viewer sentiment feedback: A QoE perspective. *IEEE Netw.*, 29, 6, 14–19, Dec. 2015.

14

A Study on Protection of Multimedia System Contents Using a Biometric-Based Encryption Technique

Pinaki Pratim Acharjya, Santanu Koley, Subhabrata Barman, Subhankar Joardar and Jayeeta Majumder*

Department of Computer Science and Engineering, Haldia Institute of Technology, Haldia, West Bengal, India

Abstract

A framework for protecting multimedia content based on user biometric information and a layered encryption/decryption system is proposed in this chapter. Encryption schemes that require a password are susceptible to issues with illicit key exchange. It is feasible to reduce the unauthorized use of protected content by using hardware identifiers and biometric data as keys. This is achieved by combining the symmetric and asymmetric key systems. The proposed method's computational needs and applicability are also discussed. The results of experiments involving time-measurement-related encryption and decryption are also presented. Watermarking technologies can be utilized in addition to the suggested approach to allow for the creative uses of protected multimedia data.

***Keywords*:** Multimedia, multimedia content, content protection, encryption, decryption

14.1 Introduction

The proliferation of large-scale computer networks (such as the Internet), increase in applications utilizing these networks (such as e-commerce and e-learning), and growing concerns surrounding identity theft have made the design of appropriate personal identification systems increasingly

**Corresponding author*: jem2003_kolkata@yahoo.co.in

Subhabrata Barman, Santanu Koley and Subhankar Joardar (eds.) Next-Generation Systems and Secure Computing, (277–292) © 2025 Scrivener Publishing LLC

important. Systems that are able to (i) accurately, (ii) rapidly, (iii) reliably, (iv) without infringing upon private rights, (v) economically, (vi), and (vii) without requiring major alterations to the existing infrastructure are desirable. Be aware that some of these needs are incompatible with one another. Conventional personal authentication techniques, which rely on a physical token, such as an ID card, or a (secret) piece of information, such as a password, are unable to meet any of these requirements because they are assumed to be used only by authorized users of the system.

Based on a previous study (Jain *et al.*, 1999; Maltoni *et al.*, 2003), biometrics-based personal authentication systems that utilize physiological and/or behavioral traits (such as voice, face, iris, hand geometry, fingerprint, etc.) of individuals are promising candidates for either replacing or enhancing these traditional systems. They are founded on entities (traits) that are actually far more deeply tied to the individual than ID cards or passwords. Therefore, as biometric data cannot be lost, forgotten, or readily inferred, they are more reliable. The fact that there is nothing to carry or remember makes this more convenient for users. By enabling the characteristics of the system to be changed to reduce the possibility of unauthorized usage, the authentication accuracy is improved.

The primary benefits of biometrics over other authentication methods are their non-repudiable nature, security, and ease of use (Jain, 2004). However, claims of security and non-repudiation are only valid if the system's overall integrity is maintained (Ratha, 2001). A hacker with physical or remote access to an authentication server can steal saved templates, which, in the case of simple templates, are irreplaceable. Privacy concerns are also highlighted because many biometrics reveal personal information other than identity. Another major privacy concern is that the widespread use of biometric authentication makes it easy to track an individual's step. The four main concerns with the widespread use of biometrics for remote and onsite authentication are (i) security of the network, (ii) privacy of users, (iii) protection of templates, and (iv) trust between users and servers. In civilian applications, these concerns often outweigh the accuracy of biometrics in isolation.

Piracy and other copyright violations involving digital multimedia content are major concerns for distributors and owners of legitimate content (Furht, 2005). Consequently, the protection of intellectual property rights for multimedia information—also referred to as digital rights management or DRM for multimedia—has attracted much attention recently. The most recently proposed DRM solutions employ digital watermarking and encryption techniques (Dittmann, 2001). By offering a basis for legal action, digital watermarking techniques can be used to discourage or prevent unauthorized copying and distribution. Encryption methods are typically used to stop unauthorized copies and distribution. However, the most recently proposed DRM solutions combine digital watermarking and encryption to increase security against unauthorized copying and their subsequent distribution (Lin, 2005). Digital watermarking techniques are widely used in DRM architectures as a supplement to encryption techniques.

It is challenging to prevent illegal content from being copied and distributed. Cryptographic techniques that provide common security objectives, such as confidentiality, authentication, data integrity, and non-repudiation, have evolved over a long period. Unfortunately, there are no easy solutions to the problem of protecting content from illegal copying or distribution using these techniques. In classical cryptography, an adversary, Eve, listens to the channel and uses cryptanalysis to decrypt the data obtained, while two communicating parties, Bob and Alice, attempt to confidentially transmit the content through an untrusted channel.

On the other hand, in a content protection scenario, Bob and Eve are seen as adversaries, and Alice's goal is to securely deliver the content to Bob's dependable hardware or software. Specifically, Bob is allowed to use the content on the trusted device but not copy or distribute it, whereas Eve is not allowed to use, copy, or spread the content. Therefore, the system's dependability and stability are crucial for DRM. The core idea behind modern DRM technology is the existence of stable, impenetrable environments.

The main goal of any DRM system is to prevent content sharing while still allowing authorized users access and use it. Consequently, rather than being sent or transmitted in its unencrypted form, the content must be packaged (wrapped) with DRM (Lin, 2005). The bundled content can only be accessed by the user, Alice, using a reliable and impenetrable device. However, Bob's device cannot be used to unlock the content purchased by Alice. Furthermore, Bob's reliable device—which Alice controls—is unable to unlock the content intended for Alice. Consequently, it is necessary to establish an authentication mechanism between users and their trusted devices.

The user applies finger F to the sensor to enroll in a fingerprint-based system. The output Fs, which is an image of the fingerprint, is then processed by a feature extractor to generate the template Ft, which is subsequently stored in a database together with the user's identity I (note that this database can be local, such as a smart card issued to an individual, or central, such as a law enforcement database). During verification, the user's digital fingerprint is obtained once more, and the generated template Fv, in contrast with the database template Ft, corresponds to the identity I that is being claimed. A "Yes" decision is generated if the matcher finds that these two representations are "near enough." Typically, this is based on a similarity (dissimilarity) measure.

To increase the security of logical and physical access systems, the use of physiological or behavioral traits, such as speech or handwriting in biometrics-based personal identification systems is becoming increasingly common. Although biometric systems offer several advantages over traditional token- or knowledge-based authentication mechanisms, such as increased user comfort and resistance to imposter users, attacks remain possible.

Biometric techniques offer inherent advantages over traditional personal identification systems and ensuring the security and integrity of biometric data remains a critical concern. For example, it is impossible to recreate a person's biometric data (such as her fingerprint image), unlike passwords, credit cards, or IDs that have been stolen. According to Schneier (1999), a biometrics-based verification system can only be successful if the verifier system certifies that the biometric data came from an authorized person at the time of enrollment. Furthermore, although biometric data are unique, confidentiality is not a features. For example, someone may leave fingerprints on everything they touch and surreptitiously see faces everywhere they look. Thus, attacks on biometric systems have the potential to reduce trustworthiness.

To promote the widespread use of biometric procedures, it is imperative to enhance the security of biometric data, particularly fingerprints. Watermarking, encryption, and steganography can be used to achieve this goal. Steganography, which translates from Greek to mean "hidden communication," is the process of encoding crucial information that is not immediately apparent in carrier data. Steganography is based on concealing the information itself, as opposed to cryptography, which looks for methods to render encrypted data unusable for unauthorized individuals. Therefore, when transmitting crucial biometric information, such as minute details, from a client to a server, steganography-based techniques may be suitable. Steganographic techniques reduce the possibility that biometric data will be unlawfully altered as a result of attackers intercepting it during transmission.

Pirate users can benefit from high-fidelity and speedy duplication when digital processes are used in the creation, editing, and distribution of multimedia data (such as images, videos, and music). The copies generated were the same as the original material, and the duplication process was completed quickly. On the other hand, analog processes (such as printing and scanning an image) take longer and produce images that are of lower quality for various reasons (e.g., printer noise). The widespread use of the Internet has created new avenues for pirates to quickly and easily distribute digital content protected by copyright to a large number of users without fear of detection. This is because digital tactics offer another advantage. Multimedia data owners and their authorized distributors are raising concerns about revenue loss, which has a negative impact on creating new content and distributing it quickly. The academic community, multimedia industry, and government regulatory bodies are now closely monitoring multimedia content security.

Digital watermarking and cryptography are two of the most frequently employed techniques for safeguarding multimedia data's intellectual property rights (IPR).

14.2 Literature Survey

Big data and cloud computing technologies have advanced rapidly, improving people's quality of life, employment, and education. But there comes a point where privacy and information security are seriously jeopardized. Data security is the primary goal of biometric authentication. Nevertheless, it has several drawbacks, such as a restricted set of biometric traits and data leakage resulting from biometric template theft. Considering these shortcomings, biometric encryption (Bodo, 1992) has been recommended as a substitute. Biometric encryption, as opposed to biometric authentication, requires a sufficient degree of similarity between biometric characteristics and can store a key securely and reliably or dynamically extract the same and stable key. Consequently, it performed better. Recently, researchers have focused on this field. Many studies have also focused on biometric encryption using fuzzy vault (Nandakumar *et al.*, 2007) and dynamic biometric-key generation schemes (Sheng *et al.*, 2012; Hoque *et al.*, 2008; Lim *et al.*, 2012).

According to Uludag *et al.* (2005), fingerprint vaults are installed with the understanding that fingerprint features are pre-aligned. Nevertheless, it is impractical to apply this assumption to a real-world setting. Then, using Helper Data, which includes the maximum curvatures on fingerprint ridges and maximum curvature points, the calibration problem was resolved. Zhang *et al.* (2011) found that if two register vault templates and Helper Data are obtained, the success rate of attacking a biometric cryptosystem can reach 60% when the order of the polynomial is nine.

Dynamic key-generation-based biometric encryption is a promising technique (Sheng *et al.*, 2012; Hoque *et al.*, 2008; Lim *et al.*, 2012). Straight from the biometric template, a biometric key is extracted. This scheme's benefit is that neither a template nor a biometric key must be stored. A highly consistent or precisely reproducible biometric sample is required to create a stable key. However, because of physiological and environmental factors, biometric samples typically do not meet this requirement. Numerous studies on this plan have been conducted to date. To derive relatively long keys, the feature space is divided into subspaces and cells (Hoque *et al.*, 2008). created a lengthy key by determining how to use fingerprint orientation fields that are not always connected to it (Sheng *et al.*, 2012). For biometric discretization, bits are dynamically allocated to each feature element using a dynamic reliability-dependent bit allocation algorithm (Lim *et al.*, 2012), which is based on a Binary Reflected Grey Code. Even though a biometric key can be extracted with these attempts, it is neither short nor relatively long with a high Equal Error Rate (EER).

Digital watermarking and encryption are two of the most used methods. Dittmann *et al.* (2001) discussed the applicability of these methods discussed for multimedia data security requirements and related issues. The digital watermarking process involves incorporating metadata such as ownership directly into multimedia content. Hartung *et al.* (1997) and Swanson *et al.* (1998) provided an overview of watermarking methods for various multimedia data. Watermarking techniques, however, are not resistant to different types of attacks on multimedia data such as cropping and filtering. Unauthorized copying and distribution issues can be resolved using encryption. However, the issue of illicit key-sharing plague encryption is shown in the following illustration. Let us say that Bob, a pirate user, or a pirate website is disseminating an encrypted multimedia file that Alice owns. Alice needs the right key to decode the data to utilize the file. For instance, by registering on the website that is linked to the content and entering her payment information, Alice can lawfully obtain the key. This way gives the content provider access to Alice's personal information when she watches, listens, or plays (this use of multimedia data will be referred to as "playing") the protected content. However, the security that encryption provides is negated because Alice can also obtain the key illegally (for instance, Bob could send Alice the encrypted file along with the correct key).

Another potential remedy for illegal key exchange is the use of users' biometric traits, such as their physiological or behavioral traits (e.g., fingerprints, faces, or irises), which are unique to each individual and can therefore be used for personal authentication (G. Lassmann, 2002). Unlike token-based authentication (like ID cards or keys) and knowledge-based authentication (like passwords and PINs), biometric data cannot be easily falsified or inferred (A.K. Jain, 2000), (Jain, A. K., 1997). If the biometrics system is secure, then incorporating the user's biometric data into the encryption/decryption process can improve the security of digital content (for a thorough analysis of possible attacks on a biometrics system, see Ratha, 2001).

The possible application of biometric data in digital signature applications was discussed by Janbandhu *et al.* (2001). In both symmetric and asymmetric key encryption systems, keys are generated using biometric information (such as an iris). However, the users' biometric signals change over time. These changes in fingerprint images can be caused by a variety of factors such as dry or dirty fingers, cuts and bruises on the fingers, improper finger placement on the sensor, and sensor noise.

Soutar *et al.* (1999) proposed a new mechanism in which the keys in encryption/decryption processes are secured using user biometric data instead of passwords. The method functions as a key management system and is called Biometric Encryption TM by the authors.

14.3 Multimedia Content Protection

Any type of content that conveys information through text, images, audio, or video is referred to as multimedia content. It can be used in marketing, education, and entertainment. The sky is limited in terms of creativity and imagination when it comes to producing multimedia material. You may engage your audience and convey your message in countless ways using various forms of media (Abdelsadek, 2014; Abdelsadek *et al.*, 2014; Aly *et al.*, 2011; Cano *et al.*, 2002; Kahng *et al.*, 1998).

Making an explainer video that may be used to introduce a new good or service is common usage for multimedia materials. Infographics is another type of multimedia material. Infographics are an excellent method for obtaining complex information and displaying it in a way that is both aesthetically pleasing and simple to comprehend. They can be used to provide advice or ideas, explain data or statistics, or simply provide a narrative.

Multimedia content has several advantages. Compared with text-only content, it is more likely to grab viewers' attention and keep them engaged. This is so that it can capture the reader or spectator using various senses. Multimedia content appeals to numerous senses, making it memorable and more likely to stick to the mind than text-only content. If you want your audience to recall important details from your study, it can be useful. Additionally, it has a wider range, increases social media share, and is simple to repurpose.

Although incorporating multimedia information (Lee *et al.*, 2013; Khodabakhshi *et al.*, 2008) has many advantages, there are a few potential drawbacks to consider. Multimedia materials can take longer to prepare than text-based content, depending on the type you wish to create. The cost of production may be higher than that of producing text-based materials. It might not be suitable for all kinds of content, it might be more difficult to monitor performance, it might not be available to everyone, and it might be more difficult to update.

There is no denying that Internet technology and multimedia signal processing are common in our daily lives nowadays. However, numerous security issues have surfaced, including biometric assaults, copy-move forgery in digital photographs and movies, and clandestine communication using multimedia files. Numerous strategies have been proposed for multimedia information security to address these issues, including steganography, watermarking, encryption, privacy protection, and deep learning. However, there are still several glaring flaws in the research methodologies. Most of the current research on multimedia content security is based on rigid requirements that are difficult to meet in practical applications. Furthermore, handling big data in a cloud-computing context is challenging because of the high computational complexity of the present approaches. All these shortcomings restrict the practical applicability of these strategies for multimedia security and require further in-depth research. This chapter presents an architecture that uses a layered encryption/decryption system and user biometric data to secure multimedia content. Unauthorized key exchange issues are common in encryption techniques that require a password. Unauthorized access to protected content can be reduced by employing hardware identifiers and biometric information as keys. This is possible by combining symmetric and asymmetric key systems. The application of the proposed method and its computing requirements are analyzed. The results of the tests on encryption and decryption related to the time measurement are also presented. Watermarking technologies offer creative uses for protected multimedia data, beyond the recommended approach.

14.4 Encryption/Decryption in Biometrics

The Biometric Encryption technique ensures that neither the biometric nor the key can be recovered from the stored template by securely affixing a PIN or cryptographic key to the biometric. Only if a valid live biometric sample is submitted during verification is key recreation.

Because managing biometric passwords requires managing both the password and biometrics, biometric encryption is a practical, secure, and privacy-friendly solution. A basic summary of the BE working steps is provided below:

14.4.1 Digital Enrollment

The digital key is generated at random during enrollment, unlike a password or PIN, so nobody, not even the user, is aware of it. Because the key is unrelated to biometrics, it can be updated or changed at any time. In the process of creating a protected BE template, also known as a "private template," a biometric sample was obtained. The BE algorithm connects the key to the biometric in a trustworthy and secure manner. The biometrics and key were encrypted. The BE template can be locally stored on a smart card, token, laptop, smartphone, or other device and offers good privacy protection. Both the key and biometrics are deleted after the enrolment procedure is complete.

14.4.2 Biometric Verification

For the BE algorithm to extract the same key or password when paired with a legitimate Biometric Encryption template, the user must provide a fresh biometric sample during the verification process. Therefore, the biometric functions as the decryption key. Once confirmed, the sample was discarded.

14.4.3 Password Management

Once obtained, the digital key, password, PIN, etc., form the basis of all applications, both physical and logical. The easiest method is to use a traditional cryptosystem, such as PKI, where a password instantly generates a set of public and private keys.

14.4.4 Encryption/Decryption Scheme

An appropriate biometric input variation is considered by the Biometric Encryption algorithm. However, a hacker with a sufficiently different biometric sample will not be able to obtain a password. Whether this encryption or decryption method is effective is uncertain because each biometric sample is different. Making the system work correctly is very challenging, given the development of many modern hacking techniques.

The benefits of biometric encryption technology can significantly security and privacy. Below is a list of this technology's principal advantages and benefits:

14.4.4.1 *No Holding of Biometric Image or Template*

Biometric system privacy and security concerns include concerns regarding identity theft by hackers, possible data matching, surveillance, profiling, and interception. Improper use and handling of biometric data by third parties may lead to costs and negative externalities that impact individuals.

Biometric encryption instantly manages such threats and hazards. Users maintain complete (local) control over the applications of their biometric data. The local government encourages increased enrollment and use of the system, which also helps build a stronger sense of confidence and trust in the system.

14.4.4.2 *Improved Authentication and Security*

In biometric encryption, the Account IDs are recalculated directly from the user's verification, where they are linked to the biometric. They offer more complex and comprehensive account identifiers (passwords), which are far more efficient, do not need to be remembered, and are less susceptible to security lapses. Substitution attacks, data tampering, Trojan horse attacks, and other such techniques are not possible because neither the attacker nor anybody else has access to a digital key. In addition, there is very little chance of a high-level masquerade attack because the system does not maintain any templates. This implies that a party that interferes cannot create a digital artifact.

14.4.4.3 *Personal Data and Communications are More Secure*

Users can easily and conveniently encrypt their sensitive or confidential data using BE technology. Because each person's unique biometric is used locally as a key, BE technology can safely be a powerful tool in their hands. Thus, biometric encryption can be considered as public encryption.

14.4.4.4 *Greater Public Acceptance, Confidence, and Use Greater Compliance with Privacy Laws*

Public trust and confidence are essential conditions for the implementation of any biometric system. A large-scale data breach involving a central database of biometric templates could have long-term negative effects on the entire industry. Users maintain total control over their biometric data in a manner that benefits them and lowers the risk of identity theft and monitoring. This will encourage the use of biometrics in a wider range of contexts and significantly aid in meeting the requirements of privacy and data protection regulations.

14.4.5 Suitable for Large-Scale Applications

The BE program uses a one-to-many, privacy-protected database to avoid "double dipping." The multimodal database includes both custom (iris templates) that manage the connection to the user's encrypted records and standard anonymous templates for a single biometric (fingerprints). The public and private templates would need to match significantly for the user's history to be decrypted and displayed. As BE technology reduces the risks associated with traditional biometric systems, it makes database applications possible. Without ever disclosing the actual biometric data, users would be able to safely use their biometrics to prove their identity to anybody for any purpose with biometric encryption.

14.5 The Process

There are two entities that can interact as server R and user F. F wants to obtain file U that is on server R. Both symmetric and asymmetric key encryption techniques are applied during file transfers [12]. K^+_R and K^-_R in Figure 14.1 stand for R's public and private keys, respectively. K^+_R (.) and K^-_R (.) signify how these keys are used in an asymmetric-key system.

The expression E(X, k1, k2,..., kn) in a symmetric key system indicates that file X should be encrypted with key k1, followed by the resultant file with key k2, etc. D(Y, kn, kn-1,..., k1) denotes the following procedure: First, using key kn, decrypt file Y; next, using key kn-1, decrypt the resulting file, and so on. The data initially accessible at R and F are shown in Figure 14.1 in the corresponding columns inside the dashed boxes. The IF, which includes the username, represents the identity of user F. The password selected by the user for use in the encryption and decryption procedures is called PF. The biometric information of user F collected at time t is indicated by the notation B^t_P, t = 0, 1, 2... Because of the previously mentioned causes, it should be noted that biometric data are not time-invariant.

There is a thorough explanation of the encryption–decryption process. The user first encrypts I_P, P_P, and B^0_F using the server's public key before

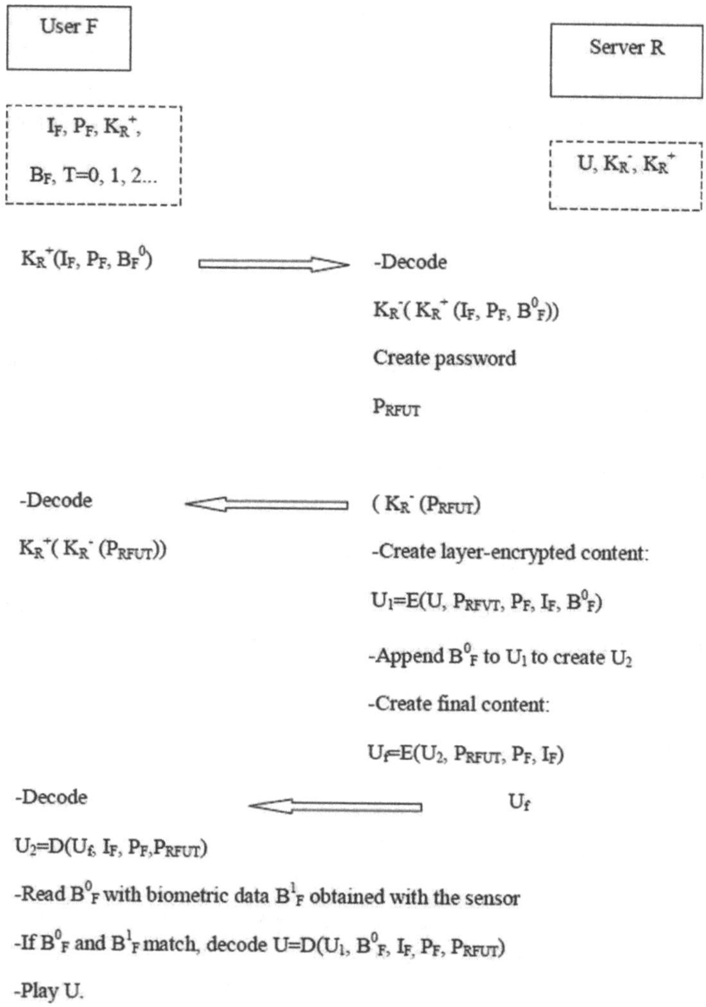

Figure 14.1 Structure of the file transfer.

sending encrypted data to the server. The server uses its private key K^-_R to decode these three pieces of data. This information can only be decoded by server R and not by an outsider owing to the asymmetric key technique. The server generates a password P_{RFUT} (which is a function of server R, user F, content U, and a time stamp T) and delivers it to the user after encrypting it with K^-_R after confirming the legitimacy of the user and any relevant details, such as payment status.

The user uses the public key K^+_R to decode the data. By layering the encryption of U using the keys produced from P_{RFUT}, P_F, I_F, and B^0_F, the server constructs encrypted content U_1. To obtain U_f, another level of encryption was performed, as indicated in Figure 14.1, after appending the biometric data (B^0_F) to U_1. The user receives this file from the server, where the encryption keys are used to locate U_2 in the reverse order. The biometric information collected from the sensor B^1_F can be matched with B^0_F because this data (U_2) contains B^0_F.

In the event of a positive match, the actual multimedia content U is obtained by performing final layered decryption (e.g., B0F and B1F are from the same finger, iris, etc.). By doing this, the media player will be able to play the U content for user F. Recall that B0F will be matched with B2F and so on the next time the user wishes to play multimedia content.

According to the previously mentioned secure file transfer system, a "closed application" is one in which the file is decrypted immediately before playback and is not saved on the user's computer. The decryption module, media player, matcher, biometric sensor, and playing medium (such as a speaker or monitor) should be securely connected to prevent manipulation.

14.6 Experimental Results

DES is applied to multimedia files, and the wall clock times for encryption and decryption are provided. A DES key typically comprises 56 bits. These values can all be used directly as DES keys because they are all 8-character strings composed of a 7-bit ASCII code: user ID (IF), user-selected password (PF), and server-generated password (PRFUT). A typical fingerprint image can yield a feature vector that is larger than 600 bits and is composed of the orientation and minute details of the fingerprint. The size of the biometric data (Bt, where t = 0,1,2...) is typically larger. Iris images, which can yield a feature vector with a length of 512 bits, can be used in the same manner. These feature vectors can be used as DES keys by first hashing one-way into 56-bit keys.

Reversed keys are used in DES, which sets it apart from the other encryption and decryption methods. It follows that the encryption (at server R) and decryption (at user F) times for the same multimedia file should be comparable. Using the Cipher Block Chaining (CBC) mode of DES, the encryption and decryption of a 5 MB file takes 3 s on a Sun Ultra 10 workstation (333 MHz). The entire time required to decrypt the file is approximately 21 s when the user's computer needs to perform seven DES decryptions (see Figure 14.1). It makes sense to wait for this long time because the decryption process only occurs before the multimedia file plays. These times can also be significantly reduced by employing specialized hardware circuits.

14.7 Conclusion

A proposed and tested multimedia content security framework is built based on layered encryption/decryption and user biometric data. Unauthorized key exchange is a problem with password-requiring encryption techniques. Unauthorized access to protected content can be reduced by employing hardware identifiers and biometric information as keys. This is possible by combining symmetric and asymmetric key systems. The application of the proposed method and its computing requirements are analyzed.

References

Jain, A.K., Ross, A., Prabhakar, S., An introduction to biometric recognition. *IEEE Trans. Circuits Syst. Video Technol.*, 14, 1, 4–20, 2004.

Ratha, N.K., Connell, J.H., Bolle, R.M., Enhancing security and privacy in biometrics-based authentication systems. *IBM Syst. J.*, 40, 3, 614–634, 2001.

Jain, A.K., Bolle, R., Pankanti, S. (Eds.), *Biometrics: Personal Identification in Networked Society*, Kluwer Academic Publishers, New York, 1999.

Maltoni, D., Maio, D., Jain, A.K., Prabhakar, S., *Handbook of Fingerprint Recognition*, Springer, New York, 2003.

Furht, B., Muharemagic, E.A., Socek, D., *Multimedia Security: Encryption and Watermarking*, Multimedia Systems and Applications, vol. 28, Springer, New York, 2005.

Dittmann, J., Wohlmacher, P., Nahrstedt, K., Usingcryptographic and watermarking algorithms. *IEEE Multimedia*, 8, 4, 54–65, Oct-Dec. 2001.

Lin, E.T., Eskicioglu, A.M., Lagendijk, R.L., Delp, E.J., Advances in digital video content protection. *IEEE Spec. Issue Adv. Video Coding Delivery*, 93, 1, 171–183, 2005.

Bodo, A., Method for producing a digital signature with aid of a biometric feature. German patent DE 42 43 908 A1, June 30, 1994, Priority date: Dec. 23, 1992.

Nandakumar, K., Jain, A.K., Pankanti, S., Fingerprint-based fuzzy vault: Implementation and performance. *Inf. Forensics Secur. IEEE Trans.*, 2, 4, 744–757, 2007.

Sheng, W., Howells, G., Fairhurst, M., *et al.*, Reliable and secure encryption key generation from fingerprints. *Inf. Manage. Comput. Secur.*, 20, 3, 207–221, 2012.

Hoque, S., Fairhurst, M., Howells, G., Evaluating biometric encryption key generation using handwritten signatures. *Bio-inspired Learning and Intelligent Systems for Security, 2008. BLISS'08.ECSIS Symposium on.* IEEE, pp. 17–22, 2008.

Lim, M.H., Teoh, A.B.J., Toh, K.A., An efficient dynamic reliability-dependent bit allocation for biometric discretization. *Pattern Recognit.*, 45, 5, 1960–1971, 2012.

Uludag, U., Pankanti, S., Jain, A.K., Fuzzy vault for fingerprints. *Audio-and Video-Based Biometric Person Recall*, pp. 310–319, Springer Berlin Heidelberg, 2005.

Zhang, R., Liu, E., Zhao, H., *et al.*, Improved cancelable fingerprint fuzzy vault system. *J. Xidian Univ.*, 4, 033, 2011.

Hartung, F. and Kutter, M., Multimedia watermarkingtechniques. *Proc. IEEE*, 87, 7, 1079–1107, July 1999.

Swanson, M.D., Kobayashi, M., Tewfik, A.H., Multimedia data-embedding and watermarking technologies. *Proc. IEEE*, 86, 6, 1064–1087, June 1998.

Lassmann, G., Some results on robustness, security, and usability of biometric systems. *Proc. ICME 2002*, Lausanne, Switzerland, vol. 2, pp. 577–580, Aug. 2002.

Jain, A.K., Hong, L., Pankanti, S., Biometric identification. *Comm. ACM*, 43, 2, 91–98, Feb. 2000.

Jain, A.K., Hong, L., Pankanti, S., Bolle, R., An identity authentication system using fingerprints. *Proc. IEEE*, 85, 9, 1365–1388, Sept. 1997.

Ratha, N.K., Connell, J.H., Bolle, R.M., An analysis of minutiae matching strength. *Proc. 3rd AVBPA*, Halmstad, Sweden, pp. 223–228, June 2001.

Janbandhu, P.K. and Siyal, M.Y., Novel biometric digital signatures for Internet-based applications. *Inf. Manage. Comput. Secur.*, 9, 5, 205–212, 2001.

Soutar, C., Stoianov, A., Gilroy, R., Kumar, B.V.K.V., Biometric Encryption. *Chapter 22 in ICSA Guide to Cryptography*, R.K. Nichols (Ed.), McGraw-Hill, 1999.

Abdelsadek, A., Distributed index for matching multimedia objects. M.S. thesis, School of Comput. Sci., Simon Fraser Univ., Burnaby, BC, Canada, 2014.

Abdelsadek, A. and Hefeeda, M., Dimo: Distributed index for matching multimedia objects using MapReduce, in: *Proc. ACM Multimedia Syst. Conf. (MMSys'14)*, pp. 115–125, Mar. 2014.

Aly, M., Munich, M., Perona, P., Distributed Kd-Trees for retrieval from very large image collections, in: *Proc. Brit. Mach. Vis. Conf. (BMVC)*, Aug. 2011.

Cano, P., Batle, E., Kalker, T., Haitsma, J., A review of algorithms for audio fingerprinting, in: *Proc. IEEE Workshop Multimedia Signal Process*, pp. 169–173, Dec. 2002.

Kahng, A., Lach, J., Mangione-Smith, W., Mantik, S., Markov, I., Potkonjak, M., Tucker, P., Wang, H., Wolfe, G., Watermarking techniques for intellectual property protection, in: *Proc. 35thAnnu. Design Autom. Conf. (DAC'98)*, pp. 776–781 , Jun. 1998.

Khodabakhshi, N. and Hefeeda, M., Spider: A system for finding 3D video copies. *ACM Trans. Multimedia Comput. Commun. Appl. (TOMM)*, 9, 1, 7:1–7:20, Feb. 2013.

Lee, S. and Yoo, C., Robust video fingerprinting for content-based video identification. *IEEE Trans. Circuits Syst. Video Technol.*, 18, 7, 983–988, Jul. 2008.

15

Deep Learning Algorithms for Detecting Network Attacks—An Overview

R. Mythili* **and A.S. Aneetha**

Department of Computer Science, Vels Institute of Science, Technology & Advanced Studies (VISTAS), Pallavaram, Chennai, Tamil Nadu, India

Abstract

The current era of the digital and communication field is driven by Deep Learning approaches, a cutting-edge artificial intelligence technique, with a limitless array of applications that learn and evolve on their own by analyzing the environment. A classification model developed using deep learning algorithms can identify any type of data from various sources, such as images, text, and audio. The models were trained using different types of multilayer network topologies with large amounts of labeled and unlabeled data. Deep learning algorithms have evolved based on data and model outcomes used in news aggregation, fraud detection, image recognition, healthcare, and child development. Cybercrime is a rapidly changing field, and deep learning is crucial for intrusion detection systems (IDS) and malware detection systems. These systems monitor network traffic and identify suspicious activities, enabling early detection and control of cyber-attacks. Deep learning algorithms trained on large datasets improve the attack response speed, with future architectures utilizing large amounts of raw data for cyber security systems and smart automation scenarios. This chapter explores the use of deep learning algorithms in cyber security, specifically in intrusion and malware detection systems, and analyzes their performance using metrics, such as precision, accuracy, f-score, and recall.

***Keywords*:** Deep Learning, algorithms, cyber security, IDS, malware, detection, network attacks

**Corresponding author*: mythili.r2011@gmail.com

Subhabrata Barman, Santanu Koley and Subhankar Joardar (eds.) Next-Generation Systems and Secure Computing, (293–324) © 2025 Scrivener Publishing LLC

15.1 Introduction

The modern linked environment makes people more vulnerable to network attacks. Because IT networks are now the foundation of every organization, businesses and stakeholders are significantly at risk of cyberattacks that try to compromise network security. Network security offers us the capacity to take preventive measures which will safeguard the networking components from malfunction, abuse, despair, modification, unauthorized get entry to and so on. Although we believe that our data are safe and secure when uploaded to the Internet, hackers can compromise these data and steal money or reveal personal information. Therefore, a network must be secured. Our network and the data stored in it are protected by network security from breaches, software and hardware infiltration, and other threats.

Network security defines a collection of significant rules, regulations, and configurations based on risks, network use, accessibility, and total threat security. We protected our data from fraudulent individuals in cybersecurity. Cybersecurity refers to the use of computer networking, software, or other technologies to protect against online dangers. It maintains a variety of practices to protect the integrity of networks, programs, and data from unauthorized access. Intrusion Detection Systems (IDS) and Malware Detection Systems use deep learning for cybersecurity. An IDS monitors network traffic and spots unusual activities, whereas malware detection systems find and stop intrusions before they cause harm.

15.1.1 Cybercrime and Cybersecurity

Cybercrime is the act of utilizing computers to manipulate cyberspace to create, distribute, alter, steal, misuse, and destroy information against the will or interest of the victim and without the use of physical force. In theory, information can be anything from government secrets to electronic money, and the victim can be an individual or a business [1]. It has two primary subtypes: illegal activities involving computers, and criminal conduct directed against computers. It performs several other types of crime which include malware transmission, illegal data, and unlawful photos. Financial and non-financial infractions are included in cybercrime [27].

Cybersecurity is crucial for leading a digital life in today's networked world. As technology advances and businesses become increasingly reliant on digital systems, protecting sensitive data, upholding customer confidence, and guaranteeing continued operation have become critical objectives.

The significance of adequate cybersecurity measures is illustrated by the statistics we gathered on the subject, which range from the increasing frequency of data breaches to the monetary losses experienced by businesses and the increasing sophistication of hackers.

15.1.2 Network Security

Network security is defined as the application of methods, procedures, and protocols to safeguard a person or organization's communication and information. The goal of network security, a branch of cybersecurity, is to safeguard both the information that can be delivered over network nodes and the veracity of any channel. We can secure our data both inside and outside an organization with the help of networking and cybersecurity. Under the supervision of network security, a variety of elements are joined to guarantee the security of the data and networks. Based on this, various network security methods exist:

1. Firewalls
2. Access Control
3. Virtual Private Networks (VPNs)
4. Intrusion Prevention Systems (IPS)
5. Wireless Security
6. Software Protection
7. Behavioral Analytics

- **Firewalls:** Services or equipment known as firewalls serve as gatekeepers in charge of making decisions on which websites, web pages, advertisement pop-up, and other services, can enter and leave a network.
- **Access Control:** Access control permits organizations to secure themselves from potential attackers to invade exclusive statistics and to block unauthorized devices and users from gaining access to the given community.
- **VPNs:** A VPN usually makes use of the Internet to further encrypt the relationship between endpoint tool and a community, and allow professionals to authenticate the communication between the network and the device. This results in the construction constructing an encrypted and secure tunnel using the net.
- **IPS:** The intrusion prevention system finds and saves assaults using scanning community visitors. This is finished by using

databases of assault strategies with which professionals are familiar and correlating them with network activities.

- **Wireless Security:** It is critical to have Wi-Fi protection mainly when cybercriminals are unexpectedly concentrated on exclusive information for extortion.
- **Software Protection:** Utility safety involves a hard and fast software program hardware and approaches that song and lock the vulnerable points of a utility to effortlessly be targeted by attackers to infiltrate the network.
- **Behavioral Analytics:** It is a concept in business analytics that offers insights into how customers behave on their websites, e-commerce platforms, mobile apps, chats, emails, connected products, and other digital channels.

15.2 Technologies of Network Security

15.2.1 Intrusion Detection Systems

An Intrusion Detection System (IDS) is a combination of the phrases intrusion and detection process of identifying cyber threats, and information should be passed to concerned authorities in the network system. Intrusion is the illegal attempt to obtain data from a computer system or network to undermine its availability, confidentiality, or integrity. A security measure for detecting illegal activities is the detection system. Therefore, an IDS is a tool for detecting harmful and illegal activity in network traffic, and it aids network admistrators in taking the necessary preventive measures

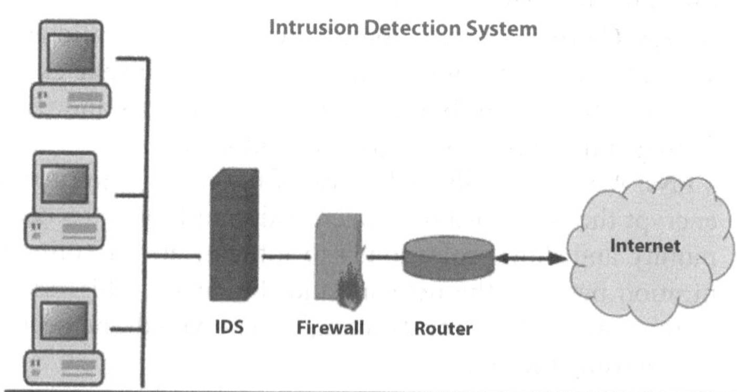

Figure 15.1 Basic architecture of IDS.

to secure the communication network infrastructure and the connected nodes [2]. Figure 15.1 shows the basic architecture of IDS:

15.2.1.1 Types of IDS Tools

Different environments can be used to implement intrusion detection. An IDS can be either host- or network-based, similar to many cybersecurity solutions.

- **Network Intrusion Detection System (NIDS)**—may include both software(console) and hardware (sensors) to manage and track network traffic packets at various places for any potential intrusion or abnormality [3].
- **Host Intrusion Detection System (HIDS)**—monitors only activity on the host system, which is a certain computer or server. Although it is restricted to only one machine, it has greater capabilities than an NIDS because it can access encrypted information traveling over the network, such as system configuration databases, registries, and file characteristics [3].

15.2.1.2 IDS Functionality

- An IDS continues to track network visitors to look for uncommon behaviors.
- The recorded network log information was examined for any symptoms of anomalous behavior.
- Signatures of the traffic are analyzed for any possibility of an attack or intrusion; the IDS compares the community activity to a hard and fast of predetermined guidelines and styles.
- The IDS notifies the system administrator if it reveals something corresponding to one of these guidelines or styles.
- The system administrator can then look at the alert and take suitable measures to prevent harm or extra intrusion.

15.2.1.3 Implementation of IDS

An IDS and firewalls are both cybersecurity solutions that can be deployed to protect an endpoint or network. An IDS may be deployed in conjunction with other security measures, including access control, authentication mechanisms, and encryption techniques, to increase the comfort of systems against cyber-attacks [4]. Many strategies have been developed over time to improve IDS utilizing deep learning techniques. Due to its increased classification accuracy and capacity to shield the network from malicious attacks, DL is superior to other approaches [5]. An IDS is a crucial component of an organization's cybersecurity system. Network security is built on a basic firewall; however, many sophisticated attacks can get around it. An IDS adds a second layer of protection, making it more difficult for an attacker to enter the network of an undetected company. Many researchers have focused on CPS and anomaly detection using deep learning algorithms. Alternatively, such designs and algorithms have their own obstacles and demanding situations for economically detecting and eliminating several varieties of cyber-attacks [6].

15.2.2 Malware Detection System (MDS)

Malware, often known as malicious software, is a type of program or part of a program designed to interfere with, change, or eliminate any software components necessary for a computer system, device, service, or network to operate properly [7]. Malware is an umbrella term that encompasses spyware, trojan horses, worms, ransomware, and other harmful software.

15.2.2.1 Types of Malwares

- **Viruses:** The term "virus" refers to an executable file containing malicious code. The virus spreads when a compromised file is transferred from one system to the other.
- **Worms:** This is a form of malware that can duplicate itself and spread frequently over a network by exploiting security flaws.
- **Trojan horse:** Malware that carries out malicious operations under the appearance of a desired operation, such as playing an online game.
- **Ransomware:** This malware encrypts personal information and documents while demanding a ransom amount to decrypt them.
- **Spyware:** This software enters a user's computer, collects data from the machine and user, and transfers it to third parties without user knowledge.

Currently, malware is one of the main cybersecurity risks. The threat posed by malware has increased over the last several years as millions of new malware samples have been found. The use of methods and technologies to recognize, stop, notify, and react to malware threats is known as malware detection. This enables the recovery of compromise indicators to identify hacked devices and, consequently, forecast future infections, analyze their effects, specify exploited vulnerabilities, and pinpoint the source. The procedure involves identifying and thoroughly examining suspicious files, codes, or records of endpoints.

Basic malware detection methods, such as signature-based detection, check summing, and application allowlisting, can aid in identifying and limiting the known risks. Advanced malware detection systems use AI to proactively search for and identify new and undiscovered malware threats.

15.2.2.2 Malware Detection Techniques

- **Signature-Based Detection:** A secured system's software applications leave a distinct digital trail known as a signature, which is used in signature-based detection. Software is scanned by antivirus systems, whose signatures are then recognized and compared to those of known malware.
- **Check summing:** This method is a type of signature analysis that involves calculating cyclic redundancy check (CRC) checksums. Check summing helps to verify that the files are uncorrupted.
- **Application Allowlisting:** Application allowlists, also known as whitelists, work in opposition to attack signature strategies. Instead, specifying which software the antivirus program should block, it maintains a list of authorized programs and disables all others.
- **Endpoint Protection Platform (EPP):** Endpoints such as workstations for employees, servers, and cloud-based resources are where the EPPs are installed. They act as the first line of defense, able to spot threats and stop them before they harm sensitive assets.
- **Endpoint Detection and Response (EDR):** An endpoint security solution known as EDR continuously scans end-user devices for malware and ransomware to identify them and take appropriate action.

15.3 Network Attacks

An attack is a facts security threat that includes a try to achieve, adjust, destroy, take away, implant, or display facts without legal admission to or permission. It is one of the most important safety threats in information technology, happens to both individuals and organizations, and comes in different forms. Network attacks mainly fall into two categories: passive and active attacks. In a passive attack, an attacker gains access to a network and can watch or steal sensitive data without altering the data itself. A good example is wiretapping. However, in an active attack, the attacker modifies the data by deleting, encrypting, or doing other harm to it. A good example of this might be viruses or other types of malware. Major network attacks are listed in Table 15.1 with its description.

15.3.1 Active Attacks

Active attacks are a type of cybersecurity attack in which an attacker attempts to change, damage, or impair a system or network's regular operation. Active attacks, as opposed to passive assaults, which simply involve monitoring or eavesdropping on a system or network, can be more harmful because they include attackers taking actual action against the target system or network.

The forms of active attacks are as follows:

- Masquerade
- Amendment of messages
- Repudiation
- Replay
- Denial of provider

15.3.2 Passive Attacks

A passive assault has no impact on system resources; instead, it attempts to gather or use information from the system. In nature, attacks that are passive eavesdrop on or watch over communication. The opponent wants to receive the transmitted information. Attackers that use passive methods observe or gather information without making changes or erasing it. Examples of passive attacks include eavesdropping, in which an attacker listens to network traffic to obtain sensitive information, and sniffing, in which an attacker takes and examines information packets to steal sensitive statistics. Kinds of passive attacks are as follows:

- The release of message content
- Traffic analysis

Table 15.1 Types of attacks.

Type of attacks	Description
Endpoint Attacks	The act of gaining unauthorized access to consumer devices, servers, or other endpoints and compromising them—usually by infecting them with malware—thus compromising the system.
Malware Attacks	Introducing malware into IT resources, which enables attackers to take control of systems, steal data, and cause harm. Ransomware assaults are also among them.
DoS (Denial of Service) [28]	This attack renders a network, host or different piece of infrastructure unusable with the aid of legitimate users.
Vulnerabilities, Exploits, and Attacks	Gaining illegal access to, compromising, or damaging systems by taking advantage of flaws in company software.
DDoS (Distributed DoS)	It is miles a kind of DoS attack, wherein more than one compromised systems are used to target a single system causing a Denial of Service.
Advanced persistent threats	These are sophisticated, multi-layered threats that encompass both network and other assault types.
Packet sniffer	A passive receiver that records a copy of every packet that flies.
IP Spoofing	The ability to inject packets into the Internet with a false source address.
A man-in-the-middle (MiTM) attack	Cyber-attack wherein the attacker secretly intercepts and relays messages between events who consider they may be communicating at once with each other.
Phishing [22]	The technique of delivering fake messages that seem to be from a reliable source.
DNS spoofing	The process of poisoning DNS server entries to send a targeted user to a malicious website under the attacker's control.
Rootkit	Software used by cybercriminals to gain control over a target computer or network.

15.4 Deep Learning Approaches

This section describes deep learning approach-based intrusion detection systems. Some deep learning approaches used for cyber security intrusion detection are as follows.

15.4.1 Feed Forward Neural Network (FFNN)

An artificial neural network, known as an FFNN, does not have loop-like connections between its nodes. The opposite of an FFNN is recurrent neural network, in which certain routes are cycled. Because the input is only processed in one direction, the feed-forward model is the most basic type of neural network. In this model, a number of inputs are multiplied by weights, as they input the layer. The sum of the weighted input values was then acquired by adding each value. A value is frequently created if the total of the values is greater than a predetermined threshold, which is typically set to zero; if the sum is less than the threshold, the output value is −1. The multilayer feed-forward neural network has numerous neuron-structured layers, such as the input, hidden, and output layers. An output layer with one or more neurons provides an output for one or more inputs. The multilayer feed forward network architecture is given in Figure 15.2.

The input to the network is an n-dimensional vector. The network carries L hidden layers having n neurons each. In the end, there may be one output layer containing k neurons (k classes). Each neuron inside the hidden layer and output layer can be split into parts: pre-activation and activation (a_i and h_i are vectors). The input layer can be known as the zero-th layer and the output layer can be called L-th layer. W_i and b_i are the weight and bias between the layers.

- The pre-activation at layer i is given by

$$\boldsymbol{a}_i(\boldsymbol{x}) = \boldsymbol{b}_i + \boldsymbol{W}_i\boldsymbol{h}_{i-1}(\boldsymbol{x}) \tag{15.1}$$

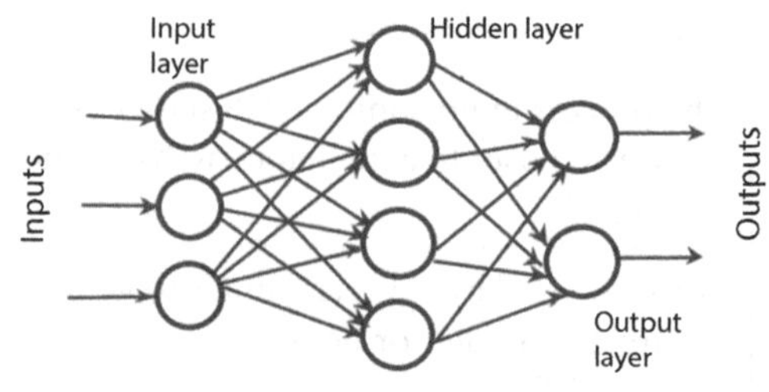

Figure 15.2 Feed forward network architecture.

- The activation at layer is given by

$$h_i(x) = g(a_i(x)) \tag{15.2}$$

where g is called the activation function.

- The activation at the output layer is given by

$$f(x) = h_L(x) = O(L(x)) \tag{15.3}$$

where O is the output activation function.

15.4.1.1 In Malware Detection

An FFDNN malware classification and prediction model was created and implemented by Singh [8] using the concept of feature concatenation. DL classifiers for malware detection were trained and validated using portable executable header (PEH) data. To train the FFDNN for prediction and classification in the first section, the functions produced by every hidden deep layer are concatenated. In the second level, parametric tuning is performed on the ML classifier, RF, SVM, and k-NN ML with the deep functions of the hidden layers applied independently or mixed. Every neuron in a layer is connected to every other neuron within the layer above it in a very connected layer, which is also referred to as a dense layer. The PEH data are used to train an FFDNN with GeLU activation characteristics and forecast the entry on the output layer of the DNN u sing the pass-entropy (Lce) and L1 loss features. The suggested FFDNN general loss (L) function is expressed as follows:

$$L = \gamma L_{ce} + +(1-\gamma)L_1 \qquad (15.4)\ [31]$$

where,

L_{ce}, cross entropy,
L_1, loss function,
γ, weight between loss function.

In a later stage, a 20-layer FFDNN was trained using various activation functions, and its deep features were returned to train the FFDNN and ML classifiers. Different activation functions, including SeLU, eLU, ReLU, and GeLU, of the DNN were used to conduct the inquiry. The best accuracy was attained by GeLU, which was 98.17%.

15.4.2 Convolutional Neural Network (CNN)

The CNN is a not unusual synthetic neural network used for object and image recognition and classification. DL techniques use a CNN algorithm to identify components in an image. The extraction of features from the image is performed through some hidden layers, consisting of the convolution layer, the ReLU layer, and the pooling layer. Learning the relevant features of the input data is the main goal of CNN. The earliest layers in this method encompass a collection of learnable convolutional feature extractors. Every item of input statistics is traversed by means of a sliding window created by means of the applied filters. The stride is the term used here to describe the overlap distance that is utilized to create various feature maps. Convolutional kernels make up each CNN layer, which is used to make one type of feature map [9], concluding the classification using one or more absolutely related layers after the convolutional and pooling layers have been built. Figure 15.3 illustrates CNN architecture.

Let width (W_1), Height (H_1) and Depth (D_1) of the original input. The Stride S and the number of filters F with padding P, the output is $W_2 \times H_2 \times D_2$ where D2 is equal to the number of kernels.

$$W_2 = \frac{W_1 - F + 2P}{S} + 1 \quad (15.5)\ [20]$$

$$H_2 = \frac{H_1 - F + 2P}{S} + 1 \quad (15.6)\ [20]$$

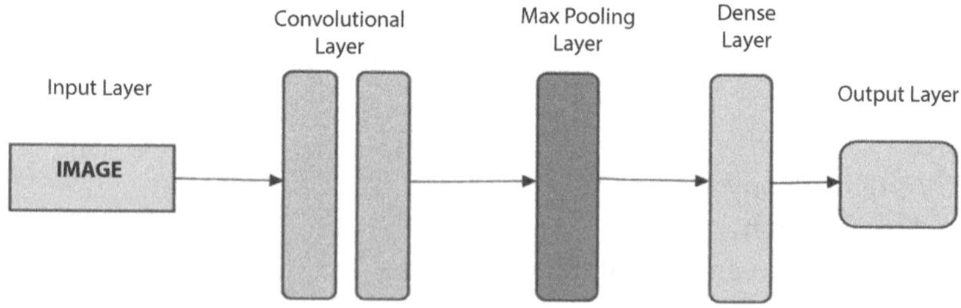

Figure 15.3 Convolutional neural network architecture.

15.4.2.1 Implementation of CNN in IDS

In the field of computer vision, CNN has achieved great progress. They [32] serve the supervised feature extraction and classification needs of the IDS. Relatively, CNNs require much less preprocessing than other image-type strategies. The implication is that, in contrast to traditional methods, the network figures out the way to optimize the filters (or kernels) on its own. First and foremost, feature extraction does not need any context or human input [10]. In order to detect network intrusion [11], we employed time series data containing a million benign and malicious connections, CNN, and a hybrid of CNN. Here, CNN consists of a convolution 1D layer, a pooling 1D layer, a fully linked layer, and a non-linear activation function as ReLU. A totally linked layer incorporates the softmax function that offers the probability distribution over each class.

15.4.3 Recurrent Neural Networks (RNN)

RNNs work on the premise that each layer's prediction is made by saving its output and feeding it back into the system's input. The nodes from multiple layers of the neural network are compacted to form a single layer of RNN.

In Figure 15.4, A, B, and C are the parameters of the network. Right here, "x" is the input layer, "h" is the hidden layer, and "y" is the output layer. A, B, and C are the network parameters used to improve the output of the model. At any given time, t, the cutting-edge input is a combination of input at x(t) and x(t – 1). The output at any given time is fetched back to the network to enhance the output.

RNN are frequently used for sequential training data learning. It uses the back-propagation mechanism to train the model. It is made to model sequence data and enhances the capabilities of the traditional feed-forward

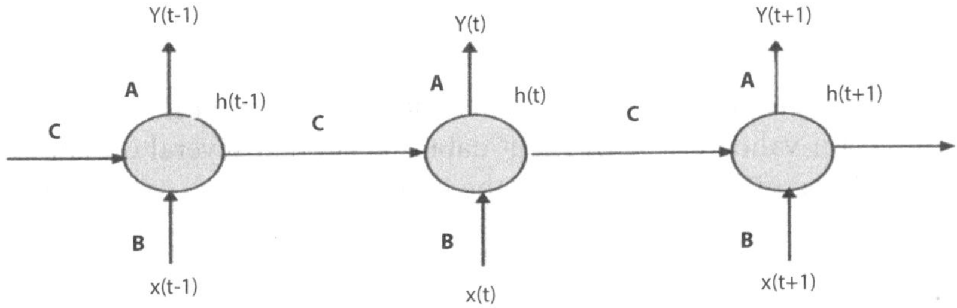

Figure 15.4 Recurrent neural network architecture.

neural network. It is composed of input, hidden, and output units, the latter two of which are thought of as memory elements. Each RNN unit uses its current input as well as the output from a prior input to reach a decision.

15.4.3.1 Implementation of RNN in IDS

RNN may be used for supervised class and feature extraction for an IDS. RNNs can often only handle sequences of a certain maximum length before experiencing short-term memory issues. These problems are addressed by means of many RNN variations, which include Long Short-Term Memory (LSTM) and Gated Recurrent Unit (GRU) [26].

In the context of binary and multiclass classification of the NSL-KDD dataset, Yin *et al.* supplied RNN-based totally IDS. The model was evaluated with various hidden node counts and learning rates. Results indicated that the number of hidden nodes and various learning rates have an impact on the model's accuracy. For binary and multi-class cases, the best accuracy was attained utilizing 80 hidden nodes and learning rates of 0.1 and 0.5.

In addition to the multilayer perceptron and a SoftMax classifier, Xu *et al.* advised an IDS primarily based on RNN employing GRU as the main memory. KDD Cup'99 and NSL-KDD datasets were used to test the proposed methodology. When compared to other approaches, experimental results indicated good detection rates.

15.4.4 Autoencoder (AE)

An autoencoder is a kind of artificial neural network, namely used to discover data encodings unsupervised. It trains the network to capture the most crucial elements of the input image with the goal of learning a lower-dimensional likeness (encrypting) for higher-dimensional data, usually for range reduction. Image denoising, image compression, and in certain situations even the invention of picture data can all be accomplished by autoencoders.

The architecture of autoencoders, shown in Figure 15.5, consists of three parts,

- ➢ **Encoder:** A component that encodes a representation of the train-validate-test set input data that is often several orders of magnitude smaller than the input data.

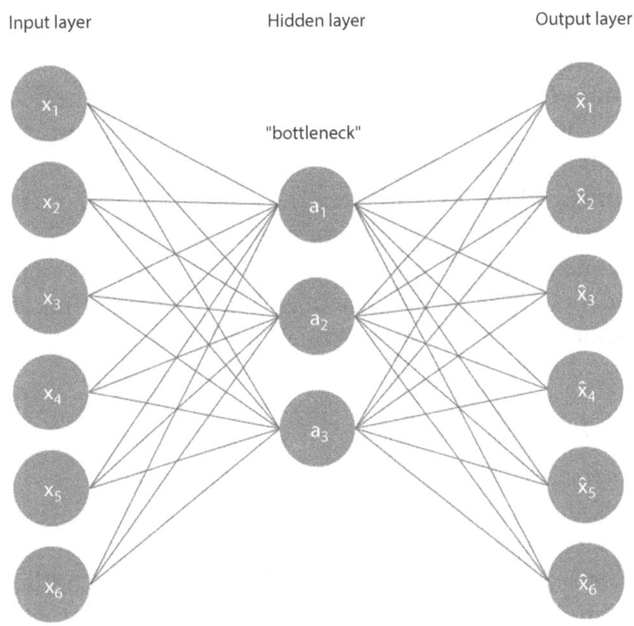

Figure 15.5 Autoencoder architecture.

- **Bottleneck:** A network component that is the most crucial because it holds the compressed knowledge representations.
- **Decoder:** A component that assists the network in "decompressing" knowledge representations and recovering the data from its encoded state. Next, the output is compared with a source of truth.

AE works at the idea of matching the output as near to the input as feasible via learning the excellent features. It includes input and output layers of equal dimension, even as the size of the hidden layers is generally smaller than the input layer. The input to the model is compressed into a small area known as the bottleneck by the encoder, which is composed of convolutional blocks followed with the aid of pooling modules. The decoder, which uses a string of upsampling modules to restore the compressed feature to its original state as an image, is the bottleneck that follows. In the case of simple AE, the output is expected to be similar to the input data with much less noise. Before training AE, a collection of four hyperparameters is required. They are:

- **Code size:** It is the primary hyper parameter used to fine-tune the autoencoder. It is also called bottleneck size.
- **Number of layers:** The depth of the encoder and the decoder are crucial tuning parameters for autoencoders, much like for all neural networks.
- **Number of nodes per layer:** The weights each layer uses are determined by the number of nodes in that layer.
- **Reconstruction Loss:** The loss function used to train the autoencoder is highly dependent on the type of input and output we want the autoencoder to adapt to.

15.4.4.1 Types of AE

The different variants of autoencoders are as follows:

1. **Undercomplete AE**
   Reconstructing the image from the compressed bottleneck region is accomplished using an undercomplete autoencoder, which accepts an input image and attempts to predict it as an output. These types of autoencoders are mostly used to create latent spaces, also known as bottlenecks, which serve as compressed substitutes for input data that are quickly and readily decompressed back with the aid of a network when necessary.
2. **Sparse AE**
   Sparse AE are much like the undercomplete autoencoders in that they use the equal image as input and floor fact. The size of the bottleneck is controlled and tuned for undercomplete autoencoders, whereas the variety of nodes at each hidden layer is controlled and tuned for sparse autoencoders.
3. **Contractive AE**
   Contractive AE works under the notion that inputs with similar characteristics should have similar encodings and latent space representations. It implies that for slight input alterations, the latent space should not vary significantly.
4. **Denoising AE**
   This is the first algorithm of its kind whose ground truth is not the input image. Send a picture that has noise added by digital manipulations to denoising autoencoders. The encoder–decoder design receives the noisy image, processes it, and compares the results to the original image.

5. **Variational AE**
   Both traditional and variant autoencoders are trained to only constitute the input in a compressed shape referred to as the latent area or bottleneck. As a result, the latent space that the model created after training may not be continuous and hence difficult to interpolate.

15.4.4.2 Autoencoder in IDS

Khan *et al.* proposed an efficient two-stage model based totally on deep-stacked AE. The preliminary stage classified the dataset into the attack and regular classes with probability values. These probability rankings are then used as an extra function and are input to the final decision stage for normal and multiclass attack types. The performance of the proposed model was tested using KDD Cup'99 and UNSWNB15 datasets. To reduce the troubles of the class imbalance of the datasets, an extraordinary technique was adopted for both datasets. For KDD Cup'99, the down sampling was performed to eliminate repeated records. While, to balance the distribution of records in UNSWNB15, upsampling of the dataset was performed with the use of SMOTE. This preprocessing of the dataset dramatically improves the DR efficiency of the attack class with lower training times.

15.4.5 Restricted Boltzmann Machine (RBM)

RBM is an undirected graphical version that has recently played a significant part in the deep learning framework. In 1986, Smolensky first introduced it under the name Harmonium. It is a method that is helpful for feature learning, collaborative filtering, topic modeling, classification, regression, and dimensionality reduction.

Restricted boltzmann machine architecture is given below in Figure 15.6, which might be shallow, two-layer neural networks, are the building blocks of deep belief networks. The first layer of the RBM is the visible, or input, layer, and the second one is the concealed layer. Each circle

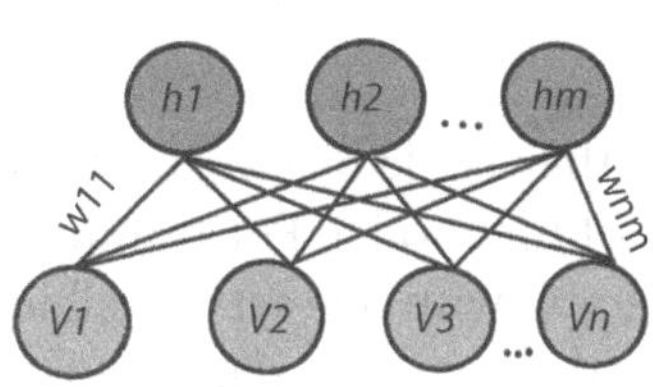

Figure 15.6 Restricted boltzmann machine architecture.

represents a node, which resembles a neuron. Nodes from the same layer are connected, despite the fact that they are connected to one another across levels. The limitation of an RBM is the lack of intra-layer communication. Each node acts as the center of computing, making arbitrary decisions about whether to transmit input or not before processing it.

15.4.5.1 Working of RBM

Each visible node gets its low-level features from a dataset learnable item. At hidden layer node 1, x is multiplied by a weight and delivered to a bias. An activation function employing the outcomes of the two processes and input x produces the node's output, or the strength of the signal passing through it. A matrix with rows equal to the input nodes and columns equal to the output nodes will always be produced by the weights between the two layers. At each hidden node, each input x is multiplied by its appropriate weight w. The four inputs are sent to each hidden node, improved by each weight. Every hidden node gets one output due to the activation algorithm after the sum of these products is once again added to a bias (which compels at least some activations to occur).

15.4.5.2 RBM in Network Intrusion Detection

For network intrusion detection [12], employed RBM with four inputs and five hidden nodes, which comprises of two layers: the visible layer (layer vi) and the hidden layer (layer hi), which has N_v and M_h nodes.Here hidden gadgets are used to seize higher level correlations in the information, and the visible units to mirror the facts themselves. The proposed system is absolutely interactive among visible and hidden gadgets, and there is no interactivity between gadgets of the same kind. Therefore, the visible stochastic binary variables are connected to hidden stochastic binary variables h. For binary RBM, the energy E(v,h) which defines the bipartite (visible and hidden) structure, is given by:

$$E(v,h) = -v^T a - b^T h - v^T\, Wh \tag{15.7}$$

The weight matrix W, the visible bias vector b, and the hidden bias vector c are the parameters of the model. For training efficiency, BMs may be restricted to a bipartite graph with one set of visible neurons and one set of hidden neurons. They used a particular dataset for intrusion detection, and their approach comprehends three major aspects—weight initialization, pre-training, and fine-tuning—plus a few parameter optimization picks like number of training epochs, mini batches, momentum, and gaining knowledge of rate.

15.5 Models of IDS

Ahmad [2] reported that network attacks are prevented by a proposed end-to-end early intrusion detection system, which also uses a deep neural network-based classifier to identify attacks. The network is trained in a supervised manner to extract relevant features from raw network traffic data. They introduced a new metric called earliness to evaluate the proposed approach. They take a dataset from CICIDS2017 and obtained a result with 0.803 accuracy. Ashiku [3] addressed network IDS, and the proposed deep learning model includes CNN with regularized MLP. The dataset used to experiment with this model is UNSW-NB15, primarily selected for its representation of real-world network traffic designed to the common vulnerabilities and exposures. The proposed model obtained overall accuracy of 95.4% and 95.6% for the pre-partitioned and user-defined multiclass classification. Alsughayyir *et al.* [5] used deep learning-based techniques including auto-encoders, CNNs, and RNN to create an effective IDS. The suggested methods try to differentiate between a network's typical behavior and an anomaly-based one. [21] The data collected by the IDS evaluation program of DARPA'98 were used to create the KDD dataset. The new NSL-KDD data that was used in this study. With an accuracy of 0.99 for training and 0.94 for testing, RNN exceeds all other methods in the experiment findings.

Based on real-time datasets or pre-existing datasets from various sources, multiple writers employed deep learning algorithms in the cybersecurity field to detect various types of assaults. Connected and Autonomous Vehicle (CAV) data was gathered by Aldhyani [13] from actual CAV traffic data, which included contained benign packets and packets subject to spoofing, flooding, and replaying assaults. The dataset was used to identify attack messages using CNN and CNN-LSTM hybrid networks, which combine CNN and long short-term memory models. They achieved a higher accuracy of 97.30%. To successfully detect and identify the trigger encoded data and defend a DNA sequencing pipeline from Trojan attacks, Islam *et al.* [14] used CNN deep learning. The outcome demonstrates nearly up to 100% accuracy in detection in such a novel Trojan attack scenario, even after applying fragmentation encryption and steganography to the encoded trigger data.

Gouveia *et al.* [12] used a UNB ISCX intrusion detection evaluation dataset to show the effectiveness of the Restricted Boltzmann machine method. The Network Training MSE and Network Validation MSE both had successful outcomes. In their study, Almalaq *et al.* [15] address cyber-attacks by putting forth a deep learning-based attack detection model for energy systems that could be trained using data and logs from phasor measuring units (PMUs). Data classification is carried out using the AdaBoost algorithm. The suggested model has ultimately been evaluated against other machine learning models using a variety of measures. The suggested model obtains a 93.6% detection rate and a 93.91% accuracy rate.

Li *et al.* [16] adopted a multilayer perceptron (MLP) model and a hierarchical RNN model to detect attacks. The four types of assaults included in the DARPA public datasets used by the authors are DoS, Probe, U2R, and R2L. Finally, the proposed method outperforms other initializations in terms of error rate (approximately 9% relative decrease). Weight initialization is also applied. Haddadi *et al.* [17] use a two-layered feed-forward neural network to address an IDS. An early halting approach is employed during the training phase of neural networks to solve the overfitting issue. The DARPA dataset is used to evaluate the suggested system. The pre-processed connections chosen from DARPA had their feature range changed to [−1,1]. Results from the experiments demonstrate that the system has reasonable performance with high precision while being simpler than similar scenarios. The Al-Abassi *et al.* [18] model was specifically created for an Industrial Control System (ICS) context. DNN and Decision Tree (DT) classifiers are used by the proposed attack detection model to identify cyberattacks. A 10-fold cross-validation on two authentic ICS datasets is used to assess the performance of the suggested model. When RF and DNN were compared, the proposed model's accuracy was 95.86%.

15.6 IDS Datasets

The CICIDS2017 dataset: Ahmad *et al.* [2] utilized it to evaluate the effectiveness of their strategy, and this dataset contains seven different forms of attack flow, such as Heartbleed, Botnet, and Web. Network traffic pertaining to web assaults like SQL injection is included. The attacker sends and injects into the database a string of SQL statements.

UNSW-NB15 dataset: In their proposed system's approach, Ashiku *et al.* [3] suggested "categorical cross entropy" to avoid overfitting using the UNSW-NB15 [23, 25] train and test datasets. Utilizing user-defined datasets and the Nadam optimization technique is suggested to prevent overfitting.

PEH dataset: The PEH was the source of the dataset used by Singh *et al.* [8] for malware detection in their proposed system. A 138,048 × 54 matrix can be used to represent the 138,048 instances of the malware dataset and the 54 features.

HTTP DATASET CSIC 2010 dataset: Ghazal *et al.* [10] made heavy use of HTTP DATASET CSIC 2010. In the dataset, there were 36,000 queries, and 25,000 of those were made fraudulently by bots. The package includes a lot of risks, including cross-site scripting, CRLF injection, SQL injection, server-side inclusion, and parameter manipulation. Just 0.20 percent of the total dataset is used for evaluation; the remaining 0.80% is used as training data.

KDD Cup 99 dataset: In 1998, the MIT Lincoln Laboratory provided the network IDS dataset. The training dataset includes 24 attacks split into four groups. A specific protocol type was used to gather sender and receiver flow data, which was used to gather TCP/IP data as one of the features. An updated version of the KDD Cup 99 dataset, the NSL-KDD dataset [30], was described by Vinayakumar *et al.* [11].

UNB ISCX dataset: This Intrusion Detection Evaluation Dataset was utilized by Gouveia [12]. This dataset's records are categorized based on three features: basic, content, and traffic. Each entry consists of a set of IP packets that flow data between two IP addresses using application- and transport-layer protocols, starting at one moment in time and ending at another. The odds of a class being normal are 0.466, whereas the odds of a class being anomalous are 0.534.

ICS cyberattack dataset: A total of 15 categories with a total of 5,000 data points each make up the ICS cyberattack multiclass classification dataset used by Almalaq *et al.* [15]. The Attribute-Relation File format (AREF) is the primary file format used for the data collection. An ASCII text file known as an ARFF file expresses a collection of shared attributes amongst various samples.

DARPA dataset: This public dataset, which was made available by the MIT Lincoln Lab in the United States and consists of a two-week test set and a seven-week train set, was used by Li *et al.* [16]. These files contain four types of assaults: DoS, Probe, U2R, and R2.F. Haddadi *et al.* [17] used a TCP dump file that contained a record of all traffic from the DARPA dataset. There were four separate sorts of attacks in the traffic: DoS, R2L, U2R, and Probe. The KDD Cup 99 data collection has 5,000,000 connections, and each connection includes 41 properties with both symbolic and numerical values.

- **Dos (Denial of Service):** Attacker to stop authorized users from utilizing a service.
- **R2L (Remote to Local):** The attacker attempts to get access because they do not have an account on the victim's computer.
- **U2R (User to Remote):** The attacker attempts to obtain superuser capabilities while having local access to the victim's computer.
- **Probe:** The attacker attempts to learn more about the intended host.

The effectiveness of the suggested approach by Al-Abassi *et al.* [18] is evaluated using two different ICS datasets. The Gas Pipeline (GP) dataset comprises 17 features and a total of 274,628 observations, of which 54,925 (20%) and 219,702 (80%) are samples for testing and training, respectively. The Secure Water Treatment (SWaT) dataset consists of 1,048,576 observations that are split into 838,860 training samples and 209,715 testing samples.

15.7 Result Analysis

- A 20-layer FFDNN that has been trained using several activation functions was utilized by Singh *et al.* [8] to recover deep features. The FFDNN [24] and machine learning classifiers are both trained using this technique. Although GeLU, an activation function with superior performance, achieved more accuracy than DNN, it was still lower than 98.17%.
- Using binary cross entropy as the loss function, Adam as the optimizer function, 15 epochs as the number of training sessions, and 128 as the batch size, Ghazal *et al.* [10] built deep learning techniques. In comparison to LSTM and CNN, this algorithm can identify these attacks efficiently and effectively. The LSTM plus CNN showed the greatest performance results.
- Experiments are carried out by Almalaq *et al.* [15] using KNN, SVM, GBDT, XGBoost, and other methods. Deep learning models are used to compare all of the methods for protecting the smart grid against various forms of cyberattacks. Distances are calculated using the Euclidean/Manhattan distances. Instead of focusing on the specific cyberattack, the proposed methodology would detect and prevent cyber-hacking at the location of reinstallation.

- In the DARPA 1998 train set, attacks make up around 65.54% of the total, while the DARPA attack proportions are 63.29, 1.99%, 0.26%, and 0.01%. Li uses error rates to verify the effectiveness of the initialization strategy [16].
- Two datasets, each with a unique collection of linkages, were utilized for training and testing by Haddadi *et al.* [17]. In each group, 20% of the data are used for tests, while the remaining 80% are for training. With dataset 1, training was stopped using the "early stopping" technique after 599 iterations. The similar event occurred in 611 epochs for dataset 2. The proposed IDS is then evaluated using test results. The results suggested that the proposed IDS performed almost as well in both experiments and that the detection rates were extremely close. Therefore, IDS with less data is more appropriate due to decreased computational overhead.

15.8 Evaluation Metrics

Evaluation metrics are quantitative measures used to rank a statistical or machine (or) deep learning model's performance and efficiency. Accuracy is the most frequently used categorization evaluation metric. When the accuracy rate reaches 99%, the model may be considered effective. However, this is not always true, and can be misleading in some situations.

Most widely used evaluation metrics are

- ➢ The Confusion Matrix for a classification problem
- ➢ The Key Classification Metrics: Accuracy, Recall, Precision, and F1-score.

15.8.1 Confusion Matrix

The confusion matrix is a matrix used to determine the overall performance of the classification models for a given set of test data. It offers greater insightful picture, which is not always the best performance of a predictive model, but additionally which instructions are being predicted efficaciously and incorrectly and what type of mistakes are being made. The below table shows four category metrics (True Positive, False Positive, True Negative, False Negative) and our predicted value compared to the actual value in a Confusion Matrix Table 15.2.

Table 15.2 Confusion matrix.

		Predicted Value	
		Positive	Negative
Original Value	Positive	True Positive	True Negative
	Negative	False Positive	False Negative

- **True Positive:** How many times the model correctly classifies a Positive sample as Positive.
- **False Negative:** How many times the model incorrectly classifies a Positive sample as Negative.
- **False Positive:** How many times the model incorrectly classifies a Negative sample as Positive.
- **True Negative:** How many times the model correctly classifies a Negative sample as Negative.

15.8.2 Key Classification Metrics

Accuracy (Acc)

A model's overall prediction accuracy can be determined using the accuracy evaluation metric. The formula for accuracy is

$$Accuracy = \frac{TrueNegative + TruePositive}{TruePositive + FalsePositive + TrueNegative + FalseNegative} \tag{15.8}$$

Precision (PR)

The precision is calculated as the rate between the number of *Positive* samples rightly classified to the total number of samples classified as *Positive* (either rightly or inaptly). The precision shows how accurate the model is in classifying samples as positive.

$$Precision = \frac{TruePositive}{(TruePositive + FalsePositive)} \tag{15.9}$$

Recall (RE)

The recall is calculated as the rate between the number of *Positive* samples rightly classified as Positive to the total number of *Positive* samples. This measures the model's capability to describe positive samples. More positive samples were found when the recall was larger.

$$Recall = \frac{TruePositive}{(TruePositive{+}FalseNegative)} \tag{15.10}$$

F1 score

The accuracy of a model is evaluated using the F1 score. It combines the precision and recall of a classifier into a single metric by taking their harmonious mean.

$$F1\,score = \frac{2(Precision * Recall)}{Precision + Recall} \tag{15.11}$$

15.8.3 Metrics Used in IDS

- Ahmad *et al.* [2] evaluated the classification performance using PR, RE, FPR, balanced accuracy (BA), bookmaker informedness (BM), and other measures for each class in the dataset. Each of the measures mentioned above might range from 0 to 1. The earliness of their approach was estimated using the technique below,

$$Earliness = \frac{T - t}{T - 1} \tag{15.12}$$

where t is the minimum wide variety of packets required to properly predict the class of a given glide and T is the total quantity of packets within the flow.

- Ashiku *et al.*'s technique [3] uses "categorical cross entropy" in conjunction with the Adam optimization algorithm with momentum to avoid overfitting. The proposed approach achieved 94.4% accuracy on the testing dataset as a consequence. The proposed architecture and hyperparameter obtained performance of 95.6% accuracy utilizing the user-defined dataset UNSW-NB15. The algorithm suggests combining the Nadam optimization algorithm with momentum and "categorical cross entropy" to reduce overfitting.
- As observed in Table 15.3, Ghazal *et al.* [10] examined the effectiveness of various models:

Table 15.3 Various model efficiencies.

Models	Accuracy	Precision	Recall	F1 score
Decision Tree	0.894	0.878	0.864	0.871
Random Forest	0.879	0.857	0.852	0.855
Gradient Boosting	0.829	0.733	0.926	0.818
XGB (extreme Gradient Boosting)	0.888	0.852	0.884	0.868
AdaBoost	0.774	0.731	0.724	0.727
Multi-Layer Perceptron	0.735	0.747	0.550	0.633

- Accuracy, precision, recall, and f-score were employed by Vinayakumar *et al.* [11] to assess the performance of the suggested system as shown in Table 15.4.

Table 15.4 Performance analysis of CNN.

Algorithm	**Accuracy**	**Precision**	**Recall**	**F-score**
CNN one layer	0.999	0.999	0.999	0.999
CNN two layers	0.998	0.999	0.998	0.999
CNN three layer	0.801	0.804	0.994	0.889
CNN one layer-LSTM	0.94	0.998	0.928	0.961
CNN two layer-LSTM	0.997	0.999	0.996	0.998
CNN three layer-LSTM	0.964	0.999	0.956	0.977

Gouveia *et al.*'s [12] study features were normalized to the range [0,1] and treated as continuous values. In order to reduce variability, the data is analyzed using the cross-validation method in many rounds. The Mean Square Error (MSE) technique, which takes into consideration the estimator's bias and variance, is used in this study to calculate the common difference between the predicted and actual output.

- Metrics like TP, FP, FN, and TN were employed by Almalaq *et al.* [15] to evaluate the performance of the suggested system. They advised that the system be evaluated using F1 score, accuracy, precision, and recall.
- Al-Abassi *et al.*'s [18] usage of Industrial Control Systems (ICSs) security revealed that identifying cyberattacks while achieving high f1-scores on unbalanced datasets is the key

challenge. The attack detection models taken into consideration in this work's performance evaluation metrics are TP, FP, TN, and FN. The proposed metrics outperform the present approaches in each of the four metrics. The SWaT dataset produces better results than the GP dataset.

➢ The measurements consisting of accuracy (ACC), precision (PR), true positive rate (TPR), recall (RE), false positive rate (FPR), true negative rate (TNR), and F1-score are used by Wu *et al.* [19].

$$FPR = \frac{FP}{(FP + TN)}, \quad TPR = \frac{TP}{(TP + FN)}, \quad \text{TNR} = \frac{TN}{(TN + FP)} \quad (15.13), (15.14), (15.15)$$

Where TP, True Positive; TN, True Negative; FP, False Positive; and FN, False Negative.

The ratio of anticipated attacks to total attacks is displayed using TPR or RE. The FNR formula is used to calculate the ratio of incorrectly classified normal data to all normal data. [29] The proportion of inconsequential occurrences that are wrongly classified as attacks is measured by FPR, also known as FAR. The balance performance in terms of precision and recall is represented by the weighted average of PR and RE, or F1-score. The percentage of threats in attack data that are accurately categorized as complete attack data is known as TNR.

15.9 Conclusion

IDS uses a range of AI approaches, such as deep learning, to strengthen performance against new attacker problems and play a significant part in safeguarding networks and computer systems all over the world. DL can independently find meaningful features in high-dimensional data, giving it substantial advantages over other traditional deep learning techniques. This chapter provides a detailed overview of a cyber-attack detection system based on CPS's deep learning algorithms. It is clear that researchers have developed diverse deep learning algorithms for detecting and mitigating cyberattacks in CPS which will enhance cybersecurity compared to traditional machine learning algorithms and other detection algorithms.

This study additionally investigates deep learning strategies and analyzes how deep learning algorithms are utilized in intrusion detection systems.

In most previous studies, the feature dimension was reduced only to reduce the computational effort required during feature extraction. Second, gaining the most in-depth knowledge of strategies is appropriate for image analysis and pattern recognition. Third, the more the data included in the experiment, the better the classification results. However, most attack-detection problems lack sufficient data. Therefore, combining supervised and unsupervised learning can enhance the overall performance. In follow-up studies, we would like to evaluate the effectiveness of these algorithms using our own dataset.

References

1. Yar, M. and Steinmetz, K., Cybercrime and Society (3rd ed.). SAGE Publications, 2019. Retrieved from https://www.perlego.com/book/1431897/cybercrime-and-society-pdf (Original work published 2019).
2. Ahmad, T., Truscan, D., Vain, J., Porres, I., Early Detection of Network Attacks Using Deep Learning. *Proc. - 2022 IEEE 14th Int. Conf. Softw. Testing, Verif. Valid. Work. ICSTW 2022*, pp. 30–39, 2022, doi: 10.1109/ICSTW55395.2022.00020.
3. Ashiku, L. and Dagli, C., Network Intrusion Detection System using Deep Learning. *Procedia Comput. Sci.*, 185, 239–247, June 2021, doi: 10.1016/j.procs.2021.05.025.
4. Ferrag, M.A., Maglaras, L., Moschoyiannis, S., Janicke, H., Deep learning for cyber security intrusion detection: Approaches, datasets, and comparative study. *J. Inf. Secur. Appl.*, 50, 1–21, 2020, doi: 10.1016/j.jisa.2019.102419.
5. Alsughayyir, B. and Qamar, A.M., Deep learning-based network attack detection using convolutional and recurrent neural networks. *Int. J. Eng. Res. Technol.*, 12, 12, 3027–3303, 2019.
6. V., N. and Shaju, B., Deep learning algorithm based cyber-attack detection in cyber-physical systems-a survey. *Int. J. Adv. Technol. Eng. Explor.*, 5, 49, 489–494, 2018, doi: 10.19101/ijatee.2018.547030.
7. Djenna, A., Bouridane, A., Rubab, S., Marou, I.M., Artificial Intelligence-Based Malware Detection, Analysis, and Mitigation. *Symmetry (Basel)*, 15, 3, 1–24, 2023, doi: 10.3390/sym15030677.
8. Singh, P., Borgohain, S.K., Sarkar, A.K., Kumar, J., Sharma, L.D., Feed-Forward Deep Neural Network (FFDNN)-Based Deep Features for Static Malware Detection. *Int. J. Intell. Syst.*, 2023, 1–20, 2023, doi: 10.1155/2023/9544481.
9. Mohammadpour, L., Ling, T.C., Liew, C.S., Aryanfar, A., A survey of CNN-based network intrusion detection. *Appl. Sci.*, 12, 16, 8162, 2022.

10. Ghazal, S.F. and Mjlae, S.A., Cybersecurity in Deep Learning Techniques: Detecting Network Attacks. *Int. J. Adv. Comput. Sci. Appl.*, 13, 11, 221–230, 2022, doi: 10.14569/IJACSA.2022.0131125.
11. Vinayakumar, R., Soman, K.P., Poornachandrany, P., Applying convolutional neural network for network intrusion detection. *2017 Int. Conf. Adv. Comput. Commun. Informatics, ICACCI 2017*, vol. 2017-Janua, pp. 1222–1228, 2017, doi: 10.1109/ICACCI.2017.8126009.
12. Gouveia, A. and Correia, M., A systematic approach for the application of restricted boltzmann machines in network intrusion detection. *Lect. Notes Comput. Sci. (including Subser. Lect. Notes Artif. Intell. Lect. Notes Bioinformatics)*, vol. 10305 LNCS, pp. 432–446, 2017, doi: 10.1007/978-3-319-59153-7_38.
13. Aldhyani, T.H. and Alkahtani, H., Attacks to automatous vehicles: A deep learning algorithm for cybersecurity. *Sensors*, 22, 1, 360, 2022.
14. Islam, M.S., *et al.*, Using deep learning to detect digitally encoded DNA trigger for Trojan malware in Bio-Cyber attacks. *Sci. Rep.*, 12, 1, 1–13, 2022, doi: 10.1038/s41598-022-13700-5.
15. Almalaq, A., Albadran, S., Mohamed, M.A., Deep machine learning model-based cyber-attacks detection in smart power systems. *Mathematics*, 10, 15, 2574, 2022.
16. Li, C., Sheng, Y., Wang, J., Cyberspace attack detection based on advanced initialized recurrent neural network. *Int. J. Innov. Comput. Inf. Control*, 15, 4, 1413–1424, 2019, doi: 10.24507/ijicic.15.04.1413.
17. Haddadi, F., Khanchi, S., Shetabi, M., Derhami, V., Intrusion detection and attack classification using feed-forward neural network. *2nd Int. Conf. Comput. Netw. Technol. ICCNT 2010*, June 2015, pp. 262–266, 2010, doi: 10.1109/ICCNT.2010.28.
18. Al-Abassi, A., Karimipour, H., Dehghantanha, A., Parizi, R.M., An ensemble deep learning-based cyber-attack detection in industrial control system. *IEEE Access*, 8, 83965–83973, 2020, doi: 10.1109/ACCESS.2020.2992249.
19. Wu, Y., Wei, D., Feng, J., Network attacks detection methods based on deep learning techniques: a survey. *Secur. Commun. Netw.*, 2020, 1, 8872923, 2020. Article ID 8872923, 17 pages.
20. Naseer, S., Saleem, Y., Khalid, S., *et al.*, Enhanced network anomaly detection based on deep neural networks. *IEEE Access*, 6, 48231–48246, 2018.
21. Peng, W., Kong, X., Peng, G., Li, X., Wang, Z., Network intrusion detection based on deep learning, in: *Proceedings of 2019 International Conference on Communications, Information System and Computer Engineering (CISCE)*, pp. 431–435, Haikou, China, July 2019.
22. AlEroud, A. and Karabatis, G., Bypassing detection of urlbased phishing attacks using generative adversarial deep neural networks, in: *Proceedings of the Sixth International Workshop on Security and Privacy Analytics*, pp. 53–60, New Orleans, LA, USA, March 2020.

23. Latif, S., Idrees, Z., Zou, Z., Ahmad, J., DRaNN: A Deep Random Neural Network Model for Intrusion Detection in Industrial IoT. *2020 International Conference on UK-China Emerging Technologies (UCET)*, IEEE, pp. 1–4, 2020.
24. Kasongo, S.M. and Sun, Y., A deep learning method with wrapper based feature extraction for wireless intrusion detection system. *Comput. Secur.*, 92, 101752, 2020.
25. Choudhary, S. and Kesswani, N., Analysis of KDD-Cup'99, NSL-KDD and UNSW-NB15 Datasets using Deep Learning in IoT. *Procedia Comput. Sci.*, vol. 167, pp. 1561–1573, 2020.
26. Mehedi, S.T., Anwar, A., Rahman, Z., Ahmed, K., Deep Transfer Learning Based Intrusion Detection System for Electric Vehicular Networks. *Sensors*, 21, 4736, 2021.
27. Singh Anand, K., Cyber Crime, Law and Social Challenges, in: *Social Media: Issues and Challenges*, N.K. Rai (Ed.), Avon Publishing House, Delhi, 2020.
28. Lippmann, R.P., Fried, D.J., Graf, I., Haines, J.W., Kendall, K.R., McClung, D., Weber, D., Webster, S.E., Wyschogrod, D., Cunningham, R.K., *et al.*, Evaluating intrusion detection systems: The 1998 darpa offlineintrusion detection evaluation, in: *Proceedings DARPA Information Survivability Conference and Exposition. DISCEX'00*, vol. 2, IEEE, pp. 12–26, 2000.
29. Zhong, W. and Gu, F., A multi-level deep learning system formalware detection. *Expert Syst. Appl.*, 133, 151–162, 2019.
30. Aslan, Ö.A. and Samet, R., A comprehensive review onmalware detection pproaches. *IEEE Access*, 8, 6249–6271, 2020.
31. Kaspersky Research, Machine learning methods for malwaredetection. *Symmetry*, 14, 11, 2304, 2022.
32. Llauradió, D.G., Convolutional neural networks for malware classification. Master's thesis, Universitat Politècnica de Catalunya, 2016.

16

Deep Learning Techniques for Detection of Fake News in Social Media with Huge Data

Namratha M.*, Rajeshwari B. S. and Jyothi S. Nayak

Department of Computer Science & Engineering, B.M.S. College of Engineering, Bengaluru, India

Abstract

The practice of reading news via social media has its pros and cons. Due to media's low cost, ease of use, and quick information transmission, people turn to it for information. However, social media facilitates the widespread dissemination of purposefully misleading information in fake news. Owing to how simple it is to create and distribute information on the internet, the dissemination of false news has recently grown more prevalent. While fake news is not actually true, it is created to appear true for a certain reason. While fake news detection is challenging for humans, deep learning and machine learning methods make the work much simpler. A variety of algorithms for machine learning can make it easier in detecting whether news is true or false. Various researchers utilized classifiers based on machine learning for checking the authenticity of news. It is simple to obtain the datasets needed to train the classifiers.

This chapter explains several deep learning method performances combined with the current state-of-the-art word embeddings on benchmark fake news datasets.

This chapter mainly focuses on various fake news detection algorithms as mentioned below.

- To create a thorough study on deep learning models for spotting fake news and the collection of significant information from recent studies along with diverse algorithms employed for achieving it.

**Corresponding author*: namratham.cse@bmsce.ac.in

Subhabrata Barman, Santanu Koley and Subhankar Joardar (eds.) Next-Generation Systems and Secure Computing, (325–346) © 2025 Scrivener Publishing LLC

- To present a complete analysis of the chronological review, their related works, and contribution to research designs and general findings on fake news detection models.
- To analyze the performance metrics, applications, datasets used, simulation platforms used, and necessary research gap along with challenges present in existing fake news detection models.

***Keywords*:** Social media, deep learning, machine learning, fake news detection system

16.1 Introduction

Online reviews can be used by customers as a very valuable resource when making purchases, but it is also possible that it will be influenced by fraudulent or unfavorable remarks.

Genuine reviews are written by the consumers who have used the product themselves or service and provide well-versed feedback about their experience. False reviews, in contrast to this, are those that have been written by people who have not actually tried the product or service or who have been paid to give a favorable evaluation.

The newest trends of posting online reviews has significantly increased in recent times, since the convenience of online shopping and home delivery services. People rely more on online purchasing these days, and thus, they feel more at ease discussing their thoughts on the goods and services they have used. Hence, the number of online reviews given by the customers has increased. Overall, the ease and efficiency of online shopping have greatly contributed to the growing trend of internet review posting. The absenceof physically inspecting products before purchasing them can result in a heavy reliance on reviews from other buyers. Ensuring the truthfulness of these reviews is important to prevent buyers from falling victim to fraudulent or misleading reviews. However, it might be a challenging task to manually read through every review to differentiate between fake and ambiguous reviews. To effectively address this issue, a systematic approach must be implemented to identify the source of the problem. Developing using a deep learning model for the review section to flag certain reviews as real or spam, this issue may be solved. One intriguing element is that by using this technique, spammers who have not utilized the product may be distinguished from legitimate users. To artificially filter reviews of the product and inflate its ranking, spam reviews or the use of various customer

IDs may be employed. One way to identify positive feedback or reviews is by looking for language that expresses enthusiasm or satisfaction. Words such as "awesome", "so good", and "fantastic" are good indicators of positive sentiment. By analyzing such kinds of phrases, one can get a better sense of the genuine sentiments of a product, service, or experience without resorting to plagiarism. Asthey frequently oversell the goods or attempt to pass off fake evaluations by repeating the samephrases again, they typically influence consumers. Thus, the problem of spam filtering requires vast data to train and be efficient with extra domain knowledge such as sarcastic words used by customers to demonstrate their disagreement towards the product; sometimes, the product is fine but not the delivery or the package that impacts the review categorization. Instead of incorrectly classifying these reviews as unfavorable as in sentiment analysis, an NLP method was used in this instance to identify such reviews. Include data preprocessing to eliminate any unfavorable product reviews.

Figure 16.1 depicts the basic steps involved in deep learning. This consists of data processing, feature selection and extraction, and classification of model generation.

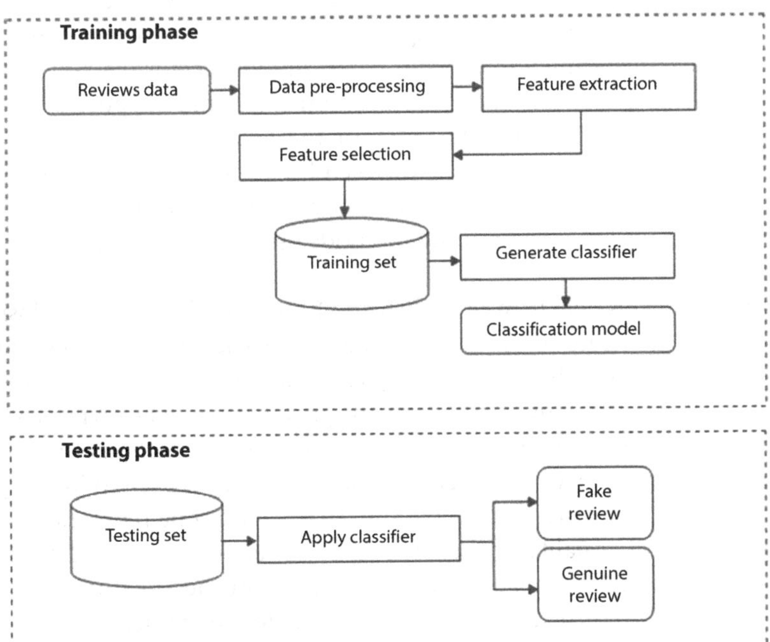

Figure 16.1 Training and testing phase.

The methodology for fake review detection works is as follows:

- **Data Collection:** In the initial phase of fake review detection, data collection is conducted by gathering reviews from various platforms such as Amazon, which couldbe for a product or service.
- **Data Preprocessing:** The next phase is data preprocessing, which involves removing punctuation marks, stemming (creating a root word from every word in the dataset), and removing stop words (frequently used words like determiners,articles, and prepositions) to retain only the important words in the dataset for the next step.
- **Feature Extraction and Selection:** Feature extraction and selection are performed after preprocessing. Features are taken beyond the preprocessed data, which canbe classified as linguistic features and relational features.
- **Classifier Model Construction and Testing:** A classifier model is built and tested using a small set of data with labels in the final stage. The practice data are already available, which are classified as a phony review or a real review. The prototype may be built utilizing various machine learning methods, including logistic regression, support vector machines, Naive Bayes classification, decision trees, and support vector machines. The efficiency of the fake review detection approach depends on a variety of variables, including the labeled information used in training, proper feature selection, and the data mining methods used for detection.

Online reviews help firms establish and keep a good reputation. Positive reviews can promote traffic and revenue; however, untrue or misleading reviews might have the opposite impact, misleading potential customers and damaging a company's reputation.The prevention of fake reviews is now a growing concern, necessitating the use of effective methods to identify them. By developing a more accurate and efficient approach to identifying fake reviews, companies may make sure that their online reputation accurately reflects the quality of their products or services. This study has the potential to make an impact on the ongoing effort tocombat fake reviews and increase the consistency of online reviews for consumers.

In this analysis, we are evaluating the performance of our classification model on a prepared dataset of images. Eighty percent of the images are used for training and the remaining 20% are used for testing. We will use precision, a measure of the accuracy of the classifier, to comparethe performance of our model with that of other methods. It is important to understand the capabilities of a predictive model in order to know how it will perform on new data that it hasnot seen before. One way to do this is to compare the performance of different versions of a model on the same prediction problem and choose the one that performs the best.

Objectives

The primary goal of the project is identifying whether the given product review is fake or real. The following are the objectives of the proposed system:

- Building a Recurrent Neural Network (RNN) model and a Long Short-Term Memory (LSTM) model to train and group the phony reviews.
- To recognize the attributes and patterns that separate false reviews from authentic ones.
- To assess the model's performance on a diverse set of review platforms and domains.
- To enhance the model's performance by incorporating additional data inputs, such asmetadata or user information.

16.2 Related Work

Two models of neural networks that incorporate conventional bag-of-words, word context, andcustomer emotions have been suggested by Petr Hajek *et al.* [1] Three sets of features arespecifically used by the models to learn document-level representation: (1) n-grams, (2) wordembeddings, and (3) distinct lexicon-based mood indicators. The classification of false reviews into four areas is done using such a high-dimensional feature representation. They compare the classification results for the given detection systems with several cutting-edgeways for detecting bogus reviews in order to illustrate the usefulness of the systems.Regardless of the datasets' sentiment polarity and product category, Dibyajyoti Baishya *et al.* [2], with an emphasis on fraudulent reviews, employed the bag-of-words model and gloveembedding matrix. On text classifications, they applied three fresh deep learning algorithmsand two various feature extraction methods. In comparison to conventional machine learningmodels, the experimental study of a public dataset produced good and even superior results. Considering the deep walk methodology using reviewers' graph data and a (modified) semi-supervised clustering algorithm, which may be considered for partial background information, Punit Rathore *et al.* [3] provided a top-down framework for possible fake reviewer groups identification. The suggested method may be further developed to identify social media groupsof opinion spammers (such as false comments or fake postings) using temporal affinity, semantic traits, and sentiment analysis.

Priyanka Gupta *et al.* proposed [4] that the internet review system has greatly expanded, allowing users to give their first-hand impressions of the goods or services. Future consumers' purchase decisions are influenced by these reviews, which may either benefit or hurt a company's bottom line. Reviews that are spam are ones that have been written with the intent to defame or exalt a company and deceive the public. Thus, it is essential to spot false reviews in order to preserve the credibility of the online review system. Combining spam-related information with a rule-based weighting system, according to Muhammad Zubair Asghar *et al.* [5], can enhance the efficiency of even the most basic spam detection approach. As more people and businesses become interested in separating bogus (spam) from real (non-spam) product reviews, this innovation may be useful to evaluate spam detection systems. The results of this effort will give insight into spam-related characteristics and feature weighting and help to create more advanced instruments for the detection of opinion spam. Previous state-of-the-art studies in the area of opinion spam identification employed fewer spam city-related variables and a less effective feature weighting technique.

Deepika Vachane and colleagues [6] introduced a named spam identification system, whichuses spam highlights to display review illuminating lists as heterogeneous information structures to configure a spam ID approach into a collection of issues. Using criticality, we wereable to get excellent results in terms of various measurements on survey informative indices. Once a person's search inquiry returns absolutely no results, the commitment endeavor is stillongoing. A machine learning strategy was suggested by Elmogy *et al.* [7] to recognize bogus reviews. To extract different reviewer behaviors, numerous engineering methods are employed alongside the reviews' feature extraction procedure. This assesses the effectiveness of a number of experiments performed on a real dataset of restaurant reviews from Yelp, both with and without characteristics derived from user behaviors. They evaluate the effectiveness of various classifiers in both situations, including KNN, Naive Bayes (NB), SVM, logistic regression, and random forest. Several n-gram language models, particularly bi-gram and tri-gram, are accounted for the assessments. A unique technique to identify bogus reviews was put out by Wang *et al.* [8] and is based on multiple feature fusionand rolling collaborative training. The technique first needs an initial index system with a variety of features, including text features, sentiment features for reviews, and reviewer behavior information. They created similar algorithms to extract all of a review's characteristics, as this strategy also needs a set of initial training samples. The review's categorization is then manually labeled. The approach then chooses the best accurate classifierto categorize fresh reviews after training 7 classifiers using the initial sample set. The method'soriginality resides in the addition of the characteristics and categorization labels of the fresh reviews to the initial sample, which are set as fresh data. Hence, the sample set's size will automatically grow.

By merging the resembling and the grid search techniques, Yao *et al.* [9] provided a unique solution to the data imbalance problem. They use stacking and majority votingtechniques to include the improved base classifiers. The meta-classifier in the stackingensemble model is also used with the suggested data mimicking technique. The results demonstrate that the proposed ensemble model outperforms some existing techniques, thereby offering a new approach to the problems of data imbalance and feature pruning in the field offake review detection. This study advances the practice of combining various methods or algorithms into a model. A challenge of fake review identification was put out by Mohawesh *et al.* [10] who summarized the datasets already in existence and their methods of gathering. It examines the currently used feature extraction methods. In order to find gaps, it also critically reviews and analyzes the available methodologies into two groups: deep learningtechniques and conventional statistical machine learning techniques. Also, carry out a benchmark research to assess the effectiveness of various transformers neural network models that have not been applied before, the identification of fraudulent reviews.

Jnoub *et al.* [11] provide a hybrid answer set programming (asp) and natural language processing-based fact-checking system. The study contains the reviewers' behavioral patternsas well as the qualitative and quantitative properties/features gleaned from the reviews' content. In a case study, they assessed the framework using a movie review dataset made up of user accounts and the reviews they are connected with, including the review's title, content, and starrating. This allowed them to determine which reviews are unreliable and designate them as such in the output. Using a dataset of hotel reviews from online sources, Hassan *et al.* [12] developed a successful supervised machine learning strategy to recognize fraudulent online reviews. This fact is abused by dishonest individuals and organizations that submit fictitious evaluations to elevate their own goods or denigrate those of rivals. The problem of identifying false internet reviews may be viewed as a binary classification task where a classifier is modeled to determine if a review is real or not.

Hassan *et al.* [13] developed a sentiment analysis model that effectively distinguishes between favorable and unfavorable emotive reviews. It displays a sentiment analysis of the distribution of positive and negative reviews. The suggested sentiment model was used to determine the influence of a probabilistic sentiment score on the identification of false online reviews using a hotel review dataset. Sentiment analysis is crucial to a system for detecting bogus reviews. Phase-wise processing is used by Dhairya Patel *et al.* [14] to automatically categorize user evaluations into "suspect", "clear", and "hazy" categories. Recursively separating components into suspicious and clear is the hazy category. Business organizations may keep track of the sales of their products, through examining, reading, and understanding what customers are telling about products.

16.3 Proposed Work

The existing system for identifying fake reviews typically relies on machine learning algorithmsuch as SVM (Support Vector Machine) and Random Forest. These algorithms classify reviews as authentic or fraudulent based on several factors, including length, sentiment, and writing style [15, 16].

In machine learning, a hyperplane is created that separates the genuine and false reviews that are created using features taken from the reviews. The algorithm maximizes the margin between the two classes, improving its capacity to adapt to fresh data. Random Forest produces a group of interconnected decision trees, contrasted to classify the reviews. A subset of the features is accustomed to train each tree, improving the algorithm's accuracy and preventing overfitting [17–19].

Numerous machine learning methods have been successful in identifying fake reviews, but they have limitations. SVM can struggle with high-dimensional feature spaces, and Random Forest can be computationally expensive. Overall, even though these techniques are effective in identifying fake reviews, they have limitations in accuracy that could be addressed through deep learning techniques [20–22].

The proposed system for identifying fake reviews using deep learning techniques involves thefollowing steps:

1. **Data Preprocessing:** The system will first preprocess the Amazon product review dataset, including removing irrelevant data and cleaning the text.

2. **Feature Extraction:** The system from the reviews and the algorithm will extract numerous features, including the review's length, sentiment, writing style, and reviewer's profile information and review history. Additionally, the apparatus will employ advanced featureengineering techniques to extract different behaviors of reviewers in addition to the review's content.
3. **Training Data Preparation:** The apparatus will divide the preprocessed data into training, validation, and testing sets.
4. **Model Selection:** The apparatus will assess the efficiency of two deep learning models, RNN and Long Short-Term Memory (LSTM), to determine the best model for the task.
5. **Training the Model:** The apparatus will train the selected model on the training set, adjusting the model's parameters to optimize its performance.
6. **Model Evaluation:** The apparatus will evaluate the trained model's performance on the validation set, adjusting the model's parameters as necessary to increase the precision.
7. **Model Testing:** Finally, the apparatus will test the trained model on the testing set to rate how well it works to spot bogus reviews.
8. **Deployment:** One can use this model to detect false reviews using a web-based application after it has been trained and evaluated.

16.3.1 Deep Learning Model

Deep learning is a technique for machine learning based on how people learn. Data science, which additionally consists of statistics and predictive modeling, includes it as a vital component. DL expedites and simplifies the process of gathering, analyzing, and interpreting vast amounts of data. Hence, it greatly aids data scientists.

Both organized and unstructured data are used to train deep learning systems. A few examplesof deep learning applications include facial recognition, virtual assistants, autonomous car vision, tax evasion, and many others.

16.3.2 Long Short Term Memory (LSTM)-Based Model

DL could be viewed as a means to automate predictive analytics at its most basic level. Figure 16.2 depicts the deep learning architecture employed

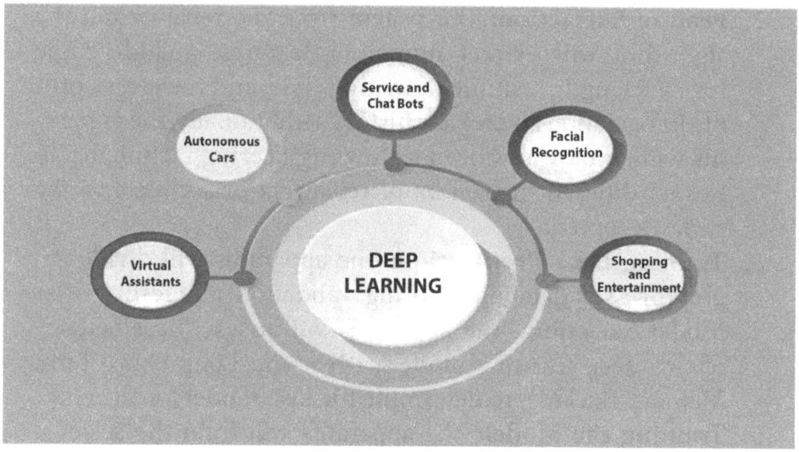

Figure 16.2 Deep learning applications.

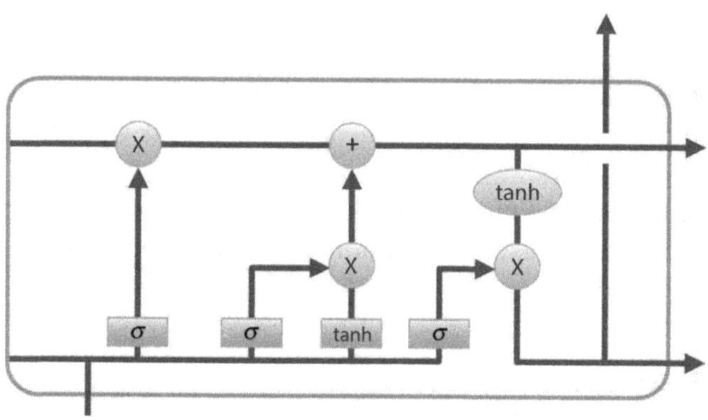

Figure 16.3 Long short-term memory (LSTM).

during the fake news detection. Unlike traditional ML algorithms, algorithms for deep learning are built in a hierarchy of increasing complexity and abstraction. You may think of DL as a branch of ML. It is seen as a subfieldin computer science that deals with algorithmic learning and self-evolution. Artificial neural networks (ANNs) are used in deep learning (DL), and they are designed to emulate human thought and learning. ML employs easier techniques. DL algorithms are used in a range of applications, including as autonomous vehicles and medical devices. Auto specialists are usingDL to automatically identify things like stop signs and traffic lights. Moreover, DL is utilizedto identify pedestrians, enabling to reduce collisions.

The results of the previous step are used as the source of the current step in recurrent neural networks (RNNs), a form of sequential data-handling neural networks. RNNs may not be able to anticipate words or patterns that are stored in long-term memory due to their difficulties with long-term dependencies. Hochreiter and Schmidhuber developed the long short-term memory (LSTM) model to deal with this problem.

LSTM is one kind of RNN that is made to keep information stored for a long time. Figure 16.3 depicts the LSTM model architecture employed during the fake news detection. This makes it particularly useful to analyze sequential data, like text, speech, and time series. LSTMcan learn long-term relationships in the data, making it well-suited for applications such as language translation, speech recognition, and time series forecasting. Overall, LSTM is an effective tool for handling sequential data and perhaps utilized to address many real-world problems.

16.3.3 Natural Language Processing (NLP) Model

Natural Language Processing (NLP) is an interdisciplinary field that focuses on the interactionbetween computers and human language. It involves creating software to handle and analyze vast volumes of natural language data. Through the aid of artificial intelligence, NLP enables computers to comprehend natural language, including spoken and written language, just like humans do. This technology has various practical applications in different industries, such as corporate intelligence, search engines, and medical research.

NLP technology allows computers to process real-world information, make sense of it, and convert it into machine-readable code. Computers are equipped with reading software and microphones that enable them to record audio, similar to how humans use their ears and eyes to sense the world around them. During processing, the computer program takes various inputsand translates them into a language that the computer can understand. Overall, NLP technologyplays an important role in advancing machine intelligence, making it easier for computers to processand analyze human language data.

The suggested system's design is depicted in Figure 16.4:

Data Preprocessing: A technique for changing crude information into a clean dataset is called information preprocessing. In different terms, whenever information is obtained from different sources, it is gathered in crude organization, which makes examination unthinkable.

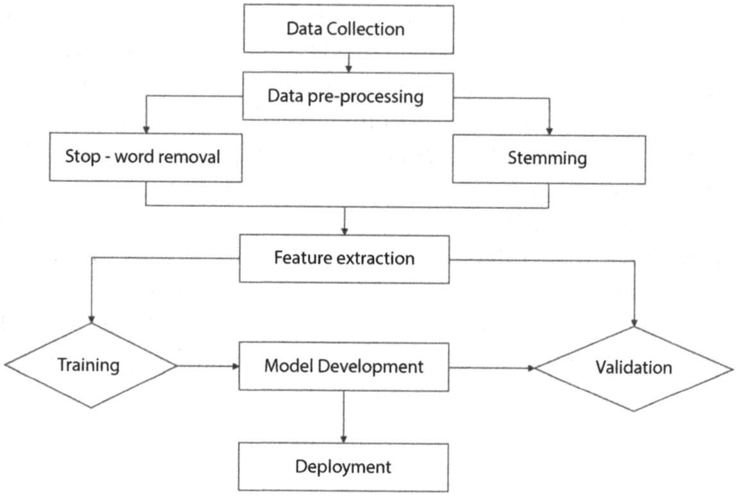

Figure 16.4 High-level design.

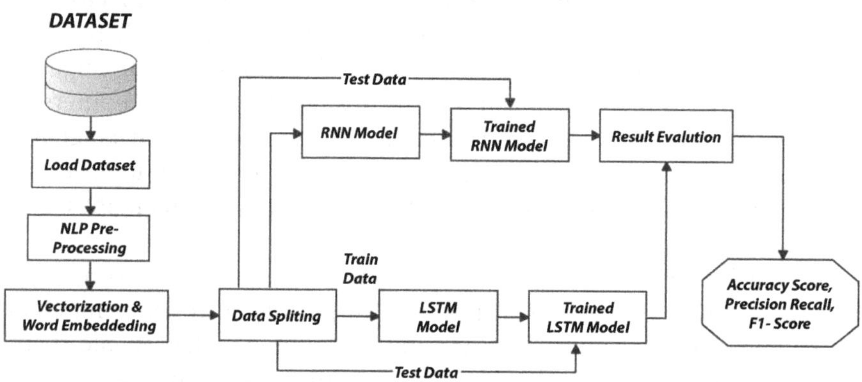

Figure 16.5 System architecture.

Thus, certain methodologies are continued to change over the information into a minuscule, clean informational collection. This strategy is completed preceding the execution of Iterative Analysis. Figure 16.5 depicts the system architecture proposed for fake news detection. Information Preprocessing is the term for the succession of steps. It consists of the accompanying advances:

- Clean-up of information
- Coordination of information

- Change of information
- Decrease of information

Since there is unstructured genuine information, information preprocessing is required. Most of the certifiable information consisted of the following:

- **Wrong information (missing information)**—an assortment of purposes behind missing information, including the inability to gather information consistently, information section mistakes, biometrics mechanical issues, etc.
- **Occurrence of boisterous information (inaccurate information and peculiarities)**—foundations for the event of uproarious information could go from a mechanical concern with the gadget that gathers information to an individual mistake while entering information, in addition to other things.
- **Conflicting information**—happens for an assortment of reasons, including information duplication, defective entering information, mistakes in cipher or names, i.e., information limitations infringement, etc.

16.4 Results and Discussion

CLSTM—Report on Classification

In machine learning, a categorization report is actually a metric for an appearance review. The trained classification model's accuracy, memory, assistance, and F1 measure are displayed using this method. Table 16.1 displays every indicator from the CLSTM classification result for the purpose of clarity.

The table gives an overview of performance metrics for a classification model. It achieves an accuracy of 99% in correctly classifying instances as either "True" or "Fake". The model demonstrates high accuracy, memory, and F1 score for both classes ("True" and "Fake"), all around 0.99. This demonstrates the model's skill in accurately identifying both categories. The macro and weighted averages of these metrics, across both classes, remain consistent at 0.99 as well. In conclusion, the model showcases excellent performance in distinguishing between "True" and "Fake" instances and has excellent levels of F1 score, recall, accuracy, and precision.

Table 16.1 Classification report for CLSTM.

Metrics	Definition			
Precision	Precision is defined as the proportion of positive examples to the sum of both true and false positives.			
Recall	Recall is the ratio of true positives to all true negatives and false negatives.			
F1 Score	The F1 is a balanced harmonic average of such memory and precision. The model's predicted capacity increases as the F1 score value gets closer to 1.0.			
Support	Number of instances of a class that truly exist in the dataset constitutes the number of supports. It does not differentiate between kinds; it only improves the performance evaluation process.			
	Precision	**Recall**	**F1 score**	**Support**
True	**0.95**	**0.37**	**0.53**	**2085**
Fake	**0.61**	**0.98**	**0.75**	**2115**
Accuracy			**0.68**	**4200**
Macro avg	**0.78**	**0.68**	**0.64**	**4200**
Weighted avg	**0.78**	**0.68**	**0.64**	**4200**

CLSTM—Confusion Matrix

It is easier to visualize the results of the categorization exercise when using a matrix of confusion, which provides the many scenarios of the prediction as well as results in a tabular style. In Figure 16.6 below, it is depicted. It creates a table with all of the classifier's predicted and actual values.

Figure 16.6 displays the confusion chart for the CLSTM model. By examining the confusion matrix,the model is clearly performing incredibly well. It has achieved an accuracy of 99.17%, indicating a high level of correctness in its predictions.

RNN—Report on Classification

In machine learning, a categorization report is actually a metric for an appearance review. The trained classification model's accuracy, memory, assistance, and F1 measure are displayed using this method. Table 16.2 displays every indicator from the RNN classification result for the purpose of clarity.

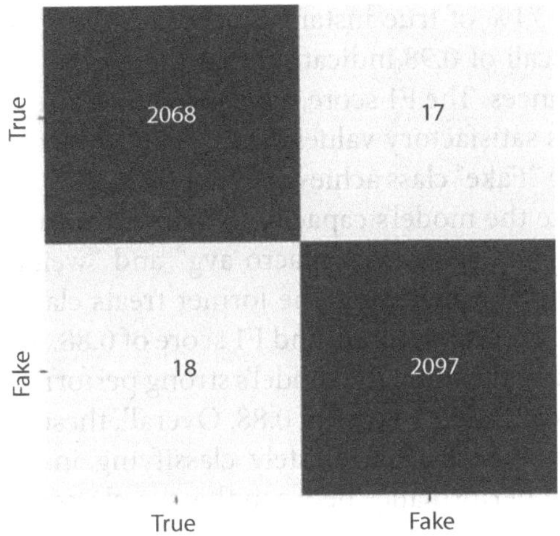

Figure 16.6 Confusion matrix for CLSTM.

Table 16.2 Classification report for RNN.

	Precision	Recall	F1 score	Support
True	**0.98**	**0.71**	**0.82**	**2085**
Fake	**0.77**	**0.98**	**0.87**	**2115**
Accuracy			**0.85**	**4200**
Macro avg	**0.88**	**0.85**	**0.85**	**4200**
Weighted avg	**0.88**	**0.85**	**0.85**	**4200**

The provided table summarizes the outcomes of a binary classification task involving the categorization of instances into "True" and "Fake" classes. The achieved metrics provide information about the model's effectiveness. An accuracy of 85% refers to the percentage of the 4200 total instances that were successfully predicted. Precision, which gauges the accuracy of positive predictions, yields noteworthy values. For the "True" class, the precision of 0.98 denotes that 98% of instances predicted as "True" are actually true, while for the "Fake" class, the value of 0.77 indicates that 77% of instances predicted as "Fake" are correctly classified. Recall, which quantifies the model's ability to capture actual positives, demonstrates differential results. The recall for the "True" class is 0.71, implying that the model identifies 71% of true instances accurately. Conversely, the "Fake" class attains a recall of 0.98,indicating that the model correctly pinpoints 98% of fake instances. The F1 score, a balanced measure between precision and recall, yields satisfactory values. The "True" class obtains an F1 score of 0.82, while the "Fake" class achieves a slightly higher value of 0.87. These scoresencapsulate the model's capacity to manage both false positives and false negatives. The aggregated "macro avg" and "weighted avg" metrics present overarching evaluations. The former treats classes equally, resulting in an average precision, recall, and F1 score of 0.88. The latter considers class imbalances, reaffirming the model's strong performance with an average precision, recall, and F1 score of 0.88. Overall, these results underscore the model's competence in accurately classifying instances, albeit with some variation in performance between the two classes.

RNN—Confusion Matrix

It is easier to visualize the outcomes of categorization exercise when using a confusion matrix,which provides the many scenarios of the prediction and findings in a tabular style. In Figure 16.7 below, it is depicted. It creates a table with all of the classifier's predicted and actual values.

The confusion curve in Figure 16.7 shows how well the RNN model performed. The example has achieved a notable accuracy rate of 84.83%, showcasing its performance in correctly predicting outcomes.

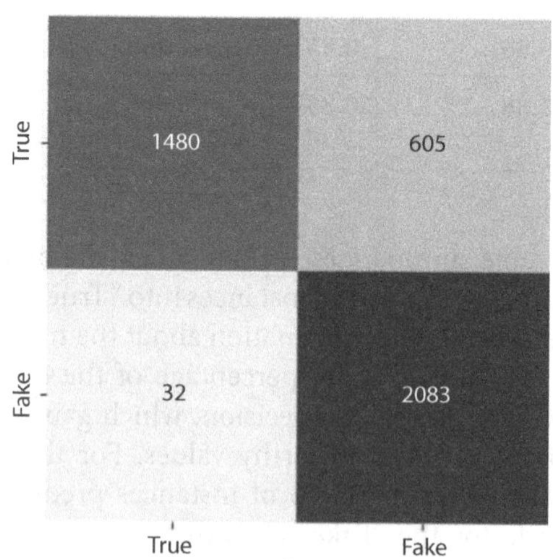

Figure 16.7 Confusion matrix for RNN.

Accuracy Plot Graphs and Loss Plot Graphs

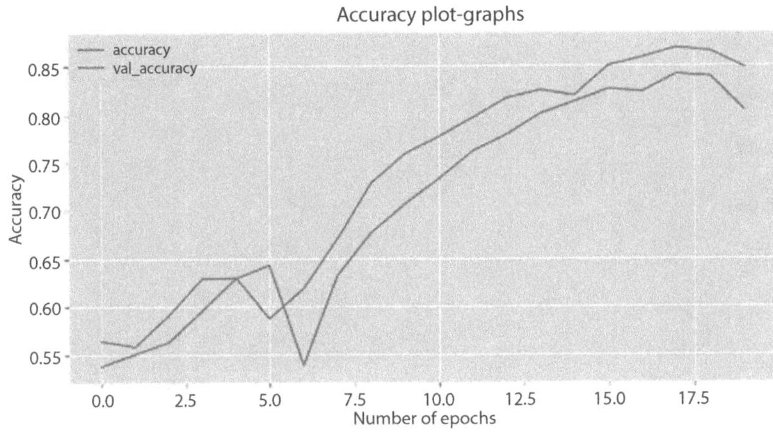

Figure 16.8 Accuracy plot graph.

An accuracy plot graph shows how a classification model performs over time or with various parameter values. It illustrates how the model's accuracy measure evolves as it is tested or trained in various scenarios. Figure 16.8 shows the accuracy plot graph for the proposed model.

The independent variable is represented by the *x*-axis of the graph and could be the quantity that represents training iterations, epochs, or parameter configurations. The accuracy value, which ranges from 0 to 1, is represented on the *y*-axis and shows the percentage of accurate predictions provided by the model.

The accuracy plot graph displays the trend of accuracy improvement or degradation while themodel is trained or evaluated. In a perfect world, we would like to see the accuracy rising or remaining steady at a high value. Nevertheless, peaks or peaks on the accuracy plot may signifyoverfitting, underfitting, or other issues with the model's functionality. We may evaluate the model's overall performance, choose the best parameters for training or iterations, and obtain insights regarding the model's development process by examining the accuracy plot graph.

Loss Plot Graphs

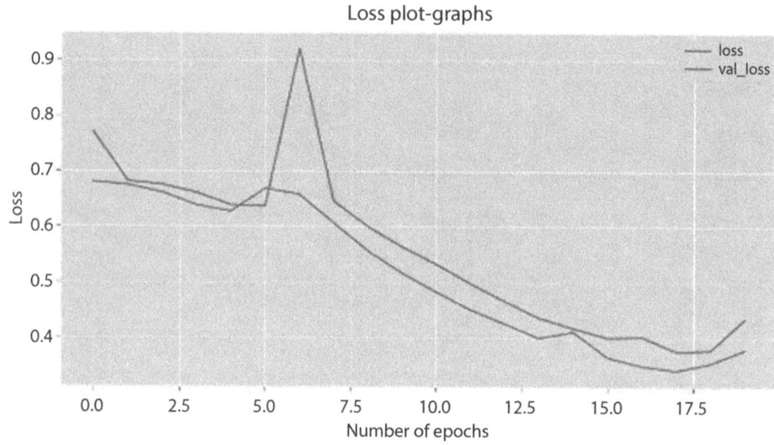

Figure 16.9 Loss plot graph.

This loss plot graph shows how the loss function evolves over time while a model based on machine learning is trained. It offers information on how effective the model is assimilating the information during its training process. The loss function represents the discrepancy between the model's predicted output and the actual targets. It is important to reduce this loss during training since it shows how well the model fits the data. The *y*-axis of the loss graph is typically the loss, and the *x*-axis is the total amount of training repetitions or epochs. The loss ought to ideally decrease during training, showing that the algorithm is improving and that forecasts are becoming more accurate, although it is typical to see changes in the loss throughout training.

The loss graph can be examined to find various patterns or problems. Figure 16.9 shows the loss plot graph for the proposed model. For instance, a loss that is consistently reducing indicates that the model is convergent. On the other hand, if the loss is substantial and continues to rise, the model may not be learning well or may be overfittingthe training set. It is essential to keep an eye on the loss plot graph to improve the model's performance and spot any potential issues as they arise during training.

16.5 Conclusion

In conclusion, the escalating prevalence of fake reviews in online platforms poses a significant challenge to consumer trust and informed decision-making. This study aimed to address this issue through the deep learning techniques, with a specific focus on the Convolutional Long Short-Term Memory (CLSTM) model. This work showcased the efficacy of the CLSTM model in accurately identifying fake reviews, achieving an impressive accuracy rate of 99%. This result significantly outperformed the traditional Recurrent Neural Network (RNN) model, which achieved an accuracy of 85%. The substantial gap in performance underscores the advantage of employing advanced deep learning architectures, such as CLSTM, for tackling the intricate task of fake review detection. Furthermore, this work highlighted the importance of utilizing methods of natural language processing to enhance the model's ability to decipher subtle linguistic cues indicative of fake content. This holistic approach improved the model's accuracy and precision, enhancing its efficacy as a strategy for preserving the integrity of review sites on the internet. Deep learning and natural language processing are used to create a CLSTM-based approach and offers a promising solution to the pervasive problem of fake reviews. The ability to achieve such a high accuracy rate holds great potential in fostering a more trustworthy online consumer environment, where users can confidently rely on genuine reviews to make informed choices. As online platforms continue to play an increasingly vital role in commerce and information dissemination, the implementation of robust fake review detection mechanisms becomes imperative to ensure the credibility and authenticity of user-generated content.

16.6 Future Work

Future research should focus on enhancing CLSTM model accuracy through iterative refinement and methodological advancements, potentially through larger and more diverse training datasets, optimized model architecture, and fine-tuning techniques, exploring hybrid methodologies that combine the strengths of both CLSTM and RNN models to produce even more durable and accurate detection systems. Additionally, delving into explainable AI techniques would enhance model interpretability and provide insights into the artificial decision-making process review detection. Furthermore, considering the dynamic nature of fake reviews, research should focus on developing adaptivemodels capable of recognizing emerging patterns and evolving deceptive tactics. Collaborativeefforts between researchers, online platforms, and regulatory bodies are vital to continually update detection algorithms and stay ahead of new deceptive techniques. User engagement could also be incorporated to improve model performance. Leveraging user feedback and reported instances of fake reviews can aid in refining models and adapting them to real-world challenges. This collaborative approach could lead to the development of more robust and accurate detection systems, ultimately fostering greater trust and reliability in the online marketplace.

References

1. Munk, M., Barushka, A., Hajek, P., Deep neural networks integrated with word embeddings and emotion mining are used to detect fake customer reviews. *Neural Comput. Applic.*, 32, 17259–17274, 2020, https://doi.org/10.1007/s00521-020-04757-2.
2. Deka, J.J., Dey, G., others, Baishya, D., Deep Learning-Based Sentiment Analysis-Based Fake Review Detection in E-Commerce (SAFER). *Comput. Sci. SN*, 2, 479, 1581–1599, 2021, https://doi.org/10.1007/s42979-021-00918-9.
3. Rathore, P., Soni, J., Prabakar, N., Palaniswami, M., Santi, P., Identifying A Groups of Fake Reviewers Using a Semi supervised Method. *IEEE Trans. Comput. Social Syst.*, 8, 6, 1369–1378, December 2021.
4. Gandhi, S., Chakravarthi, B.R., Gupta, Priyanka, Using Bert, Roberta, Albert, and Distilbert for transfer learning techniques to detect the fraudulent reviews. *Information Retrieval Evaluation Forum in 2021.*
5. Ahmad, S., Ullah, A., Asghar, M.Z., Framework for detecting opinion spam using a hybrid categorization system. *Soft Comput.*, 24, 3475–3498, 2020, https://doi.org/10.1007/s00500-019-04107-y.
6. Vachane, D., Machine Learning Algorithm for Detecting False Online Product Reviews. *Turk. J. Comput. Math. Educ. (TURCOMAT)*, 12, 1S, 29–39, 2021.
7. Elmogy, A.M., *et al.*, Fake reviews detection using supervised machine learning. *J. Adv. Comput. Sci. Appl. Int.*, 12, 1, 601–606, 2021.
8. Fake Review Detection Based on the Multiple Feature Fusion & Rolling Collaborative Training. *IEEE Access*, 8, 182625–182639, 2020, doi: 10.1109/ACCESS.2020.3028588.
9. Yao, J., Zheng, Y., Jiang, H., An Ensemble Model for Fake Online Reviews Detection Based on the Data Resampling, Feature Pruning, and Parameter Optimization. *IEEE Access*, 9, 16914–16927, 2021, doi: 10.1109/ACCESS.2021.3051174.
10. Mohawesh, R., *et al.*, Fake Reviews Detection: A Survey. *IEEE Access*, 9, 6, 65771–65802, 2021, doi: 10.1109/ACCESS.2021.3075573.
11. Jnoub, N., Brankovic, A., Klas, W., Fact-Checking Reasoning System for Fake Review Detection Using Answer Set Programming. *Algorithms*, 14, 190, 1–11, 2021, https://doi.org/10.3390/a14070190.

12. Krishnaveni, N. and Radha, V., Spam review predictions through multiple features using sentiment analysis and neural networks. *J. Crit. Rev.*, 7, 12, 2810–2817, 2020.
13. Krishnaveni, N. and Radha, V., Feature selection algorithms for data mining classification: a survey. *Indian J. Sci. Technol.*, 12, 6, 1–11, 2019, https://doi.org/10.17485/ijst/2018/v12i6/139581.
14. Visani, C., Jadeja, N., Modi, M., A study on different machine learning techniques for spam review detection, in: *2017 International Conference on Energy, Communication, Data Analytics and Soft Computing (ICECDS)*, IEEE, pp. 676–679, 2017, https://doi.org/10.1109/ICECDS.2017.8389522.
15. Hussain, N., Turab Mirza, H., Rasool, G., Hussain, I., Kaleem, M., Spam review detection techniques: a systematic literature review. *Appl. Sci.*, 9, 5, 987, 2019, https://doi.org/10.3390/app9050987.
16. Asghar, M.Z., Ullah, A., Ahmad, S., Khan, A., Opinion spam detection framework using hybrid classification scheme. *Soft. Comput.*, 24, 5, 3475–3498, 2020, https://doi.org/10.1007/s00500-019-04107-y.
17. Catal, C. and Guldan, S., Product review management software based on multiple classifiers. *IET Softw.*, 11, 3, 89–92, 2017, https://doi.org/10.1049/iet-sen.2016.0137.
18. Sun, C., Du, Q., Tian, G., Exploiting product related review features for fake review detection. *Math. Probl. Eng.*, 1–7, 2016, https://doi.org/10.1155/2016/4935792.
19. Elssied, N.O.F., Ibrahim, O., Osman, A.H., Enhancement of spam detection mechanism based on hybrid k-mean clustering and support vector machine. *Soft. Comput.*, 19, 11, 3237–3248, 2015, https://doi.org/10.1007/s00500-014-1479-2.
20. Nagwani, N.K. and Sharaff, A., SMS spam filtering and thread identification using bi-level text classification and clustering techniques. *J. Inf. Sci.*, 43, 1, 75–87, 2019, https://doi.org/10.1177/0165551515616310.
21. Ebadati, O.M.E. and Ahmadzadeh, F., Classification spam email with elimination of unsuitable features with hybrid of GA-naive Bayes. *J. Inf. Knowl. Manag.*, 18, 01, 1950008, 2019, https://doi.org/10.1142/S0219649219500084.
22. Harris, C.G., Comparing human computation, machine, and hybrid methods for detecting hotel review spam, in: *Conference on e-Business, e-Services and e-Society*, Cham, Springer, pp. 75–86, 2019, https://doi.org/10.1007/978-3-030-29374-1_7.

17

A Secure IoT-Based Heart Rate Monitoring and Analyzing System

Soumya Roy[1]*, Rajib Manna[1], Sabyasachi Samanta[2], Moumita Sahoo[1] and Somak Karan[1]

[1]*Department of Applied Electronics and Instrumentation Engineering, Haldia Institute of Technology, Haldia, West Bengal, India*
[2]*Department of Computer Science Engineering (Cyber Security), Haldia Institute of Technology, Haldia, West Bengal, India*

Abstract
This chapter tries to develop a wristband for measuring the heart rate signal of an individual followed by some encryption techniques to secure the data during transmission to the cloud-based server. The hardware-level security provides privacy in the data from measurement to the cloud-based server, which is a vital part in the healthcare sector. The cloud-based platform consists of some sophisticated algorithms and machine learning techniques that analyze the heart rate data to provide valuable insights related to potential health issues as well as actionable information. This system can generate comprehensive reports and trends based on the collected data. This enables healthcare professionals to track an individual's heart rate patterns over time, identify any recurring issues, and make informed decisions regarding treatment plans and interventions. Additionally, the system facilitates remote patient monitoring, allowing healthcare providers to remotely track patients' heart rates, and reducing the need for frequent hospital visits.

***Keywords*:** Heart rate, internet of things, encryption, decryption, machine learning, wearable device

**Corresponding author*: er.sroy9@gmail.com

Subhabrata Barman, Santanu Koley and Subhankar Joardar (eds.) Next-Generation Systems and Secure Computing, (347–378) © 2025 Scrivener Publishing LLC

17.1 Introduction

One of the simplest and most straightforward ways to monitor one's health is to monitor heart rate. It is also a quick and easy technique for medical professionals to detect or identify health issues. Heart rate refers to the frequency of cardiac contractions within a given time frame, typically measured in beats per minute. The human body instinctively adjusts its heart rate to correspond with what the individual is doing or what is going on around them. A person's heart rate is a crucial sign of their general well-being. Too high or too low a heart rate may indicate a cardiac condition or other health issues. Doctors may be able to diagnose medical issues by sensing heart rate everywhere across the body. Along with the heart rate, a different type of chest pain an individual exhibits also helps to diagnose different types of heart abnormalities. Angina, also known as cardiac chest pain or heart-related chest pain [1], is a symptom indicating that the heart muscle (myocardium) is not getting enough blood and oxygen. Because they are narrowing or clogged, the coronary arteries, which supply the heart with oxygen-rich blood, are typically to blame for this decreased blood flow. Because it can be a marker of various cardiac illnesses, including coronary artery disease (CAD) and its numerous forms, cardiac chest pain is a significant symptom.

TA—Typical Angina: Chest pain or discomfort, or angina, is a condition when the heart muscle does not get enough blood or oxygen. It is a typical sign of coronary artery disease and is frequently described as a pressure-like or squeezing feeling in the chest. Additionally, the arms, neck, jaw, shoulder, or back may also be affected. For accurate diagnosis and treatment, it is essential to distinguish between various kinds of chest discomfort in a medical setting. Patients who complain of chest pain frequently go through a thorough evaluation that includes a medical history, physical exam, and a number of tests (such as an ECG, blood tests, stress tests, and imaging) in order to identify the underlying cause of their pain and choose the most appropriate course of treatment.

ATA—Atypical Angina: Atypical angina refers to chest pain or discomfort that does not exhibit the typical angina pattern. It might possess different qualities or be situated in an unusual area. Although it does not exhibit the traditional symptoms, it may nonetheless be associated to cardiac problems.

NAP—Non-Anginal Pain: Chest pain that is not caused by a heart condition or coronary artery disease is referred to as non-anginal chest pain. Muscle strain, digestive problems, nervousness, or even lung troubles are just a few of the additional causes that it could be due to the fact that symptoms of angina are not present.

ASY—Asymptomatic: Asymptomatic refers to the absence of perceptible symptoms. This would imply that the patient is not at all experiencing any pain or uneasiness in the chest in the case of chest pain.

The healthcare industry experiences a significant transformation with the introduction of an Internet of Things (IoT)-enabled heart rate monitoring system. This innovative technology offers the capability to continuously monitor and analyze an individual's heart rate in real time. The IoT and wearable technology are seamlessly combined in this groundbreaking technology to improve the precision, usability, and efficiency of heart rate monitoring. The system typically comprises of a wearable sensor and a cloud-based platform as its two main parts. The wearable sensor continuously gathers heart rate information from the person, frequently in the form of a wristband or chest strap. The sensor measures heart rate with accuracy and reliability using cutting-edge technologies. The collected heart rate data are then transmitted wirelessly to the cloud-based platform through an internet connection. The IoT aspect comes into play as the wearable device connects to the internet and makes use of a remote server in the cloud to do analysis and processing. The health care data should be transmitted from one medical sector to another for treatment assistance. Typically, security is being provided when data are communicating form one server to another and hardware-level security is still not faithfully incorporated in the IoT-based system.

The technique of encrypting data stored or communicated by a microcontroller in a way that only authorized parties may access and decode it is known as encryption in microcontroller data. To prevent unauthorized access to or manipulation with sensitive data, this is an essential security feature in many applications, including IoT (Internet of Things), embedded systems, and communication devices.

- Data Confidentiality: The microcontroller uses encryption to make sure that the data it stores or transmits are private. Without the decryption key, an attacker will not be able to decipher the encrypted data, regardless of whether they physically access the microcontroller's memory or intercept data as they are being transmitted.
- Encryption Algorithms: To accomplish encryption and decryption, microcontrollers commonly use cryptographic algorithms. In applications utilizing microcontrollers, encryption methods are frequently utilized.

- Key Management: The management of encryption keys affects the security of encrypted data. To avoid unauthorized access to the keys themselves, microcontroller applications must implement strict key management procedures, including key generation, distribution, storage, and rotation.
- Resource Constraints: A microcontroller's computing capabilities are frequently constrained. Therefore, it is essential to build encryption techniques that are resource-efficient. For encryption, some microcontrollers may include hardware acceleration, which speeds up the operation.
- Secure Boot: To make sure that only trusted and verified code may execute on the device, microcontrollers may employ secure boot techniques in addition to encrypting data. This stops unauthorized software modifications or firmware updates on the device.
- Tamper Detection: Some microcontroller applications may include tamper detection mechanisms to detect physical attacks on the device, such as attempts to access encrypted data by physically tampering with the microcontroller. These mechanisms can trigger alerts or take protective actions.
- Secure Storage: Even if the physical storage medium is compromised, encryption can be used to safeguard sensitive data that microcontrollers store in non-volatile memory (such as EEPROM or flash memory).
- Compliance: Depending on the application and sector, microcontroller-based systems may be required to adhere to certain security requirements, such as those outlined in FIPS 140-2, ISO 27001, or sector-specific security standards.

Devices that connect across a variety of networks, such Wi-Fi, Bluetooth, or cellular, frequently employ microcontrollers. Data transmission via these networks is safe thanks to encryption, which also prevents eavesdropping and data interception. When encrypting microcontroller data, it is important to carefully analyze the application's needs, the resources at hand, and the required level of security. To safeguard sensitive data, it frequently combines hardware-based encryption modules (if available), effective software implementations, and reliable key management procedures.

IoT-based heart rate monitoring systems must be secured using a thorough and multi-layered strategy that takes into account all security concerns. To adjust and improve your security procedures over time, it is critical to remain current on new threats and security best practises.

To confirm the security of your system, think about requesting third-party security exams and certifications.

A straightforward bitwise technique called XOR (exclusive OR) may be used to encrypt and obscure data. Each bit in the output of XORing two pieces of data is set if and only if one of the corresponding bits in the input data is set. Although XOR encryption is not thought to be safe for encrypting sensitive data on its own, it can be used as part of more sophisticated encryption.

Be aware that XOR encryption cannot reliably thwart determined attackers from accessing sensitive data. It is a simple technique that is susceptible to several assaults, including frequency analysis, known-plaintext attacks, and others. We should utilize well-known encryption methods like AES or RSA for safe data encryption and adhere to standard practices for key management and security. Complex algorithms cannot be implemented due to limited memory space and temporal constraints.

Due to their constrained computing and memory capabilities, microcontrollers can present a number of difficulties when implementing complicated encryption methods. The following are some typical issues that you could run into while trying to implement sophisticated encryption methods on microcontrollers:

- Resource Restrictions: The processing (CPU), memory (RAM and flash/EEPROM), and energy resources of microcontrollers are often constrained. For key management, data buffering, and intermediate calculations, complex encryption methods frequently require a lot of computer power and memory. This might be a significant constraint, and you might need to use more resource-efficient techniques or drastically optimize your code.
- Execution speed: When used in real-time applications, complex encryption algorithms might be difficult for microcontrollers to process quickly enough. For instance, the microcontroller could not satisfy the necessary performance requirements in situations where data have to be encrypted or decrypted fast.
- Algorithm Suitability: Microcontroller contexts are not the best place for all sophisticated encryption techniques. Some algorithms could demand functions or actions that the hardware of the microcontroller cannot effectively handle. It is essential to select encryption methods that are designed for situations with limited resources.

- Energy Use: Cryptographic procedures can use a lot of energy. This may cause a quick battery drain for microcontroller devices that run on batteries. It is critical to optimize algorithms for energy efficiency, particularly in IoT applications.
- Execution Time: Complex encryption algorithms might take a long time to run on some devices.
- Code Size: The encryption implementation's code size can have a big impact. Large code sizes may cause limitations since flash memory on microcontrollers is frequently constrained.
- Hardware Support: Some microcontrollers are equipped with hardware-accelerated cryptographic modules, which may greatly enhance the speed and security of encryption operations. This capability is not provided by all microcontrollers, though.

Ultimately, the trade-offs between security, performance, and resource limitations specific to the microcontroller platform must be carefully taken into account when implementing advanced encryption on microcontrollers.

In this regard, this chapter tries to develop a wristband for measuring the heart rate signal of an individual followed by some encryption techniques to secure the data during transmission to the cloud-based server. This allows healthcare professionals, caregivers, and even individuals themselves to access heart rate information in real time, regardless of their location. Providing security with effective memory utilization and fast communication is the main challenge. The IoT-based system typically consists of a microcontroller where memory and power consumption is the key factor. Thus, the encryption technique utilized in the hardware system must satisfy both the points. This hardware-level security provides the privacy in the data from measurement to the cloud-based server, which is a vital part in the healthcare sector.

In the cloud-based platform, sophisticated algorithms and machine learning techniques analyze heart rate data to provide valuable insights and actionable information. These algorithms can detect abnormal heart rhythms, irregularities, or fluctuations that may indicate potential health issues. For instance, if the system detects a sudden spike or drop in heart rate, it can trigger immediate alerts to both the individual and designated healthcare providers.

Moreover, the system can generate comprehensive reports and trends based on the collected data. This enables healthcare professionals to track an individual's heart rate patterns over time, identify any recurring issues, and make informed decisions regarding treatment plans and interventions. Additionally, the system facilitates remote patient monitoring, allowing healthcare providers to remotely track patients' heart rates, and reducing the need for frequent hospital visits.

17.2 Literature Review

Heart rate signals are collected from the finger or ear using an IR TX-RX (Infrared Transmitter and Receiver pair) module and amplified to provide a measurable scale [2]. A low pass filter was used to remove the background noise. A microcontroller is programmed with an algorithm to run the proposed heart rate counting system. Comparing the outcomes of this method to those of the time-consuming and laborious heart rate counting test revealed promising outcomes. The proposed method can be applied for a wide variety of healthcare settings, including homes, clinics, communities, and even sports medicine.

A warning system that can track a patient's cardiac state is discussed [3]. With the help of the photo plethysmograph (PPG) technology, the heart rate is determined. The PIC16F87 microcontroller processes this signal to calculate heart rate in beats per minute. Then, it uses SMS to send alerts to medical professionals, patients' families, or their relatives' cell phones. This will also notify the family so they can get to the patients right away.

The Internet of Things is used to develop systems for heartbeat monitoring and heart attack detection [4]. The sensor is connected to a microcontroller, allowing for both internet transmission and verification of heart rate readings. The user can limit the number of heartbeats. Following the establishment of these restrictions, the system begins monitoring. When the heart rate of the patient above a predetermined threshold, the system initiates a notification to the controller, who subsequently disseminates this information via the internet, thereby alerting the medical practitioners and any relevant individuals. The technology also warns when a heartbeat is too low. Every time a user signs in for monitoring, the system also shows the patient's real-time heart rate.

A microcontroller-based heart rate and temperature monitor that uses a fingertip and temperature sensor is discussed [5]. The device, which uses optical technology to track blood flow through the finger, has the portability benefit over traditional recording methods. The device's performance on actual signals demonstrates accuracy in heartbeat measurement even during vigorous physical exercise. The system is managed by a central unit and is made up of sensors that measure a patient's body temperature and heartbeat. The sensor measurements are further analyzed and delivered through GSM module to a distant place where they are displayed on a cell phone.

With the aid of the Arterial Lumen Area model, the Blood Pressure estimate algorithm was created utilizing the maximum amplitude and maximum/minimum slope algorithms [6]. Maximum amplitude and maximum/minimum slope algorithms were compared to the Blood Pressure estimation technique, and the latter provided greater accuracy. Both healthy and ill patients were used to test this strategy [7]. Even if the optimization method uses more oscillometric pulse, it takes longer.

In order to record, store, and analyze heart sounds asynchronously, a system based on the Internet of Things and signal analysis was developed [8]. It improves data transmission speed and power efficiency. Physiological parameters were obtained through the implementation of preprocessing, segmentation, and clustering methodologies in order to augment the information pertaining to cardiovascular health. The routine for monitoring cardiac auscultation is simple to implement and provides energy and financial savings.

Constructing the ischemic stroke identification mechanism involved merging heart rate variability assessment with multivariate statistical process management [9]. A verification process for the ischemic stroke identification system was conducted using 19 rodents. Given the shared characteristics of cerebrovascular structure, its applicability to human subjects was explored. The experiment was carried out on a limited group of creatures, and the HRV analysis was not conducted with anesthesia's potential influence on the stroke detection system in mind.

Using a wrist-worn ECG and the sphere IoT platform, heart rate variability was tracked [10]. It was based on ECG and photoplethysmography methods. Raw ECG readings and heart rate are measured using Ag, Ag/Cl electrodes. Low power was required by this technology. The battery life is longer.

For the purpose of predicting ECG signals and protecting the communication channel, the ECG key that is specific to the chip was successfully retrieved through the utilization of a biomedical analyzer and a test strip [9]. Application-specific integrated circuit technology was used for its implementation [11]. This technology forecasts ventricular arrhythmia and offers security, power efficiency, and effective sharing. This system requires adaptation in order to use various resources while adapting biological platforms.

Abba and Garba [12] reported an IoT-based system for human heartbeat monitoring and control. It demonstrates accurate sensing and data transmission via an assembled prototype. Resting heart rate findings align with medical standards, and the system offers a flexible, reliable, and confidential approach for medical practitioners, aiding their work.

17.3 Methodology

The order of the steps to be taken throughout the system administration process is visualized by a block diagram and a flowchart. When the cycle stream was first established, it directed the crucial phases of any upcoming tasks from a system's start to finish. For the purpose of developing, planning, and maintaining electrical and electronic equipment, circuit diagrams were used. These diagrams were really important for a well-developed system. The overall block diagram of the whole system is demonstrated in Figure 17.1.

The sensors are so connected with the wearable band that when a heart disease patient wears that band and power on that device, it will start collecting the heart rate data from the patient body at a fixed or user-defined sampling rate. The collected data are then transferred to the processing unit, where a microcontroller is connected. The sensor unit is connected with

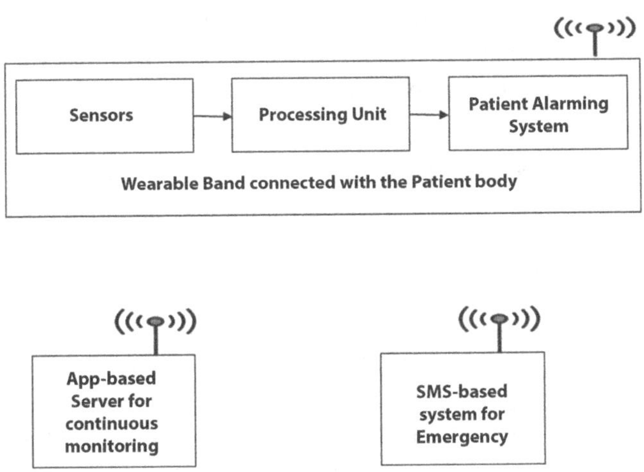

Figure 17.1 Overall block diagram of the whole system.

the processing unit via I2C communication protocol. The sensor data that are mainly in the analog format are first converted to digital with the help of a microcontroller in-build ADC. Then, those data are directly sent to the App-based cloud server through which the patient party can continuously monitor or track the heart rate of the patient through any smartphone application or personal computer. Providing security with effective memory utilization and fast communication is the main challenge. The IoT-based system typically consists of a microcontroller where memory and power consumption are the key factors. Thus, the encryption technique utilized in the hardware system must satisfy both points. This hardware-level security provides privacy in the data from measurement to the cloud-based server, which is a vital part in the healthcare sector. The App-based cloud server will also store all the heart rate data of that patient for further diagnosis by the registered medical practitioners. A small display unit is also interfaced with the processing unit via the I2C protocol for local monitoring purposes. In the processing module, a Machine Learning-based algorithm is developed that checks heart rate data and decides whether that person will have heart disease or not. The ML-based algorithm collects some other health-related information such as Age, Gender, Chest Pain Type, Resting BP, Cholesterol, and Fasting Blood Sugar. All these data are pre-inputted data based on last diagnosis result. It will generate an alarm signal as well as send a message to the registered medical practitioner. The system has the facility in which the patient or the registered medical practitioner can set the threshold values for generating an alarm signal as well as a message signal. The alarm signal that will alert the patient has mainly two types: one is in the form of a vibration signal, causing the wearable device to vibrate to alert the patient, and the other is in the form of a sound signal in terms of a buzzer to alert the patient and the surrounding personnel. The flowchart of the overall system is shown in Figure 17.2.

17.3.1 Hardware Description

The system has two prime components: one is the IoT-based smart wearable device and another one is the Application that can be operated in any smartphone or personal computer. The heart rate is measured by the health monitoring system that is installed inside the IoT-based smart wearable device. The implementation of this multifunction system requires numerous components. The circuit diagram of this health monitoring system is shown in Figure 17.3. Design implementation is crucial for the system to be successful. The components of this system and their brief descriptions are as follows:

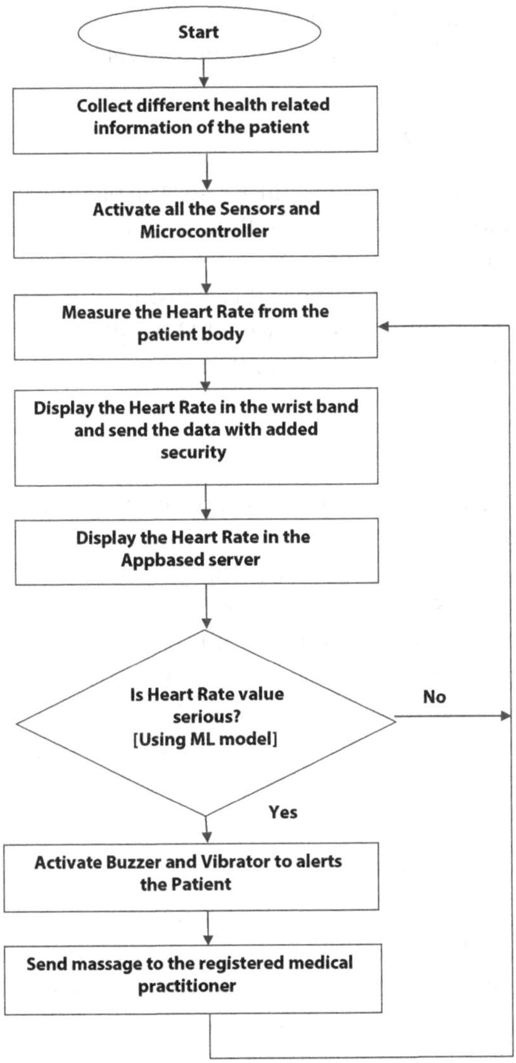

Figure 17.2 The flow diagram of the overall system.

17.3.1.1 ESP32

The ESP32 family encompasses an integrated microcontroller with attributes such as built-in Wi-Fi and dual-mode Bluetooth capabilities. It has gained popularity owing to its cost-effectiveness and energy-efficient design. Depending on the model, the ESP32 series uses a RISC-V microprocessor with either a single core or a pair of cores from Tensilica's Xtensa LX6 or LX7 families. In addition, it has built-in filters, power amplifiers, low-noise receiver amplifiers, and switches for the antennas. An illustrative depiction of the ESP32 is presented in Figure 17.4.

17.3.1.2 MAX30100

The MAX30100 sensor measures pulse rate. The pictorial representation of MAX30100 is shown in Figure 17.5. Precise results are provided by a synchronized beat oximeter and heartrate sensor combination. This sensor is appropriate for this system because it can distinguish between beat oximetry and heart rate signals using two LEDs, a photo detector, enhanced optics, and low-noise analog flag handling.

17.3.1.3 Boost Converter

A boost converter, also known as a step-up converter, is a DC-to-DC power converter designed to elevate the voltage from its input (power supply) to its output while reducing the current (load). This type of switched-mode power supply (SMPS) incorporates a minimum of two semiconductors, including a diode and a transistor, and at least one energy storage element, such as a capacitor, inductor, or both. To minimize voltage ripple, capacitive filters are typically employed on both the input (load-side filter) and output (sometimes in conjunction with inductors) (supply-side filter) of such a converter. Figure 17.6 illustrates a standard boost converter.

17.3.1.4 Display (OLED)

The term "organic light-emitting diode" (OLED) or "organic electroluminescent diode" (organic EL) refers to a specific type of light-emitting diode (LED) that utilizes an emissive electroluminescent layer composed of organic compounds. When an electric current is applied, this LED emits light. This component is utilized in the system to locally display the body's pulse rate (in BPM) and blood oxygen saturation (in SpO2). Another advantage of this module is its compact size, a crucial factor in the development of wearable devices. Figure 17.7 depicts a typical OLED.

17.3.1.5 SMS Facility

An API for SMS Gateway like FAST2SMS is used to provide the SMS facility. This bulk SMS API is compatible with languages like PHP, Java, C#, Python, Ruby, Javascript, NodeJS, and more.

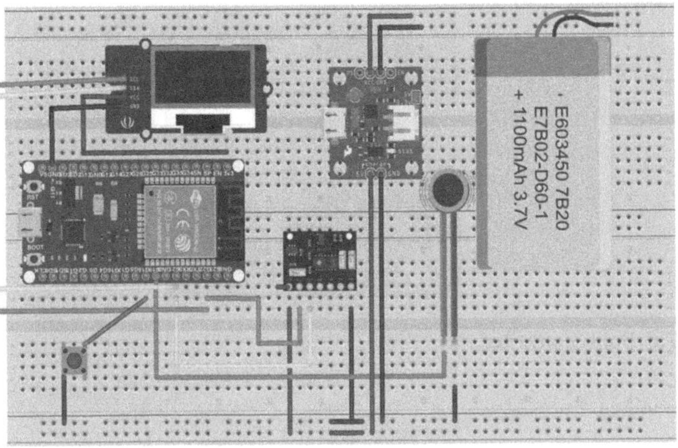

Figure 17.3 The circuit diagram of the wearable device.

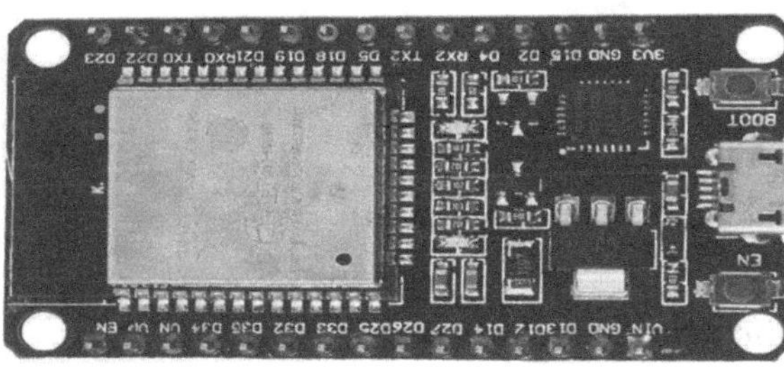

Figure 17.4 ESP32.

Figure 17.5 MAX30100.

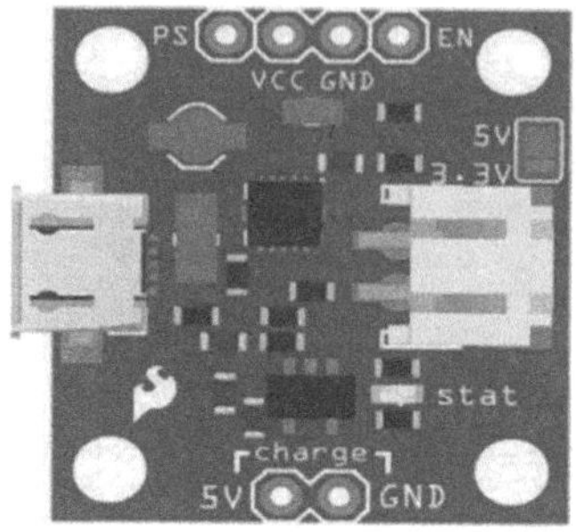

Figure 17.6 Boost converter.

Figure 17.7 Organic light-emitting diode (OLED).

17.3.2 Application Development

The development of applications for smartphones and personal computers is facilitated through the BlynkIoT platform. Blynk is an Internet-of-Things platform designed for iOS and Android smartphones, enabling users to remotely control devices such as Arduino, Raspberry Pi, and NodeMCU. With this application, individuals can compile and assign the appropriate addresses to various widgets, allowing them to create a graphical interface or human–machine interface (HMI).

17.3.3 Encryption Technique Description

A Wi-Fi-enabled microcontroller is used in this work where Wi-Fi provides the connectivity with internet. Thus, the microcontroller can send local data to the server through internet. Now, anyone can access all data from anywhere in the world. Its sounds awesome, but when we talk about the internet, one word always comes to our mind—security. In IoT-based devices, security is the most important thing.

A protocol called HTTP is used to convey data across the internet. It is known as HTTPS when the data are encrypted using SSL/TLS. To put it simply, HTTPS is basically the HTTP protocol with SSL/TLS-encrypted data. The browser's built-in tools for certificate validation, renewal, and updating automatically manage SSL/TLS certificates in web browsers. The browser examines the SSL/TLS certificate of a website when you visit it to make sure it is current and has not expired. The user will normally see a warning from the browser if there is a problem with the certificate. On the other hand, SSL/TLS certificates are not managed automatically by the device on an embedded system. Here is why manually updating SSL/TLS certificates on an ESP32 might be necessary.

There are many reasons behind this problem. The reasons are limited resources, firmware management, security policy, and more. Another problem is that HTTPS needs more resources and slows down the microcontroller workflow. The solution is a simple and easy encryption and decryption process. The easiest way to encrypt and decrypt data is run XOR operation with the data value. At first, take any 8-bit key value. This 8-bit key value is considered as the encryption and decryption key.

Now, take an example to describe this process.

17.3.3.1 Encryption Process

Consider the Data is $(85)_{10}$ and the Key is $(17)_{10}$

Now the Encrypted text = $(85)_{10}$ XOR $(17)_{10}$ = $(01010101)_2$ XOR $(00010001)_2$ = $(010\ 0100)_2$ = $(68)_{10}$

17.3.3.2 Decryption Process

The Encrypted text is $(68)_{10}$ and the Key is $(17)_{10}$ Cyphertext= 68 in binary—01000100

So, the main data = $(68)_{10}$ XOR $(17)_{10}$ = $(01000100)_2$ XOR $(00010001)_2$ = $(01010101)_2$ = $(85)_{10}$

17.3.4 Software Description

The combination of high-performance data computation with machine learning (ML) [13] has resulted in the emergence of a number of new options for analyzing and assessing data-intensive operations in a variety of different industries. ML has been successful up to this point in paving the path for abnormalities in heart rate identification. There are a lot of companies in the health care industry that are using these technologies to gain ahead. A few years ago, no knowledgeable person could have conceived of such an innovation, which can make difficult tasks easy to accomplish. ML is a tool that gives the system the ability to learn and grow on its own automatically based on the experiences it has had in the past. In ML, one of the primary goals is to enable the computer system to learn on its own without any assistance from a person. When a machine is provided with a sufficient quantity of data, it will, therefore, learn how to interpret, operate, and analyze these data by making use of ML Algorithms, for the purpose of resolving problems that occur in the real world.

This chapter presents the preparation of a feature set utilizing a smart digital watch. Next, the feature set undergoes pre-processing and is provided for the classifiers to make predictions on the presence of abnormal heart conditions in the user of the watch. The operational mechanism of the prediction model is as follows and depicted in Figure 17.8.

17.3.4.1 Extracted Feature-Based Dataset

A feature-based dataset is prepared with 7 features. Among these features, the smart watch measures maximum heart rate and the wearer through the connected app of the watch enters all other features. The wearer-entered features are gender, age, resting blood pressure, chest pain type, cholesterol, and fasting blood sugar.

17.3.4.2 Data Preparation

Quantile Transformation

In the fields of statistics and machine learning, quantile transformation [14] refers to a data transformation technique or a data pre-processing approach that is used to transform the distribution of a variable into a normal or uniform distribution. The goal of achieving a more Gaussian (normal) distribution is one that is frequently pursued since doing so can be advantageous for a wide variety of statistical and machine learning methods. The quantile transformation seeks to alter the data distribution of the

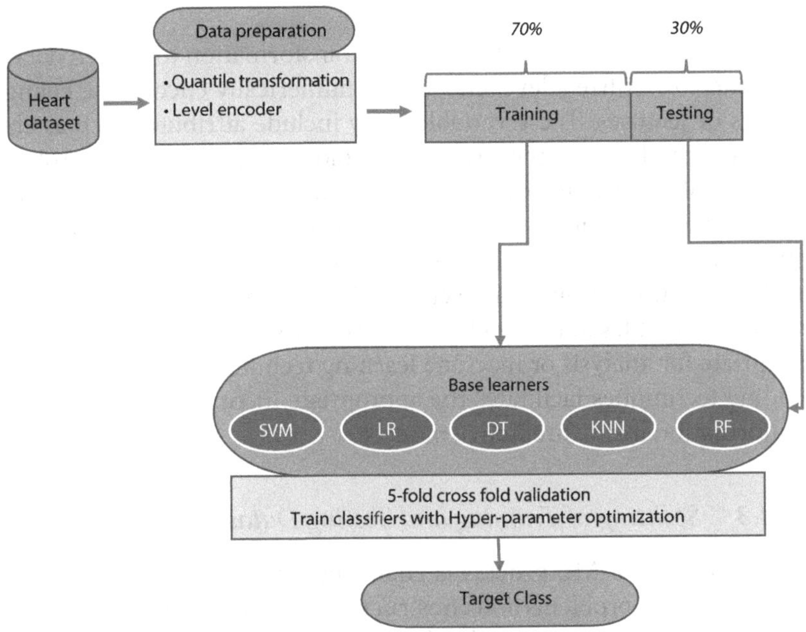

Figure 17.8 Basic block diagram of the predictive model for heart abnormality detection.

characteristics or variables that are used to describe the phishing incidents when it is applied to a dataset that has been created from smart watch measurement. We can improve the performance of some algorithms or statistical studies by altering the data so that it conforms to a target distribution that we want it to have. This can be done by making the data conform to the distribution that we want it to have. The method of quantile modification helps to reduce the severity of the impact that is caused by outliers and extreme values in the dataset. In order to improve the robustness and reliability of subsequent studies or ML models, it is possible to redistribute the data in accordance with a target distribution. In addition to this, the utilization of this method can reduce the influence that the skewness of the data has on the accuracy of ML models by reducing the impact of the skewness. When applying the quantile transformation to a smart watch dataset, one would normally perform this process on the relevant features or variables used to represent the characteristics of cardiac abnormality occurrences. These qualities include a low or high heart rate, various types of chest pain, and so on. The converted dataset can then be utilized for further analysis, feature selection, or training machine learning models to detect and categorize the wearer of a watch with a heart abnormality condition.

Level Encoder

Following the application of the quantile transformation to a given dataset, it is possible to utilize a level encoder to numerically encode the changed variables or features. These variables may include attributes such as chest pain kind, gender, and the presence of blood sugar or cholesterol. The utilization of a level encoder proves to be quite advantageous in scenarios involving categorical variables or variables that possess a constrained number of distinct levels. The application of a quantile transformation followed by the utilization of a level encoder guarantees the conversion of categorical variables in the modified dataset into a numerical format that is appropriate for analysis or machine learning techniques. The utilization of encoding techniques facilitates the appropriate incorporation of categorical information inside predictive models.

17.3.4.3 Splitting of Training and Testing Dataset

The first step in an ML process is collecting a vast quantity of data on a variety of cardiac problems and constructing the dataset with all of the necessary parameters. After that, the data that were stored are first organized into sets, and then they are processed using the processor. During this step, any unnecessary noise is eliminated. In the form of testing data and training data, the data that have been processed have been partitioned and categorized. These data are referred to as pre-processed data. The test data, in addition to the raw data, are placed through processing, which ultimately results in an output that is then added to the training data. The complete dataset is then input into the Machine Model so that it can gain knowledge and experience from it. In this study, a training set consisting of 70% of the entire data was used, while the remaining 30% served as the test set.

17.3.4.4 Machine Learning-Based Algorithms

Before deciding on the strategy to put into practice, it is important to do an evaluation to determine which one is the most appropriate for the specific dataset. When working on a machine learning problem with a particular dataset, we put a variety of models through their paces to see which ones best handle optimization issues. In this section, we will evaluate several classification models by contrasting their accuracy scores and confusion matrices:

- Support Vector Machine (SVM)
- Decision Tree (DT)

- k-nearest neighbors (KNN)
- Logistic Regression (LR)
- Random Forest (RF)

Support Vector Machine

In the realm of supervised machine learning, the Support Vector Machine (SVM) is a popular tool for tackling problems of categorical classification. The goal of this approach is to find the hyperplane in N-dimensional space that most reliably separates the data points, where N is the number of features in the dataset. Multiple hyperplanes can be produced, but the major objective of the technique is to identify the hyperplane with the maximum margin, which represents the greatest distance between the data points of the displayed features. The accuracy of the categorization will increase as the distance between the objects being classified increases. Achieving a bigger margin can be accomplished through the utilization of support vectors. Any alteration or adjustment made to the support vectors has the potential to cause a shift in the position of the hyperplane. Within the Support Vector Machine (SVM) framework, there are two primary types of classifiers, namely, Support Vector Classification (SVC) and Nu-Support Vector Classification (NuSVC). Several crucial hyperparameters utilized in Support Vector Machines (SVMs) are outlined below:

- Kernel: A kernel function is a computational method used to transform input data into a suitable format for subsequent data processing operations. The SVM utilizes a collection of mathematical functions that provide a framework for data manipulation. This framework has led to the development of a concept known as the "kernel." The kernel function is used to generally convert the training dataset from a space of non-linear decision surfaces into a space of linear equations. By using this method, you can determine the dot product of two points in terms of the usual feature dimensions.
- Gamma: The gamma parameter is responsible for determining the extent to which the influence of an individual training sample propagates. A lower numerical number corresponds to a greater distance, whereas a higher numerical value corresponds to a lesser distance. A lower gamma value leads to decreased model accuracy, similar to the effect of a higher gamma value. The gamma value that yields a model with favorable decision boundaries is the median value.

- C parameter: To reduce the overall amount of generalization error, the model's tolerance for incorrectly classified data points is set by the regularization parameter C. Increases in C reduce the trained classifier's tolerance and maximum span. In contrast to max-tailed classifiers, which are trained to be extremely specific, soft-tailed classifiers are trained to be extremely generic. The C value regulates the extent of the penalty for misclassification. A higher value of C corresponds to an increased penalty for misclassification, whereas a lower value of C corresponds to a decreased penalty for misclassification. As the value of C increases, the permissible margin for the decision functions to accurately categories all training points decreases. There is a possibility that the model could exhibit over-fitting tendencies when trained on the dataset. A lower value of C increases the number of degrees of freedom, hence simplifying the decision function at the cost of reduced training accuracy.
- Degree: The degree of the polynomial kernel function, denoted as 'poly', is a parameter that is disregarded by all other kernel functions. The default value is set to three.

Decision Tree

The DT classifier employs a greedy technique. The algorithm under consideration is a form of supervised learning that uses a tree structure to represent both characteristics and class labels. DTs are commonly employed for the purpose of training a prototype that enables the prediction of the class or value of the target variables, based on the provided training data. Decision nodes and leaves are distinct classifications that can be employed to classify DT. The ultimate result or outcome is foliage. The branches emanating from each node inside the tree symbolize the various possible solutions for the given test case, while each node itself functions as a test case for a certain attribute. The recursive approach is repeated for each subtree that is constructed from the new nodes. Several crucial hyperparameters utilized in DT include the following:

- Criterion: The setting in question pertains to the method by which the measurement of contaminants in the separation process is determined. The default metric for impurity is the Gini index, while an alternative option is to utilize entropy.
- Max depth: This factor controls the upper limit of the tree's depth. The default value is null. Frequently, the outcome of

this phenomenon is the occurrence of overfitting in decision trees. The utilization of the depth parameter serves as a means to arrange the tree or impose limitations on its growth, hence mitigating the risk of overfitting.

- Splitter: DTs choose which features to separate based on a specific methodology. By default, the method selects the optimal partition for each node, using all available attributes. If the splitter random parameter is supplied, any subset of attributes is considered. A split is constructed based on the features inside a given arbitrary subset. The max_features parameter determines the dimensionality of the random subset.

K-Nearest Neighbors

In contrast to the aforementioned classifier, the KNN technique is considered non-parametric in nature. The algorithm is commonly referred to as the Lazy Learner because of its characteristic of not taking rapid action. During the training period, the system retains the values of the dataset and subsequently executes actions on the dataset after the classification process. The process involves comparing the new data with the existing dataset and subsequently categorizing them based on predetermined criteria. The classifier in question is often regarded as one of the most straightforward classifiers employed within the framework of Supervised Learning Technique. The utilization of the KNN algorithm facilitates the straightforward identification of novel characters or categories. In the KNN algorithm, the initial step involves the selection of the number of neighbors (k). Subsequently, the Euclidean distance is computed between the data points, enabling the identification of the nearest neighbors. Subsequently, the total count of datasets inside each k neighbor may be aggregated, and the newly acquired data points can be assigned to the category that possesses the highest number of neighbors. Several crucial hyperparameters utilized in the KNN algorithm are outlined below:

- N neighbors: The number of neighbors to be utilized.
- Leaf Size: The adjustment of the trade-off between the expense of traversing nodes and A node's leaf size effectively regulates the cost of brute-force distance estimation by setting the minimal number of points that can be contained within that node. The aforementioned factor may have an influence on the speed of tree construction and querying, as well as the amount of memory required for tree storage.

- p: The power parameter for the Minkowski metric is denoted by p. The value of p in the Manhattan distance metric is equal to 1, while in the Euclidean distance metric, the value of p is equal to 2.

Logistic Regression

LR is a supervised machine learning technique utilized for binary classification tasks. It achieves this by predicting the probability or likelihood of a specific action, occurrence, or observation. This particular model exclusively yields binary outcomes, limited to the choices of yes/no, 0/1, or true/false. LR is a statistical technique that involves the division of data into distinct classes, followed by an examination of the connection between one or more independent variables. Predictive modeling commonly uses algorithms to determine the probability of a specific event being classified under a particular category.

Random Forest

The RF classification models use a group of decision trees to make a prediction. The training data for each decision tree are chosen at random. A random subset of features is considered for splitting at each tree node. Model randomization reduces overfitting and improves generality. When using a random forest for prediction, each decision tree generates its own prediction. The final forecast is then based on majority voting of the tree predictions. This strategy makes the model more resilient because the forest's other trees often offset individual trees' inaccuracies. Several crucial hyperparameters utilized in the RF algorithm are outlined below:

- n_estimators: How many trees must be built before drawing conclusions. Sklearn's defaults are 100. Data size strongly affects N_estimators; more DTs are needed to capture data trends.
- max_features: Max features of RF are considered when dividing a node. The maximum number of features for node separation might be sqrt (n_features) or $\log_2$ (n_features).
- Criterion: Measurement of split efficacy in decision trees for categorization tasks. Gini impurity and entropy-based information gain are prominent support criteria. It uses the Gini coefficient by default.
- Max_depth: Maximum decision tree limits. When applied to a null value, the decision tree divides until purity is reached.

- random_state: The modification of variables that affect sample randomness. The model will always produce the same results with a fixed random state value, same hyperparameters, and training data.

17.3.4.5 Hyperparameter Tuning Using Grid Search

Hyperparameters, referred to as model parameters in the academic context, are assigned fixed values prior to the training process. One of the most straightforward algorithms for hyperparameter tweaking is grid search. Fundamentally, it partitions the lattices of the hyperparameter space. Next, cross-validation is used to ascertain significant performance indicators following the exploration of each combination of values within this grid. The optimal combination of hyperparameter values can be determined by identifying the grid location that maximizes the mean during cross-validation. Grid search is a comprehensive methodology that systematically explores all potential combinations to identify the optimal spots inside a given domain. Nevertheless, the procedure exhibits a notable sluggishness. The process of personally verifying each room combination can be time-consuming and occasionally provide challenges. Each individual grid point necessitates the implementation of n-fold cross-validation, which entails conducting n training iterations.

17.4 Result Analysis

17.4.1 Hardware Implementation

Step 1: Design the Hardware Circuit
The hardware circuit diagram as shown in Figure 17.3 is first designed in the breadboard to check its workability. Initially, the circuit measures the body pulse rate in terms of BPM. The hardware design circuit is finalized in the veroboard. Both (breadboard as well as veroboard) circuit diagrams are shown in Figure 17.9. For local indication, an OLED display is connected with the hardware circuit as shown in Figure 17.10.

Step 2: Develop the Communication Channel to the App-Based Server
The next step is to communicate the data to an App-based server for remote monitoring. This hardware-level security plays a key role here to provide the privacy in the data from measurement to the cloud-based server. The encryption technique is discussed in the next section. The BlynkIoT

Figure 17.9 Designed hardware circuit.

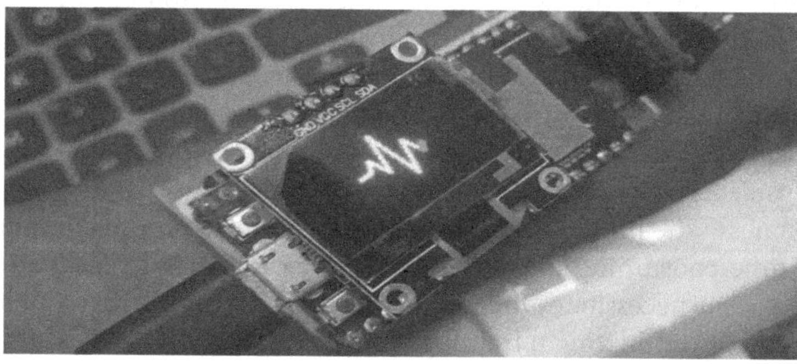

Figure 17.10 Hardware circuit with OLED display.

platform is used to develop this server-based monitoring system. Using this App, one can monitor his or her patient remotely either through any smartphone or through any personal computer. To use this facility, first the patient's parties have to register in that platform and then successfully log in with correct information every time to make this secure. The screenshot of this App-based remote monitoring is shown in Figure 17.11.

Step 3: Validate the Measure Data from the Device with the Standard One
Once the hardware circuit is developed, the first and foremost objective is to validate that circuit or the data collected from that circuit with some standard one. This will tell us the accuracy and reliability of the developed device. To do this, the developed device reading is cross-validated with the pulse oximeter, as shown in Figure 17.12. Table 17.1 represents the measure as well as standard data to calculate the inaccuracy present in the developed system using Equation 17.1.

Figure 17.11 App-based remote monitoring.

Figure 17.12 Validation of the developed system with a commercial pulse oximeter.

$$\%Error = \frac{|Measured\,Value - Standard\,Value|}{Standard\,Value} \times 100\% \qquad (17.1)$$

Step 4: Design the Configuration Page in the App-Based Server
A configuration page is designed to get all details about the patient. The page collects the patient information such as patient name, patient age, gender, chest pain type (from the last diagnosis), resting BP (last testing data), cholesterol (last testing data), fasting blood sugar (last testing data), patient address (in case of emergency, a registered medical practitioner can visit the actual location to take the necessary action), and alert number (the phone number of the registered medical practitioner). The screenshot of this activation page is shown in Figure 17.13.

Step 5: Develop the Communication Channel to the Cell Phone via SMS
A faithful communication channel is also made with the cell phone via SMS. This step is implemented with the help of the FAST2SMS API gateway.

Table 17.1 Performance index.

BPM reading			
Measured	**Standard**	**% Error**	**Avg. %Error**
82	82	0.0	1.10
75	74	1.35	
81	82	1.22	
83	82	1.22	
85	86	1.16	
88	89	1.12	
85	86	1.16	
86	85	1.18	
86	85	1.18	
80	82	2.44	
80	81	1.23	
80	80	0.0	

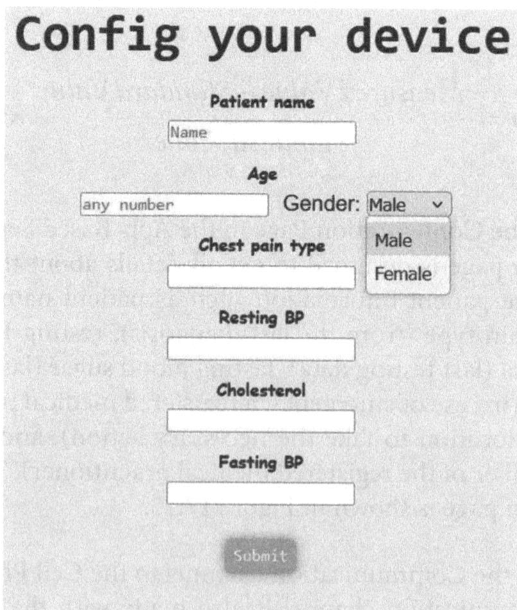

Figure 17.13 Activation page.

Once a severe heart disease condition of the patient is detected (based on the machine learning algorithm), an SMS with all details (like BPM value, patient name, patient address, etc.) is sent to the registered medical practitioner's phone number to take the necessary action to save the patient. A screenshot of such a message is shown in Figure 17.14.

Step 6: Assemble the Whole Circuit
After foolproofing each and every step, now all the parts are assembled in a single device to make the whole system workable. The system components are so connected that it will look like a wearable device and a heart patient can wear that band for his/her health monitoring purpose. With the help of this device, many lives can be saved.

17.4.2 Software Validation

The approach was designed and validated using a computer that featured a 16 GB random access memory along with an Intel Core i5 processor. Python, a programming language, was used on the Google Colab platform to implement the aforementioned solution, which was suggested. When evaluating the performance of a model, one must determine how accurately it can classify data. It can be helpful in determining how accurately

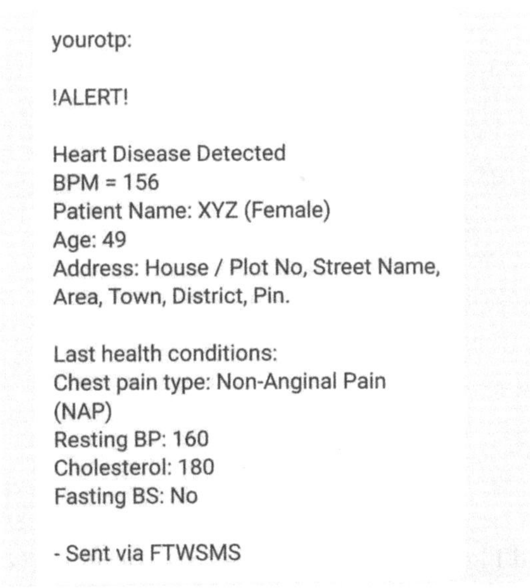

Figure 17.14 Type of message sent to the registered alert number.

the model can predict the target classes. The metrics that are applied for analysis are going to be determined by both the type of binary classification being used and the criteria that are being applied to the problem. The following are some of the measures [15] that are used to evaluate the effectiveness of a heart anomaly detection model that is based on binary classification:

17.4.2.1 Confusion Matrix and Performance Metrics

In our research, we employed a train–test split classification approach. Predictions are made using 70% of the data for training and 30% for testing. The accuracy of the classification is based on the following formula:

$$Ac = \frac{tp + tn}{tp + tn + fp + fn} \tag{17.2}$$

The abbreviations for "true positive", "true negative", "false positive", and "false negative" are "tp," "tn," "fp," and "fn," respectively.

As a tabular representation, the confusion matrix is used to evaluate a classification model's accuracy. Predictions of $fp, tp, fn,$ and tn are detailed in the statement. Measures of effectiveness including recall, precision, accuracy, and $F1-\text{score}$ can be computed using the aforementioned statistics.

$$Recall = \frac{tp}{tp + fn} \tag{17.3}$$

$$Prc = \frac{tp}{tp + fp} \tag{17.4}$$

$$F_1 - score = \frac{2tp}{2tp + fp + fn} \tag{17.5}$$

Table 17.2 and Figure 17.15 depict the confusion matrix and evaluation metrics, respectively, of the proposed heart abnormality detection model.

Table 17.2 Confusion matrix of phishing detection.

Confusion matrix representation	True level	*Predicted level*		*LR*	True level	*Predicted level*	
		P[#]	N[$]			P	N
	P	*tp*	*fp*		P	79	23
	N	*fn*	*tn*		N	18	110
DT	True level	*Predicted level*		SVM	True level	*Predicted level*	
		P	N			P	N
	P	79	23		P	79	23
	N	22	106		N	12	116
KNN	True level	*Predicted level*		RF	True level	*Predicted level*	
		P	N			P	N
	P	78	24		P	80	22
	N	13	115		N	21	107

P, Positive; $ N, Negative.

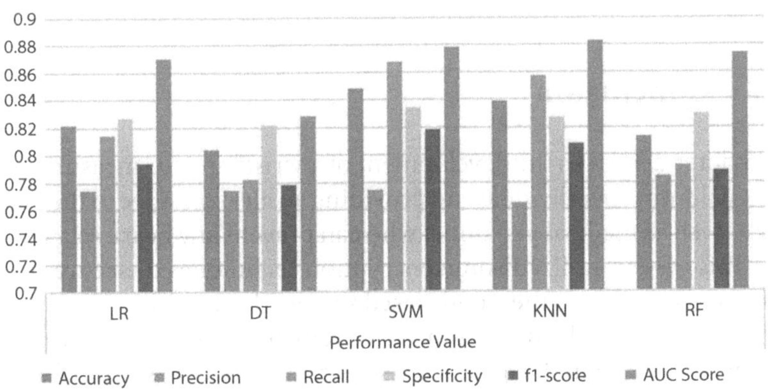

Figure 17.15 Evaluation metrics of the proposed prediction model.

17.4.2.2 Graphical Performance Analysis

The suggested prediction model for the heart abnormality detection system undergoes an evaluation of its performance based on a variety of metrics, and the outcome is compared to other existing systems or benchmarks.

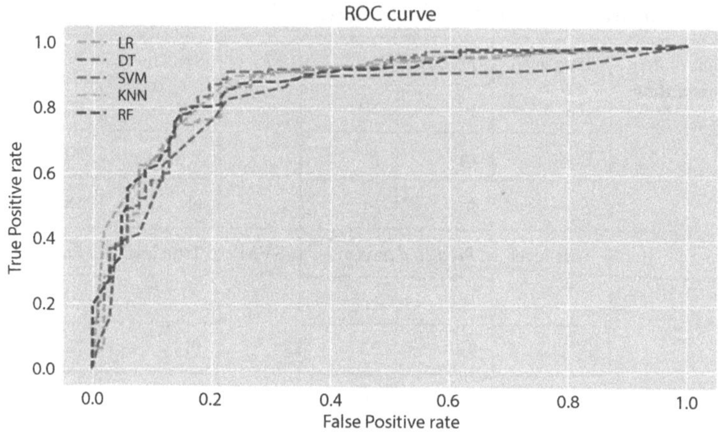

Figure 17.16 Graphical performance analysis with ROC curve of the heart abnormality detection model.

The analysis of the results of this evaluation is referred to as the result analysis. The ROC curve depicts the trade-off between the true positive rate (also known as sensitivity) and the false positive rate (also known as 1-specificity) at a number of different classification thresholds (as shown in Figure 17.16).

17.5 Conclusion

This chapter describes the development of a wristband for measuring heart rate signal from an individual and providing an alert message to the patient's party as well as medical personnel who can prevent any heart-related problems. This system utilized some encryption techniques to secure the data during transmission to the cloud-based server. This hardware-level security provides privacy in the data from measurement to the cloud-based server, which is a vital part in the healthcare sector. The cloud-based platform consists of sophisticated machine learning based algorithms that analyze the heart rate data to provide valuable insights related to potential health issues as well as actionable information. This system can generate comprehensive reports and trends based on the collected data. This enables healthcare professionals to track an individual's heart rate patterns over time, identify any recurring issues, and make informed decisions regarding treatment plans and interventions. Additionally, the system facilitates remote patient monitoring, allowing healthcare providers to remotely track patients' heart rates, and reducing the need for frequent hospital visits.

Received: ((will be filled in by the editorial staff))
Revised: ((will be filled in by the editorial staff))
Published online: ((will be filled in by the editorial staff))

References

1. Barnett, L.A., Prior, J.A., Kadam, U.T., Jordan, K.P., Chest pain and shortness of breath in cardiovascular disease: a prospective cohort study in UK primary care. *BMJ Open*, 7, 5, e015857, 2017.
2. Mamun, A.L., Ahmed, N., Alqahtani, M., Altwijri, O., Rahman, M., Ahamed, N.U., Rahman, S.A.M.M., Ahmad, R.B., Sundaraj, K., A microcontroller-based automatic heart rate counting system from fingertip. *J. Theor. Appl. Inf. Technol.*, 62, 3, 597–604, 2014.
3. Jubadi, W.M. and Sahak, S.F.A.M., *IEEE Symposium on Industrial Electronics and Applications*, Kuala Lumpur, Malaysia, pp. 1–5, October 4-6, 2009.
4. Sidheeque, A., Kumar, A., Sathish, K., Heart Attack Detection Using internet of things: IOT. *Int. J. Eng. Sci. Comput.*, 9, 1563–1571, 2007.
5. Alam, M.W., Sultana, T., Alam, M.S., A Heartbeat and Temperature Measuring System for Remote Health Monitoring using Wireless Body Area Network. *Int. J. Biosci. Bio-Technology*, 8, 1, 171–190, 2016.
6. Koohi, I., Batkin, I., Groza, V.Z., Shirmohammadi, S., Dajani, H.R., Ahmad, S., Metrological characterization of a method for blood pressure estimation based on arterial lumen area model. *IEEE Trans. Instrum. Meas.*, 66, 4, 734–745, 2017.
7. Muangsrinoon, S. and Boonbrahm, P., *14th International Joint Conference on Computer Science and Software Engineering*, NakhonSiThammarat, Thailand, July 12–14, 2017.
8. Biryukov, A., Perrin, L., Udovenko, A., *Annual International Conference on the Theory and Applications of Cryptographic Techniques*, Springer, pp. 372–402, 2016.
9. Yasin, M., Tekeste, T., Saleh, H., Mohammad, B., Sinanoglu, O., Ismail, M., Ultra-Low Power, Secure IoT Platform for Predicting Cardiovascular Diseases. *IEEE Trans. Circuits Syst. I*, 64, 9, 2624–2637, 2017.
10. Beach, C., Krachunov, S., Pope, J., Fafoutis, X., Piechocki, R.J., Craddock, I., Casson, A.J., An ultra low power personalizable wrist worn ECG monitor integrated with IoT infrastructure. *IEEE Access*, 6, 44010–44021, 2018.
11. Mohana, R.S. and Ravish, H.V., *Global Conference on Communication Technologies*, Thuckalay, India, 2015, April 23–24.
12. Abba, S. and Garba, A.M., An IoT-Based Smart Framework for a Human Heartbeat Rate Monitoring and Control System. *Proceedings*, 42, 1, 36, 2020.

13. Doupe, P., Faghmous, J., Basu, S., Machine Learning for Health Services Researchers. *Value Health*, 22, 7, 808–815, 2019.
14. Bogner, K., Pappenberger, F., Cloke, H.L., Technical Note: The normal quantile transformation and its application in a flood forecasting system. *Hydrol. Earth Syst. Sci.*, *16*, 4, 1085–1094, 2012.
15. Steurer, M., Hill, R.J., Pfeifer, N., Metrics for evaluating the performance of machine learning based automated valuation models. *J. Property Res.*, *38*, 2, 99–129, 2021.

18

A Secure IoT-Based Approach for Smart Irrigation System Using an Arduino Uno Microcontroller

Nitesh Kumar[1], Soumen Ghosh[1*], Sabyasachi Samanta[2], Abhijit Sarkar[2] and Priyatosh Jana[2]

[1]*Department of CSE (Data Science), Haldia Institute of Technology, W.B., India*
[2]*Department of CSE (Cyber Security), Haldia Institute of Technology, W.B., India*

Abstract
In this research work, an Arduino UNO microcontroller (SI-AUNO) is used to establish a smart irrigation system. Sensors assess soil humidity and wetness to estimate irrigation needs. The technology automates irrigation to maximize agricultural production and preserve water. Food demand rises with population and urbanization. Farmers are seeking effective irrigation technologies to maximize agricultural yields to fulfill this demand. The answer is smart irrigation systems, which provide real-time soil moisture data and reduce water waste. The suggested system employs low-cost sensors to monitor soil moisture and weather to predict plant water needs. Small farmers may use the cost-effective, easy-to-implement technology. The article details the system's hardware, software, and testing and assessment findings. The smart irrigation system may increase agricultural production and water savings. This chapter shows how low-cost sensors and microcontroller technologies may increase irrigation efficiency and efficacy in smart irrigation systems. The suggested approach should boost agricultural production and water saving. Farmers may also be certain that the IoT-based smart irrigation system's data, infrastructure, and control mechanisms are secure, assuring its dependability and longevity.

Keywords: Moisture sensor, temperature sensor, smart irrigation, Arduino UNO, SI-AUNO, secure IOT

**Corresponding author*: soumenghoshcse@gmail.com

Subhabrata Barman, Santanu Koley and Subhankar Joardar (eds.) Next-Generation Systems and Secure Computing, (379–400) © 2025 Scrivener Publishing LLC

18.1 Introduction

In this study, a more efficient and sustainable approach to irrigation is needed in the agriculture system. Irrigation is an essential aspect of agriculture, but traditional methods can be ineffective, leading to water waste, poor crop yields, and increased costs. To address this issue, the use of technology in agriculture has led to the development of smart irrigation systems, which are based on the Internet of Things (IoT) and use sensors and automation to optimize water usage and improve crop yields. The focus of this research is on a smart irrigation system using Arduino Uno, a low-cost, open-source microcontroller, i.e., as Smart Irrigation using Arduino UNO (SI-AUNO). The system utilizes humidity and soil moisture sensors to detect the water content of the soil and determine if irrigation is necessary. The sensors will be placed at different depths of the soil to provide a comprehensive understanding of the soil moisture levels, enabling the system to make more accurate decisions about irrigation [17]. The system will also be capable of adjusting the amount of water used for irrigation, reducing water waste and increasing crop yields. The main goal of this research is to design, implement, and test the smart irrigation system using Arduino Uno, and evaluate its potential impact on the agricultural industry. The system is designed to be user-friendly, affordable, and easily implementable, so it can be adopted by farmers of all sizes. By automating the irrigation process, the system will save time and effort for farmers, allowing them to focus on other important tasks [18]. Figure 18.1 displays a typical smart irrigation system.

In conclusion, this chapter discusses the need for an irrigation system that is more effective and environmentally friendly, as well as the possible effects of a smart irrigation system that uses an Arduino Uno on the

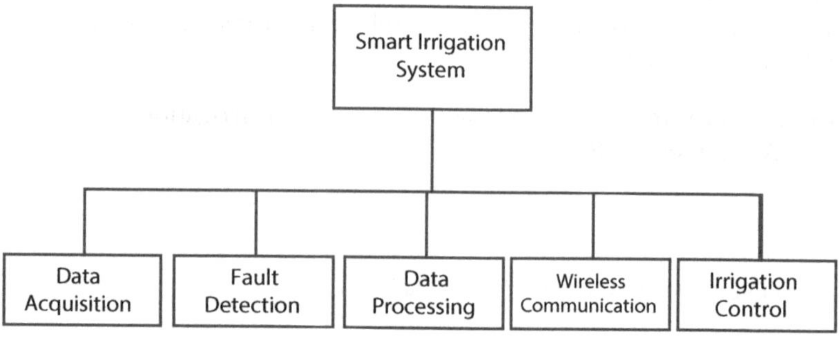

Figure 18.1 Smart irrigation system.

agricultural sector. This study will assess the design, execution, and possible effects of the system, which has the potential to revolutionize how we approach irrigation by making it more efficient, cost-effective, and sustainable [19].

Smart irrigation systems have become increasingly important in addressing the challenges of modern agriculture, particularly in the context of water scarcity and climate change. In India, agriculture is a major contributor to the economy, and there is a pressing need to modernize traditional practices in order to improve productivity and conserve resources. One major issue facing Indian agriculture is the overuse of water, which has led to a decline in groundwater levels and a decrease in overall water availability [20].

Figure 18.2 shows the different benefits of irrigation structure. This chapter proposes a smart irrigation system that makes use of low-cost sensors and automation to optimize water use and boost agricultural yields in order to address this problem. The system will use moisture sensors to measure the quantity of water in the soil and adjust the irrigation schedule accordingly. The system will also be IoT-capable, enabling remote monitoring and control. The system will be able to adjust to the unique requirements of various places within a sizable agricultural field thanks to the deployment of a dispersed network of sensor nodes and dispersed pumping units [21].

By developing a smart irrigation system that is affordable, easy to implement, and user-friendly, this research hopes to provide a practical solution for farmers facing water scarcity and other challenges in modern agriculture. The goal of this research is to conserve energy and water resources, handle the system manually and automatically, and detect the level of water. By incorporating these security measures into an IoT-based

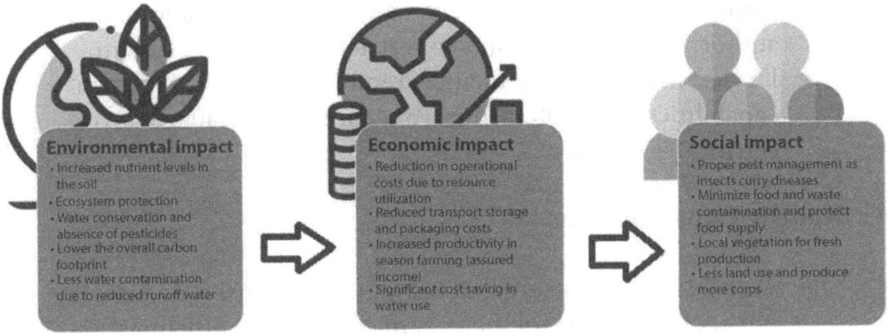

Figure 18.2 Economic, ecological, and communal benefits of the irrigation structure [17].

irrigation system, we can enhance the overall reliability, integrity, and confidentiality of the system, protecting it from potential threats and unauthorized access [23].

Creating a secure IoT-based Smart Irrigation System is essential to protect your system from potential vulnerabilities and ensure the confidentiality, integrity, and availability of data. Below are the key components and considerations for building a secure smart irrigation system:

A. Hardware Components

- Arduino or Microcontroller: Choose a microcontroller platform that supports encryption and secure communication protocols.
- Sensors: Use reliable and authenticated sensors for measuring soil moisture, temperature, humidity, and rainfall.
- Actuators: Employ secure solenoid valves and pumps for irrigation control.
- Secure Communication Module: Add a secure communication module (e.g., GSM, Wi-Fi with security features) to connect the system to the internet.

B. Software Components

- Firmware: Write secure firmware for the microcontroller to collect sensor data, control actuators, and implement security features.
- Secure Protocols: Use secure communication protocols like MQTT with TLS/SSL or HTTPS for data transmission.
- Data Encryption: Encrypt sensitive data at rest and in transit to protect it from eavesdropping.
- Access Control: Implement robust authentication and authorization mechanisms to restrict access to the system.
- Device Management: Include remote device management capabilities to update firmware securely and manage device certificates or keys.

C. Security Considerations

- Authentication: Ensure that only authorized users or devices can access and control the system. Use strong authentication methods like certificates or API keys.

- Authorization: Enforce role-based access control to limit actions users or devices can perform within the system.
- Data Encryption: Use strong encryption algorithms to protect data both during transmission and storage.
- Secure Boot: Implement secure boot procedures to prevent unauthorized firmware modifications.
- Logging and Monitoring: Keep detailed logs of system activities and establish monitoring to detect suspicious behavior.
- Security Updates: Plan for regular security updates to address vulnerabilities and improve system security.
- Physical Security: Protect the physical components of the system from tampering and unauthorized access.

D. Network Security

- Firewall: Employ a firewall to filter incoming and outgoing traffic, allowing only authorized communication.
- Intrusion Detection System (IDS): Implement an IDS to monitor network traffic for signs of intrusion or abnormal behavior.
- VLAN Segmentation: Segment the network to isolate the irrigation system from other devices and networks.

E. Cloud and IoT Platform

- Choose a Secure IoT Platform: Select a reputable and secure IoT platform that offers encryption, access control, and secure device management.
- Secure Communication: Use the platform's built-in security features for communication between the IoT devices and the cloud.

F. User Interface

- Secure User Authentication: Implement strong user authentication and session management for the web or mobile interface.
- HTTPS: Use HTTPS for secure data transmission between the user interface and the IoT platform.

G. Physical Security

- Enclosures: Use tamper-resistant enclosures for the IoT devices to protect them from physical attacks.
- Locks and Access Control: Secure access to the physical components of the system.

H. Compliance

- Ensure that your system complies with local and international regulations regarding IoT security and data privacy.

Building a secure IoT-based Smart Irrigation System requires careful planning, continuous monitoring, and regular updates to address emerging security threats. Consider working with security experts or consultants to assess and improve the security of your system. Security should be an integral part of the entire system design and operation. By following the security measures and best practices, it can significantly enhance the security of your IoT-based smart irrigation system and minimize the risk of cyber-attacks and data breaches. Remember that security is an ongoing process, and it is essential to stay vigilant and update your security measures as new threats and vulnerabilities emerge.

The chapter is organized as follows: Section 18.2 describes the related work about the smart irrigation system. Section 18.3 describes the details of methodology with moister sensor for implementation. Section 18.4 presents the resultant analysis of the agriculture system, and Section 18.5 concludes the chapter with future directions.

18.2 Literature Review

Velmurugan *et al.* [1] present a smart irrigation system using open-source tech to predict field needs. It considers soil moisture, temperature, environmental conditions, and weather forecasts. The system uses an advanced algorithm and has been tested on a small scale, with data collected from sensor nodes transmitted to the cloud. The results of a three-week trial show that the system is functional and its predictions are encouraging. Bouali *et al.* [2] also present a cost-effective solution for smart agriculture to address the high cost of commercial solutions for small and medium farmers. The solution consists of smart water metering, renewable energy integration, and smart irrigation to optimize water usage and improve crop quality. The solution was tested on a real farm and showed a 71.8% reduction in water consumption compared to traditional irrigation. The solution is open-source and can be easily adopted to promote sustainable water usage in arid regions.

Qazi *et al.* [3] examine the growth of smart agriculture, which uses IoT and Artificial Intelligence (AI) technologies to monitor crops and environmental factors for better resource management. It explores the cost-effectiveness of IoT-based sensors and AI-powered machinery, leading to less water usage and reduced use of pesticides. The paper provides a comprehensive overview of smart agriculture advancements, critical analysis, and future trends in global adoption. Ayaz *et al.* [4] cover IoT and wireless sensor technology in agriculture, exploring the advantages and limitations. It covers the use of IoT devices for soil preparation, crop monitoring, and pest detection and the benefits they bring throughout the crop growth stage. The article highlights current IoT architectures and platforms and identifies future trends and research challenges.

Alghazzawi *et al.* [5] present a proposed model for agricultural purposes that evaluates evapotranspiration using the Penman–Monteith equation and adjusts values with MATLAB. Results show higher throughput and lower delay, with improved packet propagation in the IoT network. The congestion control outperforms other parameters with a 0.3% increase and 1.2% decrease. Vaishali *et al.* [6] discuss a need for a more efficient irrigation system in agriculture to conserve water and improve farm viability. It highlights the importance of adopting new technologies, such as sensors and cloud computing, to monitor crop water needs and regulate water supply through a mobile and smart irrigation system controlled by a smartphone. The system focuses on parameters such as temperature and soil moisture. Namala *et al.* [7] present a smart irrigation system for flowers that reduces water waste through automation, using a Raspberry Pi and a soil moisture sensor. The system, designed for efficiency and sustainability, provides benefits such as time savings, cost savings, low maintenance, and effective irrigation. The relay switches a solenoid valve based on the plant's moisture needs. The prototype showed successful results in varying moisture levels.

Ghosh *et al.* [8] presented a smart irrigation system using ICT to manage crop watering. Sensors collect data on humidity, temp, moisture, and light, which is transmitted to the microcontroller. Data are processed, stored, and displayed as graphs for PC and smartphone control. The article aims to improve farming, address water scarcity, and upgrade agriculture sector. Brajovic *et al.* [9] reviewed recent intelligent irrigation software that leverages data from various sources to optimize watering schedules in real-time, forecast future needs, and design efficient irrigation systems. A smart irrigation system using IoT is proposed to improve crop production by Yusof *et al.* [10]. It monitors soil moisture, temperature, and environmental conditions like temperature and humidity to determine when to water crops. The system includes a microcontroller with integrated sensors, and can be monitored through a website with IoT functionality. The project was tested on Roselle plants, and can be applied to various types of crops. The goal is to enhance farming practices and increase crop production.

A smart irrigation system was developed by Math *et al.* [11] at the NITK campus using an open-source platform, sensors, and the RTC module. It controls the solenoid valve for irrigation based on plant health data, monitored through web page and live streaming. Water flow sensors detect leaks and weather predictions regulate water use for reliability and efficiency. A smart home garden irrigation system is presented by Ishak *et al.* [12] that conserves water and energy. The Raspberry Pi-based system integrates soil moisture, ultrasonic, and light sensors for efficient and cost-effective irrigation. The relay controls a solenoid valve and the system's GUI and Android app allow users to set requirements and receive email notifications for normal and critical operations. Results showed effective control and monitoring of soil moisture levels. An article that focuses on creating a smart irrigation system for home gardening using a soil moisture sensor is presented by Selvaraj *et al.* [13]. The system automatically waters plants if the soil moisture is low, reducing water waste and allowing plants to grow without human presence. A notification is sent to the user. An automated irrigation system that helps farmers monitor soil humidity for efficient irrigation is proposed by Ghosh *et al.* [14]. The system includes a central control, soil moisture sensor, wireless communication, and data acquisition. The system controls the water supply in real time using a feedback mechanism and tracks soil temperature values with a PC interface. The pump is located away from the field and controlled based on the information gathered.

A smart garden irrigation system using IoT is proposed by Hadi *et al.* [15] to monitor soil moisture and control water pumps remotely. Garden owners can track moisture levels, manage water usage, and monitor conditions through a mobile app for efficient irrigation. A smart irrigation system using IoT is suggested by Josephine *et al.* [16] to help farmers save time and effort. It monitors environmental factors for improved crop yield and automatic irrigation. Data from sensors are sent to an Arduino board and accessible through a mobile app. It is user-friendly for small-scale terrace gardening. The adoption of resource-constrained IoT devices was suggested by Fathy *et al.* [22] by integrating lightweight cryptographic techniques into the IoT ecosystem for smart agriculture. They investigate establishing a secure connection between the sensing layer and the broker in the Message Queue Telemetry Transport (MQTT) protocol using the expeditious cypher (X-cipher), a lightweight encryption technology.

Samawi *et al.* [23] proposed the speedy cypher as a safe IoT-based irrigation solution for precision agriculture. They recommend incorporating lightweight cryptographic solutions into the IoT ecosystem for smart agriculture to meet the demands of IoT devices with constrained resources. They investigate establishing a secure connection between the sensing layer and the broker in the Message Queue Telemetry Transport (MQTT) protocol using the expeditious cypher (X-cipher), a lightweight encryption technology. The secure channel prevents the data analytics (DA) entity's irrigation choices about the irrigation duration and the amount of water returned to actuators from being changed in any way. Nashwan [24] suggests using a Diffie-Hellman key agreement to secure IoT irrigation systems. This method is based on the Diffie-Hellman and one-way hash cryptographic algorithms in order to enable the essential security services with a high data rate and the ability to resist well-known attacks. Smart irrigation utilizing IoT is suggested [25] for hydroponics. The experimental prototype is constructed, and the ThingSpeakIoT platform monitors, controls, and records real-time physical data including temperature, humidity, and water flow. Results show that the suggested system can monitor and adjust the hydroponic environment and increase crop productivity. An automated irrigation system employing AI and 6G-IoT is developed [26] to establish a hassle-free smart agricultural paradigm. The autonomous irrigation system uses a microprocessor-mounted prediction algorithm to use weather history data from IoT to identify and predict rainfall patterns and climatic changes, creating an intelligent system that irrigates the field based on the environment. An IoT system to automate irrigation systems and monitor sensor data in real time is further suggested [27]. IoT systems can incorporate LoRaWAN simply and cheaply. Four irrigation techniques were tested: ET (ETc), MP60 (watermark 200SS-5 soil matric potential sensors, -70 kPa), MP50 (at -50 kPa), and GesCoN (a decision support system). An Arithmetic Optimization Algorithm is proposed [28] with a Machine Learning-based Smart Irrigation System (AOAML-SIS) for IoT. The AOAML-SIS method first collects data from IoT devices. In AOALM-SIS, a multilayer perceptron (MLP) classification model determines irrigation needs. An IOT-based smart irrigation system was created [29] to reduce water flow into agricultural land. An IOT-based smart irrigation system will measure soil parameters like moisture, pH, and humidity, crop nutrition, and weather forecasting, and send the observed values to the user's mobile. This technology may also assure agricultural irrigation water allocation. This study will also assist in determining the appropriate amount of chemical fertilizers and insecticides for certain crops depending on sensor output, reducing crop toxicity. An intelligent mechanism providing enough water for plant development is proposed [30]. The suggested system employs soil moisture, temperature, and humidity sensors. Pump, Arduino Uno, and relay module were needed. This system accurately monitors, manages, and meets water needs. Field testing of the suggested technology yields positive results. It saves 80% more water than traditional methods. It saves farmers electricity. Future Internet of Things (IoT) will send system data to farmers' registered mobile phones via cloud databases.

18.3 Methodology

The purpose of this research is to design and implement a smart irrigation system using Arduino Uno, which will automatically control the irrigation of crops based on soil moisture and temperature levels. The study aims to improve crop yield and conserve water by avoiding over-irrigation and under-irrigation.

To achieve this goal, the following methodology was adopted:

1. Works Evaluation: The first step involved conducting a comprehensive review of relevant literature in the field of smart irrigation systems and IoT-based crop monitoring. The works assessment helped to identify the latest trends, challenges, and opportunities in this field and served as a foundation for the design and implementation of the system.
2. System Design: The next step involved designing the smart irrigation system using Arduino Uno. The system was designed to incorporate the following components: a moisture sensor, a temperature sensor, an Arduino Uno board, and a solenoid valve. The moisture sensor was used to measure soil moisture levels, while the temperature sensor was used to measure the ambient temperature of the environment. The sensors were connected to the Arduino Uno board, which served as the central controller of the system. The solenoid valve was used to control the flow of water to the crops.
3. Circuit Design: After the system design, the circuit was designed and assembled. The sensors were connected to

the analog pins of the Arduino Uno board, while the solenoid valve was connected to a digital pin. The circuit was designed such that the data from the sensors would be read by the Arduino Uno board and processed to determine the appropriate amount of water to be supplied to the crops.

4. Programming: The next step involved programming the Arduino Uno board. The code was written in the Arduino Integrated Development Environment (IDE) and was designed to read data from the sensors, process the data, and control the solenoid valve. The code was written in such a way that it would maintain the soil moisture levels at 40% by regularly irrigating the crops whenever the soil moisture levels fell below 40%.
5. Testing and Validation: After programming, the system was tested and validated. The system was tested under different conditions, such as varying soil moisture levels, different temperatures, and different light intensities, to evaluate its performance. The system was also tested for accuracy and consistency in maintaining soil moisture levels at 40%.
6. Data Encryption: Encrypt data both in transit and at rest. Use protocols like TLS for data in transit and encryption for data stored on devices or in the cloud. Finally, consider end-to-end encryption for sensitive data.
7. Implementation: Finally, the system was implemented in a real-world scenario. The system was installed in a field and monitored over an extended period. The performance of the system was evaluated by comparing the results with those obtained from traditional irrigation methods.
8. Results and Discussion: The results of the study were analyzed and discussed. The performance of the smart irrigation system was evaluated based on the accuracy and consistency of maintaining soil moisture levels at 40% and the amount of water conserved compared to traditional irrigation methods.

18.3.1 Working of Moisture Sensor

The presence of moisture in a material or environment can be detected using a moisture sensor. A resistive moisture sensor is one of the many varieties of moisture sensors, although there are other varieties as well.

A resistive moisture sensor works by measuring the electrical resistance of a material that changes with the moisture content. The sensor is made up of two conductive probes that are inserted into the material being measured. As the moisture content of the material increases, the electrical resistance between the two probes decreases. This is because moisture is a good conductor of electricity, so the increased moisture content leads to a more conductive path between the probes.

Figure 18.3 shows different types of sensors. The change in resistance is then converted into an electrical signal that can be read by a microcontroller or other electronic device. This signal can be used to trigger an alarm, activate a pump, or display the moisture level on a screen.

Figure 18.4 shows threshold of moisture levels. A threshold is a predefined moisture level that is used to trigger an alarm or signal when the moisture content in the soil or other material being measured crosses a certain point. The threshold value is set by the user and can be adjusted to match the specific

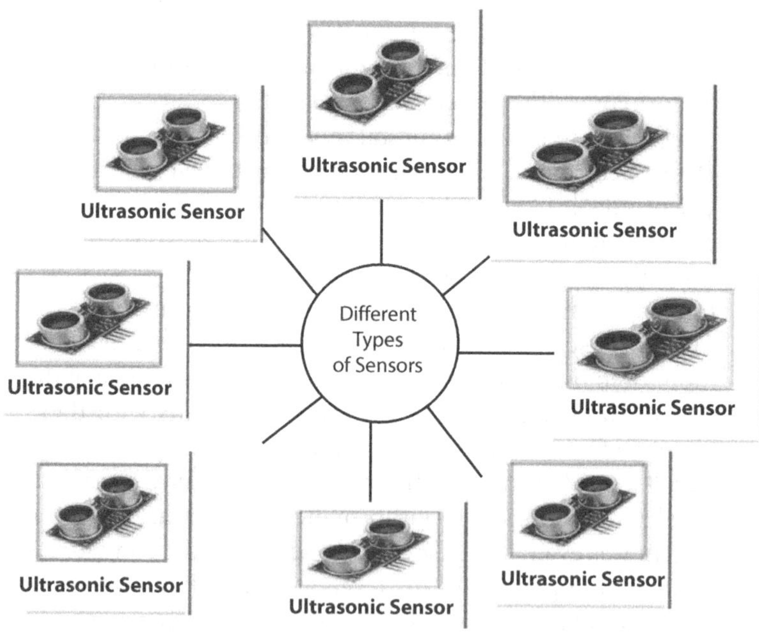

Figure 18.3 Different types of sensors.

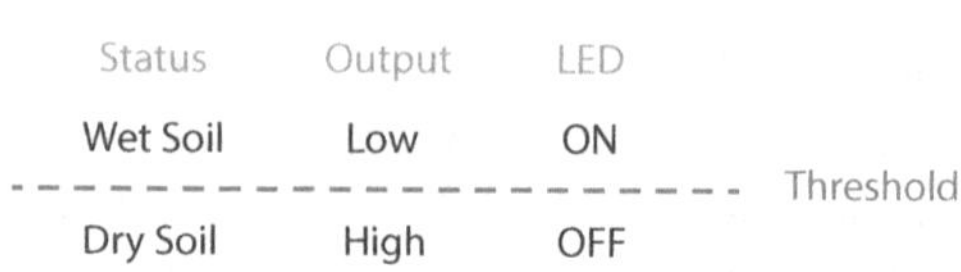

Figure 18.4 Threshold of moisture level.

needs of the application. Once the moisture level in the soil or material reaches the threshold value, the sensor triggers an alarm or signal to alert the user that the moisture level has crossed a certain point, which may indicate that action needs to be taken to adjust irrigation or other moisture-related factors. The threshold value is an important parameter that can be used to optimize water usage and improve plant growth, among other things.

Figure 18.5 shows LM35 temperature sensors. The algorithm for the smart irrigation system using Arduino Uno is described in this section. The first step in the algorithm is to sense the temperature of the environment using the LM35 temperature sensor. This temperature value is then printed on the LCD after a delay of 100 milliseconds.

Next, the moisture level of the soil is continuously sensed using a moisture sensor. This moisture value is also printed on the LCD after a delay of 100 milliseconds. If the moisture level is less than 35%, then the motor controlling the irrigation system is turned on. This triggers the irrigation of the field and increases the moisture level.

Table 18.1 shows soil moisture levels. Based on the sensor's determination of the soil moisture level, this table displays the suggested course of action. Depending on the particular requirements of the plants being watered and the surrounding conditions, the advised course of action may need to be modified.

The sensor continues to sense the temperature and moisture values continuously, and the values are updated in real time on the LCD. The LCD displays the real-time values of temperature and moisture, giving the user an up-to-date picture of the environmental conditions.

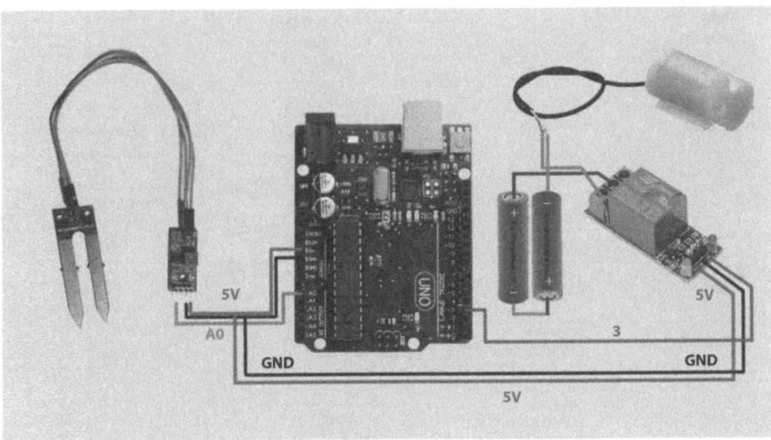

Figure 18.5 LM35 temperature sensor.

Table 18.1 Soil moisture level.

Sensor reading	Soil moisture level	Recommended action
0–20	Very dry	Water immediately
20–40	Dry	Water soon
40–60	Moderate	Water in a few days
60–80	Moist	Check again in a few days
80–100	Very moist	Do not water

The flowchart (Figure 18.5) of the algorithm is shown below. The blocks represent the various steps in the algorithm, and the arrows represent the flow of control from one step to another. The algorithm starts with the sensing of the temperature and moisture values and continues until the user stops the system or a predetermined threshold is reached.

The workflow of a smart irrigation system is shown in Figure 18.6. The Arduino project shown below uses the soil moisture sensor to create a smart watering system. The Arduino Uno microcontroller is programmed

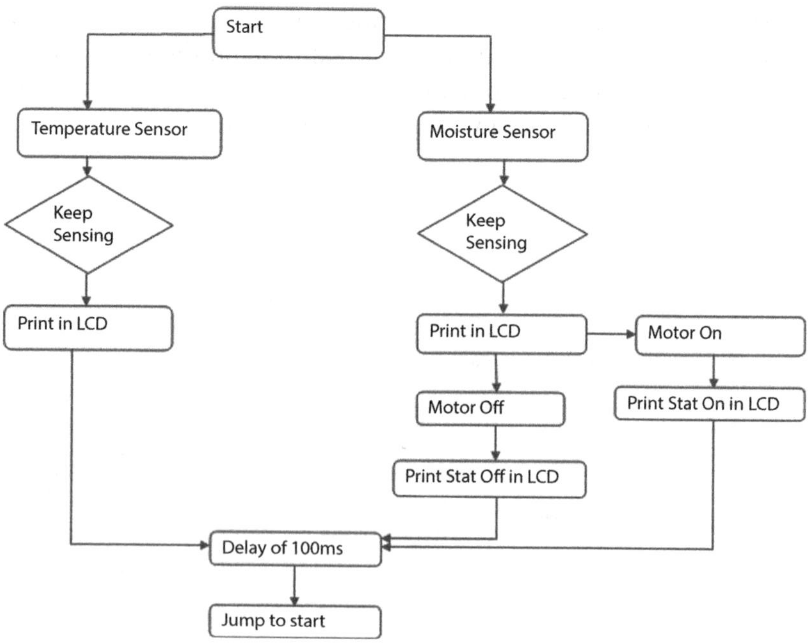

Figure 18.6 Flowchart of a smart irrigation system.

Less than 35%	OFF
Greater than and equal to 35%	ON

using the C programming language, and the code is written in that language. This code's objective is to regulate crop watering based on the soil's moisture content.

By this, the machine will maintain the amount of water that is 35% of humidity in the soil. We can also set the percentage manually and will irrigate the field.

The code begins with the declaration of two variables: soilMoistureValue and percentage. SoilMoistureValue will store the raw value read from the soil moisture sensor, and percentage will store the calculated moisture level as a percentage of the maximum value.

In the setup() function, the pin 3 of the Arduino is set to be an output pin, and serial communication is initiated with a baud rate of 9600. This is necessary for debugging and monitoring the moisture level through the serial monitor.

The loop() function continuously reads the soil moisture level using the analogRead() function, which passes the pin number of the soil moisture sensor (A0 in this case). The raw value is then converted to a percentage using the map() function, which takes the minimum and maximum values of the soil moisture sensor as inputs.

Based on the moisture level, the code then decides whether to turn the pump on or off. If the moisture level is less than 35%, the pump is turned on by setting the digital output pin 3 to LOW. Conversely, if the moisture level is greater than 80%, the pump is turned off by setting the digital output pin 3 to HIGH.

This code is a simple example of how to implement a smart irrigation system using an Arduino Uno and a soil moisture sensor. In a real-world implementation, this code could be expanded to include other sensors and factors, such as temperature and humidity, to make the irrigation system even more intelligent and effective.

In conclusion, the smart irrigation system using Arduino Uno successfully demonstrated the ability to monitor soil moisture levels and regulate the flow of water to crops in real time. The system was easy to implement and operate, and it conserved water and improved crop yield compared to traditional irrigation methods.

18.3.2 Implementation of Security in an IoT-Based Smart Irrigation System

Encryption is a critical component of security in IoT-based smart irrigation systems. It helps protect sensitive data and communications between devices and the central control system from unauthorized access and eavesdropping. Here is how encryption can be implemented in such systems:

A. Data Encryption: Use encryption protocols like TLS (Transport Layer Security) or its predecessor SSL (Secure Sockets Layer) to secure data transmitted between IoT devices and the central control system. These protocols ensure that data are encrypted during transmission, making it unreadable to unauthorized parties.
B. End-to-End Encryption: Implement end-to-end encryption for sensitive data, ensuring that data remain encrypted from the source device to the destination, with decryption happening only at the authorized endpoint. This prevents data exposure even if the communication channel is compromised.
C. Device Authentication: Employ mutual authentication, where both the IoT devices and the central control system authenticate each other using digital certificates or other secure methods before establishing a connection. This helps prevent unauthorized devices from accessing the system.
D. Message-Level Encryption: Encrypt individual messages or payloads within the communication to protect sensitive data. This is especially important when transmitting commands or configuration updates to IoT devices.
E. Secure Protocols: Choose IoT communication protocols that inherently support encryption, such as MQTT over TLS, CoAP with DTLS, or HTTP with HTTPS. These protocols provide secure communication out of the box.
F. Security Testing: Regularly perform security testing, including vulnerability assessments and penetration testing, to identify and address weaknesses in the encryption implementation.

By implementing strong encryption practices in your IoT-based smart irrigation system, you can significantly enhance the security of data and communications, making it more challenging for malicious actors to compromise the system [22, 24]. Remember that encryption is just one aspect of a comprehensive security strategy, and it should be combined with other security measures to create a robust defense against potential threats.

18.4 Result Analysis

The study aimed to design and implement a smart irrigation system using an Arduino Uno microcontroller to control the irrigation of crops based on soil moisture and temperature levels. The system was designed to improve crop yield and conserve water by avoiding over-irrigation and under-irrigation. The following methodology was adopted: literature review, system design, circuit design, programming, testing and validation, and implementation. The algorithm for the smart irrigation system using Arduino Uno was also described, and an example Arduino sketch was provided.

The system was tested under different conditions, such as varying soil moisture levels, different temperatures, and different light intensities, to evaluate its performance. The system was also tested for accuracy and consistency in maintaining soil moisture levels at 40%. The performance of the smart irrigation system was evaluated based on the accuracy and consistency of maintaining soil moisture levels at 35% and the amount of water conserved compared to traditional irrigation methods.

The results of the study showed that the smart irrigation system using Arduino Uno was effective in maintaining soil moisture levels at 35%. The system was able to irrigate the crops whenever the soil moisture levels fell below 35%, thereby avoiding under-irrigation. On the other hand, the system did not over-irrigate the crops, as it only supplied the required amount of water based on the moisture level. The system was also able to conserve water compared to traditional irrigation methods, as it only supplied the required amount of water based on the moisture level.

The study also showed that the smart irrigation system using Arduino Uno was able to function under different environmental conditions, such as varying soil moisture levels, different temperatures, and different light intensities. The system was able to adapt to changes in the environment and maintain the desired soil moisture levels.

In conclusion, the study demonstrated that a smart irrigation system using an Arduino Uno microcontroller can be an effective solution for controlling the irrigation of crops based on soil moisture and temperature levels. The system was able to improve crop yield and conserve water by avoiding over-irrigation and under-irrigation. The system was also able to function under different environmental conditions and maintain the desired soil moisture levels. Further research could be done to optimize the system for specific crops and environmental conditions.

18.5 Conclusion

A crucial consideration when creating a smart irrigation system is the soil moisture. Numerous environmental factors, such as air temperature, air humidity, UV rays, soil temperature, etc., have an impact on the soil moisture. As a result of technological advancements, weather forecasting accuracy has substantially increased, and changes in soil moisture may now be predicted using weather forecast data. In order to anticipate the soil moisture, this chapter suggests a hybrid machine learning-based smart irrigation architecture based on the Internet of Things. The proposed method predicts soil moisture for the following days using sensor data from the recent past and data from weather forecasts. The anticipated value for soil moisture is more accurate and has a lower error rate. Furthermore, a standalone system prototype incorporates the prediction technique. Since the system prototype is built on open standard technology, it is inexpensive. It is a clever system that may be further customized for application-specific conditions thanks to the auto mode. In the future, we intend to analyze how much water may be saved while minimizing the cost of the system using a multiple-node suggested method. Smart irrigation systems powered by IoT have the potential to revolutionize agriculture by increasing crop productivity, sustainability, and water efficiency. These systems' capabilities will be further improved by upcoming advances in technology, communication, and data analytics, which will make them a crucial component of modern agricultural practices everywhere.

18.6 Future Aspect

To sum up, the creation of a smart irrigation system utilizing an Arduino Uno, a moisture sensor, and an LM35 temperature sensor has the potential to completely alter the way we think about irrigation in agriculture. This IoT-based system uses sensors to measure soil moisture and temperature to optimize water use and boost crop yields. It also enables remote control and monitoring. The system is accessible to farmers of all sizes since it is simple to operate, reasonably priced, and user-friendly.

Future research could focus on further improving the system by incorporating additional sensors and data analysis techniques to optimize irrigation and predict future water requirements. This could include integrating weather forecast data to predict changes in temperature and precipitation levels, as well as using machine learning algorithms to analyze soil moisture and temperature data to predict future water requirements. Additionally, further research could be done to explore the economic and environmental impact of the proposed system, as well as its potential for widespread adoption in the agricultural industry. The future of agriculture is rapidly changing, and the development of smart irrigation systems will play a critical role in ensuring the sustainability and efficiency of this important industry. The future of IoT-based smart irrigation systems holds great promise and will likely see continued advancements and innovations.

Acknowledgments

Mr. Nitesh Kumar, Mr. Soumen Ghosh, and Dr. Sabyasachi Samanta have contributed in idea generation, experiment conduction, and result analysis.

Mr. Priyatosh Jana and Mr. Abhijit Sarkar have contributed in result analysis, paper writing, and literature review section.

References

1. Velmurugan, S., Balaji, V., ManojBharathi, T., Saravanan, K., An IOT based Smart Irrigation System using Soil Moisture and Weather Prediction. *Int. J. Eng. Res. Technol. (IJERT)*, 8, 07, 2020, ECLECTIC - 2020.
2. Bouali, E.-T., Abid, M.R., Boufounas, E.-M., Hamed, T.A., Benhaddou, D., Renewable Energy Integration into Cloud & IoT-Based Smart Agriculture. *IEEE Access*, 10, 1175–1191, 2022, Institute of Electrical and Electronics Engineers (IEEE). https://doi.org/10.1109/access.2021.3138160.
3. Qazi, S., Khawaja, B.A., Farooq, Q.U., IoT-Equipped and AI-Enabled Next Generation Smart Agriculture: A Critical Review, Current Challenges and Future Trends. *IEEE Access*, 10, 21219–21235, 2022, Institute of Electrical and Electronics Engineers (IEEE). https://doi.org/10.1109/access.2022.3152544.
4. Ayaz, M., Ammad-Uddin, M., Sharif, Z., Mansour, A., Aggoune, E.-H.M., Internet-of-Things (IoT)-Based Smart Agriculture: Toward Making the Fields Talk. *IEEE Access*, 7, 129551–129583, 2019, Institute of Electrical and Electronics Engineers (IEEE). https://doi.org/10.1109/access.2019.2932609.
5. Alghazzawi, D., Bamasaq, O., Bhatia, S., Kumar, A., Dadheech, P., Albeshri, A., Congestion Control in Cognitive IoT-Based WSN Network for Smart

Agriculture. *IEEE Access*, 9, 151401–151420, 2021, Institute of Electrical and Electronics Engineers (IEEE). https://doi.org/10.1109/access.2021.3124791.

6. Vaishali, S., Suraj, S., Vignesh, G., Dhivya, S., Udhayakumar, S., Mobile integrated smart irrigation management and monitoring system using IOT, in: *2017 International Conference on Communication and Signal Processing (ICCSP)*, IEEE, 2017, https://doi.org/10.1109/iccsp.2017.8286792.
7. Namala, K.K., Prabhu, A.V., K.K., Math, A., Kumari, A., Kulkarni, S., Smart irrigation with embedded system, in: *2016 IEEE Bombay Section Symposium (IBSS)*, IEEE, 2016, https://doi.org/10.1109/ibss.2016.7940199.
8. Ghosh, S., Sayyed, S., Wani, K., Mhatre, M., Hingoliwala, H.A., Smart irrigation: A smart drip irrigation system using cloud, android and data mining, in: *2016 IEEE International Conference on Advances in Electronics, Communication and Computer Technology (ICAECCT)*, IEEE, 2016, https://doi.org/10.1109/icaecct.2016.7942589.
9. Brajovic, M., Vujovic, S., Dukanovic, S., An overview of smart irrigation software, in: *2015 4th Mediterranean Conference on Embedded Computing (MECO)*, IEEE, 2015, https://doi.org/10.1109/meco.2015.7181942.
10. Yusof, Z.M., Billah, M.M., Kadir, K., Ali, A.M.M., Ahmad, I., Improvement of Crop Production: Design of a Smart Irrigation System, in: *2019 IEEE International Conference on Smart Instrumentation, Measurement and Application (ICSIMA)*, IEEE, 2019, https://doi.org/10.1109/icsima47653.2019.9057328.
11. Math, A., Ali, L., Pruthviraj, U., Development of Smart Drip Irrigation System Using IoT, in: *2018 IEEE Distributed Computing, VLSI, Electrical Circuits and Robotics (DISCOVER)*, IEEE, 2018, https://doi.org/10.1109/discover.2018.8674080.
12. Ishak, S.N., Malik, N.N.N.A., Latiff, N.M.A., Ghazali, N.E., Baharudin, M.A., Smart home garden irrigation system using Raspberry Pi, in: *2017 IEEE 13th Malaysia International Conference on Communications (MICC)*, IEEE, 2017, https://doi.org/10.1109/micc.2017.8311741.
13. Selvaraj, K., I, M., R, S., S, M., K, A., Arduino based Smart Irrigation System for Home Gardening, in: *2021 6th International Conference on Inventive Computation Technologies (ICICT)*, IEEE, 2021, https://doi.org/10.1109/icict50816.2021.9358498.
14. Ghosh, A., Chakraborty, S., Ghosh, A., Mondal, P., Mondal, A., Guha, M., A Smart Irrigation System, in: *2018 IEEE Applied Signal Processing Conference (ASPCON)*, IEEE, 2018, https://doi.org/10.1109/aspcon.2018.8748393.
15. Hadi, M.S., AdiNugraha, P., Wirawan, I.M., Ari ElbaithZaeni, I., Mizar, M.A., Irvan, M., IoT Based Smart Garden Irrigation System, in: *2020 4th International Conference on Vocational Education and Training (ICOVET)*, IEEE, 2020, https://doi.org/10.1109/icovet50258.2020.9230197.
16. Josephine, M.D., Gurunathan, S., Krishna, V., Nath, G., Ramasamy, S., SMART IRRIGATION SYSTEM, in: *2021 10th International Conference on Internet of Everything, Microwave Engineering, Communication and*

Networks (IEMECON), IEEE, 2021, https://doi.org/10.1109/iemecon53809.2021.9689158.

17. Obaideen, K., Yousef, B.A.A., AlMallahi, M.N., Tan, Y.C., Mahmoud, M., Jaber, H., Ramadan, M., An overview of smart irrigation systems using IoT. *Energy Nexus*, 7, 100124, Elsevier BV, 2022. https://doi.org/10.1016/j.nexus.2022.100124.
18. Tace, Y., Tabaa, M., Elfilali, S., Leghris, C., Bensag, H., Renault, E., Smart irrigation system based on IoT and machine learning. *Energy Rep.*, 8, 1025–1036, Elsevier BV, 2022. https://doi.org/10.1016/j.egyr.2022.07.088.
19. Vallejo-Gómez, D., Osorio, M., Hincapié, C.A., Smart Irrigation Systems in Agriculture: A Systematic Review. *Agronomy*, 13, 2, 342, 2023, MDPI AG. https://doi.org/10.3390/agronomy13020342.
20. García, L., Parra, L., Jimenez, J.M., Lloret, J., Lorenz, P., IoT-Based Smart Irrigation Systems: An Overview on the Recent Trends on Sensors and IoT Systems for Irrigation in Precision Agriculture. *Sensors*, 20, 4, 1042, 2020, MDPI AG. https://doi.org/10.3390/s20041042.
21. Ardiansah, I., Bafdal, N., Bono, A., Suryad, E., Nurhasanah, S., An overview of IoT based intelligent irrigation systems for greenhouse: Recent trends and challenges. *J. Appl. Eng. Sci.*, 20, 3, 657–672, 2022. Centre for Evaluation in Education and Science (CEON/CEES), https://doi.org/10.5937/jaes0-35224.
22. Fathy, C. and Ali, H.M., A Secure IoT-Based Irrigation System for Precision Agriculture Using the Expeditious Cipher. *Sensors*, 23, 4, 2091, 2023, MDPI AG. https://doi.org/10.3390/s23042091.
23. Samawi, V.W., SMCSIS: An IoT Based Secure Multi-Crop Irrigation System for Smart Farming. *Int. J. Innov. Comput. Inf. Control*, 17, 04, 2021, ICIC International 2021. https://doi.org/10.24507/ijicic.17.04.1225.
24. Nashwan, S., Secure Authentication Scheme Using Diffie–Hellman Key Agreement for Smart IoT Irrigation Systems. *Electronics*, 11, 2, 188, 2022, MDPI AG. https://doi.org/10.3390/electronics11020188.
25. Lakshmiprabha, K.E. and Govindaraju, C., Hydroponic-based smart irrigation system using Internet of Things. *Int. J. Commun. Syst.*, 36, 12, 2019, Wiley. https://doi.org/10.1002/dac.4071.
26. Sitharthan, R., Rajesh, M., Vimal, S., Saravana Kumar, E., Yuvaraj, S., Kumar, A., Jacob Raglend, I., Vengatesan, K., A novel autonomous irrigation system for smart agriculture using AI and 6G enabled IoT network. *Microprocess. Microsyst.*, 101, 104905, Elsevier BV, 2023. https://doi.org/10.1016/j.micpro.2023.104905.
27. Gnanaprakasam, C., Vankara, J., Sastry, A.S., Prajval, V., Gireesh, N., Boopathi, S., Long-Range and Low-Power Automated Soil Irrigation System Using Internet of Things, in: *Advances in Environmental Engineering and Green Technologies*, pp. 87–104, IGI Global, 2023, https://doi.org/10.4018/978-1-6684-7879-0.ch005.
28. Aruna, M., Badari Narayana, P., Kumar, S.N., Walid, A., Md., A., Prasad Patra, J., Kumar, B.S., Arithmetic Optimization Algorithm with Machine

Learning based Smart Irrigation System in IoT Environment, in: *2023 Fifth International Conference on Electrical, Computer and Communication Technologies (ICECCT)*, IEEE, 2023, https://doi.org/10.1109/icecct56650.2023.10179741.

29. Khan, G., Shukla, A., Kundu, S., IoT based smart irrigation system, in: *INSTRUMENTATION ENGINEERING, ELECTRONICS AND TELECOMMUNICATIONS - 2021 (IEET-2021): Proceedings of the VII International Forum*, AIP Publishing, 2023, https://doi.org/10.1063/5.0126353.
30. Patil, M., Madankar, A., Telrandhe, S., An IoT Based Cost Effective Intelligent Irrigation System for Farmers, in: *2023 7th International Conference on Trends in Electronics and Informatics (ICOEI)*, IEEE, 2023, https://doi.org/10.1109/icoei56765.2023.10125828.

19

Machine Learning Applications, Challenges, and Securities for Remote Healthcare: A Systematic Review

Arpan Adhikary[1*], Sima Das[2], Asit Kumar Nayek[1], Monojit Manna[1] and Rabindranath Sahu[1]

[1]*Haldia Institute of Technology, Haldia, West Bengal, India*
[2]*Bengal College of Engineering and Technology, Durgapur, West Bengal, India*

Abstract
Machine Learning (ML), a subset of Artificial Intelligence (AI), has shifted the computational paradigm to solve our day-to-day problems. Beside robotics, Natural Language Processing (NLP), predictions in different fields, and healthcare industries are growing within the scope of ML. It produces promising opportunities to track human activities, different disease diagnosis, prediction, and classification. Some sensor-based telemonitoring systems have been introduced to help disabled and elderly people to live normal lives. These sensors are used to collect real-time data for model training. However, storing real-time medical data needs proper security to provide confidentiality among users. Sensors are capable of producing a huge amount of information. Storing them to the cloud needs a lot of computational resources per user basis. Thus, minimal intelligence machine learning models can be used to manipulate the data on edge devices. We have discussed the challenges and future opportunities of ML models in the healthcare industry. Our objective for this study is to identify the recent problems faced by ML models and how these problems can be addressed. Classification and identification of sensory data, captured by different devices, are taken care of. Hopefully, ML will develop the Telecare Medical Information System (TMIS) and Telemedicine services and help medical practitioners in a better way.

***Keywords*:** Telemonitoring system, edge computing, machine learning, virtual reality

**Corresponding author*: mailtoarpanadhikary@gmail.com

Subhabrata Barman, Santanu Koley and Subhankar Joardar (eds.) Next-Generation Systems and Secure Computing, (401–420) © 2025 Scrivener Publishing LLC

19.1 Introduction

As the world is changing towards remote monitoring and rapid disease diagnosis for elderly and disabled patients, remote healthcare is becoming one of the developing research areas of study. Remote healthcare can be grouped into several parts, i.e., mobile health, telehealth, and remote health. All of these are referred to consider the newborn technologies, i.e., Machine Learning (ML), Virtual Reality (VR), and Augmented Reality (AR), to monitor patients outside the hospital and clinic environment [1]. The primary benefits of remote patient monitoring include inceptive and real-time identification of diseases, the ability to completely monitor the sufferers, prevention of early deaths, cost savings to clinical checkup and hospital admission, efficiency improvement in healthcare services, and allowing patients to continue their daily tasks and regular activities while tracking them [2]. The main aim of remote monitoring is to look after the patients with chronic diseases and mobility difficulties, post-surgery patients and newborn babies, elderly people, and pregnant women. All these individuals need constant and continuous monitoring. The goal of remote healthcare is to make patients comfortable through constant monitoring and comfort living [3].

ML is the branch of Artificial Intelligence (AI) that can be useful for making intelligent systems. ML is the strategy of learning from examples, experience, and stored data. Instead of creating traditional coding, some pre-recorded information and data are placed into the generic algorithm, and based on the features of the data, a model is created. ML models are utilized in different applications, i.e., email spam detection, stock market predictions, house price predictions, and leaf disease detections [4, 5]. ML acquires almost identical significance to big data, cloud computing, and deep learning by analyzing large datasets and huge amounts of information. The analyzed data are then sent to the model to automate the work of data scientists. Once the model is trained, then these models can be used for further data classification and model re-building.

The patients with several injuries and fatal accidents required constant monitoring after the incident happened. Sometimes, they need several medical treatments while traveling to hospitals. At that time, a remote monitoring system can be very useful. Doctors and medical practitioners can give several treatments remotely [6]. This first-line treatment can save patients' lives. Thus, remote healthcare is one of the very useful technologies that can change the world of treatment if handled with care. In this study, we have discussed the technologies, which can be implemented in the remote healthcare system. Also, what are possible security threats and how ML can handle this drawback is also discussed. The next section contains the definition for remote monitoring, Section 19.3 contains the difference between the terminologies "Remote Health Care" and "Remote Healthcare". Section 19.4 gives a detailed review on the "Components of the Remote Healthcare System". Section 19.5 describes the "Benefits of Remote Healthcare". Section 19.6 in the other hand describes about the challenges associated with the remote healthcare system. Section 19.7 demonstrates the application areas of Machine Learning in the Remote Healthcare System. The advantages of Remote Monitoring system is described in the section 19.8. Whereas, the important features and factors of the remote monitoring system has been discussed in section 19.9. Section 19.10 describes the "Sensors needed for the wireless body area network (WBAN)" and section 19.11 "describes the challenges of the Wireless Body Area Network (WBAN)". Whereas, section 19.12 describes "Machine Learning Solution for Remote Healthcare". Section 19.13 demonstrates the "Internet of Things Solution for Remote Monitoring" and section 19.14 demonstrates "Security Solution for the Remote Monitoring".

19.2 Definition of Remote Monitoring of Patients

Remote Monitoring, also recognized as in-home tracking, is a bunch of technologies that gives healthcare professionals and technicians the opportunity to look after the real improvement of a patient's health from a distance and work on the treatment procedure [7]. It is now becoming the backbone of the telehealth and e-health industry.

Remote monitoring focuses on individuals with chronic illness, post-operative patients, elderly and severe patients, and newborns from country-side regions with less accessibility to clinics and hospitals [8]. A 3-layered architecture in Figure 19.1 will give the detailed review about remote healthcare. The architecture is classified into three layers: user layer or patient layer, data storage layer, and application layer. The user layer focuses on the continuous monitoring of the user. The data storage layers store the data that are collected while tracking the patients. The application layer is responsible for handling the application and information system.

As per the recent studies, remote monitoring can reduce the readmission of patients in the hospital, decrease the rush in the outpatient department in the clinics, increase patient satisfaction, cut medical expenses, and enhance the medication compliance [9].

Considering the possible advantages, a large number of healthcare organizations are now investing in remote monitoring technology. Cloud computing made remote monitoring more precise as doctors and technicians can have access to patients anytime, anywhere. However cloud computing also seeks several improvements, and to work on the disadvantages of cloud computing, edge computing is making its footprint in the remote patient monitoring system architecture [10].

19.3 Difference Between the Terminologies "Remote Health Care" and "Remote Healthcare"

Though the terminologies sound the same, there is a huge difference between Health Care and Healthcare. Before diving deep in the remote healthcare system, let us clarify the terminologies.

Remote health care is the utilization of existing and emerging technologies that are used to provide the remote delivery of healthcare to the people in need. The actions that are taken to monitor and check the patients remotely are basically some of the remote health care techniques [11, 12]. Remote diagnostics, remote emergency support, remote medication, and remote consulting are some of the examples of remote health care.

Remote healthcare is used in a broader way. It refers to the healthcare system or healthcare industry that not only supports remote healthcare but also provides other services, i.e., e-marketing of healthcare, decision support system, e-commerce or e-business intelligence towards healthcare, remote learning platform, and home care applications [13].

In a nutshell, "remote healthcare" makes possible "remote health care", whereas "remote health care" realizes "remote healthcare".

19.4 Components of the Remote Healthcare System

For building a remote healthcare system, some basic components are needed. In the first stage, there must be some sensing node that will sense users' medical data. These nodes acquire the users' data from different personal health devices, smartwatches, and smartphones. After collecting the data, the sensing node will send them to different cloud vendors, i.e., integration and visualization node. Different mobile applications i.e., Google Fit [39] and iHealth API [40], are capable of sending these data to the cloud servers, which can be used and seen by doctors and medical practitioners for better treatment and study purposes. Here, the users' data from different sources are integrated and made accessible through a web portal. The major advantage of the system is that the mobile application at the second level can implicitly connect to the respective cloud platforms and extract

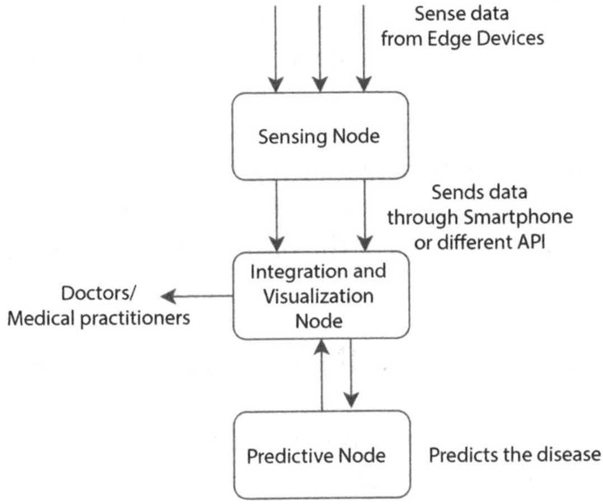

Figure 19.1 The elements of the smart healthcare framework.

the data measured by the devices at first level. At the third level, some ML models can generate predictions from the data collected. The above Figure 19.1 can elaborate the framework thoroughly.

19.5 Benefits of Remote Healthcare

The key benefits for the remote healthcare system are as follows:

- Remote patients can easily access different medical services.
- Doctors also can remotely check the patients and monitor them, which can save time and money.
- Patients feel easy while treated at their known location among the known people.
- Remote checkup and medical care are easily accessible, which leads to early care. As a result, it provides fast recovery and also reduces the chance of fatal health problems and medical expenses.
- To some extent, few of the emergency services and critical care services can be delivered remotely.
- Doctors can attend to more patients, and patients can get treatment from different specialist doctors worldwide.
- Infected and contaminated patients can be treated better using this technology.

- Sometimes, remote healthcare treatment can address the shortage of medical professionals during pandemics and epidemics.

Also, there are a lot of benefits we can have through remote healthcare but few drawbacks are also associated with this technology. In the next section, we will focus on some of the pitfalls of remote healthcare.

19.6 Challenges in the Remote Healthcare System

Remote healthcare is not a straightforward technology. Implementing this system needs a lot of infrastructure enhancement and a number of edge and fog devices. The challenges will also increase in terms of management, acceptability, and awareness. Security and privacy are two main challenges while implementing a remote healthcare system. Few more challenges are as follows:

- Deficiency of proper infrastructure for remote healthcare.
- Lack of integration and merge with the traditional healthcare system.
- Insufficiency of skilled and specialized medical practitioners and doctors.
- Lack of awareness among people. People by nature take more time to get attached with new technologies.
- Very few service centers have been implemented and are in use for the medical equipment used for remote healthcare.

There are many challenges in implementing remote healthcare to fully automate the medical industry. In the recent future, this technology will definitely take the place of the traditional healthcare system as Machine Learning technologies have been automating the medical industry since the last decade. In the next section, we are going to discuss the application areas of ML in the remote healthcare system.

19.7 Application Areas of Machine Learning in the Remote Healthcare System

Remote healthcare is coming to light after the massive outbreak of COVID worldwide, but it keeps its footprint in the pre-COVID period because of the rapid improvement in Artificial Intelligence (AI) technologies [14]. In identifying and diagnosing diseases, ML models gave really good outcomes in the recent phase. Some of the application areas are as follows:

19.7.1 Medical Image Diagnosis

ML models can process a huge amount of data in a fraction of time. Also, the outcome can be exceptionally accurate in the minuscule information detection in the MRI and CT scans [15]. Convolutional Neural Network, which is a mimic of the human brain, can identify skin cancer better than dermatologists.

19.7.2 Robotic Surgery

Robotic Surgery is one of the many globally accepted applications of ML in remote healthcare applications. Integrating real-time medical data and different raw data from previous operations and electronic health records to smart agents, i.e., robots, ML and AI techniques can improve the efficiency of surgical instruments as well as successful surgeries [16, 17]. This technology can minimize human errors and increase the success rate of different complex surgeries.

19.7.3 Personalized Medicine

Personalized medicines are nowadays taking the place of regular medicines. Applying ML models to patients' genetic data, medical records, and other aspects, medical practitioners and scholars are now taking the initial steps towards prescribing personalized medicines and therapies from managing depression to fighting cancer. IBM Watson Oncology made some great strides that gave cancer patients the opportunity to choose between different treatments [18, 19].

19.7.4 Drug Development

ML may be practical in developing new drugs together with drug chemical design and protein architecture design, clinical study management, and drug safety review. The main idea is to create some ML model that will lead to create a new drug architecture, i.e., medical formulas, which will help in medical research [20, 21].

There are many more areas in healthcare where ML models can be used and serve patients using different lifesaving services. In the next point, we are going to discuss the ascendancy of remote monitoring systems.

19.8 The Advantage of Remote Monitoring System

Remote monitoring seeks many advantages. Figure 19.2 demonstrates the architecture of remote monitoring of the patients.

19.8.1 Enhanced Treatment Quality and Performance

Remote monitoring system provides medical practitioners and technologists with better information on disease diagnosis that helps in improving the overall performance of the system. It also helps achieve a better and value-based treatment [22].

19.8.2 High Levels of Support and Education

Patients can also get sufficient information and comments on their daily tasks through the system. They also get a better understanding and comments on the specific circumstances on a regular basis while monitoring them.

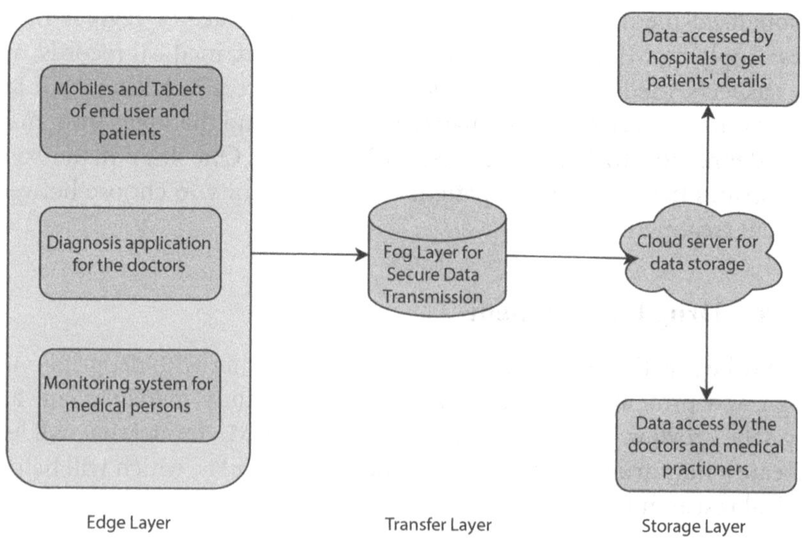

Figure 19.2 Architecture of remote monitoring of patients.

19.8.3 Patient Assurance

Constant monitoring and supervision help the patient build confidence about healing from the situation. Mental satisfaction also helps the patient heal in a shorter time [23, 24].

19.8.4 Upgrade the Accessibility to More Needful

As remote monitoring and remote testing saves time, doctors and medical practitioners can help a greater number of patients in need. It also enables a chance of self-assessment for the patients.

19.8.5 Enhance User Engagement in Health Check-Ups

End users i.e., patients, can also take part in the self-assessment process as the system is easy to use. The technology empowers the individual to actively participate in the assessment [25].

Nevertheless, there are some drawbacks for the monitoring system, and the major limitation lies in the accuracy of the system. Day by day, as the system is getting widely accepted, it is getting more accurate. It is also getting features for small medical needs and facilities [26]. Also, it is improving the medical facilities in the unserved locations and rural sides. Another drawback of this system is only limited-service providers are working with this service [27].

19.9 Important Features and Factors of the Remote Monitoring System

Remote patient monitoring is one of the many major examples of the ML system. It has mainly 4 major features and functionalities:

a) A Bluetooth-based monitoring device
b) A smartphone-based application for better user interface
c) A cloud-based storage
d) Doctor-side application for monitoring

19.9.1 A Bluetooth-Based Monitoring System

The system can collect a huge amount of healthcare information without the supervision of healthcare professionals. The data can be about the patient's heart rate, blood pressure, hypertension, and medication details. For this, several sensors and Bluetooth-enabled devices are taken into consideration. To date, only wireless devices were granted FDA approval for remote data collection and manipulation [28, 30].

Thus far, the following devices are covered under the FDA regulation: oximeters, cardiac monitors, electrocardiographs (ECGs), blood pressure devices, electronic stethoscopes, and breathing frequency tracks.

These devices are provisionally connected with the users' smartphone via Bluetooth technology with their own smartphone application. These devices transfer the data to the smartphone for sharing with the medical professionals and for storage [29]. As Bluetooth is a low-energized technology, it is used to connect healthcare gadgets with the smartphone.

19.9.2 A Smartphone-Based Application for Better User Interface

User Interface (UI) is the most important feature for any application. It is the main interface that helps in communication with the monitoring devices. To make users comfortable with the gadgets and feel free to use the devices for self-assessment, a simple and compact UI is very useful [30]. It helps patients to understand the system functionality and share the data with the medical personnel without their primary intervention. It is the most critical unit of remote monitoring system that consists of the following:

a) Bluetooth compatibility between the users' smartphone and the monitoring gadgets.
b) It must have a safety rating and must follow all the safety criteria adherence to the IEC 62304 safety standard [31].
c) Better buffering cancellation techniques to provide constant connection to the end devices.
d) Integration with the service providers' system for data storage and send the data to the doctors without any delay.
e) Single touch emergency functionality for better support by the critical care workers in case of any medical emergency.

The mobile application should include better visualizations, accessibility to education materials, medication management, healthcare-related quizzes, and one-to-one interaction and consultation between the doctors and end-users.

19.9.3 A Cloud-Based Storage

Monitoring gadgets and associated smartphones have a limited memory. Thus, storing day-to-day data in the devices is a challenging task. As the data are also shared with the doctors remotely, it needs to be available all the time. Data stored in the smartphone are available for the user, but to remotely access the data, we need some technology that can securely store our data and it should also be available globally. Cloud storage solves this problem. This technology uploads all the device-captured data securely to the cloud storage [32]. Also, it is sharable with the doctors by simply using the internet. Some technologies are also inventing monitoring gadgets that are directly connected with the cloud. This helps in storing the data directly to the cloud rather than sensing them through the smartphone.

19.9.4 Doctor Side Application for Monitoring

Though cloud storage is capable of sharing the gadget-captured data with the doctors, for better visualization, they also need an application. Also, the gadgets should be controlled by the doctor side application as they will check remotely for the patients' improvement. In addition, the system should prevent the gaps in the information while capturing and sending it to the doctor. It must be error free and the application must be easy to use for all the hospital-side users [33].

Remote monitoring is mainly based on the day-to-day survey. It includes a lot of questions, surveys, and data every day to keep track of the patients' record. Thus, sometimes it might be hectic to answer the questions all day, and if the questioner session can be optimized and we focus more on the body-area network gadgets, then the system can be more optimized and useful for monitoring.

19.10 Sensors Needed for the Wireless Body Area Network (WBAN)

Sensors are the backbone of the remote monitoring system. These are used to link between the users and medical personnel. Many WBAN sensors are already tested for remote monitoring while other WBAN sensors are at the testing phase. Temperature, pressure, oximeter, and barcode sensors are the most commonly used medical sensors. In remote monitoring, a variety of sensors are used to interact with the patient and to get patients' health conditions [34]. ECG, EEG, temperature, and oximeter sensors are the most common sensors for monitoring. Sometimes, other sensors are also used to get the details about room oxygen level, room temperature, etc. These gadgets are trained using different ML models to be utilized as the monitoring system and to correctly sense the situation. A WBAN is mainly a collection of wearable electronic gadgets or sensors that, when connected to patients' bodies, can sense different parameters from their body. These sensors can be classified into two classes: the sensors placed within the patients' body are called implanted sensors [35], whereas the sensors that are connected to the outer skin or in a short distance (not greater than 5 cm) are called external sensors. However, there are certain challenges while using WBAN sensors. These problems are discussed in the next section.

19.11 Challenges of the Wireless Body Area Network (WBAN)

Though the use of WBAN sensors can have a lot of benefits in remote health monitoring of the patients, they have certain challenges as well. These challenges sometimes limit the productivity of the system. The issues are as follows:

19.11.1 Security and Privacy of Medical Data

The most important feature of remote healthcare is to collect data and send it to the cloud. For transferring the information, the available technologies, i.e., Bluetooth and ZigBee technologies, are mainly used. However, wireless technologies have limited energy, power, and transmission range, and these technologies are prone to attack. Patients and users who use the remote monitoring system are worried about data theft. Security and privacy of the collected data are very important [36]. Different cyber security methodologies, i.e., data encryption and secure channels, are helpful to overcome the problem.

19.11.2 Sensor and Technology Compatibility

Sometimes, due to the version mismatch between the sensors and the technology used, malfunction of the sensors is possible. If this situation occurs, then the collected data may become erroneous. To overcome this situation, the software and firmware version should be the same for all the sensors and tech gadgets used.

19.11.3 Secure Challenge and Fog Computing

While uploading the data to the cloud, the data may be stolen in between. As wireless technology is more attack-prone, we need to upload data in a secure way. For this, we can use a secure channel, maybe edge and fog nodes rather than directly uploading to the cloud server [37]. These technologies can reduce the risk of log-traveling for the data. Also, these nodes can be used to train the models in a very quick and secure way.

19.11.4 Comfortability

If the sensors are worn for a long time, this can make patients uncomfortable. To reduce the comfortability and increase the acceptance of the sensors, several steps can be taken. The materials can be made with soft materials, the size of the sensors can be reduced to feel, and the wearing time can also be reduced [38].

Though there are certain problems while using the WBAN sensors, ML models can help in accepting the system in a better way. In the next section, we have discussed the machine learning solutions for remote healthcare systems.

19.11.5 Availability of Proper Internet

From transferring the data to the cloud to accessing them, a stable internet connectivity is required. However, stability for the internet is a big challenge for remote areas. Thus, some memory-based edge nodes can be developed, which can store some amount of data offline and can transfer them upon connection to the internet [36, 37]. However, storing data in edge devices is also a challenging task, as these devices are tiny, so memory management with size is a challenging task.

19.12 Machine Learning Solution for Remote Monitoring

Machine Learning models help automate things. It is considered as one of the new technologies that are adapted in healthcare. Some of the ML technologies are trained and tested well in healthcare technology, whereas some of the technologies are in the development stage for healthcare. ML models can easily analyze new problems and give better solutions after getting proper training. For this ability, many remote monitoring service providers prefer using machine learning techniques to train the WBAN sensors. After training with proper data, sensors can achieve the result as specified in the training. ML models can also be trained in the different sensors as edge computing. In this technology, the sensors are used as edge nodes. These nodes are capable to train ML models individually and send the models back to the superior. It will let the data engineers train models with different data. In this technology, at first, the data must be collected from different edge nodes. These data can be used for training and testing the ML models. However, collecting data and storing them is a bit of a hectic task. As medical data are very confidential, they should be taken as a high-priority task. For availability and consistency, the medical data can be stored to the cloud servers. The cloud server gives the doctors and patients the opportunity to access data from anywhere and anytime, but collecting data and sending them to the cloud is a very crucial event. To enhance the data transfer model, fog nodes can be used. Fog nodes work as a bridge while transferring the data from edge to the cloud. ML models can be used to automate the fog nodes and edge devices. Also, these devices can be trained about the format of data to be collected. After storing the data to the cloud, some machine learning models can be built that can analyze the type of data. In addition, it is possible sometimes to classify the type of disease or the improvement of the patient. Figure 19.3 gives a detailed review about the technologies that can be used in model training and sensor development for transferring the data.

19.13 Internet of Things Solution for Remote Monitoring

As remote monitoring is rapidly growing, data collection has become a major task. The Internet of Things has become a savior for this problem. The devices that are connected to the internet are called IoT devices. These devices can be both wearable devices and external devices. Being connected to the internet, these devices are accessible remotely and medical practitioners can connect through these devices to collect the data. Though the devices are tiny in size and have very less memory associated with them, these data can be transferred to the cloud servers or any other external devices for better use. As per studies, the Internet of Everything (IoE) is the network that is going to connect data, processes, things, and people at a time. It will be more convenient to collect the data remotely. The basic difference between IoT and IoE is that IoT focuses more on the physical objects, whereas IoE circumscribes four basic components: people, process, things, and data. For remote healthcare, IoE can become a more agreeable solution than IoT. A three-level architecture can be formed for some better IoT solution in a remote healthcare system. Here, in the 1st level, different wearable IoT devices can be used to form a body-area network. Using this, we can collect the patients' data anytime. Also, we can build a large patient dataset that can further be used to provide better treatment. Using this body-area network, the data of users' daily activities can be collected. Now, these data can be transferred to smartphones or other devices, where a bulk of data can be stored simultaneously. Then from smartphones, these data can be transferred to the cloud server. These centralized servers can be used to store and analyze huge data. These data can then be transferred to the medical practitioners for training and study purposes. Figure 19.3 demonstrates an IoT framework that can be useful for future remote healthcare solutions.

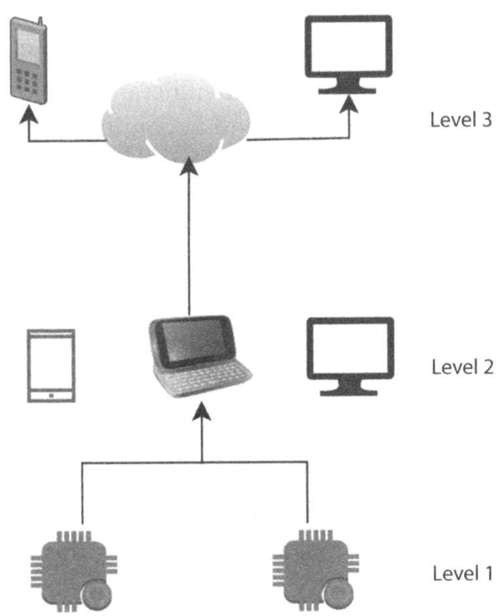

Figure 19.3 Architecture of IoT framework for remote healthcare.

19.14 Security Solution for the Remote Monitoring

Security is another prime problem that needs to be improved while automating the healthcare industry. Medical data are highly confidential, and if they are misplaced or compromised, they can be harmful for both patients and medical practitioners. Though remote data collection is made easy with the involvement of different technologies, security is a major issue for the patients' data. As IoT devices and wearable devices have very small memory associated with them, the best practice is to transfer the data to the cloud server. However, the wireless channel is the most untrusted and insecure way to transfer. The attacker can get into the system and steal the data anytime during data transmission. Thus, fog technology can be adopted to the network, and through fog nodes, the data can be transmitted from Edge devices to the cloud. Different security mechanisms and algorithms can be used during data transmission. Also, data can be encrypted through different algorithms for better protection.

19.15 Conclusion

This study explored how ML models can be used in remote health checkup and monitoring. Although it will be the most useful application in the near future, as of now, it has several security and technological issues. We have discussed different security threats and vulnerabilities in this study. These threats can be prevented using new and upcoming technologies. Some of the new age technologies have been discussed in this paper, and how these technologies can be used to build an automated system is also addressed. Also, the vulnerable areas can be explored to be averted. ML with WBAN sensors not only can capture the data, but also can be sent to the doctors in a shorter time. This technology will allow the doctors to attend to more patients at a shorter time. In addition, the hospitals can serve more patients without admitting them. Patients can also be checked up by the doctors without traveling to the clinic. This will not only save time and money, it will also let the patient be cured at home. Severely ill and disabled patients will get a big relief using this technology. If the models can be trained well, then some advanced remote monitoring system can be implemented using our research work for a better healthcare system in the future.

References

1. Spigulis, J., Multispectral, fluorescent and photoplethysmographic imaging for remote skin assessment. *Sensors*, 17, 5, 1165, 2017.
2. Qiu, J., Wu, Q., Ding, G., Xu, Y., Feng, S., A survey of machine learning for big data processing. *EURASIP J. Appl. Signal Process.*, 2016, 1–16, 2016.
3. Field, M.J., Telemedicine and remote patient monitoring. *JAMA*, 288, 4, 423, 2002.
4. Sandryhaila, and Moura, J.M.F., Big data analysis with signal processing on graphs: representation and processing of massive data sets with irregular structure. *IEEE Signal Process Mag.*, 31, 5, 80–90, 2014.
5. Lepper, J., Remote patient monitoring. *Primary Health Care*, 19, 6, 37–38, 2009.
6. Ondiege, B. and Clarke, M., Investigating user identification in remote patient monitoring devices. *Bioengineering*, 4, 3, 76, 2017.
7. Dhinakaran, M., Phasinam, K., Alanya-Beltran, J., Srivastava, K., Babu, D.V., Singh, S.K., A system of remote patients' monitoring and alerting using the machine learning technique. *J. Food Qual., 2022*, 1, 6274092, 2022.
8. Tian, Y., Peng, Y., Peng, X., Li, H., An attribute-based encryption scheme with revocation for fine-grained access control in wireless body area networks. *Int. J. Distrib. Sens. Netw.*, 10, 11, 259798, 2014.
9. Pramanik, P.K.D. and Choudhury, P., IoT data processing: The different archetypes and their security & privacy assessments, in: *Internet of Things (IoT) Security: Fundamentals, Techniques and Applications*, S.K. Shandilya, S.A. Chun, S. Shandilya, E. Weippl (Eds.), pp. 37–54, River Publishers, 2022.
10. Pramanik, P.K.D., Upadhyaya, B.K., Pal, S., Pal, T., Internet of things, smart sensors, and pervasive systems: enabling the connected and pervasive health care, in: *Healthcare Data Analytics and Management*, pp. 1–58, Academic Press, 2019.
11. Pramanik, P.K.D., Pareek, G., Nayyar, A., Security and privacy in remote healthcare: Issues, solutions, and standards, in: *Telemedicine technologies*, pp. 201–225, Academic Press, 2019.
12. Albahri, O.S., Zaidan, A.A., Zaidan, B.B., Hashim, M., Albahri, A.S., Alsalem, M.A., Real-time remote health-monitoring Systems in a Medical Centre: A review of the provision of healthcare services-based body sensor information, open challenges and methodological aspects. *J. Med. Syst.*, *42*, 1–47, 2018.
13. Shah, T.I., Milosavljevic, S., Bath, B., Measuring geographical accessibility to rural and remote health care services: Challenges and considerations. *Spatial Spatio-temporal Epidemiol.*, *21*, 87–96, 2017.
14. Al-Khafajiy, M., Baker, T., Chalmers, C., Asim, M., Kolivand, H., Fahim, M., Waraich, A., Remote health monitoring of elderly through wearable sensors. *Multimed. Tools Appl.*, *78*, 17, 24681–24706, 2019.

15. Abdolkhani, R., Gray, K., Borda, A., DeSouza, R., Patient-generated health data management and quality challenges in remote patient monitoring. *JAMIA Open*, *2*, 4, 471–478, 2019.
16. Ahad, A., Tahir, M., Yau, K.L.A., 5G-based smart healthcare network: architecture, taxonomy, challenges and future research directions. *IEEE Access*, *7*, 100747–100762, 2019.
17. Albahri, O.S., Albahri, A.S., Mohammed, K.I., Zaidan, A.A., Zaidan, B.B., Hashim, M., Salman, O.H., Systematic review of real-time remote health monitoring system in triage and priority-based sensor technology: Taxonomy, open challenges, motivation and recommendations. *J. Med. Syst.*, *42*, 1–27, 2018.
18. Terkamo-Moisio, A., Karki, S., Kangasniemi, M., Lammintakanen, J., Häggman-Laitila, A., Towards remote leadership in health care: Lessons learned from an integrative review. *J. Adv. Nurs.*, *78*, 3, 595–608, 2022.
19. Shah, T., Yavari, A., Mitra, K., Saguna, S., Jayaraman, P.P., Rabhi, F., Ranjan, R., Remote health care cyber-physical system: quality of service (QoS) challenges and opportunities. *IET Cyber-Phys. Syst.: Theor. Appl.*, *1*, 1, 40–48, 2016.
20. Clifford, H.D., Pearson, G., Franklin, P., Walker, R., Zosky, G.R., Environmental health challenges in remote Aboriginal Australian communities: clean air, clean water and safe housing. *Aust. Indig. Health Bull*, *15*, 2, 2015.
21. Bornheimer, L.A., Li Verdugo, J., Holzworth, J., Smith, F.N., Himle, J.A., Mental health provider perspectives of the COVID-19 pandemic impact on service delivery: a focus on challenges in remote engagement, suicide risk assessment, and treatment of psychosis. *BMC Health Serv. Res.*, *22*, 1, 718, 2022.
22. Fitts, M.S., Russell, D., Mathew, S., Liddle, Z., Mulholland, E., Comerford, C., Wakerman, J., Remote health service vulnerabilities and responses to the COVID-19 pandemic. *Aust. J. Rural Health*, *28*, 6, 613–617, 2020.
23. Maharatna, K., Mazomenos, E.B., Morgan, J., Bonfiglio, S., Towards the development of next-generation remote healthcare system: Some practical considerations, in: *2012 IEEE International Symposium on Circuits and Systems (ISCAS)*, pp. 1–4, IEEE, 2012, May.
24. Seto, E., Smith, D., Jacques, M., Morita, P.P., Opportunities and challenges of telehealth in remote communities: case study of the Yukon Telehealth System. *JMIR Med. Inf.*, *7*, 4, e11353, 2019.
25. El-Rashidy, N., El-Sappagh, S., Islam, S. R., M. El-Bakry, H., Abdelrazek, S., Mobile health in remote patient monitoring for chronic diseases: Principles, trends, and challenges. *Diagnostics*, 11, 4, 607, 2021.
26. Hensen, B., Mackworth-Young, C.R.S., Simwinga, M., Abdelmagid, N., Banda, J., Mavodza, C., Weiss, H.A., Remote data collection for public health research in a COVID-19 era: ethical implications, challenges and opportunities. *Health Policy Plann.*, *36*, 3, 360–368, 2021.

27. Campbell, N., McAllister, L., Eley, D., The influence of motivation in recruitment and retention of rural and remote allied health professionals: a literature review. *Rural Remote Health, 12*, 2, 153–167, 2012.
28. Kalasin, S. and Surareungchai, W., Challenges of Emerging Wearable Sensors for Remote Monitoring toward Telemedicine Healthcare. *Anal. Chem., 95*, 3, 1773–1784, 2023.
29. Li, Z., Xu, D., Guo, X., Remote sensing of ecosystem health: opportunities, challenges, and future perspectives. *Sensors, 14*, 11, 21117–21139, 2014.
30. Majumder, S., Aghayi, E., Noferesti, M., Memarzadeh-Tehran, H., Mondal, T., Pang, Z., Deen, M.J., Smart homes for elderly healthcare—Recent advances and research challenges. *Sensors, 17*, 11, 2496, 2017.
31. Shaik, T., Tao, X., Higgins, N., Li, L., Gururajan, R., Zhou, X., Acharya, U.R., Remote patient monitoring using artificial intelligence: Current state, applications, and challenges. *Wiley Interdiscip. Rev.: Data Min. Knowl. Discov. 13*, 2, e1485, 2023.
32. Kalid, N., Zaidan, A.A., Zaidan, B.B., Salman, O.H., Hashim, M., Muzammil, H. J. J. O. M. S., Based real time remote health monitoring systems: A review on patients prioritization and related" big data" using body sensors information and communication technology. *J. Med. Syst., 42*, 1–30, 2018.
33. Abelsen, B., Strasser, R., Heaney, D., Berggren, P., Sigurðsson, S., Brandstorp, H., Nicoll, P., Plan, recruit, retain: a framework for local healthcare organizations to achieve a stable remote rural workforce. *Hum. Resour. Health, 18*, 1, 1–10, 2020.
34. Onnis, L.L., What is a sustainable remote health workforce?: People, practice and place. *Rural Remote Health, 16*, 3, 1–13, 2016.
35. Sagahyroon, A., Remote patients monitoring: Challenges, in: *2017 IEEE 7th Annual Computing and Communication Workshop and Conference (CCWC)*, pp. 1–4, IEEE, 2017, January.
36. Saura, J.R., Ribeiro-Soriano, D., Saldana, P.Z., Exploring the challenges of remote work on Twitter users' sentiments: From digital technology development to a post-pandemic era. *J. Bus. Res., 142*, 242–254, 2022.
37. Fernandez, F. and Pallis, G.C., Opportunities and challenges of the Internet of Things for healthcare: Systems engineering perspective, in: *2014 4th International Conference on Wireless Mobile Communication and Healthcare-Transforming Healthcare Through Innovations in Mobile and Wireless Technologies (MOBIHEALTH)*, IEEE, pp. 263–266, 2014, November.
38. Selvaraj, S. and Sundaravaradhan, S., Challenges and opportunities in IoT healthcare systems: a systematic review. *SN Appl. Sci., 2*, 1, 139, 2020.
39. Google Fit, Google Fit, https://www.google.com/fit/. Accessed 29 June 2020.
40. OAuth 2.0 – OAuth, https://oauth.net/2/. Accessed 23 Oct 2020.

20

Enhancing Video Steganography Security for Cross-Platform Applications: A Focus on High-Definition Formats and Streaming Environments

Santanu Koley[1*] **and Ankur Kumar**[2]

[1]*Department of Computer Science & Engineering, Haldia Institute of Technology, Purba Medinipur, West Bengal, India*
[2]*Department of Civil Engineering, Buddha Institute of Technology, Gorakhpur, Uttar Pradesh, India*

Abstract
The objective of this chapter is to create a cross-platform video steganography program that can safely conceal data inside a video container. The research has been restricted to a particular video format due to the vast and intricate nature of the field of video editing. High-definition video is worn in a format that is frequently used. It takes more than a few weeks or months to thoroughly verify the security of any system or solution. Although a system's security can be partially understood in this amount of time, many security experts think a system is secure only if it has not been compromised after a number of years. Steganography and cryptography are combined in the software solution to ensure a minimal level of security. Over the last decade, online video streaming has grown immensely in popularity. Several steganographic techniques have been suggested; however, they ignore some contextually significant features. These techniques were specifically designed for "real time video" and "streaming". Several steganographic techniques, including some basic ones that have been reported in the literature, have been reviewed in this chapter. Additionally, a study has been done on the operation of pertinent video formats and coding techniques. Lastly, thought has been paid to the security of steganographic techniques and how steganography might be used to strengthen them.

**Corresponding author*: santanukoley@gmail.com

Subhabrata Barman, Santanu Koley and Subhankar Joardar (eds.) Next-Generation Systems and Secure Computing, (421–440) © 2025 Scrivener Publishing LLC

Keywords: Steganography, encoder, decoder, algorithm

20.1 Introduction

Even though steganography has been around for thousands of years, it is a unique and little-known facet of security. The origins of steganography can be traced to the Ancient Greeks, who gave us the first detailed account of a method that was dubbed "steganography" 1500 years later. The Greek terms *stegano* and *graphia*, which translate to "covered" and "writing", respectively, are the source of the phrase. Steganography, to put it simply, is the art of secret communication in which the existence of a message is concealed.

Even though the word "steganography" has Greek roots, it is not used in literature until the 17th century, when Johannes Trithemius employs it in a trilogy that was released in Frankfurt in 1606. The remaining two volumes, Polygraphia and Steganographia, focus on steganography and cryptography in particular.

20.2 Video Steganography

Image and audio files are frequently used by digital steganography systems as carriers for their hidden data. With 52% of steganography software supporting picture containers, photographs were by far the most used type of steganographic container between 1992 and 2007 [1]. Though just 15% of steganography software uses audio files, they are the second most frequently supported format. With just 3% of steganography software supporting video files, the use of these files as steganographic containers is still a relatively new area of the field.

20.3 The Compressed Domain

The spatial domain is where images are first represented. It can be thought of as a function represented as I: Z2 -> N3, where each coordinate in 2D coordinate space maps to a 3D RGB color vector. Video is represented in the spatiotemporal domain since it is a series of images.

Now let us look at the effects of keeping these functions' output in an uncompressed format. A single 1920×1080 image would require somewhat more than 2 million values to be stored [2]. For a single image, this is a significant amount of information to retain. A single second of video at 1920 × 1080 resolutions would require between 49 and 63 million pixel values in a normal video file. Large amounts of data are contained in images and videos, and since it is usually not feasible to save these data in an unprocessed, raw format, picture and video formats usually employ an alternate representation. Two of the more often used techniques for portraying images and videos in a different way that are both in the compressed domain are DCT and DWT.

20.4 Coding Concepts

A codec (enCOder/DECoder) is a complementary pair of encoders (compressors) and decoders (decompressors). An alternate (compressed) version of the original raw video format is created by the encoder and used to store or transmit video. The compressed version is converted back to the original video by the decoder. The block-based motion correction, transform, quantization, and entropy coding are the four primary parts of the H.264 codec. A codec reconstructs an approximate version of the original video les using a model, which is an efficient alternative representation. A codec should make an effort to balance two competing objectives: high compression levels and high-fidelity (high-quality) video. When decoding a different, lower-quality video representation that employs less bits, the decoder frequently produces an inaccurate approximation.

Three essential parts make up a video encoder: an entropy encoder, a spatial model, and a temporal model. After reading in a series of video frames, the temporal model looks for similarities between the neighboring frames in an effort to reduce temporal redundancy; this analysis typically entails predicting the current video frame. The prediction can be calculated using several past or future frames when using H.264. Motion compensation prediction is a technique used to improve predictions by accounting for frame-to-frame variations. A residual frame and a set of motion vectors are the outputs of the temporal model. Motion vectors are utilized to describe how the motion was corrected, and the residual frame is calculated by subtracting the prediction from the current frame.

The spatial model's input is subsequently filled with the temporal model's residual frame. Like the temporal model, the spatial model aims to eliminate redundancy within its domain; in this instance, the spatial model does this by analyzing nearby samples of the residual frame that the temporal model produces in order to lessen the spatial redundancy. In H.264, spatial reduction is accomplished by quantizing data after a transform is applied. The output of the spatial model is the quantized transform coefficients, which are obtained as a set of transform coefficients from the transform step. Insignificant values are then removed using quantization.

The last part of the video encoder, the entropy encoder, uses the output of the spatial and temporal models to generate an encoded output. After processing the coefficients from the spatial model and the motion vectors from the temporal model, the entropy encoder creates a compressed bit stream that includes header data, residual transform coefficients, and motion vectors. As a result, the decoder mechanism functions in reversal of the encoder mechanism, even though the quantization stages result in an information loss. Because of the quantization phases, the output generated by the decoder mechanism can only ever be approximated to the original input.

20.5 Temporal Model

The predicted frame is subtracted from the actual video frame to create the residual frame that the temporal model generates. The accuracy of the prediction method determines the residual frame's resizing; the smaller the residual frame, the fewer bits required to code it. The accuracy of the prediction can be increased by computing and propagating motion correction from the reference frame or frames through to the current frame.

Since there is typically a strong correlation between two consecutive video frames, motion correction can greatly enhance prediction computations. Since the movement of the objects in the scene accounts for the majority of the information recorded in subsequent residual frames, accounting for this motion variation between frames might result in a more accurate prediction. Motion of objects, alterations in the surrounding environment, and changes in light intensity can all result in changes between video frames. These adjustments are directly correlated with the movement of pixels between frames, with the exception of lighting and scenery modifications. It is possible to estimate the movement of individual pixels between consecutive frames. An optical flow is the displacement movement of pixels within a video frame.

If all goes according to plan, one may theoretically utilize the optical flow to forecast most of the pixels in the current frame by relocating each pixel according to the optical flow's description. Due to the fact that every pixel must be changed and every frame decoded using the optical flow vectors, this is regrettably an extremely computationally demanding procedure. This would produce a lot of residual data, which is contrary to the need for a small residual frame, even though it is theoretically feasible.

20.6 Macroblocks Motion Estimation

A block in the broader context of block-based motion estimation is any N M sample of a frame; a macroblock is typically a 16 × 16 pixel block of the current frame. Many codecs, such as MPEG-1, MPEG-2, H.261, H.263, and H.264, use macroblocks [3].

Creating macroblocks out of each frame is the first step in macroblock motion estimate. Every macroblock is taken in turn, and then a search is conducted for a corresponding macroblock in the reference frame. By selecting a candidate block that minimizes the difference between the macroblock in the current frame and itself, macroblocks from the current frame are matched with macroblocks from the current frame to create a residual block. Ultimately, the motion vector—a difference between the current macroblock and the candidate macroblock—is encoded and stored with the leftover block.

There are various motion and object outline issues when using a 16 × 16 size macroblock. The bit rate will increase and more bits will be needed to code a macroblock if there is a significant difference (residual energy) between it and its equivalent candidate macroblock. By breaking up a macroblock into smaller 8 × 8 or even 4 × 4 macroblock sizes, this problem can be resolved very easily. More blocks are produced while using smaller macroblocks, which might be detrimental. For this reason, using H.264's adaptive block size technique is a preferable alternative.

20.7 Steganalysis

The art and science of steganography-assisted message detection in container objects is known as steganalysis. It is the Warden's responsibility to utilize steganalysis in the Prisoners' Problem in an effort to ascertain whether a message is present in communication channels. Similar to steganography, there are many alternative approaches to steganalysis, but in theory, a good steganalysis merely requires that the data demonstrate a greater likelihood of discovery than chance [4]. Steganalysis is also defined as the process of identifying the existence of hidden communication through innocent multimedia dissemination with a high probability and low complexity [5]. It may be important to note that forensic steganalysis is responsible for precisely figuring out what the embedded message says; steganalysis merely needs to identify the existence of a hidden message.

20.7.1 Steganalysis Techniques

Targeted steganalysis is one of two groups into which steganalysis approaches fall. Steganalysis without blinding yourself. A statistical method known as statistical steganalysis can be applied to both targeted and blind steganalysis.

20.7.1.1 Targeted Steganalysis

The warden can do targeted steganalysis if they are aware of the algorithm or any other feature of the stegosystem being utilized. Targeted steganalysis is typically less complicated than blind steganalysis as the attacker is partially aware of the stegosystem's workings. Let us consider a stegosystem that uses three bytes (one for each RGB component) to represent each pixel in a palette-based image in order to encode a message in the lower left corner (LSB).

It is possible to create a straightforward targeted attack to uncover this steganographic method. The next step is to examine the frequency of ASCII characters represented in the string that was formed by stringing together the LSB characters. A spike that corresponds to the frequency of the characters that make up the Latin alphabet indicates if a message is encoded.

The frequency of ASCII values 32, 65–90, and 97–122 has significantly increased. The space character as well as upper- and lowercase A–Z characters are reflected in these values. This shows that embedded data may be detected based on ASCII frequency using the most basic type of LSB encoding. This method is similar to the analysis done in cryptography for replacement cyphers. The language of the plain-text, or covert data in this case, will contain attributes unique to that language, such as the fact that the English language's most common letter is E.

20.7.1.2 Blind Steganalysis

The warden in the context of blind steganalysis is unaware of the steganographic method that might be utilized to conceal communications within a container object. Because an optimal steganalysis algorithm should be able to identify any potential steganographic scheme, blind steganalysis is far more complicated.

20.7.1.3 Statistical Steganalysis

Finding evidence of steganography can be difficult, particularly if a multi-dimensional container file—like an image or video—is being utilized. In actuality, the container le is represented as a set of numerical functions, which solves the "detection problem" that steganalysis addresses. Both targeted and blind steganalysis can be performed with statistical steganalysis.

20.7.1.4 Video Steganalysis

Whether it is in the spatial or transform domain, covert data are embedded in a container le with any stegosystem. Zhang *et al.* note that concealed data typically has a greater signal frequency than the rest of the image. Using this insight, they suggest an aliasing detection-based video steganalysis system. Their technique separates the concealed data from the container using Haar wavelet filters. A high-pass filter in a Haar wavelet filter can recover the higher-frequency concealed data, while a low-pass filter only approximates the container. The Laplacian distribution [6] is used in additional statistical analysis to separate hidden data from the natural container frame. It has been demonstrated that this method produces satisfactory findings, with minimal false-positive and false-negative rates for the tests carried out.

The field of video steganalysis is not well-studied, as most studies focus on steganographic techniques rather than steganalysis [7]. Videos are modeled as images in current steganalysis research, where the embedding process alters the Gaussian noise of

Plaintext: the quick brown fox jumps over the lazy dog
Ciphertext: wkh txlfn eurzq ira mxpsv ryhu wkh odcb grj

A frame serves as an example of a Caesar cypher [8]. This model will probably lose significance when more steganographic techniques that use motion vectors to conceal data become commonplace. This is because motion vectors' features are being taken advantage of.

A method for identifying motion vector-based encoding for less-than-ideal data hiding techniques is put out by Cao *et al.* [9]. Changes made to the motion vectors have the potential to drastically alter the internal dynamics of video compression. Their re-examination is based on the basic idea of first decompressing the video to the spatial domain and then re-compressing. They contend that this cycle of decompression and recompression is likely to return the motion vector values to their original state, where statistical analysis can be carried out at different phases of the recompression process using prediction errors.

20.8 Cryptography

Secret writing is studied and practiced in cryptography. Cryptography has been around for thousands of years; the earliest written records trace back to this period. Even with the eld's advanced age, advancements and breakthroughs are rare, with numerous schemes being created and reimagined since its founding.

20.8.1 Substitution Ciphers

One of the first and most well-known substitution cyphers is Caesar's cypher. By substituting the character that appears three positions to the right for each character in the alphabet, one can encrypt a message using the Caesar cypher.

Between 1400 and 1850, substitution techniques dominated the field of cryptography. The Caesar cypher and most other methods employed a predetermined table of letter substitutions. Because substitution cyphers do not modify the letter frequencies, they are incredibly vulnerable. Since "E" is the most often occurring letter in the English language, the most common letter in a fixed replacement cypher (assuming the original message is written in English) is probably E.

Another well-liked substitution-based cypher that gained popularity in the 19th century was the Vigenere cypher. Because this cypher uses more than one substitution alphabet, it is considered a polyalphabetic substitution. This article describes the encryption and decryption procedure. In mathematics, the ciphertext is denoted by C, the plaintext by M, and the key by K. |K| indicates the size of the key.

20.8.2 Vigenere Encryption

$C_i = E_k(M_i) = (M_i + K_{i \bmod |K|}) \bmod 26$

Vigenere decryption:

$M_i = D_k(C_i) = (C_i K_{i \bmod |K|}) \bmod 26$

Apart from polyalphabetic cyphers such as the Vigenere, another type of cypher that uses group encryption is the polygram substitution cypher, or Playfair cypher. Developed in 1854, the Playfair cypher was employed by the British in the First World War.

20.8.3 Symmetric Algorithms

Symmetric encryption techniques encrypt plaintext and decrypt ciphertext using a single cryptographic key, which is treated as a shared secret. While some symmetric algorithms operate by deriving the encryption key from the decryption key, or vice versa, most symmetric encryption algorithms employ exactly the same key for encryption as they do for decryption.

The security of the key is ultimately responsible for the security of symmetric algorithms. For as long as the encrypted contents are required to stay secure, the key must also remain secure. By nature, symmetric algorithms are either stream cyphers or block cyphers. Bit groups, or "blocks", are the focus of a block cipher's operation. The majority of block cyphers used today contain 64-bit blocks. Stream cyphers, on the other hand, will function bit by bit.

20.8.4 Data Encryption Standard (DES)

Data Encryption Standard (DES) is one of the oldest and most well-known methods for encrypting electronic data, despite the fact that it is currently thought to be insecure. Horst Feistel created the 56-bit block cypher known as DES during his time working for IBM in the 1970s [10]. It was standardized as the US Data Encryption Standard in 1979. Up until January 1997, DES was the accepted encryption standard for eighteen years.

20.8.5 Advanced Encryption Standard (AES)

The AES is the *de facto* encryption algorithm that is currently in use by militaries and governments worldwide to protect sensitive data. The U.S. Department of Commerce's National Institute of Standards and Technology (NIST), a division, began searching for an alternative to the DES encryption standard in January 1997. DES had been in use for almost 20 years.

NIST received candidate algorithms to review as potential DES substitutes. NIST and the general public reviewed and analyzed each and every algorithm that was submitted. CAST-256, CRYPTON, DEAL, DFC, E2, FROG, HPC, LOKI97, MAGENTA, MARS, RC6, Rijndael, SAFER+, Serpent, and Two sh were the candidate algorithms that were first presented to NIST. Then, a shortlist of these 15 algorithms was created, consisting of MARS, RC6, Rijndael, Serpent, and Two sh.

In the end, Rijndael—pronounced "rain dahl"—was selected as the AES from the shortlist of potential algorithms. Belgian cryptographers Joan Daemen and Vincent Rijmen created the Rijndael algorithm. There is a thorough discussion of the precise operation of AES and symmetric cypher block modes in another section.

20.8.6 Asymmetric Algorithms

A public key and a private key are the foundation of asymmetric algorithms, often known as public-key cryptography. The owner of the private key should keep it a secret and is used to decipher ciphertext; the public key is used to encrypt plaintext and is known to all. The encryption and decryption keys in symmetric cryptography are the same or can be obtained from each other. The foundation of asymmetric cryptography is the idea that it is impossible to quickly and readily determine the private key from the public key.

It is interesting to read about the literature's history of public key cryptography. Die and Hellman first presented the concept of public and private key cryptography in their 1976 work New Directions Cryptography [11]. The RSA cryptosystem was published two years later by Rivest, Shamir, and Adleman [12]. Asymmetric cryptography techniques have previously been described in private papers by mathematicians and cryptographers James Ellis and Clifford Cocks of the UK's Government Communication Headquarters (GCHQ).

The first practical reference of public key cryptography is found in Ellis' 1970 article, The Possibility of Non-Secure Digital Encryption [Ell70]. Up to its publication with four other articles in December 1997, the piece remained a confidential document. One of those other articles was "A comment on non-secure encryption", a 1973 research paper by Cocks that essentially defines the RSA technique as it is known today [13].

20.8.7 RSA Cryptosystem

Two huge and unique prime numbers, p and q, are used by RSA to generate the public and private keys. The most difficult aspect of the RSA algorithm is creating the keys. The RSA algorithm's security stems on the fact that prime factorization is an extremely costly computer procedure. Prime factorization can take several hours, days, months, or even years, depending on the size of the number. The private and public keys for the RSA algorithm are created as follows [FSK10, Sti02]:

1. Two distinct primes p and q are chosen at random.
2. Compute n = pq
3. Compute $\phi = (p - 1)(q - 1)$
4. Choose an integer e such that e and phi are co-prime.
5. d is calculated as the inverse of e mod ϕ.

20.8.7.1 Encryption Process

Assume for the purposes of this explanation that Sukanya wishes to communicate with Saunak, M. Sukanya needs Saunak's public key, which consists of the letters n and e, before she can send anything encrypted. Sukanya initially turns the message M into an integer m. After that, the associated ciphertext is computed as follows:

$$c\ m^e mod\ n \ldots \tag{20.1}$$

Sukanya then sends c to Saunak. This process of encrypting is not reasonably reversible, as it is computationally hard to derive m from x, e and n.

20.8.7.2 Decryption Process

Saunak can decrypt Sukanya's ciphertext, c, by using his private key, d.

$$m\ c^d mod\ n \ldots \tag{20.2}$$

Encryption and Decryption Key

The pair (e; n) makes up the public encryption key, and the pair (d; n) makes up the decryption key. In addition, p, q, and ϕ need to be kept private. The cryptography section illustrates the similarities between the encryption and decryption methods. Despite their similarities, the procedure is still safe because it is computationally difficult to identify n's prime factorization. It is impossible to deduce d from e if (d; n), p, q, and υ stay safe. An attacker might know p and q, and hence υ, and d, if they could factorize n in an acceptable amount of time.

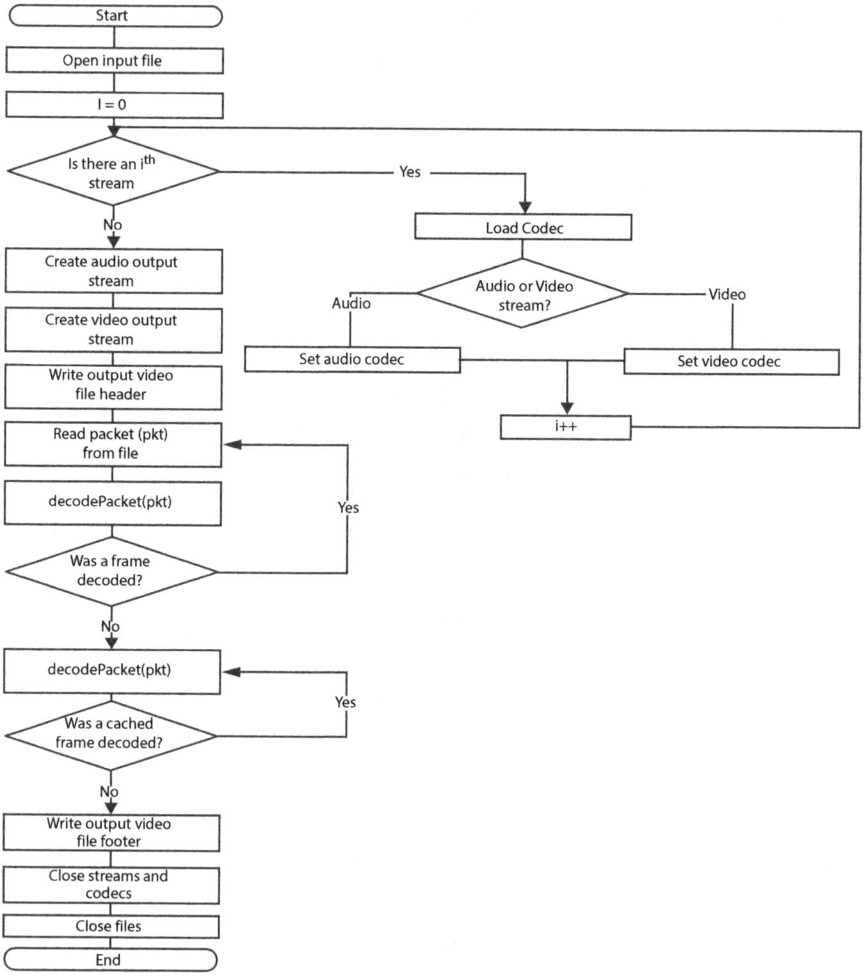

Figure 20.1 Transcode processor chart.

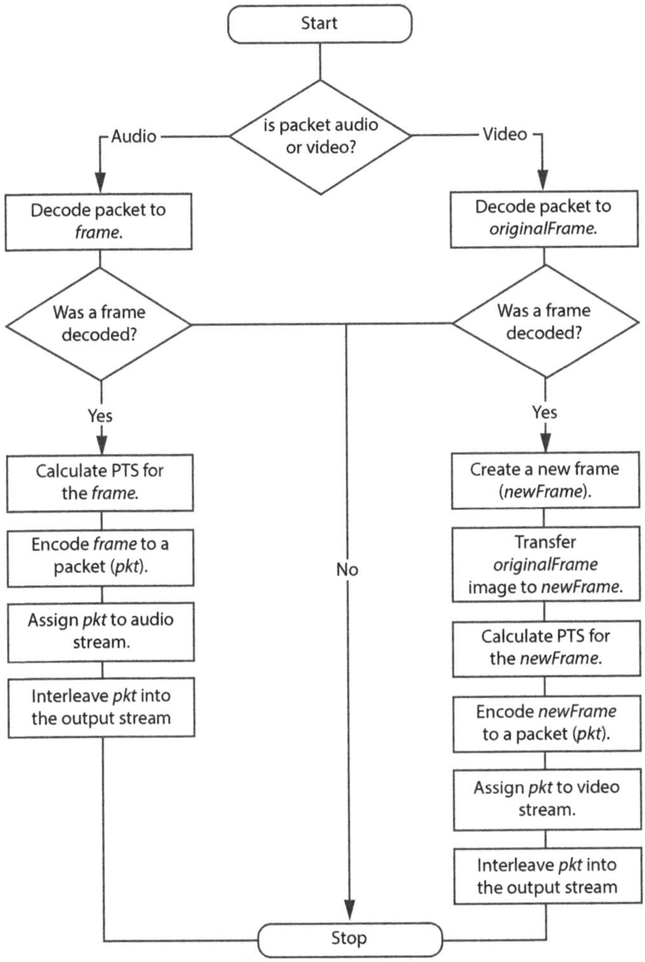

Figure 20.2 Transcode process: decode packet flow chart.

Figure 20.3 Encoder architecture overview.

It is simple to develop several steganographic encoding systems, provided that the encoder is informed about any extra coder modules. Because all of data are included in a single Decoder, the decoding procedure is significantly easier (Figure 20.4). The decoder calls the appropriate packet decoding method after looping through the packets of the designated video clip.

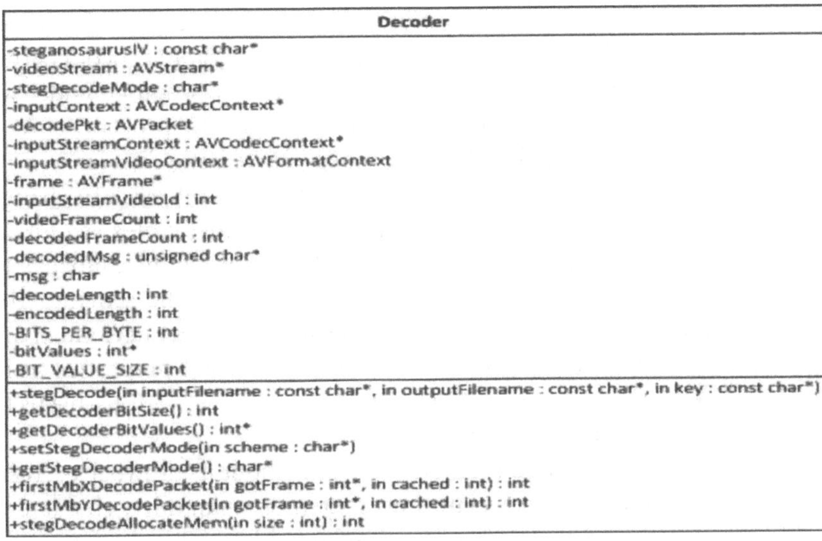

Figure 20.4 Decoder architecture overview.

20.9 Steganographic Encoder

Originally, the command line utility was designed to link to the libraries used by FFmpeg for its component parts (avcodec, avformat, etc.) during transcoding. Since this idea proved to be effective for standard transcoding, we looked into changing the AVFrame that was parsed to the avcodec encode video2 method in order to encode it into a compressed packet when we began developing the encoding procedure. It seems that we had to change the AVFrame's motion_val attribute before invoking the encode function based on the FFmpeg documentation. We were trying to modify motion_val_, but the changes were not showing up in the coded packet. Before using the avcodec encode video2 technique, it became clear that would not be able to modify the motion vectors by altering the motion_val attribute.

It is determined that editing the FFmpeg source code is the only viable option after more research and fruitless attempts to alter the compressed packet. Thereafter, the focus switched to breaking down the 850,000+ lines of code that make up the FFmpeg core. Eventually, it is determined that the motion vectors of macroblocks in P-Frames may be changed by modifying the behavior of ff_estimate_p_frame_motion in libavcodec/motion est.c.

We can now alter a frame set's motion vectors, so we can start working on creating a callback mechanism for the steganographic encoder. This would mean that in addition to changing the FFmpeg source code, we would also need to incorporate the source code into the procedure. As a result, it has been combined with the FFmpeg source code thus far.

As of 2013, the steganographic encoder only uses a bit mask to change the X component of motion vectors. The main encoder.c file's stegEncodeMx receives a callback, and it is this function that chains callbacks to the proper methods based on the selected steganographic scheme. The motion vector's X component's integer value and an MpegEncContext are required by the stegEncodeMx function. We can extract properties from the MpegEncContext, including the frame number, which will enable us to insert the necessary information.

The previously mentioned method was not without its drawbacks. Tests and trials revealed that only brief messages, no more than thirty characters, could be inserted, and that 50% of the implanted bits flipped on average, leading to an imprecise decoding of the secret message. Additional testing revealed that while bit masks varied somewhat, they sometimes significantly reduced the number of bits that could be recovered.

The following problems are eventually found to have contributed to the incorrect data embedding, in the following sequence of discovery. The covert data were inserted prior to quantization when the callback was implemented in the libavcodec/motion est.c ff estimate p frame motion method. This led to more manipulation and alteration of the motion vector values' range, sometimes completely erasing the alterations. Following more investigation into the FFmpeg source code, the callback was shifted from the libavcodec/motion est.c ff_estimate_p_frame_motion method to the libavcodec/mpegvideo enc.c encode_mb_internal method. This means that the motion vector manipulation happens right before the coding process.

Following additional examination, it was discovered that the bit mask in the decoder was returning values that fluctuated randomly. For example, if a \1" bit is encoded using a bit mask of 7, then the bit mask of 7 should return either 7 or 0 depending on whether a \1" or \0" bit is encoded. Additionally, it is discovered that would randomly return a \4" or \3"; as these were non-zero values, they were understood to \encode a 1 bit". This bit mask problem was traced back to a motion vector's coding procedure that involved a right-shift operation.

A distinct decoding bit mask was therefore used to overcome this issue; an encoding bit mask of 2 would guarantee that a decoding bit mask of

1 would extract the same bit value. The original encoder architecture's improvements were nearly always successful. The last bit flipping problem was traced back to macroblocks with a motion vector designation of "none." It seemed that the motion vectors of macroblocks that had been reported as lacking motion vector coding might be changed.

Therefore, every macroblock designated as having no motion vector is simply skipped. Through the use of motion-vector-free frames, bit shift compensation, and encoder callback movement, our transcoding system was able to embed data into video. The object _le, which contains the message to be embedded, is encrypted and saved in the encoder prior to the transcoding and embedding process starting. Bits of the video are read from the encrypted buffer and incorporated using the steganographic approach while it is transcoded.

20.9.1 Steganographic Decoder

The logic for the steganographic decoder is kept in a single file, making it somewhat easier. The choice of packet decoding function is determined on the type of steganographic approach selected. The decoder functions by decoding the video stream of a file and parsing the pertinent packets to a packet decoding function.

Since the steganographic techniques now in use only hide data in the video stream, the decoder only decodes data from the video stream. Since only one packet decoding function needs to be implemented, implementing a decoder is a rather simple operation. Parsing AVPackets to avcodec decode video2 is how a video packet is decoded until an entire AVFrame is returned. After that, the AVFrame can be handled by examining the motion_val and pict_type characteristics.

20.10 Conclusion

The goal of the study has been to investigate if data may be embedded using the LSB Technique in suitable file formats from the beginning. Many publications on video steganography were found in the literature review; however, the majority of these materials dealt with rather more antiquated DCT-based methods. There were very few studies that covered steganographic methods that might be used with contemporary video file formats like MP4. The literature, in all cases, provided high-level instructions on how to use the technique, presumably based on an understanding of how video coding functions and how to create a system that can manipulate videos, and constructing a video transcoder with the ability to alter video frame data prior to video packet coding.

The next attempt involved utilizing FFmpeg, Opencv, and Javacv instead. It was attempted to alter the RGB vector attributes of the AVFrames before they were passed to the encoder methods using the original Java code, which used FFmpeg as a linked library. However, it turned out that altering the behavior of the FFmpeg encoder was necessary to apply the necessary manipulations. Consequently, the final solution includes a modified version of the FFmpeg source code. It is possible to successfully construct a Windows and Android system that uses AES encryption to conceal data in MP4 video files.

20.11 Future Work

A little more work could be put towards solving these issues. Many ideas for different steganographic schemes have been generated by studying the mechanisms involved in changing video data; therefore, there is a lot of room for further system development and research on the subject of video steganography.

References

1. Mansour, A.M. and Bdour, N.A., Steganographic Method For Reserving Hidden Information Based On Edge Extraction Operators. *J. Theor. Appl. Inf. Technol.*, 100, 7, 2325–2333, 2022.
2. Salvi, C.M., Acharya, U.R., Molinari, F., Meiburger, K.M., The impact of pre- and post-image processing techniques on deep learning frameworks: A comprehensive review for digital pathology image analysis. *Comput. Biol. Med.*, 128, 1–13, 2021.
3. Bull, D.R. and Zhang, F., The block-based hybrid video codec, in: *Intelligent Image and Video Compression*, Second ed., 2021.
4. Chaeikar, S.S. and Ahmadi, A., Ensemble SW image steganalysis: A low dimension method for LSBR detection. *Signal Process. Image Commun.*, 70, 2019.
5. Bouzegza, M., Belatreche, A., Bouridane, A., Tounsi, M., A comprehensive review of video steganalysis. *IET Image Proc.*, 16, 13, 3407–3425, 2022.
6. Thakur, R., Malik, S.C., Raj, M., Neutrosophic Laplace Distribution with Application in Financial Data Analysis. *Neutrosophic Sets Syst.*, 13, 1, 224–233, 2023.

7. Shehab, D.A. and Alhaddad, M.J., Comprehensive Survey of Multimedia Steganalysis: Techniques, Evaluations, and Trends in Future Research. *Symmetry*, 14, 117, 2022.
8. Manepalli, D.P., Security Enhancement Using Caesar Cipher. *Int. J. Res. Publ. Rev.*, 3, 11, 9–16, 2022.
9. Yao, Y. and Yu, N., Motion vector modification distortion analysis-based payload allocation for video steganography. *J. Visual Commun. Image Represent.*, 74, 1–17, 2021.
10. Sathananthavathi, V., Ganesh Kumar, K., Sathish Kumar, M., Secure visual communication with advanced cryptographic and ımage processing techniques. *Multimed. Tools Appl.*, 83, 45367–45389, 2023.
11. DSoroceanu, T., Buchmann, N., Margraf, M., On Multiple Encryption for Public-Key Cryptography. *Cryptography*, 7, 49, 2023.
12. Christopher, A.A., Addo, H., Opoku-Mensah, E., Effective Information Security Management in Enterprise Software Application with the Revest-Shamir- Adleman (RSA) Cryptographic Algorithm. *Int. J. Eng. Res. Technol. (IJERT)*, 02, 08, 2013.
13. Rivest, Shamir, A., Adleman, L., A Method for Obtaining Digital signatures and Public-Key Cryptosystems. *Commun. ACM*, 21, 120–126, 1978.

Index

Also of Interest

Other books in the series, "Advances in Cyber Security"

Securing the Digital Frontier: Threats and Advanced Techniques in Security and Forensics, Edited by Kavita Sharma, Vishnu Sharma, Parma Nand, Anil Kumar Sagar, and Gulshan Shrivastava, ISBN: 9781394268887. Secure your understanding of vital security and forensic strategies by purchasing *Securing the Digital Frontier: Threats and Advanced Techniques in Security and Forensics,* a definitive guide that empowers you to protect sensitive information and tackle cyber threats with insights from leading experts and real-world case studies.

Artificial Intelligence and Cybersecurity in Healthcare, Edited by Rashmi Agrawal, Pramod Singh Rathore, Ganesh Gopal Devarajan, and Rajiva Ranjan Divivedi, ISBN: 9781394229796. *Artificial Intelligence and Cybersecurity in Healthcare* offers a vital exploration of the intersection of artificial intelligence and cybersecurity within healthcare Cyber Physical Systems, equipping readers with knowledge on how to navigate the transformative yet complex technological landscape shaping modern patient care and data protection.

CYBER SECURITY AND DIGITAL FORENSICS: Challenges and Future Trends, Edited by Mangesh M. Ghonge, Sabyasachi Pramanik, Ramchandra Mangrulkar, and Dac-Nhuong Le, ISBN: 9781119795636. Written and edited by a team of world renowned experts in the field, this groundbreaking new volume covers key technical topics and gives readers a comprehensive understanding of the latest research findings in cyber security and digital forensics.

CYBER SECURITY AND NETWORK SECURITY, Edited by Sabyasachi Pramanik, Debabrata Samanta, M. Vinay, and Abhijit Guha, ISBN: 9781119812494. Written and edited by a team of experts in the field, this is the most comprehensive and up to date study of the practical applications of cybersecurity and network security for engineers, scientists, students, and other professionals.

DEEP LEARNING APPROACHES TO CLOUD SECURITY, Edited by Pramod Singh Rathore, Vishal Dutt, Rashmi Agrawal, Satya Murthy Sasubilli, and Srinivasa Rao Swarna, ISBN: 9781119760528. Covering one of the most important subjects to our society today, this editorial team delves into solutions taken from evolving deep learning approaches, solutions allow computers to learn from experience and understand the world in terms of a hierarchy of concepts.

Other related titles

Cybersecurity in the Transportation Industry, Edited by Imdad Ali Shah and Noor Zaman Jhanjhi, ISBN: 9781394204267. This book offers crucial solutions and insights on how transportation companies can enhance their cybersecurity management and protect their corporate reputation and revenue from the increasing risk of cyberattacks.

SECURITY ISSUES AND PRIVACY CONCERNS IN INDUSTRY 4.0 APPLICATIONS, Edited by Shibin David, R. S. Anand, V. Jeyakrishnan, and M. Niranjanamurthy, ISBN: 9781119775621. Written and edited by a team of international experts, this is the most comprehensive and up-to-date coverage of the security and privacy issues surrounding Industry 4.0 applications, a must-have for any library.

MACHINE LEARNING TECHNIQUES AND ANALYTICS FOR CLOUD SECURITY, Edited by Rajdeep Chakraborty, Anupam Ghosh and Jyotsna Kumar Mandal, ISBN: 9781119762256. This book covers new methods, surveys, case studies, and policy with almost all machine learning techniques and analytics for cloud security solutions.

ARTIFICIAL INTELLIGENCE AND DATA MINING IN SECURITY FRAMEWORKS, Edited by Neeraj Bhargava, Ritu Bhargava, Pramod Singh Rathore, and Rashmi Agrawal, ISBN: 9781119760405. Written and edited by a team of experts in the field, this outstanding new volume offers solutions to the problems of security, outlining the concepts behind allowing computers to learn from experience and understand the world in terms of a hierarchy of concepts.

SECURITY DESIGNS FOR THE CLOUD, IOT AND SOCIAL NETWORKING, Edited by Dac-Nhuong Le, Chintin Bhatt and Mani Madhukar, ISBN: 9781119592266. The book provides cutting-edge research that delivers insights into the tools, opportunities, novel strategies, techniques, and challenges for handling security issues in cloud computing, Internet of Things and social networking.

DESIGN AND ANALYSIS OF SECURITY PROTOCOLS FOR COMMUNICATION, Edited by Dinesh Goyal, S. Balamurugan, Sheng-Lung Peng and O.P. Verma, ISBN: 9781119555643. The book combines analysis and comparison of various security protocols such as HTTP, SMTP, RTP, RTCP, FTP, UDP for mobile or multimedia streaming security protocol.

Printed in the USA/Agawam, MA
September 16, 2026

910661.143